The Colombian Civil War

For Francisco and Aura
(my parents)
for everything

The Colombian Civil War

by Bert Ruiz

McFarland & Company, Inc., Publishers
Jefferson, North Carolina, and London

ISBN 0-7864-1084-1 (softcover : 50# alkaline paper)

Library of Congress cataloguing data are available

British Library cataloguing data are available

Manufactured in the United States of America

On the cover: Colombian National Police stand guard
before destroying an illicit coca field carved out of jungle.
Courtesy of Retired Marine Corps Major Gil Macklin

*McFarland & Company, Inc., Publishers
Box 611, Jefferson, North Carolina 28640
www.mcfarlandpub.com*

Contents

Acknowledgments

I wish to express my gratitude to my wife Clare, the all–American pragmatist, whose love, strong sense of fairness and down to earth honesty, helped me put the pieces of the puzzle in place. I also want to thank my sons, Bert, Justin, Jack and Jamie. Without their love, patience, understanding and humor this book would not have been completed in three years.

In addition, I want to state my heartfelt appreciation to a dear friend in Bogotá (who would like to remain anonymous) for his spiritual guidance and generous hospitality during my long stays in Colombia. His impressive network of contacts opened many important doors for me and provided valuable insights that helped me decipher mountains of research material. Moreover, his mother, uncle, aunt, sisters, cousins, nephews, nieces, in-laws, many friends and colleagues accepted me as one of their own, and showed me firsthand how Colombians can rise above the violence and despair in their country and live their lives with determination, kindness and dignity. I wholeheartedly agree with President Pastrana: Colombia's greatest asset is its people.

I also want to officially salute Joe Toft, the former Dea Bogotá Station Chief, and Gilbert (Gil) A. Macklin, a retired United States Marine Corps major and former military advisor to the Colombian National Police, for insisting that I get it right. Additionally I want to thank the staff of the Library of Congress in Washington, D.C., and the National Archives in College Point, Maryland, for teaching me how to navigate the corridors of knowledge in their respective institutions.

And I must thank Jim Cassidy, my friend, hiking companion and next-door editor for his careful copyediting skills. I also want to thank his energetic Californian bride Elena, for her professional encouragement and delightful meals.

In conclusion, *The Colombian Civil War* is a collection of words from historians, journalists, political actors, revolutionaries, human rights activists, think tanks, social scientists, military veterans, law enforcement officials, intelligence community experts, Congressional investigators and professional staff, financial analysts, coffee executives, oilmen, bankers, lawyers, Roman Catholic priests, peace organizations and ordinary citizens. I wish to thank them all, particularly the graybeards: Robert W. Drexler, David Bushnell, Herbert Braun, Richard E. Sharpless, John D. Martz, Jorge Pablo Osterling, Harvey F. Kline, and Germán Arciniegas. And finally I want to salute all the front-line reporters who cover or have covered Colombia, especially Douglas Farah, Tod Robberson, Diana Jean Schemo, John Otis, Tim Johnson, Juanita Darling, Jared Kotler, Karl Penhaul, Ana Carrigan, and Scott Wilson.

DIVISIÓN POLÍTICA
C O L O M B I A
Departamentos

PROVIDENCIA

SAN ANDRÉS

LA GUAJIRA

ATLÁNTICO

MAGDALENA

CESAR

SUCRE

NORTE DE SANTANDER

CÓRDOBA

BOLÍVAR

ANTIOQUÍA

SANTANDER

ARAUCÁ

CHOCÓ

BOYACÁ

CASANARE

RISARALDA

CALDAS

CUNDINAMARCA

QUINDIO

BOGOTÁ D.C.

VÍCHADA

VALLE DEL CAUCA

TOLIMA

META

CAUCA

GUAINÍA

HUILA

GUAVIARE

NARIÑO

CAQUETÁ

VAUPÉS

PUTUMAYO

AMAZONAS

N
W   E
S

Colombian Provinces. From *Defense of the Pueblo, Republic of Colombia*

SAN ANDRÉS · PROVIDENCIA

RIOHACHA ·
SANTA MARTA
BARRANQUILLA ·
VALLEDUPAR ·
CARTAGENA ·
SINCELEJO ·
MONTERÍA ·
CÚCUTA ·
BUCARAMANGA ·
ARAUCA ·
MEDELLÍN ·
QUIBDÓ ·
PUERTO CARREÑO ·
TUNJA ·
YOPAL
MANIZALES ·
BOGOTÁ D.C.
PEREIRA ·
ARMENIA ·
IBAGUÉ ·
INÍRIDA ·
VILLAVICENCIO ·
CALÍ ·
NEIVA ·
POPAYÁN ·
SAN JOSÉ DEL GUAVIARE ·
PASTO ·
FLORENCIA ·
MITÚ ·
MOCOA ·

DIVISIÓN POLÍTICA
C O L O M B I A
Capitales de Departamento

N

LETICIA ·

Provincial Capitals. From *Defense of the Pueblo, Republic of Colombia*

Introduction

This book is dedicated to the honest hard-working people of Colombia. The basic principles underlying the researching and writing of *The Colombian Civil War* are that love is better than hate, peace is preferable to war, truth to deceit, brotherhood to elitism, joy to sorrow, health to sickness, nourishment to hunger, and life to death.

A peace activist in Colombia asked me to imagine a beautiful young woman from another land that you fall in love with at first sight. You look deep into her eyes with sincerity and she smiles. You try to speak to her but she is silent. You send her flowers. You write her letters. And yet, she remains hushed. Her stoic beauty is so great; you are determined to win her love.

So you dedicate time to study her. You determine she is a child of the countryside. She is intelligent. She is strong. You also find that she has witnessed the savage web of victims and executioners. And you discover that her eyes have not seen the heroic qualities of men from your land. Therefore, she guards her privacy with the fierceness of a tigress. You think her heart is pure and are saddened that she cannot trust.

You are pleased when she finally opens her lips and uses the wholesome logic of the countryside. She insists that knowledge does not keep any better than fish. She wants to keep knowledge of the countryside alive, vital and potent. She wants this knowledge to serve a purpose. She wants it to be applied to the solution of human life in Colombia.

Patience is an admirable virtue. But you do not have a surplus of time. Your choices are few. You can continue the romance and hope to attain her trust. You can walk away and never know her love. Or you can be a barbarian and try to take her by force.

This analogy in essence is Colombia. Except President Pastrana cannot walk away. He is the peacemaker. He has courted the revolutionaries to extend the boundaries of understanding and destroy the ruling elite's culture of denial. He has made concessions to establish trust. He is committed to conflict resolution with a historical consciousness. But the revolutionaries give nothing in return. Except to proclaim that war is better than servitude.

No, Pastrana cannot walk away. He was elected president with the mandate to search for peace. He must continue to seek an accord and resist the call for annihilation from the enemies of peace. Yes, Pastrana can try to take her by force, but then he would never know her love. And Colombia would *never* live in peace.

1

The voice of the poor may not always be just
But if we don't listen to it
We will never find justice

CHAPTER ONE

The Red Carpet

William Jefferson Clinton and First Lady Hillary Rodham Clinton were awaiting the start of the White House arrival ceremony. With them was the guest of honor, "The Peacemaker," Andrés Pastrana, the President of the Republic of Colombia, complete with his charming good looks, and a grand total of 82 days in office. Alongside the young President was his elegant wife, Nohra. Nearby, behind the gold rope, watching with pride under cool gray skies, were the best and brightest of Colombia's political and business elite.

The state visit, America's highest diplomatic tradition of etiquette and precedence, was the first in 23 years for a Colombian President.[1] Regrettably, during that long stretch of time, diplomacy between the United States and Colombia had slipped backwards. Up until that day in 1998 the relationship between the two nations had all the signs of a bad marriage: miscommunication, misunderstanding, and ultimately ... mistrust. Fortunately, that would all change. Mothers throughout Bogotá were explaining to their children that Colombia and the United States would kiss and make up this morning. The White House ceremony was a fresh start. So after the playing of Colombia's anthem, the "Himno Nacional," and the "Star Spangled Banner," the honor guard rendered the official 21-gun salute.

The date would be marked in Colombian history. At approximately 9:50 A.M., on Wednesday, October 28, 1998, after the joint presidential inspection of the assembled troops, President Clinton proudly welcomed President Pastrana, Mrs. Pastrana, and the members of the Colombian delegation to the United States and to the White House. President Clinton delivered an upbeat welcome.

"Two months ago when Andrés Pastrana stood in historic Bolivar Plaza, the people of Colombia inaugurated not just a new President, but a new spirit of hope. Hope for change; hope for reconciliation; hope for the fulfillment of his citizens' most profound dreams.... Colombia is the last site of major civil strife in our hemisphere. All around the world today men and women who have suffered too long from the poison of hatred are choosing the path of peace.... With your leadership Mr. President, peace can come to Colombia, too. As you embark on your mission to build an honorable and enduring peace, count on the United States as a friend and partner. This is a new beginning for Colombia. It is also a new opportunity to strengthen the bonds between our peoples. So let us begin!"[2]

The optimistic welcome by President Clinton set a new era in motion. The undisputed leader of the free world put an end to a troubled period in Colombian–American relations. In effect, the United States was officially blessing Pastrana. Out with the old, in with the new. The United States and Colombia were now on the same track. There would be no more mistrust. From now on, the United States would treat Colombia with dignity and respect. And just like that … with a mythical wave of a wand, the black cloud that hovered over Colombia disappeared.

Clinton covered a lot of ground in his opening remarks. He condemned the violence of guerrilla rebels, he bashed the brutality of the paramilitary death squads and he deplored the insidious corruption of drug traffickers. But most of all, he noted the need for peace. He also steered clear of controversy. He never addressed the painful Samper relationship. Not one word of it. Clinton at no time uttered the term "narcodemocracy." He never mentioned the explosive issue of the extradition of Colombian nationals found guilty of breaking U.S. laws. And he neglected to address the controversial U.S. annual certification process.[3]

It was truly magic. After kicking Colombia into the doghouse for nearly four years, an enormous eraser wiped clear any memory of the schism. Yes, Ernesto Samper was no longer the President of Colombia. His term had expired months earlier. Therefore, the United States was welcoming the Harvard-educated Pastrana with open arms. He lost the 1994 presidential election by a razor-thin margin because Ernesto Samper's campaign greased the wheels of the Liberal Party's powerful political machine with millions of dollars. More exactly Pastrana lost the election because the Samper campaign took six million dollars from the notorious Cali Cartel in the spring of 1994.

Eventually, this and a number of other negative factors angered the United States to the point that it publicly revoked Samper's American visa in July 1996. It was the first time a president was barred from entering the country because of a drug scandal and only the second time since Kurt Waldheim that a democratically elected president had to surrender a visa in the whole of the last century.[4] No, the United States did not like the former President of Colombia, make no mistake about that. But by not mentioning the acrimony of the past four years and by bestowing the prestigious honor of a state visit on Pastrana's new government, it appeared the United States was telling the people of Colombia, "We know we went overboard with Samper, but now we are going to make it up to you in a very big way."

Back in Colombia, deep in the harsh terrain of the Colombian frontier, surrounded by a natural jungle canopy that made detection from the air virtually impossible, Manuel Marulanda Vélez, otherwise known by his battlefield nickname "Sureshot," was drafting his own blueprint for peace.[5] Marulanda picked up the nickname Sureshot sometime in the early 1960s. The sinister rumor among the military in Colombia was that the reason he never missed was not because of his remarkable marksmanship but because he would put his weapon to his enemy's head before pulling the trigger. However, many Colombians had little faith in what the military said and attributed the army's remarks to frustration at not being able to capture or kill Marulanda.

Known as the Comandante, Sureshot was the leader of the 20,000 or more rural-based and urban guerrillas that made up the Fuerzas Armadas Revolucionarias de Colombia — Ejército del Pueblo (Revolutionary Armed Forces of Colombia–Army of the People, FARC-EP). The FARC was the largest and oldest of Colombia's leftist guerrilla groups and in certain regions of the nation they could move about unhindered "like fish in the sea." Sureshot had been living in the mountains and the vast tracts of thick Colombian jungle since 1947 and, at the age of 69, had put together the largest insurgent force in the hemisphere. He had been fighting the government for over 50 years. During the marathon struggle he took a ragtag group of poor illiterate peasants and made them a devastating fighting machine. Sureshot taught the poor to abandon the *mentalidad mendicante* or beggar's mentality and to demand a piece of the pie from the government. The Comandante and his guerrillas were ready to negotiate peace with the Pastrana government, but not with a cup in their hands.

Sureshot was a careful man. He was rarely seen in public. He was also the master of a crack intelligence and counterintelligence network that could whisk him critical information from around the country in a matter of minutes. This enabled him to keep one step ahead of the armed forces. Originally, he was allied with the Moscow-oriented Colombian Communist Party but now he had developed his own homegrown socialist ideology. He was the invisible man, who could be heard but not seen. The key to his success was his trustworthy spies: they were everywhere, and made him the best-informed general in Colombia. The Comandante was the target of army manhunts for over 50 years. In the 1960s alone, the army boasted of killing him at least a dozen times. He had countless close brushes with death but always survived. Now that he had systematically infiltrated the Colombian armed forces and police with his spies, he knew in advance when and where they would make a move. Sureshot had little formal education but had studied the enemy with a passion. In doing so, he had picked up a firm understanding of warfare. Furthermore, he used his intimate

A pensive Manuel "Sureshot" Marulanda Vélez, orchestrating the revolution from a guerrilla stronghold. Sureshot, the oldest and most powerful guerrilla in the Western Hemisphere, is the undisputed leader of the Revolutionary Armed Forces of Colombia — Army of the People (FARC-EP). *El Tiempo*

knowledge of Colombia's mountains, rivers, jungles and savannas to disadvantage the enemy.

The FARC Comandante was distrustful of the Colombian armed forces and he considered Pastrana's Defense Minister Rodrigo Lloreda a war hawk. Sureshot was well aware the people of Colombia wanted peace. He did too. For years he would tell anyone who listened he "lived in hope of peace." Sureshot also knew that the military secretly opposed any reconciliation with him, however, and they lived for the day that they could annihilate him. They betrayed him in 1984. He agreed to President Belisario Betancur's cease-fire and watched his comrades try to join the political mainstream in 1985 with the establishment of the left-wing political party, Patriotic Union (UP). He watched Jaime Pardo Leal become the leader of the UP and run for President in 1986. Then the military and drug traffickers started the Dirty War. The UP were butchered. Pardo was buried along with hundreds of other Patriotic Union party members. One by one, they were tracked down like dogs. In the first four years of the UP's existence, a party member was murdered every 39 hours.[6] The military did it. The police did it. The death squads did it. The narco-mafia assassins did it. And the government ... did nothing. They watched and never lifted a finger to intervene; they allowed the blood to flow. There was no justice. Sureshot was sure the military did not want peace. He was certain they wanted to wage war. As a consequence, he attacked the Colombian armed forces regularly and was quite pleased when his guerrillas routinely routed them.

Sureshot could no longer lead the charge in battle. He was far too old for that. Fortunately he didn't have to, he had a second generation of ferocious young Turks to do that for him. He could now orchestrate the war from afar. He single-handedly decided the 1998 presidential elections. It brought him tremendous satisfaction to do so. He knew that agreeing to meet with Andrés Pastrana in the jungle to discuss peace would tip the election toward the Conservatives. He had watched the Cali drug cartel manipulate the 1994 presidential elections and observed how the grieving teenage son of Luis Carlos Galán decided the 1990 presidential elections, so he had no qualms about altering the course of the 1998 vote. He did so for good reason.

Horacio Serpa, the Liberal Party presidential candidate running against Pastrana, was too popular with the poor. He was a potent rival. Serpa had promised the poor a platform of social reforms. Despite his role helping Samper survive impeachment, Serpa had strong credibility among the lower classes. The Comandante was certain that it would be easier to manipulate Pastrana, the rich son of a former Colombian president. It was easy for the poor to dislike Pastrana; he was the oligarchy. Therefore, Sureshot helped elect Pastrana as the 14th Colombian president he would match wits with and wage war against.

Sureshot knew the government routine. Pastrana would do as the other presidents before him had done, talk peace, grow frustrated, and then unleash the army. He was ready. He could handle the army. The FARC Comandante knew the Colombian generals were great beauty pageant judges and poor battleground leaders. He knew they were not organized. After all, Sureshot took comfort in knowing his FARC soldiers were better trained and better paid than the regular Colombian army. More importantly, though, his troops were fighting for a cause and entered battle knowing the government was corrupt. The Colombian army soldiers were inept. Sureshot realized the armed forces would rather bomb his revolutionaries from the air than fight them on the ground. He was also familiar with the peace pattern of the government, and so were the poor. All talk, no action, and no changes.

Sureshot wanted to curb the large

holdings of capital in the country. He did not want the poor to continue dying of hunger, without homes, without cars, without a roof over their heads, without education, without health, while others had huge buildings filled with dollars. Sureshot was a guerrilla leader who was determined to force change. He knew it would not be easy. The state had shown the guerrillas over many years that they were not willing to help the poor. As a result, Sureshot was determined to teach the government how to be more generous. He would have to do it at rifle point, because he was convinced revolution was the only solution to poverty in Colombia.

Sureshot concluded Pastrana was capable of peace, and he admired the young President's courage. So far Pastrana was keeping his word. He was in the process of clearing out government troops and preparing for talks in a safe haven. Sureshot was convinced Pastrana was acting with the full-fledged support of the Americans, and realized Pastrana would use this to his advantage as much as possible. Sureshot wanted the Americans to understand his struggle; he knew the FARC had to reach out to the United States and realized they had to set up direct talks with the Americans quickly. Sureshot hoped the FARC could one day visit the U.S. to ask for international funding for social development projects.

Pastrana had the support of President Clinton, but Sureshot wanted to establish a dialogue with other powerful Americans to make them aware of the murderous alliance between the Colombian army and paramilitary death squads. He wanted the Americans to know about all of the death squad massacres before they sent sophisticated equipment and trained the corrupt army to increase the bloodshed in the country. The FARC needed to tell the United States that the Colombian armed forces collaborated in mass murder by allowing death squads through roadblocks, providing ammunition and sharing intelligence. In addition, he hoped to tell the Americans that it was the civilian elites who provided funding for the paramilitary death squads.

At the end of the day, though, Sureshot was certain that the Americans would not join the battle against him in Colombia. The jungle and full-fledged guerrilla warfare had humiliated the Americans in Vietnam, and he knew that the costly lesson the Americans had learned in Asia, would not allow the Washington politicians to risk that kind of engagement again. Plus, Sureshot was aware the American people did not want Bill Clinton to send their sons and daughters to die in Colombia. However, if the Americans did invade Colombia, Sureshot and the other FARC leaders believed all of the Americas would rally around the FARC. They were convinced their guerrilla brothers in Venezuela, Brazil, Ecuador, Panama, Peru, Bolivia, Guatemala and El Salvador would join the fight against the Americans. The FARC welcomed the idea of a "people's war" against any American soldiers who set foot in Colombia. Sureshot was well aware the poor had nothing to lose, and that a father or mother would do anything to prevent their children from dying of hunger, including fighting the U.S.

The Comandante had a master plan. He would teach Pastrana an important lesson in guerrilla warfare by showing the new President the limits of his army. Sureshot had seen too many of his comrades captured, tortured and killed to back off now. The FARC would be the aggressor, and it would have the upper hand. He was determined to plot a course that maintained FARC dominance in the civil war and in peace negotiations with the government.

Sureshot wanted to educate President Pastrana. His mission was to convince the new President that the cost of peace included social reforms and political inclusion, and if that cost was not net, the FARC would see to it that Colombian soldiers would continue to die on the battlefield. In that eventuality, the Comandante had a blueprint that had elements of political and military genius in it. The government's plans for a November 7 military pullback from an area larger than Connecticut, Massachusetts and Rhode Island combined was the start of the campaign for control of Colombia. The FARC was confident that the demilitarized zone trial period of 90 days would be observed, but knew the true day of reckoning would be February 7, when the 90 days were over. Pastrana would tip his hand then — either he would continue to pursue peace in earnest, or he would attack. Sureshot wanted Pastrana to enjoy the festivities in Washington, because he was planning to whack him when he returned to Colombia.

Within hours, the skies in Washington cleared. At noon, a bright sun greeted the Colombian and American VIPs as they arrived at Foggy Bottom for a special State Department luncheon hosted by Vice President Al Gore. Once again, the guests of honor were President Pastrana and Mrs. Pastrana, and once again the agenda was the renewal of bonds. The event was staged in the State Department's prestigious Diplomatic Reception Room, which was filled with treasures of American art and exquisite American antique furniture. The elite Colombians up from Bogotá, realized the red carpet treatment that was evident in the morning, carried over to the State Department. The only difference was that the afternoon function was less formal and was oozing with good old-fashioned American hospitality.

Gore, Bill Clinton's loyal friend, and the democratic front-runner for the presidential elections in the year 2000, welcomed Pastrana, his lovely wife Nohra and

the Colombian and American dignitaries to the State Department. Some Colombians were puzzled: the American media regularly reported that Al Gore was a stuffed shirt; but on this day the Vice President looked energized; one could see it in his eyes. He opened the ceremony by mentioning how former President John Fitzgerald Kennedy (JFK) visited Colombia during his first year in office. Gore expressed "An appreciation of the courage" in Colombia and cleverly linked it to JFK's award-winning book, *Profiles in Courage*. The son of a beloved Tennessee Senator condemned the lawless aims of the guerrillas, paramilitaries and drug traffickers, he decried their criminal logic of "If they can't buy you, they kill you!" and stated that the lawless were responsible for killing three presidential candidates in Colombia. The Vice President then turned his attention to the guest of honor, and skillfully mentioned that Pastrana was elected President by the widest margin in the history of Colombia. At that point, he softened his delivery and stated it was unfortunate that the President's father, former President Misael Pastrana, could not see his son in office.[7] Gore went on to cite Misael's environmental laws that were "The most comprehensive in the world at that time!" Fully in control, Gore then complimented Andrés Pastrana on his courage during the campaign in going out to the jungle and talking to the guerrillas in the search for peace. He finished by imploring, "Let the Americas work with you to accelerate peace; let it begin; the change starts today!" The Colombians were impressed by the Vice President's uplifting speech and commented afterwards that the American media misrepresented Gore.

Pastrana was moved by the Vice President's generous remarks. It was now his turn to address the guests. He calmly approached the podium, greeted everyone, and immediately launched into a speech that essentially said that the long suffering people of Colombia had given much, and that the drive for peace would not allow a sanctuary for drugs. He then turned to the American Vice President and proclaimed, "No one in the world has done more for the environment than Al Gore!" Pastrana then saluted Gore with a toast of his wine glass, and the 250 or so dignitaries in attendance rose and joined in the tribute.

The Colombians at the luncheon glanced at one another in quiet disbelief. Had they entered "Macondo," the surreal world of the fabled Colombian author, Gabriel García Márquez? Collectively, they just could not believe that relations with the United States could improve so rapidly. Only a few months ago, Colombia was considered a pariah nation. Could it be, they asked? Did the United States finally realize that the ordinary Colombian citizen was sick and tired of the violence that was ripping their country apart? Could it be that the Americans now realized that Colombia was coming apart at the seams and that unless something was done soon, the nation would explode in further violence? Or — some of the calculating minds thought — is there some hidden agenda behind all the new fanfare. Has a deal been struck that we are not aware of, they wondered.

Late that afternoon, Clinton and Pastrana held a joint news conference at the White House. Many of the pleasantries of the morning arrival ceremony were repeated. However, the two Presidents apparently had brainstormed again and now the remarks featured less rhetoric and more substance. Clinton reiterated the significance of the new beginning for Colombia and the opportunity for "Our nations to renew our bonds." From there he said, "Our hemisphere is increasingly working together for democracy and opportunity, for justice and human rights, for the peace-ful resolution of conflicts." But then he delivered the most important words of the state visit.

"For Colombia, the insurgency looms over all other challenges today! The narcotics trade and the civil conflict have fed off each other as rebels and paramilitaries do business with violent drug traffickers. However, we know peace can come, even in the most difficult circumstances, if the will and the courage for peace are strong. President Pastrana has the will, the courage and the support of his people to build peace. I welcome his efforts for open talks with insurgent groups. We stand ready to help. We hope the insurgents and paramilitaries will seize this opportunity the President has offered them by ending terrorism and hostage taking and involvement with drug traffickers.... As I said, the fight against drugs is our joint responsibility. It must unite us, not divide us. In that spirit, I am pleased to announce that we will provide more than $280 million in assistance to Colombia in the current fiscal year: not just for the front-line battle against drugs today, but for development to build a better future."[8]

Pastrana's comments were equally forthright. "On behalf of our people, I would like to express our thanks to the people of the United States, and personally, I would like to state that although I've only been president for three months now, it would be very difficult, I think, for Nohra and I to be welcomed so warmly anywhere else. I came here with the hope of forging an alliance with President Clinton and the United States, and I will leave having established a true friendship with the President and I hope with his nation.... Finally, before answering your questions, allow me to say that my country and my compatriots feel deep respect for President Clinton and for his role as a world leader. And as a rarity in history, he is one who forges world peace. President Clinton is a friend of Colombia, and in this visit, we have solidified our friendship."[9]

The press conference questions initially ranged from the Mideast Peace agreement and what the United States could do to prevent the agreement from unraveling, to questions about the peace process in Colombia, which both Clinton and Pastrana answered in a unified fashion. Other questions were directed to the U.S. midterm elections and Republican party campaign ads. But then the going got tough for both presidents. The press started to show its teeth. Pastrana was asked, "Why have you been going down in the polls, and do you believe in those polls?"[10] Pastrana looked slightly annoyed and answered, "I don't think life is about doing well in the polls or not…. We have the highest fiscal deficit in Colombian history. We were given a country with the highest rate of unemployment the country has had in the last few years…. I think that to a great extent this decline in polls is due to the policies we've had to adopt and the policies we will continue to have to adopt to overcome the crisis…. In four years we will know if these measures we've adopted were right or not."[11]

Without missing a beat, Clinton tossed in his support. "I think he's making the right decision. If you come into office and you face a difficult challenge, and keep in mind he now faces two difficult challenges; he has a big economic challenge and he has the challenge of peace. It's better to be high in the polls than low. We all run for office. everyone would rather be loved than hated. Everyone would rather be liked than disliked." On that note, it was quite clear to the group of journalists covering the joint press conference, that the bond between the two presidents was much more that mere diplomatic posturing.

As expected, the questions directed to Clinton were about Monica Lewinsky. "In

their campaign commercials, Republicans argue in essence that you are not trustworthy, and therefore, you need a Republican Congress to balance against your presidency. And number two, they asked the question what do you tell your kids about your relationship with Ms. Monica Lewinsky. I wonder how you would answer these two questions, sir?"[12] Clinton turned solemn and weighed his words carefully. "On whether I've been trustworthy, I think you can look at the record. Go back and look at what I said I would do in 1992 when I ran for president…. A noted presidential scholar said a couple of years ago, before we had the success of the last two years, that I have kept a higher percentage of my promises than the last five presidents, in spite of the fact that I had made more detailed commitments to the American people when I ran. And the consequences are good. We have an economic boom. We have declining social problems. We are a force for peace in the world.

"I've never … I'm not trying to sugarcoat the fact that I made a mistake and that I didn't want anybody to know about it. I think I've talked out that. The American people have had quite a decent amount of exposure to that. I hope very much that they have seen that I'm doing my best to atone for it. I hope they can sense the rededication and the intensified efforts I am making for the cause of peace around the world, for the cause of prosperity at home."[13]

It was a painful moment for Clinton, one of many. No matter how hard he tried to handle the nation's business, he was constantly subjected to probing questions about his private affairs. It was torture, but he dogmatically continued to demonstrate contrition and highlight his good deeds in the hope the nation would forgive him. One thing was sure to all the Colombians at the news conference — they knew that few Latin American presidents would ever have to endure the unrelenting spotlight on their private lives. It was exclusively an American practice.

As the White House joint press conference drew to a close and preparations immediately started for the glamorous state dinner later that evening, the two Presidents were showing the world not only that they had had some successful private behind-closed-doors meetings, but that they were also developing a strong mutual respect for one another. Moreover, it was now crystal clear to all observers with a special competence in Colombian affairs that the United States fully understood that the war raging in the Colombian countryside posed a gigantic danger to Pastrana. The new President had promised peace. Thus, he was now the peacemaker.

However, in assuming the role of the peacemaker he had wagered his entire presidency on the peace process. The absence of a hedge was politically risky. To some, the new President was doing a high-wire act with no safety net. Pastrana wanted to mark his place in history by bringing peace to Colombia, but what if he couldn't deliver; What if he failed? After all, Presidents Alfonso López Michelsen 1974–78, Julio César Turbay Ayala 1978–82, Belisario Bentarcur 1982–86, Virgilio Barco 1986–90, César Gaviria Trujillo 1990–94, and Ernesto Samper Pizano 1994–98 could not end the conflict.

Furthermore, the guerrillas, paramilitary death squads, and drug traffickers had bulked up over the years. They were much stronger and much wiser than in the past. What did Pastrana have up his sleeve? It better be good, thought the observers, because it was quite clear to them that the prospect of this bloody conflict spreading to Colombia's South American neighbors was real to the United States intelligence community and absolutely terrified them.

The highlight of the Washington visit took place Wednesday evening at the black-tie state dinner in the White House East Room. The guests, who arrived at the North Portico at 7:15 P.M., were a virtual who's who of Colombian and American political, economic, and cultural affairs. By far the most glamorous Colombian on the guest list was the 71-year-old Gabriel García Márquez, the 1982 Nobel Laureate. *Time* magazine designated García Márquez one of the 100 most influential individuals of the century. In the opinion of many, he was the greatest living novelist in the world. Also present was Colombia's other famous artisan, Fernando Botero, whose works were known worldwide for their unique mastery of volume. The White House staff had the crystal and vermeil candelabras in the East Room filled with red charlotte roses, pink snowberries, burgundy hydrangeas, and cream gracia florabundas.

Interestingly enough, the best-known Colombian politician in attendance at the state dinner was César Gaviria, the Secretary General of the Organization of American States, and President of the Republic of Colombia from 1990 to 1994. Gaviria's policy of inclusion and timely implementation of *Apertura* (the opening of the Colombian economy) had a handful of Liberal leaders in Bogotá wishing they could change the constitution to allow him another Presidential term. García Márquez, Botero and Gaviria were selected by *Semana*, Colombia's prestigious weekly magazine, as three of the most important individuals in Colombia in the 20th century.[14]

The American VIPs at the state dinner were the crème de la crème of the Clinton government. They included Madeleine Albright, the Secretary of State who was quietly telling the White House that Colombia was a democracy under attack, and Janet Reno, the Attorney General who quickly rose to the status of national folk hero for her blunt and honest approach to law and the Clinton point person for co-ordinating the 1997 extradition treaty with the Colombian government.

Also present was General Barry R. McCaffrey, the down-to-earth Director of National Drug Policy who knew the score in Colombia better than anyone in the Clinton White House; Samuel R. Berger, the overworked Assistant to the President for National Security Affairs who had concluded long ago that secrecy and democracy were incompatible; and Thomas "Mack" McLarty the quintessential gentleman's gentleman, who was Clinton's childhood friend, ex–White House Chief of Staff and former Special Envoy for the Americas.

The mood at the White House gala was festive. Both First Ladies were dressed in red satin: Nohra Pastrana in a strapless gown; Hillary Clinton in a raspberry ball gown by Oscar de la Renta.[15] Everyone adored the limelight. An interesting morsel of the evening glitter reported to the nation the following day by the *Washington Post* was that Mrs. Clinton was seated next to Jimmy Smits, the actor, who they said was the best-looking man of the night and who they noted arrived without a date.[16]

After the guests settled in at tables set with Eisenhower gold-based plates and Kennedy Morgantown crystal, Clinton started his toast. It was now his moment to shine. "Today President Pastrana and I worked hard to advance the partnership between Colombia and the United States. Tonight we celebrate our friendship, among friends. It is a long friendship indeed, going back to our struggles for independence, including, as President Pastrana discussed today, an alliance in war as well as peace. After all these years the United States remains captivated by Colombia ... by the power of Colombian art, the force of Colombian literature, and, I might add, the strength of Colombian coffee. [Laughter] Indeed, if ever a prize is given to any of the people who negotiated the Peace

Treaty at Wye, something will have to be given to Colombia, for without the coffee it would not have occurred. [Laughter and applause.]

"Mr. President, your election this summer marks the beginning of a new era in your country's history and in our long relationship. Bravely, you have placed Colombia on the path to peace. You have taken hard steps toward renewed prosperity. We look forward to walking with you into the 21st century. We still have much to learn from, and to give to, each other.... We live in a hemisphere on a planet growing ever smaller. In our independence, every day we grow more interdependent. If we would be strong, we must lift others. If we would fulfill our own promise, we must help others live their dreams. We must, in short, go forward together.

"In the last phrase of what has famously become known in the United States as my favorite novel, *One Hundred Years of Solitude*, our guest and friend tonight, Gabriel García Márquez, says ... races condemned to one hundred years of solitude did not have a second opportunity on Earth. In the 21st century let us move away from isolation, solitude, loneliness, to build one hundred years of an American family together. Ladies and gentlemen, I ask you to join me in a toast to the President and First Lady of Colombia and to the people of their great land."[17]

As the buzz from Clinton's speech subsided, Pastrana rose and followed with a toast of his own. "Mrs. Clinton, you are an inspiration to women here and everywhere. You are the First Lady of the world.... This is a critical time for Colombia, for the United States and I must tell you, Mr. President, that my country and others everywhere have the highest respect and the highest hopes for your leadership. We are fortunate that in you the man matches the moment ... the world needs your nation. And, Mr. President, we need your vision and strength now more than ever. For us in Colombia, this moment in history is especially important. For us, the issue is not only the international economy but the integrity and soul of our nation. I became President on a pledge of change ... we are determined to make peace. After too many years of being devastated by drugs and the violence it brings, we are determined to win the war on drugs. After too many decades of economic want, we are determined to lift the standard of life for all our people. This is our new opportunity and our enduring challenge.

"As your predecessor President Kennedy said on his memorable visit to Bogotá in 1961, a man is not really free if he doesn't have a roof over his head or if he cannot educate his children or if he cannot find work or security in his old age. We are resolved to send the next generation of our young to school and not to war. In that spirit I say to each of you here, let us stand side by side for peace and human rights, and against drugs, in a tireless pursuit of prosperity for our hemisphere, our nations, and all our peoples.

"Let us end all conflicts, close down the drug supply and the drug demand, open up trade and investment, teach our children, and raise up the horizons of our future. Finally, in so many ways in these years, President Clinton, you have shown the world a new and better way. You are admired from South Africa to South America. You are the peacemaker of this generation. You have become my friend, and you are Colombia's friend. Ladies and gentlemen, let me raise my glass on behalf of the people of Colombia and offer a toast to the President of the United States."[18]

It was a powerful moment. Two leaders committed to conflict resolution: the peacemaker of this generation and the peacemaker of Colombia, hoping to implement initiatives to push back the frontiers of war and spread the zones of peace.

The entertainment in the East Room was at the request of the opera-loving Pastrana — soprano Ainhoa Arteta, a protégé of Placido Domingo, and pianist Alejandro Zabala. However, there was an additional treat that evening. In order to liven things up, after dinner, the Clintons broke tradition and offered the guests high-octane Latino entertainment. It was an extremely popular decision. After the first round of entertainment, the guests gravitated to the State Dining Room to gyrate to the "super-hot" sounds of Marc Anthony, the world's best-selling salsa singer and overall young hero of the new salsa generation. It was said afterwards that the party was one for the record books, and that everyone had a sensational time, dancing to the vibrant salsa sounds blasting away in the White House.

That same evening, Colombians in the political parlors of Bogotá studied the early news from Washington. All the television and radio giants in the country reported the new aura of trust and friendship communicated by President Clinton and Vice President Gore. Thursday morning, many of the seven million plus citizens of Bogotá would rush to buy one of the two most influential newspapers in the country, *El Tiempo* or *El Espectador*, and read the good news in detail. Overall, the Colombian people wholeheartedly welcomed the renewal of bonds and promises of peace taking place in the United States.

However, unspoken, and lurking in the back of some minds in Bogotá, was the thought, "At what price?" Up until this date the only significant United States policy in Colombia had been the counternarcotics war. Yet, Andrés Pastrana was elected President of the Republic to end the violence in the country, and indeed, the local public opinion polls prior to the presidential elections of 1990, 1994 and 1998 had shown that the number one concern of the Colombian people was security for the family. Therefore, many people were scratching their heads in wonderment and asking why the United States was embracing Pastrana with such gusto. He was elected president to bring peace; the Americans wanted war — a war on drugs in Colombia. The two policies didn't exactly mix. So why all the fanfare? Had the Americans changed policy, they asked?

Furthermore, Colombia was recently designated the seventh most violent country in the world by a United Nations Commission,[19] thus for the 40 million citizens in the nation,[20] peace, not the war on drugs, was what the will of the people demanded. A common expression heard on the streets was that only the coffin-makers benefited from war. Colombians wanted to create a future for the next generation. They wanted a future without enemies of peace. Despite the confusion regarding U.S. policy, the people welcomed the news from Washington. President Pastrana was getting high grades for rehabilitating the relationship with the Americans and Colombians around the country were starting to feel more upbeat about the chances for peace. Colombia was stronger with the United States at its side. Whatever the differences, the people hoped that the United States and Colombia would find a way to achieve peace and fight the war on drugs without increasing bloodshed.

Collectively, Colombians silenced their doubts and prayed that the president's controversial 90-day peace plan would work. The plan — to withdraw all police and army troops from a vast area in Southern Colombia and effectively relinquish control of it to the FARC — was scheduled to take place on November 7. Even Pastrana's political enemies hoped the plan did not backfire for fear of what it would do to the nation.

On his last day in Washington, President Pastrana, the former television anchorman and award-winning journalist, spoke at the National Press Club. The President made a good impression, and his speech was an eye-opener. What made it special was his honesty in describing the problems plaguing Colombia. "We must recognize and respond to a fundamental reality. The cause of Colombia's present crisis is not violence or even drugs; it is the poverty that fuels both guerrilla recruitment and the drug trade. The key solution is an all-out frontal assault on that poverty by substituting crops, by providing jobs, and by bringing investment for setting up more plants and factories. We must bring the world to Colombia and take Colombia to the world. In short, our first priority of peace depends on our second and third priorities: fighting drugs and growing the economy."

The President's remarks won over the audience. Many made an effort to get a copy of the speech. Several members of the audience commented how they liked the President and how his enthusiasm was contagious. Pastrana did not take Washington by storm — he was not the talk of the town by any stretch of the imagination — but what he did do during the state visit and in other meetings a very good impression. His modesty, sincerity and realistic determination to search for peace was applauded everywhere. Pastrana was the peacemaker. The American press placed a white hat on his head, in stark contrast to the black hat they put on former president Ernesto Samper. To the Americans at the National Press Club, Pastrana represented much more than a fresh start, he was an extremely rare political specimen in the Republic of Colombia — a dove.

The Pastrana peace process was courageous, but his critics in Colombia said he was giving away too much. However, Pastrana was merely duplicating a tactic from the previous government. President Samper had temporarily demilitarized the jungle region in the state of Caquetá in

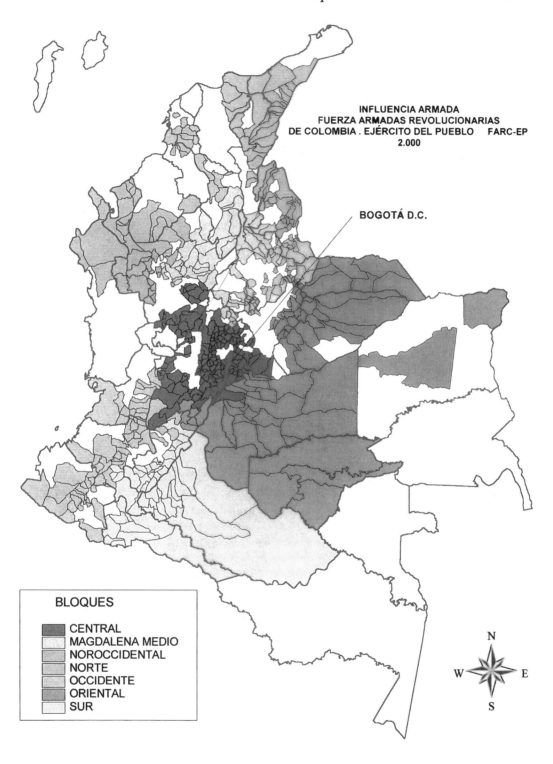

Armed Influence of the Revolutionary Armed Forces of Colombia — Army of the People, FARC-EP (2000). From *Defense of the Pueblo, Republic of Colombia*

1997 in order to complete a prisoner exchange with the FARC. Given the long history of guerrilla violence in Colombia, Pastrana was well aware his 90-day pullout and creation of a safe haven were open to criticism. The FARC had demanded the demilitarization zone to start the talks. Because he had promised the people he would abolish war, he had no choice but to agree to the FARC demand. It was his job to encourage and strengthen the peace talks, and Pastrana knew he needed to demonstrate cooperation and patience, which were two of the essential ingredients for making peace. But the most important factor for him was his positive policy of peacemaking; a policy that tries from the start to solve problems, promote justice, and to make a huge difference for good.

Pastrana wanted to be known as a peacemaker. He wanted to offer new initiatives and foster a body of disciples for peace never seen before. He knew he could not do this alone. That's why he was counting heavily on his two trusted friends Víctor Ricardo, the Peace Commissioner, and Rodrigo Lloreda, the Defense Minister. Ricardo set up the first contacts with the FARC before the presidential elections. He would be the point man with the FARC. Lloreda was a loyal friend and the President was counting on him to keep the generals from becoming enemies of the peace process. The three men — Pastrana, Ricardo and Lloreda — held Colombia's future in their hands. The trio knew there had to be a direct dialogue with the guerrillas without layers of bureaucratic red tape. They wanted the FARC to accept the government's strategies of conflict resolution. Above all President Pastrana knew injustice was a major cause of war, and he vowed to fight for justice in order to attain peace. Pastrana realized the pursuit of justice would not be popular with the Colombian armed forces who were dealing with a legacy of human rights abuses. Nonetheless, he had no choice but to fix the problem for the sake of the whole country.

After the speech, the first query during the question and answer period came from the moderator of the National Press Club event. In a rather blatant attempt to be a gracious host, he lobbed a soft question to the president. "What are you most proud of in your country?" he asked. Without hesitation, the president answered, "The people of my country!" With that straightforward and humble statement, President Pastrana's growing American popularity increased.

Notes

1. Colombian President Alfonzo López Michelson paid a "State Visit" to President Ford in September of 1975 and held constructive discussions on a wide range of issues with Ford and Secretary of State Henry Kissinger. Robert W. Drexler, *Colombia and the United States: Narcotics Trade and a Failed Foreign Policy* (Jefferson, N.C.: McFarland & Company, 1997), pp. 90–91.

2. Official transcript of President Clinton's remarks at Colombian President Andrés Pastrana's Arrival Ceremony as released by the White House, Office of the Press Secretary, October 28, 1998.

3. The Foreign Assistance Act of 1961, as amended (FAA), requires the President every year to submit to Congress a list of those countries he has determined to be major illicit drug-producing and or drug-transit countries. Section 490 (b) (A) requires that the President determine and "certify" under the certification process, first enacted in 1986, that the major illicit drug producing and/or major illicit drug transit countries have cooperated fully with the United States, or have taken adequate steps on their own, to achieve full compliance with the goals and objectives of the 1988 United Nations

Convention Against Illicit Traffic in Narcotic Drugs.

4. Austrian President Kurt Waldheim was barred from entering the United States by President Ronald Reagan in May 1987 after a Justice Department probe found incriminating evidence of his involvement in 1944 Nazi death camps.

5. Manuel "Sureshot" Marulanda Vélez's true identity is Pedro Antonio Marin. He was born into a large farming family in rural northwestern Antioquía province and first took up arms as a traditional Liberal partisan against Conservative paramilitary bands in 1947, at the start of Colombia's decade-long fratricidal slaughter between the traditional parties, known as "La Violencia."

6. In 1993, Colombia's Human Rights Ombudsman was asked by the country's Constitutional Court to report on the progress of criminal investigations into the murders of UP party activists. Of the 717 cases he examined (merely a third of the total number of victims), only ten had resulted in a completed investigation. Amazingly the accused in six of those ten cases were acquitted. Javier Giraldo S. J., *Colombia the Genocidal Democracy* (Monroe: Common Courage Press, 1996), pp. 68–69.

7. Misael Pastrana Borrero died in Bogotá on August 21, 1997, at the age of 73. He was the Conservative Party President of Colombia from 1970 to 1974 and former Colombian Ambassador to the United States during the years 1968–69. As an elder statesman, Misael Pastrana was appointed a member of the Constituent Assembly in 1991, which tried to resolve Colombia's political turmoil by reforming the Constitution in a way that would allow more sectors of society to play a role in national politics. However, Misael Pastrana resigned out of disgust at the maneuvers going on to make it constitutionally impossible to extradite suspected drug traffickers to the United States.

8. Official transcript of Joint Press Conference by President Clinton and Colombian President Pastrana as released by the White House, Office of the Press Secretary, October 28, 1998.

9. *Ibid.*

10. *Ibid.*

11. *Ibid.*

12. *Ibid.*

13. *Ibid.*

14. *Semana*, "Informe Especial, Los 15 del siglo XX," Bogotá, Octubre 12 de 1998.

15. Roxanne Roberts and Peter Carlson, *Washington Post*, "Salsa Soiree, Fete for Colombian President a Strange Brew," Washington, D.C., 29 October 1998.

16. *Ibid.*

17. Official transcript of President Clinton and Colombian President Andrés Pastrana's remarks at official dinner, as released by the White House, Office of the Press Secretary, October 28, 1998.

18. *Ibid.*

19. On April 6, 1997, the United Nations High Commissioner for Human Rights established a Special Human Rights office in Bogotá headed by Ambassador Almudena Mazarrasa. The office was staffed by five experts and a deputy director and was financed by the European Union. This action took place because the U.N. concluded that Colombia was the seventh most violent country in the world. The top seven were: 1. Cambodia, 2. Rwanda, 3. Burundi, 4. Bosnia, 5. Serbia, 6. Croatia, and 7. Colombia.

20. National Statistics Department (DANE), the official Colombian government statistics agency, reported a population of 40 million Colombians on July 21, 1998.

CHAPTER TWO

They Fought Like Lions!

Within the span of 48 hours the bubble burst. No sooner had President Pastrana and his elite entourage salsaed out of Washington for a round of important talks in Caracas with Venezuelan President Rafael Caldera, than devastating news arrived from Mitú of the biggest guerrilla military offensive in the history of the nation. The news from Mitú shocked the country. The guerrillas demonstrated their savage strength by using a new strategy. They took over a town in broad daylight and defiantly waited for the government to oust them. The hope established during the state visit immediately started to vanish. The citizens of Colombia were again compelled to accept the cruel truth that they were caught in the middle of seemingly endless civil war.

They wanted to cling to the hope generated in Washington, but they could not. Every day they absorbed news of people fleeing the countryside for refuge in the big cities.[1] Tragically, they were now forced to confront the reality that President Pastrana was not the most powerful person in the Republic. From the very bottom of their souls they wanted to believe he could restore law and order, but they could not. The President's army could not deliver decisive victories against the guerrillas roaming the countryside; in fact, the nation was

forced to accept the fact that the guerrillas had grown stronger. The FARC had shown time and time again that it, not the government based in Bogotá, was the law in many parts of the country.

Therefore, the most powerful man in the country was the President's disingenuous FARC antagonist, Comandante Manuel "Sureshot" Marulanda Vélez, the oldest and most powerful guerrilla in the hemisphere. Sureshot had assembled 65 fighting fronts (units) that could move around the country with astonishing mobility and knock off army units with ease. The other major guerrilla army in Colombia was the Cuban indoctrinated National Liberation Army (ELN), with 5,000 fighters and headed by Nicolas "Gabino" Rodríquez along with Felipe Torres and Francisco Galán who were in jail. The ELN controlled tracts of oil-rich eastern Colombia and Torres had repeatedly declared, "In our territories, we are the law." The two groups primarily worked independently of one another, with different approaches to conducting war against the government. However, on occasion, they collaborated on crimes against the state, or campaigns against the hated paramilitary death squads. The ELN was scheduled to have its own talks with Pastrana's Peace Commissioner Víctor Ricardo and was angry that it had been designated the second fiddle in the negotiation process.

But there was now no doubt in Colombia about who was calling the shots in the countryside. Sureshot had spoken, and Mitú was his message. His years of experience in guerrilla warfare and skill in portraying his movement as the social savior of the poor had made the FARC a formidable opponent. Sureshot realized over one third of Colombia's 40 million citizens lived in poverty.[2] The gap between the rich and poor helped him recruit new troops, and over the past few years the ranks of his army had swelled to the point that the FARC could not be defeated when they implemented their guerrilla warfare tactics. Consequently, Sureshot's influence in the country was immense. So much so, that *Semana* magazine selected him the "Man of the Year" in 1998. It was the first time that *Semana* had crowned a person who lived outside the law.

What made Sureshot and his FARC army even more dangerous were the ambitious plans to increase the size of the guerrilla armed forces to 30,000 men, women and children[3]: large enough, they thought, to form a people's army capable of toppling the government by force. The FARC logic was simple — until the Colombian armed forces proved that they could stop them, the sky was the limit. Few intelligence experts in the United States seriously thought the FARC was capable of winning a complete victory in Colombia, but because the Colombian army was incapable of neutralizing their efforts, the Americans studying the situation grudgingly acknowledged that the FARC's political influence would grow.

In reality, the Colombian armed forces were grasping at straws. They had been fighting a dirty war against the guerrillas for years and no matter how below the belt they tried to hit the guerrillas, they kept coming up short. The Colombian generals prayed that combat ended up on an open battlefield. They knew if the guerrillas engaged in conventional warfare, they would crush them once and for all. When army informants or former guerrillas did manage to feed them good information about FARC secret bases they were always surrounded with innocent villagers to act as "human shields" thereby preventing the armed forces from bombing the camps into oblivion. The army was seething that Sureshot had humiliated them in the eyes of the world and was extremely unhappy that Pastrana had handcuffed them with the peace process. To them, he was the devil. The army's anger was such that many Colombians knew that there would be few guerrilla prisoners if Pastrana let the armed forces take full control of the war.

The FARC had humiliated the Colombian army on several occasions in 1998. In March, the revolutionaries launched a fierce attack near the hamlet of El Billar in the southern state of Caquetá, about 260 miles south of Bogotá, and annihilated a unit of the Third Mobile Brigade, an elite Colombian army antiterrorist force. The battle erupted when the unit attempted to penetrate a coca-growing jungle area outside of El Billar. The elite force of approximately 150 soldiers never had a chance. They were overwhelmed by 500 battle-hardened guerrillas that took them by surprise. The episode was a classic example of how army intelligence repeatedly underestimated FARC capabilities. The Associated Press reported that the army managed to evacuate 40 soldiers. However, bad weather set in before the evacuation could be completed and the fighting went on for days.

The *Houston Chronicle's* John Otis filed a sorrowful story from Bogotá about the remaining soldiers. "Low on rations, their radios dead, and pinned down by guerrillas, members of an elite Colombian

Colombian Army soldiers are dazed after suffering one of their worst defeats in a fierce battle with FARC guerrillas near the hamlet of El Billar in the southern province of Caquetá, March 1998. *El Tiempo*

army counterinsurgency battalion were picked off, one by one, during five days of jungle combat last week."[4] A total of 62 soldiers were killed in action and 43 taken prisoner, according to the Bogotá daily newspaper, *El Espectador.*

Another distressing army defeat took place in early August 1998, a few days prior to Pastrana's official inauguration ceremony on the 7th. The attack was part of a massive nationwide guerrilla offensive that included 55 raids on military and economic targets in 18 of Colombia's provinces. During the offensive, the Colombian army insisted they did not lose control of the nation and guaranteed security in the country. One month earlier the new head of Colombia's armed forces, General Fernando Tapias, told a conference in Key West, Florida, "The military situation is improving ... the army is not losing the war." However, given what was taking place

across the country, it was very hard for the Colombian people outside the five major cities of Bogotá, Medellín, Cali, Barranquilla, and Cartagena to take Tapias seriously. It was common knowledge in Colombia that the army could talk a good game but was impotent when it came to backing up its macho words with action. The military had lied to the nation. For nearly 50 years they had said that the guerrilla situation was nothing to fear, and that the guerrillas were only small groups of bandits who were about to be eliminated, and that they had everything under control. The nation had heard it over and over. As a result, the army had no credibility whatsoever now that Sureshot and his forces were intimidating the country. The fear in Colombia was so great, that few citizens would venture to the countryside for weekend retreats.

The deadliest attack of the August

offensive took place in the town of Mira-flores, located in the southeastern province of Guaviare, about 250 miles from Bogotá. A force of 600 FARC guerrillas completely obliterated a key U.S.-financed police antinarcotics base located in the heart of a major coca-growing region. In blowing the well-fortified facility to pieces, the guerrillas killed 68 soldiers, wounded 87, and took numerous prisoners. The frightening aspect of the devastation in Miraflores was that the FARC forces were now entering battles with the complete confidence that they would win. On the other hand, the front-line army soldiers in the bush combating the FARC realized from the very beginning of attacks that, for them it would probably be a fight to the finish. Overall, the military precision and logistical execution by the FARC guerrillas confirmed the darkest fears of many Colombians. The army was losing the war and the situation was spinning out of control.

The guerrilla victories also supported the findings of a "Top Secret" American report leaked to *Washington Post* journalist Douglas Farah months earlier when Samper was still President. Farah reported the contents of an ultrasensitive United States Defense Intelligence Agency (DIA) document which concluded that Marxist insurgents could defeat Colombia's military within "five years" unless the armed forces drastically restructured.[5] The DIA was the principal military intelligence service in the United States and many American officials were quick to downplay the contents of the "Top Secret" report. They vehemently asserted the information was for internal use only and that its findings did not represent the official position of the United States government.

In 1998, Farah was arguably the best reporter of Colombian–American affairs in the world. He cannily obtained a summary of the report, prepared in November 1997, and added information provided by

two senior U.S. officials with direct knowledge of the full text. His article hit the country with force. In detail, it read: "The DIA assessment notes that the guerrillas now have small aircraft for surveillance operations and for moving rebel leaders and munitions around the country, as well as surface-to-air missiles and sophisticated heavy weapons bought with drug money from countries of the former Soviet Bloc.... According to the report and senior U.S. officials, the Colombian military has proved to be inept, ill-trained and poorly equipped. Of the 120,000 armed forces members only 20,000 are equipped and prepared for combat, according to U.S. intelligence sources.

"Standard military doctrine holds that a regular army needs a 10 to 1 advantage in size to defeat a well-equipped and steadfast insurgency.... The guerrillas have been fighting the government for the past three decades but have never before evinced the strength now attributed to them. According to U.S. and Colombian officials, the rebel groups control more than 40 percent of Colombia. Ten years ago, according to Colombian intelligence officials, the guerrillas maintained a presence in 173 municipalities; now, sources say, they are operating in close to 700.

"About two-thirds of FARC units and half of ELN units are involved in drug trafficking, according to U.S. and Colombian intelligence sources, providing the two groups with tens of millions of dollars to finance their operations.... The pessimistic assessment of the situation in Colombia, which produces 80 percent of the world's cocaine and a growing share of the heroin consumed in the United States, was echoed by general Charles Wilhelm, chief of the U.S. Southern Command, which is responsible for U.S. security in Latin America.... The primary vulnerability of the Colombian armed forces is their inability to see threats, followed closely by

FARC guerrillas successfully obliterated a key U.S.-financed Colombian National Police antinarcotics base in Miraflores in August 1998. *El Tiempo*

the lack of competence in assessing and engaging them, Wilhelm told a congressional hearing on March 31.

"In an April 6 letter to General Manuel José Bonett, commander of the Colombian Military, Wilhelm said that, at this time the Colombian armed forces are not up to the task of confronting and defeating the insurgents.... Colombia is the most threatened in the area under the Southern command's responsibility, and it is in urgent need of our support. Bonett, who made the letter public, agreed, saying the Colombian armed forces are in a position of inferiority to the rebels and adding that he would gladly accept U.S. military aid, even atomic bombs!

"F. Andy Messing of the Washington-based National Defense Council Foundation, which studies guerrilla warfare, warned that unless Colombia receives sustained U.S. military and economic aid, the insurgents would be unbeatable. When

one side has the advantage, there is no stopping them, Messing said."

It's been many years now that we've been in this struggle. We've had, I think, one enemy, the worst of all enemies. You know what it is? I'm talking about the isolation of this struggle, which is worse than going hungry for a whole week. Between you, you of the city and us, we who've been out here, there is a huge mountain. It's not a distance of lands and rivers, of natural obstacles. Your voices and ours don't speak to each other. There's little about us that's known among you, and around here there's little of your history that we know.— Sureshot, speaking sometime in the 1960s, somewhere in the isolated mountains of Colombia .[6]

Sureshot wanted the world to know that he could launch a devastating strike on the armed forces at will. The stage was set for a major showdown. Sureshot code-named the attack on Mitú, "Marquetalia";

The government assesses the death toll after retaking Mitú. Sureshot codenamed the November 1998 invasion of Mitú "Marquetalia" in retaliation for the brutal government bombardment of the tiny village of Marquetalia in June of 1964. *El Tiempo*

it was revenge for the brutal government bombardment of the tiny village of Marquetalia in June of 1964. What made the invasion on Mitú so brazen was that the FARC guerrillas did not beat a quick retreat after the attack. They stood their ground and challenged the army to dislodge them. Sureshot was not a loose cannon; not a reckless gambler. He studied the Colombian armed forces' tactics with a passion. He used risk-reward ratios that made absolutely sure that he inflicted dramatically higher casualties than he suffered. The man refused to use his troops as fodder, and this added to his legend.

Sureshot needed a major victory. Something outrageous. Something never done before. Therefore, he decided to take over a capital of a province. He picked an isolated target, less than 25 miles from the remote Brazilian border, and astutely cal-

culated that the Colombian armed forces would take days to muster sufficient firepower to defeat him. By timing the offensive right after the state visit, he sent President Pastrana the disturbing message that the peace process would be strenuous.

The attack took place nearly 400 miles from Bogotá in the remote southern state of Vaupés. Sometime during the sleepy predawn hours, on Sunday, November 1, 1998, the FARC quietly assembled an army of 1,000[7] heavily armed guerrillas outside the tiny capital of Mitú. Sureshot's number two in command, the chief military strategist Jorge Briceño, alias "Mono Jojoy," orchestrated the FARC forces. The unit, named Front 53, staged a crushing assault on the small garrison of approximately 120 soldiers and police protecting the town of 15,000 inhabitants. One of the front-line leaders, who led the FARC

This captured FARC photograph shows guerrilla military mastermind Jorge "Mono Jojoy" Jorge Briceño (front right center with beret and both hands on hips) proudly posing with his dangerous second-generation "Young Turks." To Mono Jojoy's right in rear with beret and beard is the legendary Henry "Romaña" Castellanos; superstitious peasants claim he made a pact with the devil so bullets could not harm him. *Courtesy of Gil Macklin*

charge on Mitú, was Comrade Romaña,[8] an extremely dangerous second-generation FARC guerrilla who was known throughout the nation for his symbolic "Che"[9] beret. Romaña was legendary; superstitious countryside peasants said he had made a pact with the devil, and that was why bullets could not enter him.

At about 5 o'clock that morning the FARC stormed Mitú on three fronts using rockets and powerful homemade gas cylinder bombs[10] to blast its way to the police station that housed the majority of the defense forces. What ensued was a fierce pitched battle as the greatly outnumbered force of 120 soldiers and police engaged the invading guerrilla army. The garrison immediately radioed for assistance, but shortly thereafter communications were severed. As a consequence, the isolated defense forces of Mitú were left to fight for their lives. Tragically, help didn't arrive in time to save them.

The first official report from the battlefield came from the Director of the Colombian Red Cross who stated that the garrison, "Fought like lions!"[11] Moreover, the Red Cross reported a grisly scene: 80 soldiers and police killed, 40 taken prisoner; ten civilians killed. (The government subsequently lowered those figures dramatically.) Overall, the battle for control of Mitú lasted 14 hours; unfortunately, it would take the Colombian armed forces "three days" to take back Mitú from the entrenched FARC guerrillas. Amazingly, few FARC dead or wounded were left behind—unlike the Colombian army, the FARC ordinarily refused to abandon their dead or wounded comrades.

Romaña was born in Medellín on March 20, 1965. His guerrilla activities dated back to 1982 and were typical of the second-generation FARC leaders, according to Colombian military intelligence. In 1982, he was with the FARC's Front 11 and was largely responsible for the assassination of at least 100 individuals in the Rio del Guaguaquí zone of Cundinamarca and Boyacá. The criminal dossier also stated Romaña coordinated an attack on an anti-narcotics patrol in 1991 that took the lives of 11 agents. Additionally, the file contained information indicating Romaña was responsible for the kidnapping of the American missionaries Timothy Van Dike and Steve Welsh on January 16, 1994, and for their subsequent murders in June 1995.

Finally, Romaña reportedly led the attack on a metropolitan police station in the southern Bogotá district of Kennedy in May 1995. Colombian military reports considered Romaña an intellectual lightweight as well as a cold-blooded killer. They would now be compelled to update the file and add that he was also an excellent field commander as he repeatedly repelled government attempts to drive him out of Mitú.

When the Colombian armed forces finally regained control of Mitú Wednesday morning, November 4, they found a town in ruin. The FARC reduced the Mitú police station to rubble. They also blew up the town bank, Caja Agraria, and emptied the vaults of $400,000. Other damage in Mitú included the destruction of the airport tower, three airplanes and the telephone communications station.

The battle for Mitú also touched off an international incident with Colombia's southeastern neighbor Brazil. The Brazilian government considered the situation grave. They registered a "vehement" protest with the Colombian government over the use of Querarí, a small Brazilian military airstrip on the frontier. Apparently, the Colombian military command had formally requested permission of the Brazilian government to use Querarí for humanitarian reasons; to evacuate its dead and wounded in the battle to recapture Mitú on Monday, November 2.

Brazil immediately granted Colombia permission to use its base for humanitarian purposes but implemented a deadline of six that evening. The dispute took place when the Brazilians alleged that the Colombian armed forces ignored the terms of the agreement and used Querarí as a strategic staging center to launch military operations to recapture Mitú. General Fernando Tapias, the Commander of the Colombian army, denied the allegations and insisted that his troops only used the Brazilian base to evacuate its dead and wounded. Ultimately, the issue was resolved in a diplomatic fashion, but not before news of the schism was splashed on the front pages of *El Tiempo* and *El Espectador,* the two dominant Bogotá newspapers, on Tuesday, November 3.

The FARC attack on Mitú forced President Pastrana to delay his visit to Venezuela in order to attend to a nation in turmoil. Strangely enough, he did not appear on national television to condemn the attack for days. The President knew the goodwill generated in Washington, D.C., was now pushed to the very back of the political landscape. And he also realized the nation was horrified by the devastating show of force by Sureshot. The lead editorials in both *El Tiempo* and *El Espectador* on Tuesday deplored the brazen attack on Mitú. *El Tiempo,* in its lead editorial called "Abrir Los Ojos," criticized the cold-blooded attack and openly questioned the wisdom of pulling troops from a vast zone of the country as a precondition to jumpstart the peace process.

The *El Espectador* lead editorial titled "Pulso Firmo" said the FARC attack was like getting hit with a bucket of cold water and that it put a totally different perspective on the peace process. It went on to say that the FARC conduct was absurd and that it advanced war, not the peace process. Overall, the two editorials stated that morale in the country was in terrible shape and suggested that the government should take a tougher, less tolerant position with the violent FARC. Another point that gnawed at the public's confidence and was commonly grumbled about on the street concerned President Pastrana's complete revamping of the army leadership when he took office. As a result of the shake-up, the country expected its armed forces to improve their combat record; they never dreamed the country's ability to defend itself would *deteriorate.*

The President was taking a beating for assuming the role of peacemaker. It was a modern day paradox. They elected him to find peace, knowing from the beginning that it would not arrive overnight, and then they immediately set about to question his every move. Sureshot had seen presidents come and presidents go. Surely he wanted to know what mettle Pastrana had. The most powerful guerrilla leader in the hemisphere was merely tossing out depth charges, to see how the young President would react. After all, the FARC had all the time in the world — Pastrana only had the four years the people elected him to the presidency for. If the President was desperate to make peace, he would agree to Sureshot's radical terms: the dismantling of Colombia's paramilitary death squads and the wholesale redistribution of the nation's wealth to the poor. In other words, Pastrana would have to make Colombia a socialist regime.

Naturally, the toughest criticism was targeted at Pastrana's surprising agreement with the FARC guerrillas to withdraw all police and army troops from five municipalities covering 15,000 square miles in

As part of President Pastrana's peace process, Colombian troops board helicopters on November 7, 1998, to evacuate the 15,000 square mile area in southern Colombia chosen for the historic establishment of a FARC demilitarized zone. *El Tiempo*

southern Colombia. The demilitarized zone was to be established in a few days, November 7, and would last for 90 days. On February 7, the plan called for the Colombian military to re-enter the zone and restore state control. Pastrana's critics said the new zone would allow the FARC to assume de facto control over a swath of territory. They complained that the FARC would be free to train for large offensives without fear of attack, that they would be allowed to replenish and expand supply lines, that they would have time to carve secret caves in the mountains to stash weapons in, and, more importantly, that they would be permitted to recruit new soldiers for more fronts and new agents to join their sophisticated intelligence and counterintelligence network. Worst of all, they would continue to operate their lucrative drug business, which gave an enormous cash flow to continue to buy more arms to escalate the conflict.

The November 7, 1998, demilitarization took place as planned. President Pastrana was a man of his word. He ordered the police and army to withdraw from the designated countryside as a precondition for the important peace talks that would take place on January 7. He was well aware that in order to resolve Colombia's gigantic conflict he would have to take risks to find common ground. He was willing to make himself vulnerable in order to create space for resolution and in order to encourage others to do the same. Pastrana was seeking a long-term solution that would prevent future conflict. He was willing to use power for peace rather than try to overpower in war. Cooperation, not domination, was the key. The President knew creative approaches to peace would challenge cultural practices and normal ways of seeing things.

Not surprisingly, the press attacked him. *The Dallas Morning News* reported the move was "One of the riskiest peace gambits ever undertaken by a Latin American leader."[12] The article stated the obvious, that the FARC had won concessions and surrendered nothing in return. On the positive side, the *Manchester Guardian* in England saluted Pastrana for his "Prolific gesture" with the FARC prior to taking office and for his "diplomatic triumph" during the State Visit.[13] However, complicating matters in Colombia was the belligerent manner of the FARC leadership who made it known that the surrender of weapons was not negotiable. Consequently, the Colombian army secretly grumbled about the lopsided arrangement but obediently followed the President's instructions nonetheless.

The FARC forces immediately entered the area and established law and order without incident. Their rules included fines for slack farming practices, neglecting animals, and leaving property and paths untidy. Some Colombians called the FARC "ecoguerrillas" because they prevented environmental abuses such as excessive forestry and hunting as well as the cheating practice of fishing with dynamite. Also seeking to head off any foolish mishaps, the FARC ordered a four-beer consumption limit for everyone in the demilitarized zone. Fortunately, the transition was peaceful. Then both sides set about to prepare for the groundbreaking January 7, 1999, talks in the southern ranch town of San Vicente del Caguán that would give birth to an honest dialogue for peace.

With the arrival of the 1998 Christmas holidays, the country was relatively free of warfare. However, most Colombians continued to venture into the countryside with extreme caution, knowing the guerrillas were predictably unpredictable. On December 24, Reuters Bogotá reported a Gallup survey conducted in Colombia and published by the local media which indicated that 74 percent of respondents believed the FARC and the ELN had no will for peace. Moreover, 48 percent of those surveyed in the poll said the peace process had got off on the wrong foot. The disheartening news for President Pastrana was that 52 percent of those surveyed said they hoped a foreign power would send in ground troops to help Colombia's military defeat the rebels.[14] Many Colombians considered the evidence in the poll as an obvious welcome mat for American troops and the possible start of another Vietnam.

A month prior to the holidays, the United Self-Defense Forces of Colombia, Autodefensas Unidas de Colombia (AUC), otherwise known as paramilitary death squads, launched its own Internet website at www.colombialibre.org. The AUC was irritated that the FARC refused to allow them a seat at the same peace table and demanded that the FARC guerrillas free all the civilians they had kidnapped and to cease all further abductions while peace negotiations continued. The web page had a logo of a peasant sowing seeds against the backdrop of a map of Colombia colored in the yellow, blue and red of the national flag. It also had an open letter to Pastrana advocating peace and politely requesting a role in the process.

The letter was coherent and professional in tone, which was quite a contrast to how the death squads conducted business in the countryside. Inside Colombia, the paramilitary death squads had one of the bloodiest reputations in the nation. The ultra right-wing group had very strong links to the Colombian army and police, hated communists, and made it their mandate to hunt down insurgents and eliminate them in the most gruesome manner possible. It was the death squads that introduced chain saws to mutilate victims inside Colombia. It was one of their signature styles of murder.

The leader of the death squads was Carlos Castaño, who was the most vicious warlord in the nation and had been fighting the guerrillas for a decade.[15] Castaño had been elected supreme commander of all paramilitary death squad fighters in April 1997 and his 5,000 fighters had spread terror across the country, gunning down, burning, and chopping up guerrillas and their suspected collaborators. The death squads were so bloodthirsty and ruthless that they were known to kill peasants who offered water to guerrillas.

There were at least seven paramilitary death squad groups allied under the name AUC: the Peasant Self-Defense Group of Córdoba and Urabá, the largest and most public group; the Eastern Plains Self-Defense Group, also known as Los Carranceros, after their leader, Víctor Carranza; the Cesar Self-Defense Group; the Middle Magdalena Self-Defense Group, the group with the longest history; the Santander and Southern Cesar Self-Defense Group; the Casanare Self-Defense Group; and the Cundinamarca Self-Defense Group.

Colombia's paramilitary death squads were legally set up by the armed forces in the late 1960s as part of an official antiguerrilla strategy, but were outlawed in 1989 as they threatened to spin out of government control. However, human rights organizations continued to accuse the Colombian military of heavy involvement and the FARC had made allegations for years that Central Intelligence Agency (CIA) advisers had provided funding to the death squads in the early 1990s.

Castaño was a high school dropout who served in the armed forces as a guide for the army counterinsurgency units. He considered himself an anti–Communist and declared that massacring leftist sympathizers was the only way to destroy rebel support bases.[16] Before leaving office in August 1998, President Samper vowed to hunt Castaño to "hell and back" and offered a $1 million reward for his capture.

On December 20, 1998, Carlos Castaño

called an 18-day cease-fire to the hostilities with the FARC and ELN guerrillas and ordered his troops to observe the holy season. The FARC and ELN leadership flatly rejected Castaño's overture. Nonetheless, with the cease-fire declaration in place, Castaño and his most trusted lieutenants went to a death squad secret fortress in the tiny village of Nudo de Parmillo in Córdoba province located in northern Colombia. The reportedly impregnable and heavily guarded encampment was near the larger town of Tierra Alta and was said to be funded by large landowners, cattle-ranchers, drug traffickers, and arms smugglers. This did not dissuade Sureshot, however; he had a score to settle with Castaño. The death squads were randomly killing unarmed men, women and children — *campesinos* that they suspected were sympathetic to the guerrillas. Sureshot was angry that they were not pursuing his guerrillas, and considered Castaño and his paramilitary cowards for butchering unarmed villagers. Sureshot had hoped for a military showdown with Castaño but realized that the death squads wanted no part of an all-out confrontation with his fighting machine. Therefore, the Comandante decided to hunt Castaño down and give him some of his own medicine.

On December 28, 1998, Sureshot's FARC guerrillas attacked their archenemies in Nudo de Paramillo. The clash lasted for two days. When it was over the camp and the village were completely destroyed. Initially, the FARC reported that they had killed the hated Castaño, but the report proved false: the death squads took heavy losses but Castaño survived. After the battle, Héctor Acosta, mayor of the town of Tierra Alta, said the FARC had killed 30 peasants during the attack on the paramilitary stronghold. "These guerrillas are the pagans of the armed conflict. There are 30 corpses mostly of women, children and old people," he said.[17]

The next day, the Reverend Joaquín Pachón, the local priest, spoke of finding headless corpses strewn among the smoldering remains of houses close to the paramilitary camp, which had served as Castaño's headquarters for the last 18 months.[18] "We found bodies without heads, it was terrifying. Nearby there's a paramilitary camp and it seems the rebels attacked the camp first and then turned on the civilians and burned all the houses in the village," Pachón told the Radionet radio network.[19] The FARC attack would spark a violent death squad backlash against the FARC. Castaño wanted blood — an eye for an eye: he was determined to get even. In the process, he was going to do what no one else in the nation had been able to do for over 50 years, and it was going to make him a national hero— he, Carlos Castaño, was going to kill Sureshot!

Thursday, January 7, 1999, was President Pastrana's day to shine. He was going to meet face to face with Sureshot and, if all went to plan, silence his critics. The peacemaker was going to introduce a menu of independent initiatives designed to decrease threat perception and distrust. He would truly put the peace process in motion, and once in motion it would stay in motion, he hoped. The weather was marvelous, bright blue skies and a warm sun. Hundreds of reporters from around the world gathered in San Vicente del Caguán, to witness the historic meeting.

A stage was set up in the town plaza with a table and chairs for the press to record the first public handshake of the peace process. The stage was adorned with the colors of Colombia and with smaller flags strung by the FARC guerrillas which read, "Opening Paths to a New Colombia." The nation had planned a great national party in expectation of the historic moment when the Peacemaker and the Phantom (Sureshot) would embrace. National television coverage was live and several

An empty seat next to President Andrés Pastrana (lower right) symbolizes Sureshot's failure to attend the opening round of peace talks on January 7, 1999. *El Tiempo*

international dignitaries as well as the news organizations were in attendance. Thousands of residents of the ranch town crowded the plaza. The President's 60-man bodyguard mingled elbow to elbow with guerrilla sentries. Overlooking the plaza were guerrilla sharpshooters in the church bell-tower, on rooftops and in strategic windows. Everything was in place for the official start of the long-awaited peace process. Expectations were high.

Prior to leaving Bogotá, Pastrana said he trusted Sureshot and believed he could work with him to end the civil conflict in Colombia. He was optimistic peace was attainable through ballots rather than bullets. All the positive rhetoric was there. This was the moment the Peacemaker longed for, the chance to start talking in earnest. This was his opportunity to convince Sureshot that everyone could work together for a greater Colombia, that there was a voice for him and his people in the Colombian government, and that he, Pastrana, was committed to a healing process. Everyone in the country was anticipating good news.

Then the worst thing short of hostilities took place. Sureshot didn't show up. Suddenly, the peace talks stumbled. The commandant of the FARC's feared Southern Bloc Joaquín Gómez announced that Sureshot had received death threats and would boycott the San Vicente del Caguán meeting. "Pastrana is like the bride all dressed up and left at the altar," said the governor of the Valle del Cauca, Gustavo Alvarez Gardeazabal.[20]

FARC commandant Gómez went on to read a speech that complained, "Pastrana had created two new mobile counterguerrilla battalions, one financed by the United States, to maintain a ring around Sureshot under the guise of fighting drug trafficking and said the President was creating an American-backed intelligence unit in southeastern Colombia with equip-ment that can vastly multiply the government's information about guerrilla troop movements."[21]

Visibly disappointed, Pastrana put on a brave face and nobly responded. "As head of State ... I am here to express the voice of a country that wants peace, that seeks social justice and is ready to carry out politics as an exercise of the common good. Colombia cannot go on divided into three irreconcilable countries, where one country kills, the other dies, and a third, horrified, scratches its head and shuts its eyes."[22]

Daniel Ortega, the former head of Nicaragua's Sandinista rebels, who attended the ceremony in San Vicente del Caguán as a guest of the FARC, angered many Colombians with his revolutionary rhetoric. He became an enemy of the Colombian paramilitary death squads when he observed, "Logically, if a revolutionary group is getting stronger, then the possibilities increase that they could overthrow the established order and take power by force."

The following day *El Espectador* published a poll indicating that 50 percent of the Colombians questioned believed the peace talks would drag on indefinitely, 27 percent believed the talks were leading nowhere, and only 23 percent believed they would result in peace. Clearly, the mood of the country had turned dour. Fortunately, the President knew all along that the peace process was fraught with risk, and was prone to setbacks. His determination to continue the role of peacemaker did not waver. President Pastrana had prepared for obstacles.

Sureshot's information was good. The death squads allowed the holy season cease-fire to expire on January 8th and then unleashed total mayhem against suspected FARC collaborators. Carlos Castaño publicly stated the FARC took advantage of the paramilitary cease-fire to launch a bloody assault on his mountain stronghold killing 30 people including three children, one of them an infant less than one month old. He vowed to avenge the attack. Sureshot was a marked man.

One of the most savage death squad attacks was in the river-front village of Playón de Orozco, in northern Magdalena province, where the death squads dragged 27 worshippers from a church and riddled them with bullets under the horrified gaze of the parish priest. In Curumaní, a town in Cesar province, Castaño's forces dragged at least ten people out of their homes and riddled them with automatic gunfire. In the same town, an 80-year-old woman died trapped in her burning house after it was set ablaze by death squads.

Four days later the *Miami Herald* reported, "As more bodies turned up along river banks from a savage offensive by right-wing militias, authorities raised the death toll from four days of violence to 136 people and said more deaths may be in the offing."[23] A week after the death squad campaign started the death toll was 150 and counting. In addition to getting even, the death squads were seeking talks with the government and wanted an equal footing with the FARC.

Juan Manuel Santos, a member of Pastrana's government-appointed peace commission and one of the giants of Colombia's Liberal Party, offered this analysis: "We would be ingenuous and stupid if we didn't take them into account in this peace process. They have shown their tremendous capacity for devastation." Consequently, Pastrana was in a quagmire, forced to juggle peace talks with the FARC, ELN, the death squads, and more importantly, conclude a successful outcome in four short years.

Unfortunately, the FARC announced a week latter that they were suspending the peace talks until the government produced what it called "satisfactory results" against the paramilitary death squads. The FARC announcement was a bitter disappointment to Pastrana and caused his already declining international prestige to dip even further. Auspiciously, however, a restart date for the peace talks was established for April 20, 1999.

President Pastrana was a man of strong conviction. He believed his people were trapped in the politics of war and the peace process was the only solution. Not a believer in hype, he knew actions were stronger than words, and he was going to prove that he was capable of conflict resolution. His enthusiasm was contagious, and those close to him couldn't help but share his conviction. Nonetheless, critics everywhere attacked him.

One of the biggest blows came from *Time Magazine International*. It printed a doomsday report stating that Colombia was in danger of being divided into three parts.[24] Another troubling blow to the peace process was delivered by Peruvian President Alberto Fujimori, who criticized Pastrana's peace plan during an official visit to Washington, in early February 1999.

Time Magazine International openly questioned Pastrana's leadership. "It [is] doubtful that the country can achieve peace without partition," the magazine said. "Pastrana's peace bid is a gamble, and a tall, perhaps impossible, order to fill. But the process is already in motion, and it will not be easy to halt. In a real sense, the question of who will rule Colombia in the future may now be in play."

To his credit, Pastrana responded in a diplomatic letter to the editor, which *Time* published.[25] The President protested the magazine's skepticism and pointed out that his government would not accept peace at any price. Moreover, Pastrana explained that he did not become President in order to preside over the country's dissolution. He openly admitted the state of

Colombia had ignored the needs of rural southern provinces for decades but added, "I believe it is only fair to ask for a reasonable period in which we will be able to work toward a realistic peace instead of the confrontation that could endanger the unity of my country and the security of the region."

Pastrana's reply fell on deaf ears as *Time* followed up with a far more critical report on January 18, 1999. It said, "Today Americans have to consider what might be called Yugo-lombia, the possibility that the country could soon be cleaved into three volatile, Balkan-like states as a result of a boiling war."[26]

The criticism from Fujimori carried a far greater sting. The Colombian government officially sent a letter of protest to the President of Peru for his undiplomatic remarks about Pastrana's peace process. "We are making our displeasure [known] with the inopportune statements by Fujimori and with the place that he chose to make his speech. Colombia's peace process is a reflection of the magnitude of the problem but not of any fear that [the guerrillas] are a threat to regional security," voiced Foreign Relations Minister Guillermo Fernandez de Sota.[27]

Fujimori, who took office at the height of a leftist guerrilla uprising, used heavy military force to virtually wipe out Peru's radical Maoist Shining Path rebels and Cuban-inspired Tupac Amaru Revolutionary Movement. Therefore, he felt well positioned to boast of his success and jab at Pastrana for not negotiating any visible concessions from the FARC for the 90-day demilitarization period.

The first five months in office for the young President were filled with highs and lows. The state visit was the highest high of his presidency and Sureshot's no-show at the peace talks in San Vicente del Caguán the lowest. Pastrana was vividly aware that the eyes of the world were watching his every move and he was determined to use this to his advantage. He took particular comfort in the knowledge that the most powerful nation in the world was at his side. During the state visit, a new priority communication system was put in place with Washington. Pastrana now had a hot line to Clinton, and he wouldn't hesitate to use it.

The young President was determined to continue to play the role of a dove. He had studied the failures of the past and he was not going to repeat them. History instructs, the future invites—this was his attitude. However, the guerrillas were stoic and the President knew he would need to establish trust to move forward. He realized the nation did not have his patience and that, in time, they would demand action—the window of opportunity would not last forever.

Pastrana was going to withstand the pressure to strike back, because he knew to retaliate would cause an escalation of the violence in the nation which had already caused so much damage. A recent report by the Colombian Health Ministry stated that it badly needs cash to deal with the psychological effects of the conflict. The ministry calculated that one Colombian family in four has lost a close relative to violence, and that one person in three who moved house in the past five years did so to escape violence. Moreover, it reported that 25 percent of mental illness in Colombia was directly related to violence, compared with 3.5 percent elsewhere in Latin America.[28]

The President's solution required patience, especially from the armed forces, and he was determined to prevent them from breaking the peace. He knew the military wanted to escalate the war and that, given the chance, they would try to settle old scores. Without restraint, they would continue well-documented history of human rights abuses and allow the violence to go on for another 100 years. Pastrana was aware the Americans were suspicious of the Colombian armed forces and were watching them closely. By law, the U.S. could not give money to militaries with controversial human rights records, so, Pastrana realized, he needed to teach the military to respect peace. The odds were against him succeeding. However, in order to secure a lasting settlement, to lead Colombia into a new era of peace, he was forced to make the attempt, even at the risk of failure.

Pastrana intuitively realized the task before him was immense. He would not shy away from unpopular decisions, though, and would prove to the world that he was worthy of the challenge and that he could bring peace, not at any expense, but at a cost that the country could afford. It was not ego driving him; it was not fame he sought. He was a loving father. Both he and his wife Nohra adored their children and all the children of Colombia, and they knew the children had no future without peace. The President had four years to establish it. In one speech he quoted a wise saying, "Without peace, there is no bread." It was as true to him as he knew it must have been to Sureshot. Nonetheless, Pastrana understood that Sureshot was not a fool and that he would try to outfox him. The FARC had said they would never lay down their arms; they would continue to prepare for war. Therefore the President, although he would restrain his armed forces, would make sure that they prepared for war as well.

Colombia was in absolute turmoil in January of 1999. The peace process was losing momentum and the country was growing impatient. However, Pastrana still had widespread support among the powerful figures in the nation. One of them, Enrique Santos of *El Tiempo*, the most respected columnist in Colombia, succinctly observed, "If talks break down, Pastrana

will be able to say he was unable to cope with subversives hell-bent on destroying the country, thereby forcing him to ask for foreign help to fight an internal war."

On another front, Nobel laureate Gabriel García Márquez was publicly defending Bill Clinton. Márquez, the owner of *Cambio Magazine,* wrote in the January 25 issue that President Clinton made some "unpardonable" mistakes thanks to his tryst with Monica Lewinsky, but lying about it wasn't one of them.[29] Márquez commented on the White House scandal in an article headlined "Unfinished Lover."

It was Márquez's first article published in *Cambio* since he and six other prominent writers and journalists had taken control of the weekly magazine earlier in the month.[30] "Puritanism is an insatiable vice that feeds on its own shit," he wrote in his commentary, which was peppered with scathing remarks about the religious right and the feeding frenzy over Clinton's private life.[31] Márquez, who met Clinton on three occasions, recalled in his article how he was impressed by the American President's "power of seduction" and "the splendor of his intelligence" when he spoke with him for the first time on Martha's Vineyard in 1995.[32]

"The President only wanted to do what every man has done and hidden from his wife since the beginning of time," according to Márquez.[33] Clinton's problem was that he betrayed his initial instinct to lie about Lewinsky, and carry on like any other "self-respecting adulterer with his head held high…. Unfortunately, he accepted his guilt with the same determination that he had denied it … and that was one of his fatal mistakes…. It's one thing to lie to fool people and something very different to hide the truth to protect your private life," wrote Márquez.[34]

On February 7, 1999, the 90-day demilitarization period expired. Sensing he

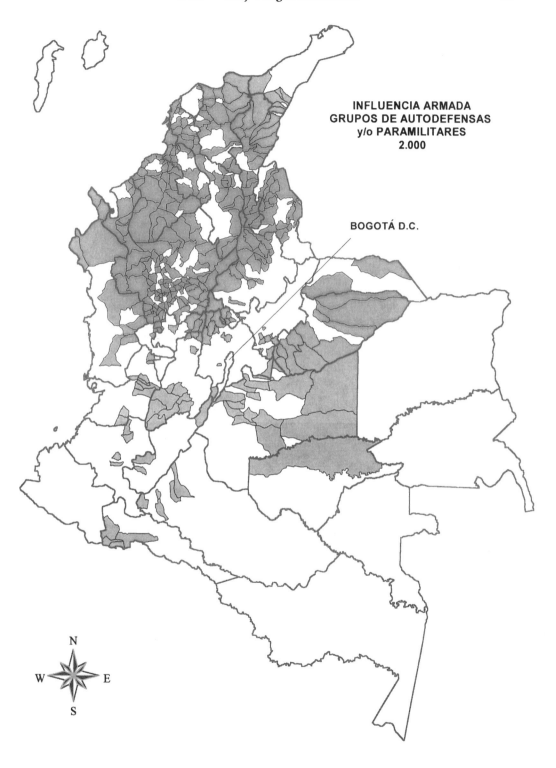

INFLUENCIA ARMADA
GRUPOS DE AUTODEFENSAS
y/o PARAMILITARES
2.000

BOGOTÁ D.C.

Armed Influence of United Self-Defense Forces and/or Paramilitary Groups (2000). From *Defense of the Pueblo, Republic of Colombia*

had few choices, and wanting to continue the disciplined practice of conflict resolution, President Pastrana extended the deadline another 90 days, until May 7. He wanted to show the world, as well as Comandante Sureshot and his well-trained army of FARC guerrillas, that he was truly committed to the peace process. Unfortunately, hawks in Colombia bashed the move and openly questioned the wisdom of granting Sureshot and his FARC guerrillas a safe haven from which to operate and to stage attacks against the government.

Notes

1. The independent Consultancy on Human Rights and Forced Displacement (Codhes) reported from Bogotá on 29 November 1998 that 241,312 Colombians from 48,000 separate families had abandoned their homes by the end of September 1998. No comparison was given for the same period the previous year. "Some 240,000 Colombians have been displaced so far this year which could make 1998 the worst year for forced displacement in the last 15 years," Codhes researcher Jorge Rojas told *El Colombiano* newspaper, which published parts of the report.

2. The Colombian National Statistics Department (DANE) released a report on 21 July 1998 stating that 36 percent of, or 14.4 million, Colombians are poor. Moreover, about 9 percent live in extreme poverty, according to DANE. The government's National Planning Department (DNP) reported that families making less that $372 per month were poor and households making only $149 per month lived in extreme poverty. The figures were based on a 1997 survey of 10,000 households. Also included in the DANE report were statistics that indicated that most Colombians had access to public utilities. About 85.6 percent of the population had running water, 93.8 percent electricity and 70.8 percent sewerage service, according to the report.

3. Karl Penhaul, Reuters, "Colombia Rebels Map Out Plan to Topple Government," 15 January 1999.

4. John Otis, *Houston Chronicle,* "Colombian Army Suffers One of Its Worst Defeats in Fight with Rebels," 8 March 1998.

5. Douglas Farah, *Washington Post,* "Colombian Rebels Seen Winning War; U.S. Study Finds Army Inept, Ill-Equipped," 10 April 1998.

6. Herbert Braun, *Our Guerrillas, Our Sidewalks* (Niwot: University Press of Colorado, 1994), pp. IX.

7. *El Tiempo,* Miércoles 4 de Noviembre de 1998, p. 6A.

8. Commandant Romaña's true identity is Henry Castellanos Garzone. Romaña is in his thirties, heavyset and reportedly lacks the intellectual powers of the Argentine revolutionary hero he worships, Che Guevara, according to Colombian Military and Police Archives.

9. Che Guevara, the Argentinean Revolutionary who joined Fidel Castro's guerrillas in the overthrow of the Batista government in Cuba. The complete story of Che can be found in the masterpiece by Jon Lee Anderson, *Che Guevara, A Revolutionary Life* (see bibliographical essay).

10. *El Tiempo,* Bogotá, Martes 3 de Noviembre de 1998, p. 6A.

11. Colombian Red Cross Director Teddy Tormbaum's firsthand account upon arriving at the battle scene in Mitú after the 14-hour siege Sunday, 1 November 1998.

12. Tod Robberson, *The Dallas Morning News,* "Colombia Turning Over Land to Rebels, Hoping for Peace. Risky Move Gives Guerrillas Too Much," 6 November 1998, p. 1A.

13. Isabel Hilton, *Manchester Guardian,* "Forget the Drugs War by Taking the First Step; Man Deserves a Salute from Us All," England, 16 November 1998.

14. Reuters, "Colombia Gloomy on Peace, Back Military Option," Bogotá, 24 December 1998.

15. Karl Penhaul, Reuters, "Castano [*sic*] dubbed Colombia's Most Vicious Warlord," Bogotá, 29 December 1998.

16. *Ibid.*

17. Reuters, "Colombia Rebels Say Top Death Squad Leader Killed," Bogotá, 29 December 1998.

18. Karl Penhaul, Reuters, "Colombia Death Squads Deny Leader Castano [*sic*] Killed," Bogotá, 30 December 1998.

19. *Ibid.*

20. Diana Jean Schemo, *New York Times* "Colombian Rebel Leader Misses Peace Meeting," San Vicente del Caguán, 8 January 1999.

21. *Ibid.*

22. *Ibid.*

23. Tim Johnson, *Miami Herald,* "Toll of Militia Terror on Rise in Colombia," Bogotá, 12 January 1999.

24. Tim Padgett, *Time Magazine International,* "A Shift in the Balance of Power," On the Caguán River, Colombia, 28 September 1998, Vol. 152, No. 13.

25. *Time Magazine International,* Letters, 30 November 1998, Vol. 152, No. 22.

26. Tim Padgett, *Time Magazine International,* "The Backyard Balkans, Colombia's President Isn't Only Fighting Drug Lords, He's Also Struggling to Hold His Country Together," Caqueta, Colombia, 18 January 1999.

27. Reuters, "Colombia Protests Fujimori Comments on Peace Talks," Bogotá, 7 February 1999.

28. *The Economist,* "Living with Death in Colombia," Bogotá, 13 February 1999.

29. Rueters, "García Márquez Slams Puritanism, Defends Clinton," Bogotá, 24 January 1999.

30. *Ibid.*

31. *Ibid.*

32. *Ibid.*

33. *Ibid.*

34. *Ibid.*

CHAPTER THREE

The Genesis of Violence

Thirty-three year-old Rosalba Sánchez de Santana lived in a ramshackle house about 18 miles north of Bogotá and each day she prayed to be rescued. Every night she went to sleep hoping she could end the grinding nightmare she was trapped in. Her shameful husband had quit and walked out. He never returned. Now, she and her two boys and two little girls were left to fend for themselves. The children were very young, all between five and eleven. They loved her and looked to her for safety. She loved them and tried her best to sustain them. But every barren morning the hunger returned and she struggled to put food on the table. She had no skills. She could not find work. The newspapers said twenty per cent of the country was looking for jobs. Consequently, every dismal day she searched to find scraps and crumbs to eat.

It hurt her knowing the children were suffering. It pained her knowing that the life ahead for the children was bleak. It saddened her knowing that she could not provide for the children. Rosalba was surrounded by the darkness of poverty. Her government was invisible. The poor around her were joining the ranks of the guerrillas and preparing for war. She was abandoned and realized that if she continued the disheartening act of survival she would be condemned to a life of misery. So on Monday night she arranged a special meal. She summoned all her courage, secretly slipped the poison into their final meal, and informed the children that tomorrow there would be no more hunger. She told them that they would finally escape the heartache. She told them their love for one another would keep them together forever. Shortly after finishing supper, she reached out and held her children in her arms one last time. She smiled for them, and watched them close their eyes. Then she wept and surrendered her spirit.[1]

Colombia has had a long relationship with violence. Historians will never compare it to the colossal catastrophe of the Fall of Rome, or to the carnage of the American Civil War. However, no one would dare approach the history of violence in Colombia without a profound degree of awe and even apprehension. The civil war has been an event so tragic and so terrible, the level of personal suffering and anguish so incomprehensible, that the phenomenon defies the basic instincts of humanity. As a result of this dreadful distinction very few foreigners immigrate to Colombia.

On the surface, the country has enormous potential. Economically, it has a reputation for diversification and stability and, up until recently, had Latin America's most consistent record of growth over the last several decades. The gross domestic product (GDP) expanded every year for more than 25 years, and unlike many other South American countries, Colombia did not default on any of its official debts during the "Lost Decade" of the 1980s.

Despite all of these economic laurels, severe poverty fueled the violence in the country. Two respected economists, R. Albert Berry and Miguel Urrutia, examined the subject in 1976 and predicted that income distribution would be an important policy question in Colombia.[2] The economists observed that "Inequality (poor vs. rich) was at a high absolute level in Colombia, compared to other countries."[3]

Berry and Urrutia conducted an exhaustive study on the skewed income distribution system and were pioneers in forecasting that the issue would be an important factor for the nation's economic well-being in the future. Today, Colombia's wealthiest ten percent absorb 40 percent of the nation's income while the downtrodden 20 percent obtain only five percent.[4] The most striking example of income disparity can be found in the countryside, where 30 percent of the population resides. The top three percent of the landed elite own 71.3 percent of arable land, while 57 percent of the poorest farmers subsist on 2.8 percent.[5] Unfortunately, Colombia's political leaders had largely ignored poverty. As a result, the issue had managed to become a crucial fundamental consideration in the nation's longstanding internal conflict.

Politically, Colombia's two-party system bears much of the responsibility for the poverty in the country. The system originated in 1826 when Simón Bolívar was elected the first President of Colombia and Francisco de Paula Santander, Vice President. The two parties grew out of conflicts between the followers of Bolívar and Santander. Bolívar's supporters formed the nucleus of what would be the Conservative Party and Santander's followers were the forerunners of the Liberal Party. Since the early days of the republic, the government's resources have gone primarily to the well-being of the country's major cities and their surrounding areas. The rural areas have received very little.

One result of this disparate policy can be seen in the educational system today. In urban areas, Colombia has a nine-year compulsory education program and 80 percent of the children enter school. In rural areas only five years of primary school were offered. As a result of this imbalance, literacy in the countryside is only 67 percent, compared with nearly 93 percent in the cities.

The social animosity and competition between the two traditional parties triggered two long civil wars in the past 100 years and ignited hundreds of other conflicts that accounted for the loss of approximately 400,000 lives. The deciding factor for violence in Colombia was whether a moderate or extremist dominated the ruling party. During the periods when moderate political actors of both sides were in power, the parties were able to work together in peaceful coalitions, but when extremist elements took over, conflict often followed. Consequently, during the competitive periods, one party usually sought to limit or completely eliminate the rival party's participation in the political process. These actions often resulted in further outbreaks of political violence.

Therefore, Colombia has a history rare for Latin America in that it has had limited military rule and has been dominated by civilian governments and regular free elections. Yet since the start of the republic the elites divided into two rival groups to contend in the political arena. A troubling aspect of this exclusive rule was that both parties ignored the poverty in the countryside and discouraged other nontraditional groups from maintaining an active voice in the ruling process. The resultant poverty and exclusion from political involvement planted the seeds for the problems that plague the nation today.

In the 1960s, three major left-wing guerrilla organizations— the Revolutionary Armed Forces of Colombia (FARC), the National Liberation Army (ELN), and the Popular Liberation Army (EPL)— along with several smaller groups established bases in the Colombian countryside. In the 1970s, a fourth major organization, the 19th of April Movement (M-19), began guerrilla operations in urban areas. (As of today, only the FARC and ELN exist.) The guerrilla leaders found fertile conditions among the poor. They encountered little difficulty recruiting and immediately sought to undermine public order through kidnappings, murders, robberies, assaults on military and police facilities, and destruction of key economic installations. Nearly all the guerrillas, with the notable exception of the middle-class M-19 Movement, were recruited from the poorest elements of Colombian society. Therefore, the groups forsaken by the political establishment gravitated to the guerrillas as a means to combat poverty and to acquire a voice for change.

At the beginning, the guerrillas sought refuge in the remote areas of the country: the jungles, the mountain ranges and along the isolated borders. The frontier was desirable because it represented the furthest distance from the army and the weakest area of government influence. However, this created a problem with the indigenous Indians. On first contact, most of the Indians sought to be independent from the guerrillas. The Indians fended off attempts by the guerrillas to infiltrate their political organizations and enlist their support. But after suffering continuous attacks by the Colombian armed forces, which assumed the majority of the Indians supported the guerrillas, and after having been forced off

valuable territories by large landowners, cooperation with the guerrillas increased.

The violence in Colombia did not start in the 1960s with the arrival of the first insurgents. The chronology of major civil unrest in Colombia dates further back, to the War of One Thousand Days in 1899. The three-year war was the first major clash between representatives of the Liberal and Conservative parties. Overall, 100,000 lives were lost. Unfortunately, the violence did not stop at the conclusion of the conflict. Widespread land disputes, particularly in the coffee zones, and strikes by banana and oil workers, in addition to tenant struggles involving the payment of rents made the Colombian countryside a dangerous place to live. Moderate Conservative and Liberal politicians attempted to cooperate, but the extreme party factions would continue to find ways to contribute to the great destruction of life after the War of One Thousand Days.

With time, the nation turned numb to the violence in the countryside. The elites who resided in the big cities and controlled the political process in the country developed an "out of sight, out of mind" mentality toward the rural poor. With the exception of *La Violencia* from 1948 to 1953 and Pablo Escobar's reign of terror in the late 1980s and early 1990s, the big cities were relatively free of prolonged periods of violence, allowing the elites to live in relative security. The government-sponsored growth in the big cities afforded them the luxury of overlooking the hardship of the countryside.

The two-party system that we know today was officially launched in 1849. David Bushnell, the author of the superb narrative *The Making of Modern Colombia: A Nation in Spite of Itself,* explained that in 1849 the Conservatives abandoned the *Ministeriales,* or Ministerial party name, and the Liberals dropped the *Progresista* label.[6] The Liberal-Conservative dichotomy was described by Bushnell as one of *tienda* (store) and *hacienda* (farm), with the Liberals representing the commercial and professional interests and the Conservatives primarily the party of the large landowners.[7] The description appropriately identifies the core of the two political parties. More specifically, the Conservatives were closely aligned with the Roman Catholic Church, whereas the Liberals attempted to reduce the power and influence of the church because they saw them as obstacles to the nation's material and intellectual progress.[8] Both parties were originally multiclass and nationwide and were created to promote collaboration across class lines. Bushnell comments, though, that the parties also worked "To serve as one more mechanism of social control whereby upper-class leaders manipulated lower-class followers.[9]

Over a period of time the Liberal Party embraced urban areas, industrialization and labor. It was profederalism, anticlerical and advocated the expansion of individual rights. The Conservative Party was strongest in the rural areas, and maintained a platform that favored the military, large landowners, limited suffrage and a centralized government. A negative policy of the Colombian political system was that the parties consistently used the perquisites of government to create and maintain popular support through patronage. The result was the party in power controlled the national budget, government jobs, and a good portion of the economy. Consequently, the lower and middle classes were bound to the political elites through patron-client relationships in the urban areas or through tenant–large landowner arrangements in the rural zones.

The patron-client relationships tied the masses into a political system that revolved around bodies of voters mobilized and controlled by local political bosses. The affiliations adopted by the lower and middle classes depended upon their relationship with influential patrons and wealthy families and became what the noted scholar of Colombian affairs Robert H. Dix famously termed, "Inherited hatreds."

In 1997, Fernando Rojas, the President of the Inter-American Legal Services Association and Visiting Scholar at the David Rockefeller Center for Latin American Studies at Harvard University, described the patron-client relationship in this fashion: "It is a culture where beliefs such as, I give to you, you give to me, and we exclude the rest of the population, dominate the mind frame of many Colombians in power."[10]

The highly regarded historian John D. Martz examined the unique relationship of dependence in his book, *The Politics of Clientelism: Democracy and the State of Colombia.* Martz explained that the state was the prime regulator, coordinator, and pacesetter of the entire national system, the apex of the pyramid from which patronage, wealth, power and programs flow.[11] The form of the government dated back to 1899, and at that time no real system of checks and balances existed. The lack of accountability prompted extremist elements of the Conservative Party to exploit the resources of the government for its political benefit and to exclude the Liberal Party, according to Martz. Complicating matters further in 1899 were Liberal allegations of tainted elections. Conservative Party repression and denial of executive office to others at all levels increased, and triggered the 1899 War of One Thousand Days.

The Liberal Party rushed to muster forces for battle. Unfortunately, the poorly organized Liberal army suffered a defeat in Bucaramanga on November 13, 1899. However, they managed to regroup and were victorious in the battle of Peralonso, in the province of Santander, the following month. Morale soared with the victory and Liberals anticipated further gains, but the tide turned. Just five months later, from May 11 to May 26, of 1900, they were decimated at Palonegro by Conservative forces which vastly outnumbered them. The Liberals were then short of soldiers and munitions, and faced a bleak outlook on the battlefield. So, out of necessity, the Liberals changed strategy, and unleashed a force that would haunt the nation forever. Out of pure desperation, they switched the code of combat from one of conventional military tactics to one of guerrilla warfare. In doing so, they transformed the war into a bitter struggle that lasted for two more years and gave birth to a form of violence that fighters would employ with frightening results for the next 100 years.

Ultimately, in November of 1902, the Liberals succumbed. The defeated army was forced to negotiate a peace agreement with the ruling Conservative government. The war took more than 100,000 lives and created a small warrior class among the poor. The War of One Thousand Days coincided with a sharp economic downturn, resulting from a worldwide weakening of coffee prices that left the economy mangled. The war also caused the government to neglect foreign affairs; its preoccupation with the aftereffects of the conflict can be partially blamed for Panama's secession from the Republic of Colombia in 1903. Eventually, the War of One Thousand Days discredited the militant factions of each party that instigated it, and led to reconciliation between the moderates of both.

The man responsible for bringing the country back together was Conservative Party leader General Rafael Reyes, who was elected President in 1904. Reyes implemented strong economic measures to spur domestic industrial growth and created a National Assembly that included representation for the Liberal Party. Still smarting from the loss of Panama, the President nonetheless set out to normalize relations with the United States, a decision that was quite unpopular in Colombia. Reyes considered the move essential in improving the prospects for trade, in restoring Colombia's credit abroad and in attracting foreign investment.

Another major directive by Reyes was the 1909 decision to strengthen Colombia's military establishment. The President turned to Chile for military advice and training. The Chilean army with over 20 years of Prussian military training behind it, succeeded in developing a well-organized and well-trained Colombian army of 8,000 men by 1911. Today one can still see the influence of that training in the Casa de Nariño, the President's Palace, where the Honor Guards wear the armored spiked helmet, or *Pickelhaube,* a vestige of the Prussian Army.[12] Historian Charles W. Bergquist traced the origins of the War of One Thousand Days in his study of the political implications of the coffee export economy of Colombia between 1886 and 1910.[13] Bergquist explored the powerful economic, political and cultural currents of the era in impressive detail, and concluded that weak commodity prices, particularly that of coffee, also contributed heavily to the outbreak of civil war in 1899.

Despite the good faith efforts by Reyes to make the political process more democratic, he had little success eliminating the simmering discontent of the poor in the countryside. Moreover, extremists in both parties continued to agitate against his government. Nonetheless, his actions were noteworthy because of the groundbreaking effort to foster a period of reconciliation with the bold experiment of sharing power.

The lack of land reform and the absence of adequate working conditions for laborers accounted for conflict over the next three decades. At the conclusion of the war, the poor gradually started to migrate to the thinly populated mountain hillsides well outside the cities, and attempted to carve out a living growing coffee. The poor settlers also migrated into the lower or medium elevations of the country to try to raise cattle or grow cotton. This migrational movement served as an outlet for population growth and resulted in the diversification of the frontier.

However, as more settlers attempted to escape the poverty of the city, land invasions by squatters became a common practice. The squatters clashed with the large landowners who practiced appropriating, legally or illegally, great stretches of the public domain, more than they ever needed for production, to assure themselves, in part, a steady supply of labor and, in some cases, a pool of voters. Over time, the government tried to step in and buy up a few large estates for distribution and resale to squatters but the problem of unclear titles resulted in endless litigation and violence. In 1926 the Colombian Supreme Court ruled that unless a clear title could be proven, the land reverted to the state. The unpopular ruling did little to resolve the tense situation and thereafter many disputes were settled by armed conflict. The death of Roman Catholic priest Mariano de Jesús Euse Hoyos in 1926 also contributed to the violence. De Jesús Euse dedicated his entire life to helping poor countryside *campesinos* deal with poverty. Without his passive leadership many poor resorted to violence to settle accounts.

Other parts of the country were experiencing a different kind of violence. Workers were starting to organize against difficult labor conditions. One of the largest targets of organized labor in Colombia was the United Fruit Company (UFCO), a Boston based American concern that started an ambitious investment in the northeastern coastal region of Colombia. UFCO entered Colombia with the full support of the government and built a massive apparatus in Santa Marta that included its own transportation system, communica-tion network, irrigation mechanism and company stores.

The UFCO complex created a virtual state within a state. Its management quickly alienated local banana growers by forcing them to sell their perishable commodities to the company at dishonestly low prices. UFCO also angered local merchants by issuing workers scrip for wages earned for use only at company stores. With time UFCO banana workers started complaining to the government about miserable working conditions, but, the government failed to aid them. As a result leftist leaders, both socialist and communist, joined the banana workers. The fact that the employer, UFCO, was a foreign company made it easier for the agitators to mobilize worker sentiment against it and obtain the sympathy of the general population.

In 1918, the workers approached UFCO management and demanded improved working conditions. Management immediately responded with a tough position. They adamantly rejected the demands and refused to bargain with the workers. Shortly thereafter, at the calling of UFCO, the government entered the picture with its well-trained army and intimidated the workers into submission. However, the net impact of the military force displayed by the government on behalf of UFCO management was to harden the position of the workers and intensify their efforts to organize.

By 1925 there were isolated reports of foreigners arriving in Colombia and spreading out to actively assist banana and oil workers unite. The Conservatives in power, led by President Pedro Nel Ospina, considered these foreigners a danger to society and labeled them Communists—a term they would regularly use to describe political activists who sought change for the poor, and a term that would rally the Conservative party regulars who were strong anti–Communists. The government frowned on the arrival and influence of the foreigners and increased efforts to assist UFCO and other similar foreign companies suppress worker unrest.

Gradually, the workers formed unions and grew in numbers and organizational strength. On November 11, 1928, the unified workers decided to stage a major banana, railroad, field workers and port strike against UFCO management. Their leader was Alberto Castrillón, the head of the newly formed Revolutionary Socialist Party (PSR), which would in 1930 become the Colombian Communist Party. Another key PSR figure assisting the banana workers was María Cano, the "Revolutionary Red Flower," who afterwards would be a strong pioneer in the struggle for women's rights. Castrillón demanded higher wages, Sunday rest, compensation for accidents, better housing, hospital facilities, the end of company stores, recognition of unions and other benefits.

UFCO refused to negotiate and sought the assistance of the Conservative Party President Miguel Abadía Méndez, who had been a professor of constitutional law at the time of his election in 1926. Abadía apparently could find no better solution and dispatched the army to suppress the strikers. General Cortés Vargas led the government troops and immediately jailed hundreds of union workers when he arrived on the scene. General Vargas also provided UFCO with nonunion workers and established protection for the strikebreakers.

The striking workers reacted violently to the military measures, and General Vargas wasted little time responding to the worker's acts of defiance. He ordered his army to destroy the strikers and all their sympathizers, which resulted in the ruthless death of hundreds. The bloodshed started in the town of Ciénaga and spread. The violence prompted Vargas to call a state of siege, allowing him to implement highly irregular military courts-martial of the civilians that resulted in 31 severe jail sentences.

Gabriel García Márquez, born on March 6, 1928, was raised in the nearby UFCO town of Aracataca and used the history of the region for the horrific banana company sequences in *One Hundred Years of Solitude*.[14] Moreover, the American role in the confrontation heightened the view in Latin America among some leading intellectuals and politicians that the United States was a greedy, irresponsible, even brutal imperialist power whose affluence was the result of the same exploitation that had caused the region's underdevelopment.

News of the atrocities and highly arbitrary legal military proceedings jarred the nation. The unnecessary force General Vargas used to put down the strike outraged many leaders in the country. The event galvanized a dynamic young politician in Bogotá, a man who began then on a long career of defending the poor underprivileged class in Colombia. The public servant who stepped forward was Jorge Eliécer Gaitán. A flamboyant dresser from a humble background, Gaitán would evolve to be one of Colombia's most important politicians.

Gaitán would shake the nation in the years to come with his fiery demands of equality for all. If Simón Bolívar was Colombia's George Washington, then surely Jorge Eliécer Gaitán was its Abraham Lincoln. Both Lincoln and Gaitán wanted to break the chains of bondage: Lincoln wanted to end the barbaric expansion of slavery; Gaitán wanted to abolish an aristocratic system of elite rule where the underprivileged were merely spectators in the political process.

Gaitán would attempt to bring the country together and give all Colombians, rich and poor, equal standing in the eyes of the law. Gaitán attacked poverty rather than wealth and soon became the undisputed leader of the underprivileged class. He had hard words for Colombia's "directing class" whom he accused of looking after its own interests while ignoring the suffering of the poor.[15] In doing so, Gaitán would become the object of scorn and loathing from some of the economic elite and leaders of the traditional two-party structure.

Jorge Eliécer Gaitán was a firebrand. "I am not a man! I am a people!" became his legendary political cry. He managed to change the direction of politics in Colombia by convincing the poor that his interests were their interests. His politics were eventually christened "Gaitanismo." The integration of capitalism and socialism within the framework of democracy was his challenge. Like all aspiring Colombian politicians, Gaitán realized that the only way to power was within the traditional two-party system. Therefore, he fought hard for admittance to the mainstream political structure and attempted to drag his poor following with him. Initially, the sheer number of devotees with him paved the way for acceptance. Afterwards, he had to rely on his political wits to gain admittance to the rarefied upper echelons of major political decision-makers.

Gaitán was not born of wealth. Historically, the underprivileged did not rule in Colombia. The noteworthy exception was Marco Fidel Suárez who became President in 1918. Suárez was born in a hut, the illegitimate son of an Antioquía peasant girl, and was cited by the elite as an example that a narrow oligarchic caste did not dominate Colombian politics. However, by the time Suárez reached the presidency, he was a religious mystic, literary dilettante, and long-time Conservative functionary who did very little for his fellow peasants. In fact, during the Suárez presidency the working class received what one labor historian called its "Baptism of Blood" when he suppressed a Bogotá tailors demonstration with force, killing seven and wounding others.[16]

Gaitán was from a lower-middle class mestizo family and sacrificed to get an education. His academic excellence was noted at an early age and, after finishing university in Colombia, he managed to scrape together the funds to study law in Italy under the penal law scholar Enrico Ferri. Gaitán worked hard in Italy and demonstrated his capacity for brilliance by finishing first in his class. Upon graduation the distinguished Ferri said Gaitán was one of the most extraordinary students he had ever taught.[17] Determined to make an impact, Gaitán returned to Colombia in 1928 and was elected to the lower Chamber of Representatives by a poor neighborhood of Bogotá.

In early 1929, Gaitán instinctively took up the banner of the banana workers and conducted a number of groundbreaking investigations into the government's handling of the bloody 1928 strike. By September of 1929, a debate was arranged to examine the violence of the banana strike. The stage was set; Gaitán now had a national forum to attack the government for the brutal use of force on the banana workers. The debate of 1929 convinced Gaitán that his future should be committed to defending the interests of the lower classes. It electrified him. He published articles, he gave speeches, and refused to accept the government's ruling that military courts try the workers.[18] Upon one fact-finding trip to the banana zone Gaitán reportedly turned to a colleague and said that he must leave because if he stayed with the horrors about, he would end up in an insane asylum.

The debate went on for 15 consecutive days. The galleries in the National Assembly were filled with spectators. Gaitán seized the moment with his emotional delivery. At one point, he dramatically pledged to donate his modest Chamber salary to the widows of slain workers although he himself was economically pressed. The crowds adored him. Gaitán was an excellent speaker, a master of slogans, and he soon taught the lower classes

The beloved Jorge Eliécer Gaitán (on balcony) speaks to a large gathering of the pueblo. *El Tiempo*

to fully comprehend and detest the word, oligarchy. As the debate progressed revelations of army atrocities and corruption by the government agencies investigating the strike brought denunciations of President Miguel Abadía Méndez and his Minister of War.

The national newspapers followed the debate closely and reported stories of General Vargas's drunkenness as well as gruesome stories and photographs of pitiful widows and children. During one emotional session, a skull of a decapitated banana worker child was brought in as evidence. The probing debate uncovered information that UFCO bought the army. Evidence was brought forward that the company paid officers 500 pesos apiece and loaded up the troops with beer and

cigarettes. Vargas suffered further embarrassment when it was disclosed that he received an official banquet in his honor by UFCO brass for his work on their behalf. The debate forced the Minister of War to resign in disgrace for signing the declaration of siege and authorizing the massacre.

In taking up the cause of the miserable banana workers Gaitán created a populist image that would stay with him the rest of his career. He managed to develop an emotional link to the lower classes with his moralistic speeches of equality. Liberal Party bosses applauded his splendid exploitation of the Conservative government's cozy corruption with UFCO. The debate hurt the Conservatives, but it was another scandal shortly thereafter involving widespread misuse of Conservative Party funds in Bogotá that doomed President Méndez.

In 1930, Liberal Party candidate Enrique Olaya Herrera was swept into the presidency, ending nearly 50 years of Conservative Party rule. With the Liberal victory, rural Conservative Party members now feared for their safety and clandestinely started to organize their own small bands of armed groups to defend against the Liberal guerrillas still operating among them. Subsequently, for the first time in the history of the nation, the two traditional parties had roving bands of armed vigilantes, working completely outside the law of the land, to practice an eye for an eye justice. A nasty outgrowth of the traditional Colombian two-party system (a system superficially taken as evidence of the country's political stability by the outside world) was this handy way of keeping alive old grudges and passing them on from father to son to grandson.[19] A major problem in 1930 was simply that the Liberals had been out of power for a half century. At most, they had held whatever minor share of jobs and spoils the Conservatives had seen fit to give them. Conservatives, on the other hand, had grown used to having the public payroll almost as their private possession. Therefore, scattered outbreaks of violence occurred in a number of departments. In some instances trouble began when jubilant Liberals set out to settle old scores, to take revenge for real or imaginary injustices received under the rule of their adversaries; in other instances local Conservative bosses were not prepared to hand over power gracefully.[20] Unfortunately, the toll of dead and wounded attracted little attention outside Colombia.

Gaitán was now a rising star. His performance in the banana strike debate hurled him into national prominence. However, his strong defense of the poor and his role in undermining the Conservative Party still did not gain him immediate access to the decision-making process in the Liberal Party. In fact, his attacks on the oligarchy alienated many party bosses. As a result, Gaitán would have to bide his time before party leaders would embrace him and trust him for a national role. He was promised that day would come. Determined, he continued his work on behalf of the poor and took a strong position on improving working conditions in the country. Gaitán advocated an eight-hour working day, accident and health insurance, paid holidays, and protection for women and minors. However, the ascension of the Liberal Party resulted in worker protests throughout the country, particularly in the coffee sector. Large landowners resisted Liberal attempts to improve working conditions, touching off bouts of violence. Some of the large landowners deeply resented the demands the local workers imposed on them and longed for the days when the poor obediently followed orders.

Gaitán gravitated to explosive issues. In August of 1930, he investigated the problem of land disputes and subsequently disclosed critical information of widespread abuses by large landowners. He sided with the poor *colonos* (squatters) trying to scratch a living from small parcels of land. Gaitán demanded that the state protect the *colonos* and warned that the intolerable conditions in the countryside would lead to violence if conditions were not revamped. He advocated a fair and even distribution of state land for the poor, an outlandish idea that had Conservatives and even some Liberals thinking he was a closet Communist. Gaitán viewed the ownership of vast territories by a few large landowners as inhibiting the natural development of the individual in Colombia, while his opposition considered the uneducated as undeserving of such opportunity.

Gaitán's popularity with the poor soared, so much so that Liberal leaders privately stepped in and asked him to tone down his fiery rhetoric, so as not to inflame the masses. The bosses promised the energetic Gaitán a greater role in Liberal Party politics if he became more pragmatic and accepted less vigorous land reform legislation. He accepted the advice despite opposition from some of his closest advisors.

In 1931 Gaitán advocated a social democratic movement that was unfriendly to foreign companies. He warned of foreign imperialism and strongly debated the need for big North American companies in Colombia. Oil companies soon found the negotiation of concessions much more tedious because of rising nationalistic pressure. Gaitán also attempted to force the state to pay attention to the individual. He wanted liberalism to embrace socialism. He encouraged the masses to have an active voice in politics for the first time in the history of the nation; he realized the only way this was possible was to unite the poor into a political block of votes that could not be ignored.

As his popularity grew his problems with Liberal bosses increased. Liberal leaders recognized that Gaitán and his growing movement would eventually circumvent the power of the economic and political elite. They considered him an extremist and were frightened that the young were flocking to his side. Traditional and non-traditional voters supported Gaitán's fresh ideas, which created resentment from veterans of the ruling elite and inspired plans among them to isolate Gaitán in order to contain further gains. The plan worked. Suddenly important doors were shut in Gaitán's face as the rich and powerful attempted to neutralize Gaitán's popularity. Sensing the conspiracy, Gaitán sought alternative support in a move that had dangerous implications. He impulsively decided to break away from the traditional

Liberal Party machine and start his very own left-wing organization.

Consequently, in April 1933, Gaitán and Carlos Arango Vélez, a long-term admirer of Lenin, started the Revolutionary Leftist National Union, Unión Nacional Izquieroista Revolucionaria (UNIR). Gaitán and Vélez formally drafted a manifesto describing dissatisfaction with the existing Liberals and called for the creation of a national radical left movement independent of all other political parties. The new party wanted social change and the development of class-consciousness. UNIR did not draw support from the elite. Undaunted, the pair of radicals pushed forward, using all the limited funds available and launched the new party with the provocative slogan, "Death to the Past, Revolution to the Future." From the outset, support for UNIR came from workers, *campesinos,* small merchants and disaffected intellectuals.

Gaitán warned the elites that if the government continued to disregard the intolerable conditions in the countryside or maintained a deliberate pattern of indifference, violence would only accelerate. His critics in the Liberal and Conservative parties responded that he built UNIR on dangerous class resentment and never offered a viable political program to help the poor. They argued that President Olaya Herrera had implemented a number of credible reforms from 1930 to 1934 to help the standard of living of the lower classes, and some of these reforms, particularly those to improve worker conditions, included many Gaitán initiatives. Therefore, the oligarchy was baffled by Gaitán's demands for further reform when a number of positive changes had already taken place. Colombian elites bitterly resented the "gun to the head" mentality that Gaitán represented.

Nonetheless, the Liberal Party won the presidency again in 1934. The new President was Alfonso López Pumarejo. To the surprise of everyone, López introduced a whirlwind of strong reforms, with his "Revolution of the March," that were the most far-reaching the nation had ever known. The President was reportedly heavily influenced by the reforms of the Mexican Constitution of 1917, the progressive ideas taking place in Peru by the Alianza Popular Revolucionaria Americana and Franklin D. Roosevelt's New Deal. López recognized the growing importance of the forsaken poor and set about to make sweeping changes in social, labor and land policy.

President López also understood that Gaitán was entirely too dangerous outside the Liberal Party. The reform-minded President reached out to Gaitán and managed to lure him back into the Liberal Party fold where he would stay the rest of his life. The merging back into the Liberal Party angered many of Gaitán's left-wing allies, but he realized, even if they could not, that the only change possible in Colombia was within the framework of the traditional two-party system. To Gaitán, any political organization outside the scope of the Liberal or Conservative Party was doomed to failure. He realized that it was better to work for change from the inside looking out, than from the outside looking in. Therefore, with his movement legitimized, he re-entered the Liberal Party in order to expand his influence within the ranks of the elite decision-makers. The country was changing. In 1929 there had been only eight legally recognized working class associations; within three years of taking office in 1934, López allowed over 100 unions to form. Moreover, López passed fresh agrarian reforms that allowed peasants to obtain land titles after having worked a plot for ten years.

In 1936 the Liberals enjoyed the sixth year of political control. By this time the Conservatives could no longer hide their contempt for the abrupt changes in the social order. Reforms, particularly for the Conservative large landowners, were difficult to accept. As a result, Laureano Gómez Castro started an extreme right-wing segment of the Conservative Party. Gómez thought the Liberals were ruining the country and his group threatened to incite a civil rebellion against the many reforms that López put in place. Gómez and his radical right-wing followers considered the reforms in agrarian policy, education, labor, and health services for the poor a subversion of the existing social order. Moreover, he himself repeatedly said the Conservatives were the only legitimate representatives of constitutional order in the country. He advocated a civilized community led by educated men of reason. Unsaid in the Gómez party propaganda was that they wanted a society whereby the poor lived in deference to the rich.

Thus the country now had two extremists: Gómez on the far right who guarded the privileges of the rich, and Gaitán on the far left who demanded a better life for the poor. Gaitán had a huge advantage in that he was far more popular and a vastly superior orator. But Gómez was a force to be reckoned with nonetheless, because of his dangerous, combative nature.

Gaitán continued to grow in popularity despite the harsh presence of Gómez. His support with the underprivileged classes eclipsed the popularity of all other Liberal Party leaders, But he was still considered a maverick to the Liberal elite and denied entry to the small circle of influential decision-makers in the party. This changed on June 8, 1936, when Gaitán was selected Mayor of Bogotá. Liberal bosses thought the job would drown Gaitán's passion for reforms but were proved wrong when his first official act as Mayor was announced — he ordered a 44-hour week for all municipal employees. The Liberal elite disagreed with the move but supported it because of the popular response among workers throughout the country.

Things were looking up for Gaitán. Months earlier, he married Amparo Jaramillo, a stunning Colombian beauty from a wealthy Medellín family. Amparo was a strong-willed, independent woman who complimented the fiery makeup of the populist politician. The best man at the wedding was Eduardo Santos, the publisher of the influential *El Tiempo* newspaper and the next Liberal President of Colombia in 1938. Santos, like López before him, was reform-minded. However, he directed his energy to modernizing Colombia's weak industrial sector and grew apart from Gaitán who insisted that the people came first. Santos was good for Colombia. López had allowed the nation's foreign debt to fall into arrears and Santos set about to reverse this trend and establish badly needed new credit, particularly with the United States.

Santos looked at the big picture. He realized that Colombia had to have its economic house in order, to gain access to capital markets abroad. Although he no longer agreed with all of Gaitán's social issues, he nonetheless appointed him Minister of Education in early 1940. It was a difficult time for the President as he sought to nurture the confidence of businessmen to build up Colombia's industrial base, while having Gaitán urging him to continue to seek additional advances for the labor movement. Santos proved to be a pragmatist who clearly fell short of Gaitán's expectations but, nonetheless, improved Colombia's financial reputation internationally.

Gómez attacked Santos for his position on World War II. President Santos fully supported the United States in the conflict but put off declaring war on Germany. This infuriated Gómez and his right-wing followers. They complained that Santos had sacrificed Colombia's neutrality. Gómez expressed his ultra nationalistic view on the Senate floor with the

following speech: "There is talk of the dangers to the Panama Canal in the event of the war spreading to the American continent. So what! Is the Canal ours? Are there not certain past events that would hardly incline the patriotic Colombian to become greatly exercised over a route that was built at the cost of our territorial integrity? Would we have cause for alarm or regret if tomorrow, when the spoils of the conquerors are divided up, the zone of which we were plundered were to pass under the control of England, Japan, or even of Germany? Do you think the life of a single Colombian should be sacrificed so the United States may hold continued possession of the Panama Canal? The people of North America should have realized that to seek us as an ally when a foreign enemy is knocking at their gates is to ask of us a sacrifice that is a path of abjection for us."[21]

Robert W. Drexler, the former American diplomat and author of the brilliant book titled *Colombia and the United States: Narcotics Traffic and a Failed Foreign Policy,* discovered a far darker side of the Conservative leader. "Gómez's line went hand in hand with his admiration for Hitler and the Spanish Dictator Francisco Franco as well as with his hatred for liberals, Masons and Jews. He ranted that the United States was 'controlled by Semitic elements' and rejoiced that Hitler's smashing of the Jews would 'redound to the good of Latinity,'" according to Drexler.[22]

President Santos detested Gómez but proceeded carefully with him so as not to inflame the Conservative Party's nationalistic temper. However, the butt of Gómez's political ridicule was Gaitán who he now commonly referred to as, "the nigger who could read."

The Conservatives were denied power again in 1942, as Alfonso López Pumarejo returned to win a second term as President. Facing tough opposition on reforms from the Conservatives, López wanted to unify the Liberal Party and appointed Gaitán Minister of Labor in 1943. The President worried about Gaitán's faction of the party. The movement had become an expression of resentment against the existing system. Consequently, Gaitán faced a difficult challenge integrating the swelling ranks of his movement into the political mainstream and maintaining his duties to the existing system as Minister. Nonetheless, he continued to set about attacking corruption, widespread fraud and watched with growing discontent as the terrible conditions of the poor did not improve. As Minister of Labor, Gaitán added to an impressive array of government jobs that enabled him to acquire the experience needed to run for president.

Unlike in his first term as President, López slowed the pace of reforms because he believed that Colombia was not ready for further changes. Gaitán knew that López was simply avoiding a confrontation with the militant Gómez who was gaining support with leaders in the armed forces. Gaitán cringed when López attempted to placate critics in the Conservative Party. Complicating matters further, Gaitán had sharp words for López when he discovered that the President was calling him an extremist. Ultimately, López lost popularity with Liberals as well as Conservatives. At this point Gaitán was absolutely certain the only hope for a greater Colombia was to make plans to mount a bid for president in the 1946 elections. He was determined to alter the democratic makeup of the country so that it better represented the hopes of the broad masses, not just the views of the select few. Unfortunately, the Liberal Party machine rejected him.

Gaitán was the underdog in the 1946 presidential elections. He openly stated he did not expect to win, particularly when the official Liberal nomination went to Gabriel Turbay, a trusted party loyalist. The Conservatives endorsed Mariano Ospina Pérez, a respected member of the coffee sector whose wealthy family had dedicated itself to the Conservative Party since independence. Ospina had wide appeal in the country because of his moderate political platform and his desire to form a coalition government with Liberals.

Gaitán knew from the start that a presidential bid as an Independent Party candidate would split the Liberals and hurt Turbay. However, he was determined to enter the contest despite being hampered by an acute shortage of funds. Subsequently, it came as no surprise when he lost and the soft-spoken Ospina was elected President with only 42 percent of the vote. Ospina presided over a Conservative Party that was split into two factions: the new President represented the moderate faction of the party called the Ospinistas; the hardliner Gómez headed the militant segment of the party called the Laureanistas. Ultimately, the right-wing portion of the party would control the National Police, firing Liberals and hiring loyal men to settle old scores.

The Conservatives wasted no time having the police enforce party privileges. The right-wing element of the party provoked waves of violence when they went out to grab control of nearly every government operation the Liberals had directed over the past 12 years. Ospina was guilty of allowing Gómez to openly use the National Police to carry on the political aims of the Conservative Party. Subsequently, Ospina's government became competitive and exclusionary, similar to the situation that triggered the War of One Thousand Days a half-century before. Beaten, Gaitán had no choice but to look ahead to the 1950 presidential elections to change the course of the nation. However, it would be much more difficult now with the Conservatives holding the reins of power and with the contempt that the dangerous Gómez had for him.

The political situation exploded in September 1947. Not surprisingly, Gaitán was the catalyst. He publicly disclosed a secret government document exposing the Ospina government's plans to illegally import massive United States arms into the country to deal with the growing Liberal unrest. Gaitán told the public that the United States was shipping the Conservatives tear gas, rifles, automatic weapons, antitank rocket launchers, medium and light tanks, armored cars and armored personnel carriers.[23] Gaitán used his new position in the Senate to take the floor and read details of the secret operation that was coordinated with the military attaché at the U.S. embassy in Bogotá.

The United States was reportedly sending Ospina the arms on Air Force planes based in Panama. The arms and tear gas were designated for the revamped National Police and was a sure sign that the government expected further eruptions within the nation. Gaitán realized the Conservatives were going to smash the opposition in the name of law and order. He therefore pointed out to the nation that under Colombian law only the armed forces were authorized to import arms and that the Ospina government had violated the President's constitutional authority. The revelation inflamed the Liberals, and the crisis ballooned when the lower house, the House of Representatives, and the Senate appointed commissions to investigate the scandal.

Antigovernment demonstrations spread to the streets and Liberal politicians aggressively attacked Ospina for his role in the scandal. Initially the President and several key Ministers denied Gaitán's allegations, but as the commissions progressed and official documents verified the charges, President Ospina confessed. He sheepishly stated that the use of tear gas was a humane method of maintaining public order, and added that the rise of violence in the country warranted his actions. To the Liberals, the scandal was clear evidence that the extremists in the Conservative government had no intentions of working with the moderates. The fears were confirmed when Ospina asked Gómez to join the government as Foreign Minister. Armed with American weapons, the Conservatives were going to use force to put down demonstrations. The Liberals of course were now going to answer with equal or more degrees of violence to protest the strongarm measures. In doing so, the country was nearing civil war.

By December of 1947, the friction between the two parties escalated in the House of Representatives. At one point during the proceedings, Conservative Representative Pablo A. Toro pointed a pistol at Liberal Representative César Oroñez, threatening to shoot him. Conservative rage was also directed at Protestants, a reaction born of the strong association the party had with the Roman Catholic Church. Gaitán was caught in the middle of the conflict. Moderates in the Liberal Party begged him to try to bring an end to the violence in the country. On the other hand, extremists in the Liberal Party were demanding drastic action to counter the brutal Conservative National Police. Meanwhile, ties between the Colombian and American military establishments grew stronger. Colombia received its first modern combat aircraft from the United States, including three B-25 bombers and 35 P-47 fighters. Tragically, the weapons were to be used by the Colombian armed forces against Colombians.[24]

The situation was desperate. Only the big cities were safe. In an attempt to stop the killing, Gaitán approached Ospina. It was January 17, 1948. Gaitán informed the President that countryside Liberals were fleeing to the cities for fear of their lives, and he pleaded for an end to the violence against members of his party. Ospina in return asked Gaitán for his support in stopping the violence. To the extremists in the Liberal Party, the message was clear: obey our law … or be whipped into submission.

By the beginning of 1948, the flamboyant Gaitán was wearing expensive suits and driving around Bogotá in a newly acquired 1947 green Buick Roadmaster. Nonetheless, his dedication to the defense of the poor had made him a hero in Colombia. Gaitán and his wife, Doña Amparo, had captured the hearts and souls of the nonruling class, and the people of the *pueblo* believed he could deliver on promises of a better Colombia. Like other politicians, Gaitán was now using radio to widen the scope of his message. Moreover, funds were pouring in from the publication *Jornada,* a high-circulation populist paper edited by one of his closest allies, Darío Samper.

Gaitán and his army of political helpers had learned from their mistakes. His organization was starting to get major Liberal Party professionals to join the campaign and they were certain to win the 1950 presidential election. The nation was now ready for his reforms—anything was better than the bloody violence sweeping the country with Ospina in charge. Even his toughest critics in the Liberal Party were jumping onto his bandwagon, knowing that nothing could stop him from becoming President in 1950.

However, there were more than two years to go before the elections took place and the Ospina government was making full use of the National Police and armed forces to suppress the opposition while it could. As support for Gaitán grew, Conservative hatred for him increased. The Conservatives were convinced that Gaitán would ruin the country with land and labor reforms. To them, he represented chaos. They were loath to accede to the idea that the voice of the underprivileged poor was equal to that of the privileged wealthy. So the country had extremists on both sides: Gómez the unrelenting preserver of Colombian tradition, and Gaitán the trailblazing hero of the poor. One represented the past, the other the future.

As the conflict within the country increased, Ospina appeared willing to make concessions to avoid further bloodshed. However, Gaitán considered Ospina's offering crumbs in exchange for peace and he knew that the people of the *pueblo* wanted something much more substantial. The Conservatives were outraged by Liberal behavior and secretly held Gaitán responsible for the nation's woes. The extremists in the Conservative Party were fuming. They could not and would not accept the civil disobedience of the lower class. As a result, the countryside was aflame with Liberal and Conservative clashes. One raided the other at day or night to even the account of the day or night before. *La Violencia* had started. Surrounded by comforts, the elites in the big cities shut their eyes: they saw the population of the cities bulging with people; they heard accounts of the terror outside the cities; but they didn't act.

In late 1947 the Conservative newspaper *El Deber,* located in the city of Montería, called for Gaitán's elimination.[25] The Liberals took note — they knew the sure sign of a death notice. The Gaitanistas were frequently subjected to police and army harassment. Now they didn't know what to expect. Gaitán's inner circle made plans to protect their leader because they understood that everything that they had worked for to date would mean nothing if Gaitán was killed. Some, who had been with him since 1930, could not bear the thought of any harm falling on their chief. They were unable to communicate the danger to him, though. Gaitán boldly refused bodyguards; he kept repeating that protection would define him as a regular politician, not a man of the *pueblo.*[26]

"I will not be killed. If I am killed, not one stone will be left unturned," he said.[27] It was true; if someone dared harm Gaitán the *pueblo* would revolt. There was no one else like him, no one like him in the shadows. He was one of a kind. No one in the history of Colombia had become a champion of the poor and underprivileged like Gaitán. He was the rudder; they were the ship. Without him, they would be out of control.

Unprotected, Gaitán was a perfect target for his Conservative enemies. The moderates in the party realized that he represented the voice of the *pueblo* and, given the violence taking place in the countryside now, they instinctively knew things would only get worse in his absence. However, the extremists in the party differed. They knew the *pueblo* was a keg of dynamite, but they thought that if they could extinguish the fuse, Gaitán, then they could short-circuit the explosion. Without Gaitán, the *pueblo* would retreat into oblivion, they thought.

Gaitán reacted angrily to the Conservative attacks on Liberals in the country; he wanted calm until the 1950 presidential elections arrived. Consequently, in an attempt to stop the violence and bring peace he asked the *pueblo* to make a disciplined and somber "Manifestación del Silencio." He sincerely wanted to play the role of the peacemaker. He chastised the militant elements in the Liberal Party who wanted an all-out war with President Ospina and his Minister of Foreign Affairs Gómez. He criss-crossed the country, traveling as much as possible to speak with the *pueblo* directly. It was to no avail—the violence continued.

In a frantic attempt to stop the bloodshed Gaitán assembled the *pueblo* for one last direct plea to President Ospina. It took place on the afternoon of February 7, 1948. The speech he delivered was called "Oración por la Paz" and Gaitán delivered it

from a balcony overlooking the plaza with 100,000 silent onlookers waving white handkerchiefs. It was a crucial moment in Colombian history. The speech was succinct, persuasive and considered the most important of his career.

> Señor Presidente. Today we do not make economic or political demands. We ask only that the actions of our country not bring shame upon us. We ask for the building of peace and civilization. We ask that the persecution by the authorities stop. Thus asks this immense multitude. We ask a small but great thing: That our political struggles be governed by the constitution. Do not believe that our silence, this impressive silence, is cowardice! We, Señor Presidente, we are not cowards. We are the descendants of the heroes who annihilated the tyrants of this sacred soil. We are capable of sacrificing our lives to save the peace and liberty of Colombia!
>
> Señor, stop the violence. We want human life to be defended, that is the least a people can ask.... Señor Presidente, our flag is in mourning; this silent multitude, this mute cry from our hearts, asks only that you treat us ... as you would have us treat you. We say to you finally, Your Excellency; Fortunate are those who understand that words of peace and harmony should not conceal sentiments of rancor or enmity. Badly advised are those in the government who conceal behind kind words their lack of respect for all people. They will be marked in the pages of history by the finger of infamy![28]

In April 1948, the Ospina government was preparing an ambitious beautification of Bogotá for the start of the Ninth Inter-American Conference, a two-week summit meeting of hemispheric foreign ministers, who, under United States auspices, had gathered to sign the charter of the Organization of American States (OAS). Bogotá was getting a fresh coat of paint and bright flowers adorned the city. Rumors swirled that funding for the face-lift went directly to Conservative Party cronies and that a large portion of the funds were being misappropriated. Aggravating matters further was a weak economy that left many lower class families out of work and hungry.

Consequently, the disenchantment with President Ospina resulted in more student protests, marches, and in some cases small riots. However, the skirmishes in the city never matched the violent conditions of the countryside where in some cases, entire families were being slaughtered with machetes.

The militant element of the Liberal Party wanted Gaitán to be more combative. They begged him to be more forceful with the Conservatives. They realized that he was the key to the *pueblo* and that the underprivileged would answer his call. But Gaitán refused to call for an insurrection. He was still looking ahead to the 1950 elections and knew any militant behavior would taint him forever. He wanted to bide his time and wait to assume the Presidency. He was too close to attaining power now to lose it. The road had been too long. He wanted the *pueblo* to be patient. He urged calm.

United States Secretary of State George C. Marshall, a retired five-star general, arrived in Bogotá on March 31, 1948. Other foreign dignitaries arrived daily. Secretary Marshall had received intelligence reports warning of possible danger in Bogotá, but they were not taken seriously and the conference continued its work on a number of economic and organizational issues without incident during its first week.[29] Gaitán was aware of the global attention enveloping Colombia and did not want to be labeled a bloody revolutionary. He wanted the world to know that he could be a responsible leader of the people and did not want to be held accountable for the needless loss of life. Foreign Minister Laureano Gómez was also worried about his reputation. He wanted the world to see him as an important diplomat and prayed his hostility towards the United States during World War II never generated much attention in Washington.

April 9, 1948, was the darkest day in the history of Colombia. A week earlier, all key Liberals in the Ospina government resigned in protest at his harsh regime. Gaitán and a small group of loyal friends, Plinio Mendoza Neira, who joined the Gaitanistas in the March 1947 congressional elections, Alejandro Vallejo, the co-editor of *Jornada*, Jorge Padilla, the Treasurer of Bogotá, and Pedro Eliseo Cruz, a Gaitanista Senator from Cundinamarca and a respected doctor, then planned to lunch together.

Gaitán was upbeat that Friday afternoon, having won an important court case the day before. He had scheduled a 3:00 meeting in his office with a 21-year-old Cuban law student named Fidel Castro, whom he had met a few days earlier. Castro was in Bogotá as a delegate to a congress of Latin American University students.

The group of friends exited Gaitán's law office for lunch at 1:00. Mendoza Neira and Gaitán were ahead of the three other companions and stepped out from the building first. On the open Bogotá street a nondescript man casually walked up to Mendoza Neira and Gaitán, brandished a gun, fired three shots, and then a fourth. They all found their mark. Jorge Eliécer Gaitán, "El hombre que fué un pueblo," was crumbled on the street bleeding. The news spread like lightning.

Mendoza Neira witnessed it all. So did Vallejo, who said afterwards that the killer "Was perfectly in control of himself ... in his eyes there was a look of hatred."[30]

The cry in the street was "Mataron a Gaitán!" (They killed Gaitán.) The assailant tried to flee but was grabbed by two nearby policemen. Officer Carlos Alberto Jiménez Díaz arrived first, and then was assisted by Officer Silva González who dragged the gunman away from the murder scene and into a drugstore across the street. González immediately called police headquarters but, to his surprise, received no answer.[31]

Sensing the danger building outside, Jiménez screamed at his captive, "Tell me who ordered you to kill, for you are going to be lynched by the pueblo!" "Oh, Señor," the man answered. "Powerful things that I can't tell you! Oh, Virgin of Carmen! Save me!"[32] They were his last recorded words.

The crowd gathered outside the drugstore. It could not be restrained for long without reinforcements from police headquarters. Emotions were running strong. One by one, the members of the crowd shook off the initial shock and replaced it with rage. The crowd approached the drugstore. Threatened, the owner quickly shut the gates, but to no avail. The crowd ripped the gates open, overwhelmed Díaz and González, and dragged the gunman back onto the street. It was there that the angry mob kicked him to death. Then they dragged him to the Presidential Palace and left him at the doorsteps of Ospina's residence.

Shortly afterwards, witnesses reported seeing mourners returning to the spot where Gaitán had fallen and watched them dip handkerchiefs into the puddle of blood left on the Bogotá street.

The riot that followed was called the Bogotazo. The bloodshed and destruction caused during the Bogotazo was recorded in modern history as the greatest riot in the Western Hemisphere. Wild rumors spread through the city. Most of the blame for Gaitán's death was immediately attributed to Ospina and Gómez. However, no one knew for sure what had happened, only that Gaitán, had been killed. Reckless radio announces broadcasted accusations that the Conservatives had murdered him. What was certain to the pueblo was that their leader had been taken from them. Gaitán had guaranteed them a voice in his government. He had rallied the pueblo and heightened expectations and now he was gone.

Nearly every government building in Bogotá was reduced to rubble. Churches, long the symbol of the Conservative Party, were ransacked and set ablaze. Conservatives fled for their lives. Upon hearing the news of Gaitán's assassination, Ospina summoned his cabinet and immediately sought refuge in the Palace where the well-trained Presidential Guard managed to send the unarmed crowds into retreat. The fear of a revolution was great. Ospina repeatedly rebuffed Gómez when he sought to meet with him for fear the mob outside would be incited to storm the gates of the Palace.[33] Conservatives everywhere expected the worst. The President's wife, Doña Bertha, admirably took matters into her own hands. "On hearing the news, she went to her private chambers, took off her gloves, placed her purse on a chair, and took two revolvers from her closet, strapping one to her waist ... she then joined her husband downstairs."[34]

The young Cuban Fidel Castro said he saw "Crazed people running ... with an indescribable fear in their eyes ... a state of indescribable rage was created."[35] Castro took up arms in the uprising but avoided arrest by escaping to the Cuban embassy. The world press managed to record the horrors of the Bogotazo, as did the hundreds of foreign dignitaries in Bogotá for the Inter-American Conference. Secretary of State Marshall and Secretary of Commerce Averell Harriman saw it and reported it all back to President Truman in the White House. They all reported Ospina's silence throughout the Bogotazo; they all reported the deadliness of the Palace Guard; they all reported the mashing of defenseless demonstrators by army tanks, the drunkenness, the looting, the senseless killing — all were noted to the

Bogotá is aflame after the April 9, 1948, assassination of Gaitán. The "Bogotazo" is widely regarded as the greatest riot in the modern history of the Western Hemisphere. *El Tiempo*

shame of the Conservatives, who prided themselves on being the only legitimate representatives of constitutional order.

Laureano Gómez fled the country and was given asylum by his idol Francisco Franco, the Spanish dictator. Amazingly, the angry mobs did not harm one foreigner. Nor did they damage the offices of the two Liberal newspapers, *El Tiempo* and *El Espectador.* Gaitán's beloved green Buick Roadmaster also managed to escape damage. However, the luckiest event for the Conservatives was that it started to rain at 4:00 that afternoon. By nightfall, the rain was heavy, thus preventing the entire city from burning to the ground and sending most of the cold and wet *pueblo* home.

The murder of Gaitán destroyed the *pueblo's* faith in Colombia. The violence quickly spread out to other regions of the country. In the town of Puerto Tejada, south of Cali, on the Río Cauca, Liberal Gaitanistas murdered Conservative bosses, cut off their heads and then went out to the town plaza and played soccer with them. No one will ever know exactly how many people died in the Bogotazo. Late that night, the Colombian marines were ordered to collect the corpses from the streets and to pick up the dead piling up at the hospitals. They reportedly worked until the next evening depositing truckloads of dead at the Cementerio Central. Many family members and friends secretly buried their dead for fear of reprisals. Although no reliable accounting of the dead can ever be made, the number generally accepted by most historians is over 2,000 dead and about 5,000 injured.

The death of Gaitán sent many Gaitanistas into the hills to fight the Conservatives. Some never rejoined Colombian society. Armed bands were formed to fight back. Police and assassins under the control of one party or the other killed entire villages. Victims of violence suffered horrendous deaths. Some were chopped up into pieces, scalped and decapitated.

Colombian scholar Herbert Braun captured the *Zeitgeist,* the spirit of the time. "Consistently reviled for being slovenly and ignorant by those who called themselves cultured and intelligent, the pueblo had been shown a more positive image of itself by Gaitán. Those who claimed to be the natural leaders of society were shown by Gaitán to be mere mortals, fearful men behind masks, who ruled in their own interests and those of the powerful and the rich rather than for the pueblo."[36]

April 9, 1948, has long been considered the official start of *La Violencia.* In reality, the violence started well before that date. However, the death toll started in earnest with the assassination of Gaitán. A total of 43,000 Colombians died in 1948; experts said the majority perished violently. After the Bogotazo, the Ospina government became more repressive. Ospina himself banned public meetings in March of 1949 and fired all Liberal governors in May.

In November of the same year, Ospina ordered the army to forcibly close Congress. His government also had rural police forces heighten the effort to intimidate and harass Liberals. As a result, Liberals refused to present a candidate in the 1950 presidential elections. Unopposed, Gómez was able to assume the presidency of Colombia on August 7, 1950. One of his first acts as President of the republic was to send Colombian troops to Korea to aid the United States and improve his relations with the White House. Consequently, Colombia was the only Latin American country to fight in the Korean War.

Gómez did not take long to live up to his nickname, "Monster." He ruled with absolute authority and was contemptuous of universal suffrage and the law of majority rule. He acquired broad powers, curtailed civil liberties in an attempt to confront the mounting violence, and circumvented all Liberal attempts to regain a real political voice. Gómez attributed all of his problems to the work of Communists, but the cold war rhetoric was cover for protecting Colombia's image abroad — in reality, poverty and political abandonment were killing Colombia.

The former priest, Walter J. Broderick, published a chilling eyewitness account of the terror inflicted on Colombia by Gómez in his book *Camilo Torres: A Biography of the Priest-Guerrillero.* The vision of *La Violencia* captured by Broderick was horrid.

My eyes have seen many sights. I have seen men coming into the cities mutilated, women raped, children flogged and wounded. I saw a man whose tongue had been cut out, and people who were lashed to a tree and made to witness the cruel scene told me that the policemen yelled, as they cut out his tongue: *You won't be giving any more cheers for the Liberal Party, you bastard!* [Italics are the author's.] They cut the genitals off other men so that they wouldn't procreate any more Liberals. Others had their legs and arms cut off and were made to walk about, bleeding, on the stumps of their limbs. And I know of men who were held bound while policemen and Conservative civilians took it in turns to rape their wives and daughters. Everything was carried out according to a preconceived plan of extermination. And the victims of these bloodthirsty policemen were poor, humble country people who were members of the Liberal Party. Their wives, their old folk and their children were shot in the full light of day. The official police took possession of the property of Liberal farmers, killed the owners, requisitioned their barns and disposed of their money, their livestock; in a word, of all that had been the livelihood of their families. It was an avalanche of pillage and an orgy of blood. At times these atrocious crimes where committed under the cover of night, with the encouragement of high government officials. And all this in the false name of God, with holy medals jingling around their necks, and without remorse.[37]

Gómez never considered the *pueblo* a part of his Colombia. He embraced the cold war hatred of Communists and viciously attacked anyone opposed to his rule. In his first year as President 50,000 Colombians perished in *La Violencia.* All totaled, up to 200,000 Colombians would die as a result of Gaitán's death. The President was indifferent to the bloodshed. He curtailed civil liberties and used the rural police as his party's agents— actions that would serve to polarize the nation and escalate the violence. Once in office, Gómez abandoned his anti–American rhetoric and cozied up to the United States to maintain power.

On January 4, 1952, a 24-year-old intellectual named Ernesto Guevara decided to interrupt his medical studies and start a journey that played an important role in his eventual departure from his birthplace in Argentina. Guevara and his childhood friend Alberto Granado set out to explore the South American continent. They left on a vintage 500cc Norton motorcycle and headed for the Atlantic coast. From there they criss-crossed the continent, abandoned the broken motorcycle, and eventually ended up in Bogotá on July 2, 1952. Guevara kept a diary of his travels and recorded this account of Colombia.

Of all the countries we have traveled through, this is the one in which individual guarantees are the most suppressed; the police patrol the streets with their rifles on their shoulders and constantly demand one's passport.... It is a tense calm that indicates an uprising before long. The plains are in open revolt and the army is impotent to repress it; the Conservatives fight among themselves and can't agree on anything; and the memory of the 9th of April 1948 weighs like lead over everyone's spirit.... In summary, an asphyxiating climate, which the Colombians can stand if they want, but we're beating it as soon as we can.[38]

No one will ever know for certain what impact *La Violencia* had on the young

Argentine. But given the extraordinary life he later committed to the red flame one can argue that the mythic figure that eventually deserted his comfortable Argentine upbringing to join the battlefields of the Cuban revolution at the side of Fidel Castro was moved by the oppression he saw in Colombia.

The legendary high priest of international revolution, "Che" Guevara saw *La Violencia* with his own eyes and a dozen years later actually toyed with the idea of joining the Cuban-backed guerrilla organization in Colombia. He made the fateful decision instead to go to Bolivia.

In conclusion, the evidence is overwhelming that Castro, who thought himself another Simón Bolívar, destined to bring a new "freedom and unity" to Latin America, and Che, the hardened revolutionary who considered it his "historic duty" to spread the armed struggle, were both intent on establishing other Cubas and Vietnams in Latin America.[39]

Notes

1. Reuters, "Colombian Mother Kills Self and Four Children," Bogotá, 23 February 1999

2. R. Albert Berry and Miguel Urrutia, *Income Distribution in Colombia* (New Haven: Yale University Press, 1976).

3. *Ibid.*, p. 252.

4. Washington Office on Latin America (WOLA), "Colombia Besieged: Political Violence and State Responsibility," 1989, p. 9.

5. *Ibid.*

6. David Bushnell, *The Making of Modern Colombia: A Nation in Spite of Itself* (Berkeley: University of California Press, 1993), p. 92.

7. *Ibid.*, p. 93.

8. *Ibid.*, p. 94.

9. *Ibid.*, p. 93.

10. Law and Democracy in Colombia, Proceedings of a Conference, The David Rockefeller Center for Latin American Studies, Harvard University, Cambridge, Massachusetts, May 7, 1997, pp. 5–6.

11. John D. Martz, *The Politics of Clientelism: Democracy and the State of Colombia* (New Brunswick: Transaction Publications, 1997).

12. Robert W. Drexler, *Colombia and the United States: Narcotics Traffic and a Failed Foreign Policy* (Jefferson, N.C.: McFarland & Company, 1997), p. 51

13. Charles W. Bergquist, *Coffee and Conflict in Colombia, 1886–1910* (Durham: Duke University Press, 1978), Part I.

14. Gene H. Bell Villada, *García Márquez: The Man and His Work* (Chapel Hill: University of North Carolina Press, 1990), p. 31.

15. Richard Sharpless, *Gaitán of Colombia: A Political Biography* (Pittsburgh: University of Pittsburgh Press, 1978), p. 55.

16. Bushnell, p. 164.

17. Sharpless, p. 50.

18. *Ibid.*, p. 55.

19. Bushnell, p. 182.

20. *Ibid.*

21. Drexler, p. 54.

22. *Ibid.*

23. *Ibid.*, p. 57.

24. *Ibid.*, p. 58.

25. Herbert Braun, *The Assassination of Gaitán: Public Life and Urban Violence in Colombia* (Madison: University of Wisconsin Press, 1985), p. 132.

26. *Ibid.*, p. 133.

27. *Ibid.*

28. Sharpless, p. 171.

29. Drexler, pp. 59–60.

30. Braun, p. 134.

31. *Ibid.*, p. 135.

32. *Ibid.*

33. *Ibid.*, p. 142.

34. *Ibid.*, p. 141.

35. *Ibid.*, p. 177.

36. *Ibid.*, p. 202.

37. Walter J. Broderick, *Camilo Torres: A Biography of the Priest-Guerrillero* (New York: Doubleday & Company, 1975), pp. 57–58.

38. John Lee Anderson, *Che Guevara: A Revolutionary Life* (New York: Grove Press, 1997), p. 90.

39. Cuban Subversive Activities in Latin America: 1959–1968, Central Intelligence Agency Secret Report, 16 February 1968, declassified and reproduced by author with permission of LBJ Library.

CHAPTER FOUR

The Mistake from Hell

The White House did not want to do it. If something went wrong, the Republicans would have a field day attacking the Democratic leadership. Ultimately, the Central Intelligence Agency, the National Security Council and the State Department persuaded the White House to agree. The clincher was Bill Clinton's pledge to President Pastrana during the state visit in October that he would do everything possible to help Colombia attain peace. The fact that Pastrana made the request himself weighed heavily in the final decision. Nonetheless, the plan was risky. Republicans would argue it was against the law. That depended on how you looked at it of course. But as a matter of policy, the United States did not have face-to-face meetings with leaders of terrorist groups, particularly those suspected of abducting and killing Americans.

Consequently, after long and careful consideration, it was decided that the United States would have clandestine meetings with the FARC in Costa Rica. The Costa Rican government was consulted and gave a quick thumbs-up. The friendly site would allow the United States to pull out the American representative and his note taker unhindered in case something went wrong. The meetings were to be held in mid–December 1998, in San

José. The capital city would be filled with vacationers during that time of year. Fortunately, many successful Latin American businessmen would be on holiday after the first two weeks of December. The festive tourist activity would provide a good cover for the rendezvous. Of utmost importance for all the Americans involved in the operation was that everything be kept under tight wraps. If news of the covert meetings leaked, Republicans would attack the wisdom of the White House decision.

There would be two meetings.[1] The first was in the private home of the FARC liaison, Alvaro Leyva. The other site was a dingy hotel. The second location was selected because it was feared the tousled guerrillas would stick out in a good hotel. Plus, few influential Americans or inquisitive reporters would stay in a dump. Sophisticated security measures would be in place at both sites. The FARC guerrillas would make a big mistake if they tried something outside of the scope of the mission. When it came to cloak and daggers, they were out of their league. If the guerrillas attempted something underhanded, the CIA would be there to deal with it.

Leyva had a Rolodex of guerrilla contacts. The 56-year-old lawyer was one of the few Colombian politicians the guerrillas trusted. The self-appointed guerrilla

61

liaison could communicate with Manuel "Sureshot" Marulanda, Supreme Commandant of the FARC, within minutes. His access was impressive. He boasted of how quickly he could reach Sureshot. "It depends on where he is. If he's in Colombia, five minutes. If he's abroad, ten."[2] Leyva, a former Conservative Party Senator, fled Colombia after he was ordered arrested on charges of corruption. He was granted political asylum in Costa Rica where he kept close contact with the FARC.[3]

The American representative selected for the secret meetings was Phillip (Phil) T. Chicola, the Director of the Office of Andean Affairs in the Bureau of Inter-American Affairs. The State Department veteran was a trusted confederate of Peter F. Romero, the highly regarded Acting Assistant Secretary for Western Hemisphere Affairs. Chicola was a career officer in the Foreign Service. He joined the State Department in 1979 and served overseas at American embassies in Guatemala, Nicaragua, El Salvador and Chile. Following short tours as Intelligence Analyst for Cuba in the Bureau of Intelligence and Research and as political officer at the American embassy in Managua, Nicaragua, he was assigned to the American embassy in San Salvador. Between 1988 and 1993 he served there as a political counselor, Deputy Chief of Mission, and Chargé d'Affaires during the period when the country's civil war was brought to a negotiated end, and the former insurgents joined the political process. In 1997, he was asked to serve as Senior Adviser to the United Nations Transitional Administrator for Eastern Slavonia, Croatia, where his experience in dealing with civil conflicts was useful. Following the successful completion of that assignment, Chicola became Director of the Office of Policy Coordination in the Bureau of International Narcotics and Law Enforcement in the State Department. His cool demeanor, impeccable credentials and nearly 20-year professional relationship with Romero made him the perfect man for the job.

Chicola was astonished by the speed of the unauthorized contact. Shortly after he was posted on his hush-hush assignment he received a direct call on his personal line in the State Department from Alvaro Leyva, who wanted to give him the details of the secret San José meetings.[4] Unsettled, he parried the call and checked with his superiors for instructions. They confirmed the connection. The United States had signaled Pastrana that the meeting was approved and the Colombian President wasted no time relaying the information to the FARC. Chicola was surprised Leyva did not go through proper channels and was trying to contact him directly on an unsecured line. Moreover, he wondered how the FARC had obtained his direct number: to his knowledge, it was not authorized for contact. He came to the quick conclusion that the FARC was anxious to see the meetings take place, wanted the Colombian government out of the loop, and knew something about the American chain of command.

Chicola and his note taker arrived in San José and checked into the hotel without incident. The weather was pleasant and was a welcome change from the climate in Washington. He was unarmed and confident he would not be in danger. His primary responsibility was to deliver three concise messages. He was not authorized to negotiate; he was basically instructed to be a good listener. He understood his presence was a major score for Pastrana, that the Colombian President had accomplished an important feat. The FARC had a wish list, but they wanted direct contact with the United States as a prerequisite for advancing the peace talks. Now that Pastrana had delivered, the gamesmanship would start in earnest. Certainly, there would be posturing, filled with guerrilla propaganda, but there had to be something very important the FARC wanted to tell Uncle Sam privately.

They arrived at Alvaro Leyva's home in San José Sunday afternoon and received a warm reception. To Chicola's trained eye, the guerrillas were not armed. The home was comfortable and Leyva was a gracious host. The introductions were informal, everyone was smiling and the discussions immediately took on a friendly air. The senior guerrilla representative was Raúl Reyes,[5] Sureshot's handpicked peace negotiator and a member of the FARC's seven-man General Secretariat. Reyes was extremely thankful that President Pastrana was able to fulfill the FARC request. He also expressed appreciation for the opportunity to meet with officials of the American government. He then went on to give the FARC view of the universe.

As Reyes brought his remarks to a conclusion he politely awaited the American's feedback. Chicola now had the opportunity to fulfill his mission and deliver the three official U.S. messages. First on the agenda was to inform the FARC that the United States—Colombian counternarcotics efforts, including aerial eradication, were nonnegotiable and would be continued. Secondly, he demanded a full accountability of the three American missionaries abducted by the FARC and believed to be the longest-held United States hostages in the world. David Mankins, Mark Rich and Richard Tenenoff, members of New Tribes Missions (NTM), were kidnapped from the Kuna Indian village of Pucuro in the Darién Province of Panama by FARC guerrillas and taken into Colombia on January 31, 1993.[6] Finally, Chicola said the United States was committed to President Pastrana's peace process but that it would be impossible to have long-term contact with the FARC if they continued to kidnap Americans and de-

stroy American property. To Chicola, his mission was now completed. From an official view, he was merely a listener, there to absorb information to be reported to the government; there was no implied or nonimplied understanding that the United States would respond to any requests made by the guerrilla terrorists.

Reyes adamantly denied any FARC responsibility for the three American missionaries. It was not the work of his troops, he said. However, in a gesture of goodwill he pledged the FARC would do everything possible to find out what had become of them. He then went on to say the FARC was against narcotics. He openly acknowledged, though, that his organization did receive funding from taxes that were collected for the protection of illicit crops and added that the FARC did depend on drug traffickers to buy the narcotics. The taxes were necessary because the FARC was functioning in the region well before narcotics arrived and they deemed it necessary to finance their own operations from the production of the profitable crops there now, he explained. Reyes then delivered "a reasonably crafted argument"[7] favorably comparing the FARC taxation system to that imposed by the American Congress which triggered the Whiskey Rebellion of 1794.[8]

Reyes indicated the FARC was willing to work toward the destruction of illicit crops and that the State Department officials could tour coca, poppy and marijuana fields in areas under the rebels' control. The drug cultivation could be eradicated "within three to five years" if the Colombian government suspended spraying programs and gave support to farmers willing to switch to growing legal crops, he said.[9] Alas, Chicola realized the FARC was placing an expensive apple in front of the peace process donkey-cart and wanted Uncle Sam to pay for it. He then advised Reyes that any U.S. aid for redeveloping alternative crops in areas of heavy drug production would not start until the civil war was over.[10]

Reyes concluded by making it perfectly clear that until there was peace, the war would continue. He stoically explained that it was the FARC's obligation to continue the struggle, especially at the early stages of the peace talks. He wanted the United States to understand that the FARC intended to negotiate from a position of strength. Reyes then diplomatically went out of his way to praise Pastrana. "We trust him. The President has shown courage and honesty. We understand he has constraints," he said.

Chicola explained that the United States had no intention of involvement in the peace process. The United States was an interested observer. He reminded them that the Colombian government made a special request for the meeting and absent that request, the gathering would not have taken place. "If you want clarification on a particular issue, we may help, but we have no right or desire to get involved," he stated. The time passed quickly. The talks went on for nearly four hours. There was still plenty of energy in the room but as evening approached, it was agreed to meet again the following morning in Chicola's hotel to continue the definition of positions.

The next day, the casually attired guerrillas and Alvaro Leyva arrived at the hotel lobby on schedule. There were very few people milling about and no one raised an eyebrow. Confident that everything was in order, greetings were exchanged all around. Chicola suggested they eat breakfast. On that note, everyone inconspicuously strolled to the empty hotel coffee shop. The group grabbed an isolated corner table, leisurely ordered coffee and food, then picked up where they had left off at the previous meeting.

Chicola opened up the discussions and went on to explain that the leadership of the United States government and that of the entire international community wanted one country, one government and no separate states in Colombia. "The nation cannot be divided," he emphasized.

Reyes calmly responded, "We are all Colombians ... we don't expect not to be Colombians. Whatever government emerges must be legitimate ... it must respect democracy and human rights ... a state that lives up to the laws of international foreigners cannot say no to counternarcotics."

Chicola expanded further and said that the United States would like to see a full integration of the FARC army back into society. Moreover, "The United States would like to see all the FARC's weapons turned in. If you do become ... as a result of the peace process ... members of the police force or the legitimate army we are neutral on that point. However, there must be one Colombian army, one Colombian police, and one Colombian nation," Chicola explained.

At this point in the discussions, Reyes turned strict. He then made it crystal clear that the FARC planned to keep their arms until President Pastrana did something about the death squads. "We cannot have a situation where the paramilitaries exist without checks," he said. "Therefore, there will be no peace agreement until the government does something about the paramilitaries," he warned.

Throughout the discussions there were only general references to Sureshot. Other topics that morning included FARC questions about the cost of the American counternarcotics budget and U.S. questions regarding future announcements on prisoner exchanges with the Colombian government. In September the FARC had released a list of 245 soldiers and police they were holding but the prisoner exchange was at a standstill. During the talks

Reyes spoke with complete authority, and, according to Chicola, he did not give the impression that the FARC was a one-man show.

The discussion ended on a positive note. In his parting words, Reyes assured Chicola that the FARC could be trusted as it began peace negotiations with the Colombian government. Reyes did not say that the FARC trusted the United States. It was well known that Sureshot was deeply suspicious of Americans and for that reason missionaries, reporters, tourists, coffee buyers, oilmen or Wall Street executives, were often regarded as envoys of the CIA. Reyes was well aware that Sureshot's suspicions would never change.

Therefore, the FARC returned to Colombia, Leyva headed back to his home, and Chicola rushed back to Washington to report the contents of the conversations to Bogotá. The game plan was for everyone to brainstorm and lay out the next step in the peace process.

It took exactly three weeks for the world to find out about San José. The news broke in Colombia. *El Espectador,* the Bogotá daily newspaper, reported the clandestine U.S. meetings with the FARC on Sunday, January 4, 1999. Republican Congressman Dan Burton of Indiana said that the meeting with the FARC showed "A lack of common sense."[11]

The White House immediately went into damage control and left the State Department to deal with the press inquires. "We participated in this meeting to demonstrate our support for the Colombian peace process," State Department spokesman James Rubin said. Rubin denied that the encounter violated a U.S. policy of isolating any of 30 groups it designated in late 1997 as foreign terrorist organizations. "Nothing in this determination precludes the U.S. government from meetings with the FARC or any other foreign terrorist organization if we deter-

mine that such a meeting is consistent with our interest, including bringing an end to Colombia's long-running civil conflict and to the terrorist attacks that accompany it," Rubin added.

"Talking to them is the right thing to do," a State Department official told the *New York Times.* "They are very intelligent and shrewd, but incredibly naive, and we got a glimpse of how unsophisticated their world view is on some issues," the official added.

A Colombian official in Bogotá familiar with the government's peace overture told the *Washington Post,* "We felt the more they are exposed to people outside the government and outside Colombia, the better…. We believed the more they get out of the mountains, the less isolated they are, the better the chance for success in the talks."

The Americans attributed the leak to Comandante Sureshot. They were certain he was quite proud of his ability to arrange face-to-face meetings with Uncle Sam; it was a sign of his power and had terrific propaganda value. He was an influential political actor and he wanted everybody to know it. Now the world would know that President Pastrana had cashed in a very big chip with the United States. They would also wake up to the fact that Bill Clinton had made a sharp change in U.S. policy toward the hemisphere's longest-running conflict.

Of critical importance was the decision to "cautiously reengage" the Colombian military by supplying it with sophisticated new weapons. However, it was also rather apparent that the decision was made because the Colombian armed forces were losing the war with the guerrillas. Consequently, when Sureshot did not show up at the San Vicente del Caguán talks on January 7, and then shortly afterwards postponed the peace talks until April 20, the doves in the U.S. government were visibly

Congressman Dan Burton of Indiana, Chairman of the House of Representative's Committee on Government Reform. *Courtesy of Dan Burton*

dejected. The American advocates of the Colombian peace process realized that the hawks in the Colombian government were gaining valuable ground.

In 1996, the U'wa Indians, a 5,000-member rain forest tribe, made headlines around the world when they declared they would commit mass suicide if an American oil company started drilling on their ancestral lands in northeastern Colombia. Occidental de Colombia, an affiliate of Occidental Petroleum Corporation of Bakersfield, California, acting on impressive geological data indicating a major discovery, was attempting to explore the Samoré block, covering more than 500,000 acres, which included the U'wa official reservation.

The American firm was very excited about Samoré. Occidental analysts thought that the block was a potential gusher with reserves of between 1.5 and 2.5 billion barrels of crude oil. Up until that date, Colombia's largest oil field was the Cusiana field, with proven reserves of 2.5 billion barrels. Cusiana was developed in the late 80s and was the largest oil discovery in the western hemisphere since the 1969 discovery of Prudhoe Bay in Alaska.[12] Therefore, Occidental, and the Colombian state-owned oil company Ecopetrol, thought that the nation was on the verge of developing another major bonanza. The Samoré block was significant because it would guarantee Colombia's oil self-sufficiency far into the next century, according to Wall Street investment bankers.

The U'wa Indian opposition touched off a nasty political, economic, and social dispute. Colombia earned $2 billion in 1995 from oil revenue. The Samoré block could potentially double that figure in four to five years. So many Colombian officials were upset in July 1996 when U'wa Indian leader Roberto Cobaria went to meet Occidental management in Los Angeles "to plead for no drilling." This trip was inconclusive. However, upon Cobaria's return to the reservation, he was dragged from his bed in the middle of the night by hooded civilian gunmen who demanded that he sign an agreement allowing Occidental to operate on the Indian land. Cobaria refused, was severely beaten, and dumped into a river to die.

Fortunately, he survived. Undaunted, the U'wa leader promptly contacted Amnesty International and other human rights organizations to complain about the growing violence against his tribe. The publicity that followed Cobaria's actions caught the attention of a young Californian environmental scientist who was graduating from the University of California at Santa Cruz in the spring of 1997. Terence (Terry) Freitas, a then 22-year-old biology major, would eventually decide to devote himself fulltime to the U'wa Indian cause. The lanky environmentalist helped establish the U'wa Defense Working Group in Malibu, California.

The group was a coalition of international environmental organizations that helped the U'wa Indians win the legal battle that same year that prevented Occidental from drilling on the reservation. The Colombian Supreme Court agreed with the anthropologists and environmentalists who held that the drilling would devastate the U'wa and their ancestral land. Ultimately, the legal moves by the U'wa and the international group headed by Freitas, prompted Occidental senior management to shelf the Samoré block project after investing $12 million from 1992.

Freitas continued his work with the U'wa Indians after the 1997 legal victory. He had their trust and would make five trips to Colombia over the next two years. On one of his first trips to the U'wa reservation he accompanied John Vidal, a British journalist working for the *Manchester Guardian*. "We invited Terry Freitas to travel to U'wa with us as fixer and translator, but I had not expected to be met in Bogotá by the all–American Californian kid that was just 22, a graduate biologist, burning with energy, cutting his political teeth, idealistic yet careful to a point, no liker of great risk," explained Vidal.[13]

"Together with photographer Paul Smith, we traveled to U'wa territory and then over to the militarized Occidental camp to confront the oil men. It was often frustrating days and nights together, living in infested barns and aware of the rebel paramilitary groups and the possibilities of kidnap. We talked at length; Terry could barely explain his love for the U'wa. It was partly emotional, partly intellectual, he would say," Vidal added.[14]

With time, the U'wa and their international supporters became a giant headache for Occidental and the Colombian government as they labored to secure the long-term economic future of the nation with additional crude oil production. Initially, the U'wa refusal to sign a deal allowing Occidental to go ahead with the exploration in the Samoré block was attributed to the National Liberation Army's (ELN's) manipulation of the Indians. However, Occidental as well as the Colombian government soon realized that Roberto Cobaria and the U'wa tribe were getting critical assistance from Freitas and his coalition of international supporters.

Meanwhile, Occidental was suffering heavy ELN attacks on its facilities near the Cano Limón field. The pipeline that served the Occidental facility was bombed 78 times in 1998, the highest number in its 13-year existence. The Cano Limón field produced about 142,443 barrels daily in January of 1999, about 17 percent of Colombia's daily output of 843,000 barrels of crude. Revenue from oil, Colombia's main source of export earnings, rose 11 percent to $491.7 million in the first quarter of 1999 from $339.4 million in the same period a year earlier, according to Ecopetrol.

In 1999, twenty-four-year-old Terry Freitas was the key activist in the United States for the U'wa Indians. However, by this time, the serious-minded Freitas was investigating the role of multinational oil companies in the ongoing cycle of violence in the U'wa region. He realized his work had dangerous consequences, but he diligently continued his investigation, even when he became the target of threats. Those who considered Freitas an enemy included the Colombian army and the right-wing paramilitary death squads, as well as the FARC and ELN guerrillas.

"He had problems with every violent actor in the region," according to Coletta Youngers, a Colombia specialist at the Washington Office on Latin America, a U.S. human rights group.[15] Freitas angered most armed groups active in the lawless border region in his attempts to assist the U'wa Indians preserve their culture.

"Terry was finding direct evidence that linked the oil companies to the paramilitaries, and that was very dangerous," said Melina Selverston, director of the Washington-based Coalition for Amazonian People and the Environment, a group that worked with Freitas.[16] Selverston said FARC militiamen had approached Freitas in 1998 year and told him the rebels didn't want to see him back in the area. "It was a sort of informal, street-corner type of conversation," she said. "He took it seriously, he told us about it, but it wasn't enough for him to stop working there," she added.[17]

In February 1999, Terry Freitas decided to return to Colombia. He went with Ingrid Washinawatok, 41—a member of the Menominee Indian nation of Wisconsin, who lived in Brooklyn, New York, with her husband and 14-year-old son — and with Lahe'ena'e Gay, 39, Director of the Hawaii-based Pacific Cultural Conservancy International (PCCI), The trio accepted an invitation from U'wa leaders to go on a one-week cultural mission to help develop a school system. Freitas and Washinawatok were also members of PCCI, which was sponsoring the trip, and assumed the humanitarian project would not touch any sensitive nerves with violent Colombian actors.

In light of previous threats against Freitas, including anonymous phone calls from suspected rightists to his Oakland, California, home, some colleagues had counseled him not to go on the mission.[18] One message was explicit: "Back off or die."[19] However, Freitas's passion for the indigenous culture and his deep conviction that would not allow him to abandon their struggle, forced him to overlook the threats and venture back to the U'wa reservation on February 18, with the two female activists.

Exactly one week later, on February 25, 1999, Freitas, who was two months shy of his 25th birthday, had packed up his gear and was leaving the U'wa reservation for the return home. Freitas, Washinawatok, and Gay had successfully completed the humanitarian mission and were accompanied by U'wa leader Roberto Cobaria who was driving the trio to the airport in the town of Saravena in northeast Arauca province.

Tragically, the four friends never made it to the airport. They came upon a roadblock near the village of El Royota, where two civilian men with ski masks and pistols forced the car to a halt, left Cobaria alone, and abducted the three Americans.

Initially, authorities were not sure who engineered the abductions. Arauca province was a right-wing paramilitary stronghold where death squads dressed as civilians systematically waged a campaign of extermination against trade unionists, leftists, human rights activists and suspected rebel supporters. Also covering Arauca was the FARC's 43rd Front, which normally organized its fighters into squadrons of 12 uniformed rebels in full

combat gear and headed by a veteran combatant.

Back in April 1998, four American bird watchers drove into the belly of rebel territory to study Colombia's rare Cundinamarca Antpitta bird.[20] A FARC front that operated just south of Bogotá captured the four bird watchers. One escaped captivity and the other three youths were released 33 days latter when FARC leaders were confident they were not CIA intelligence agents. Some Colombians thought the release was a sign that the FARC now considered Americans untouchable. More importantly, it was well known in February 1999 that the FARC did not want to ruin its political image with the Clinton White House. Politically, it was widely assumed that the FARC would do nothing to jeopardize the official unfreezing of relations with Washington.

Therefore, most journalists assumed the FARC was not stupid enough to kidnap three Americans ten and one-half weeks after meeting with the U.S. in San José. Moreover, officials in the American embassy were well aware that Freitas and the FARC had two very important things in common: a hatred of the paramilitary death squads and a distrust of the multinational oil companies. So, early news reports assumed that the paramilitary death squads had kidnapped the Americans. Kidnappings of Americans was not rare in Colombia — between 1980 and April 1998, some 92 U.S. citizens had suffered that fate. Eleven were murdered, one died in captivity of starvation, and the whereabouts of several others remain unknown, according to U.S. Embassy officials.

After a week in captivity, sometime during the morning of March 4, 1999, Terry Freitas, Ingrid Washinawatok and Lahe'ena'e Gay were taken across the Arauca River into Venezuela. Their captors marched them to a cow pasture 100 feet from the river that separated the two countries. From his farmhouse, local rancher Segundo Salamanca heard bursts of automatic gunfire. He waited ten minutes, and then went out to investigate.

"I got halfway across the road and I put my hands on my head," 49-year-old Salamanca told the Associated Press. "Who could have committed such a barbarity?" he said.[21] The three bodies were lying face up within ten paces of one another, and their bound hands were folded across their chests, said Salamanca. Gay was found first, shoeless, wearing a beige dress and with a white handkerchief covering her face. Washinawatok was also barefoot and had on beige pants and a blue shirt. Freitas was dressed in gray sweatpants and black boots.[22]

The three Americans were shot with 9mm weapons—Washinawatok and Gay four times each in the face and chest, and Freitas six times. Terry Freitas was hit twice in the back from long range, an indication he made an attempt to flee, according to the Venezuelan police and army unit that arrived on the murder scene four hours afterwards.[23]

Devastated relatives and friends of the slain activists, who had been hoping a release was imminent, struggled to understand the killings. An ashen President Pastrana addressed the Colombian press and condemned the killing of "defenseless" humanitarians. Pastrana lamented the fact that the world would again be reminded that Colombia had the highest kidnapping rate anywhere on earth. He wished the world would understand that the killing of foreigners in Colombia was rare.

Raúl Reyes said the FARC was not involved. "The FARC has no responsibility in these incidents," he said. The FARC blamed the killings on "enemies" of the country's fledgling peace process, a reference to illegal paramilitary death squads or disgruntled sectors of the military.

Occidental was swift to reject FARC insinuations that it may have stood to benefit from the deaths of the three American human rights activists. "We energetically reject those type of claims," said Juan Carlos Ucros, chief legal adviser for Occidental's Colombian operations.

Carlos Castaño's paramilitary AUC death squad organization also issued a statement denying any involvement in the murders.

The killings came on the same day that United States Attorney General Janet Reno was leaving Colombia. On Wednesday, March 3, the Attorney General had toured Armenia, the western city that was hardest hit by the January 25, 1999, earthquake, which killed at least 1,171 people and left 250,000 homeless. Reno concluded her two-day visit with a speech at the Bogotá Lawyers' Club where she prodded Colombia to resume extraditing jailed drug suspects for trial in the United States.

The murder of the three Americans also occurred just days after peace negotiator Raúl Reyes said the FARC was seeking a second meeting with U.S. officials to follow up on the San José, Costa Rica, December gathering.

"We are outraged by the murders of the three United States citizens," White House Press Secretary Joe Lockhart said in a statement. "We have strong indications they were kidnapped and murdered by members of the Colombian rebel group, the Revolutionary Armed Forces of Colombia, or FARC. We demand that the FARC accept responsibility for these crimes and immediately surrender those who committed them. The United States will not rest until those who have committed these crimes have been brought to justice.

United States Ambassador in Colombia, Curtis Kamman, reiterated Washington's call for the FARC to turn over any rebels responsible and fully cooperate with the government's inquiry into the killings. Until the FARC did so, said Kamman,

Washington would be unable to resume contacts with the group. The U'wa Indians also sharply condemned the FARC for the slayings of their American friends.

During the State Department daily press briefing on Monday, March 8, spokesman James Rubin commented on the tragedy. "Our deepest sympathy and prayers go out to the family and friends of the three American hostages who were kidnapped February 25 in Colombia and whose bodies were found in Venezuela on March 4. We have no additional information on the murder of Terence Freitas, Ingrid Washinawatok and Lahe'ena'e Gay, of Hawaii, who were affiliated with American rights organizations working on education projects with the Indians there.

"True to form, the FARC continues to deny responsibility for its action. When the FARC has killed or kidnapped other American citizens, they also denied responsibility for their actions. In the case of the kidnapping of the three American New Tribes missionaries, we have concrete information that the FARC was responsible, contrary to their denials. In another case, we also have concrete proof that the FARC killed two American citizens. So we're not surprised that they have denied responsibility."

Colombian Defense Minister Rodrigo Lloreda issued a statement the evening of the murders that put the blame squarely on Germán Briceño, alias "Granobles" the brother of Jorge Briceño, the military mastermind of the FARC and a member of its seven-man General Secretariat.[24] Jorge Briceño, known by his nom de guerre "Mono Jojoy," was widely seen as the most likely successor to FARC commander-in-chief Sureshot. Colombians knew a public admission that the brother of one of the FARC's top leaders was behind the killings would be a serious setback at a time when the group was striving to boost its political image at home and abroad.

Despite the strong allegations that the FARC was behind the murders, many Colombians expressed disbelief. Colombian Attorney General Jaime Bernal Cuéllar cautioned against "jumping to conclusions," saying the FARC's possible role in the murders could only be established after a painstaking investigation. But, added Bernal, "it's a blow to the peace process."

Noemí Sanín, a political independent who ran a strong third in Colombia's presidential vote in 1998, demanded a full-scale government investigation. "We have to find out who did this, and why they did it, because a lot of peace processes have been broken off by provocations," she said.[25]

"It's extremely bad for the peace process if it is proven that guerrillas killed the three Americans," said Augusto Ramírez Ocampo, a prominent member of Colombia's church-backed National Peace Commission.[26]

It did not take long to pinpoint the blame. On Friday night, March 5, the Colombian army broadcast what it said were intercepts of a radio-telephone contact between Germán Briceño, the commander of FARC forces in the Arauca province, and one of his guerrilla subordinates in which they discussed the U.S. hostages.

"Take them over to the other side and burn them," a voice identified as that of Germán "Granobles" Briceño said at one point, allegedly referring to the Arauca River separating Colombia from Venezuela. "Let the bitch die," he then said. "She's nothing to us." Military sources said the man identified as Briceño was referring to either Washinawatok or Gay.

The news stunned the country. Few people in the nation thought the FARC would commit such a stupid act against Americans. "It strips the FARC of all credibility in terms of their supposed will to make peace," said Enrique Parejo, a former Colombian justice minister. "You can't have peace with crimes like this."[27]

The army broadcast shattered the FARC. They immediately started a high-level cover-up. Senior Commander Raúl Reyes announced a confession on March 11, and said a local squad leader named Gildardo had acted without his superior's orders and killed the three Americans. Reyes said the Americans were picked up after straying onto rebel-held territory "without guerrilla authorization." The Americans were executed on orders of the six-year veteran Gildardo, he declared. Gildardo may face the firing squad for his actions after a tribunal of rebel leaders considers the case, said Reyes, who pleaded for forgiveness and urged that the slayings not derail the faltering efforts to negotiate an end to Colombia's conflict.[28]

Colombian military leaders, however, challenged Reyes' account and said the highly hierarchical rebel group was covering up the participation of higher-ranking commanders. State Department spokesman James Rubin called the FARC response "woefully inadequate," and added that the guerrilla should hand over the guilty rebels to authorities and fully cooperate with the Colombian government's investigation.

On March 29, 1999, arrest orders were issued against Germán Briceño on suspicion that he personally ordered the crime that drew the strong international outcry. Also included in the arrest order was an U'wa Indian, Gustavo Bokota, who allegedly assisted the FARC in its crimes against the Americans, according to Colombian Chief Prosecutor Alfonso Gómez. The prosecutor provided no further details on the investigation or whether other arrest orders would be issued in relation to the killings.

In one of the army's radio intercepts, Jorge "Mono Jojoy" Briceño, can allegedly be heard talking to his brother "Granobles." They were discussing the devastating political impact the killings were having on the FARC. During the radio intercept Mono Jojoy told his brother to come up with "any name" to put forward as the murderer of the Americans. "This is the biggest political screw-up of all," he said. "This is a mistake from hell."[29]

In Los Angeles, Julie Freitas told the Associated Press, "I'm proud of my son. He lived the life that he wanted to live. He had such a passion for the indigenous culture … and he risked his life preserving that culture." She admitted she was "totally devastated" by her son's murder, and added that she would take no solace in the FARC execution of her son's killer, particularly if there was any chance the rebel Gildardo was innocent. "Our family is not interested in revenge or any more bloodshed." The mother said she was grateful that her son's "life was so full of passion and that he fought to help people and did what he believed in."

Leslie Wirpsa, a former girlfriend of Terry Freitas, raised questions about the FARC's story. "There still needs to be a lot more clarity and a full investigation and not just by the FARC," she said. "On a trip last March, Terry called me and said he and an Indian leader were being followed by one or two people, and they had every reason to believe they were paramilitaries," Wirpsa said. Freitas also told her that on the same trip he was hauled into the police station in Cubará, the main town on the U'wa Indian reservation, and questioned about his visit. The police told Freitas they could not guarantee his safety and forced him to sign a document absolving them of responsibility if anything happened to him, a copy of which Wirpsa had in her possession.

Another friend of Freitas, from the U'wa Defense Working Group, Stephen Kretzmann, said Freitas had told him he was convinced the people following him during the Cubará visit were paramilitaries allied with oil companies in the area. An associate whose group operated in the resource-rich region where Freitas worked said the FARC had granted them permission to carry out their work. "I knew Freitas and asked the FARC on his behalf last November if he could work in the region," a respected international aid worker in Arauca said on condition of anonymity.[30] "The FARC gave me the assurance that there were no problems, and they understood his job."[31] Freitas contributed to a report in July 1998 that was critical of the oil industry and progovernment paramilitary groups.

Forty-one-year-old Ingrid Washinawatok had worked on behalf of native peoples since she was a teenager. "Everyone is in shock," said Myra Scheer, a spokeswoman for the Rainforest Foundation, on whose board Washinawatok served. "They went there to help people. We just can't understand why they were killed." In a toughly worded statement, Washinawatok's family and the Menominee nation tribe condemned U.S. policy in Colombia. "Earlier last week the family communicated to the State Department their concerns over Janet Reno going to Bogotá to deliver $230 million to the Colombian government to escalate the war against the FARC," it said.[32]

The chairman of Washinawatok's Menominee nation in Wisconsin, Apesanahkwat, said relatives and friends had been in touch with the rebels through the Red Cross and other groups and had received an e-mail message from the FARC in which it "sent greetings and expressed solidarity" with American Indians.

He found difficulty talking about the loss of Washinawatok. "They were indigenous people. They were working toward a humanitarian purpose. It's just too incredible for us to unravel and to know with any certainty what actually happened down there," Apesanahkwat told the Associated Press. "We're just in shock and a lot of grief." Apesanahkwat speculated that the deaths of the three Americans might have been in retaliation for a Colombian army victory in nearby Arauquita, just across from the Arauca River from where their bodies were found. The army killed 60 guerrillas during the February 19 battle. The guerrillas were not accustomed to taking losses, he noted.

Washinawatok had worked on behalf of native peoples around the world, including in Guatemala and El Salvador, and was married to a Palestinian she met in Cuba, said Apesanahkwat. She was also a filmmaker and a lecturer on Native American issues and was active with the American Indian Community House in lower Manhattan. The American Indian Community released a statement saying, "Ingrid Washinawatok was an integral part of the lives of many native Americans and other traditional peoples, nationally and internationally. Her place in our community will not soon be filled, if ever." The group serves the estimated 36,000 native Indians living in the New York City area.

Lahe'ena'e Gay's PCCI group worked to preserve native cultures on and inside the Pacific Rim. The U'wa Defense Working Group in California, of which Gay was a coalition member, issued a statement. "We call for a full investigation by the U.S. government and independent human rights observers into the deaths of our three colleagues. We call on the U.S. State Department to ensure that the possible role of paramilitary groups is fully investigated, and we call upon the FARC to clarify their involvement, if any."[33]

Gay's friends said they had hoped the three human rights workers would be released like the American bird watchers the previous year. They added that, politically, the killings made little sense.

In January 2000, the U'wa Defense Working Group said that Vice President Al Gore was inextricably linked with

Occidental Petroleum, the U.S. oil group that planned to start drilling on the U'was' ancestral lands in search of an estimated 1.5 billion barrels of oil.[34] Gore's official public financial disclosure report for 1998, the latest information available, indicated the Vice President owned between $250,000 and $500,000 in Occidental stock inherited from his father, Albert Gore, Sr., who died in 1998.

Mr. Gore, Sr., became a board member of Occidental Petroleum after losing his Senate seat in 1970.[35] According to the Center for Public Integrity, a nonprofit organization that studies ethics in politics, Ray Irani, the Occidental chief executive, made a donation of $100,000 to the Democratic National Committee in the early '90s following a stay in the Lincoln Room of the White House.[36]

Stephen Kretzmann, the U'wa campaign coordinator for Amazon Watch, a California-based environmental group, said, "This will not look good for Al Gore in the midst of an election campaign. It is clear that he could stop the drilling with a phone call and if he doesn't do something about this he will lose the environmental and human rights vote too."[37]

The Colombian government said that the Occidental drill site was outside the legally recognized U'wa Unified Reserve; however, tribal leaders maintained that the site was within the larger traditional ancestral territory. The U'wa Defense Working Group claimed development of the site would be damaging to the tribe and the environment because of the likely increase in oil-related violence between different armed factions in the politically unstable region. The group added that Occidental's existing pipeline was attacked more than 600 times in the last 12 years leading to 2.1 million barrels of crude oil spilling into the soil and rivers, and that U'was and humanitarian workers had been killed or injured in crossfire.

Occidental said that it planned to start building roads to the test site at the end of January 2000 and would sink the first test well at the site in May.[38] Ken Hufmann, Occidental's vice president of investor relations, refused to comment on Vice President Gore's stock holding in the company or any political donations that it had made. He would say only that "We're moving ahead with plans to drill the well but I have no specific dates."[39]

Kretzmann urged environmentalists not to vote for Gore and to protest about his links to Occidental on the campaign trail.[40]

On February 11, 2000, four helicopters from Bogotá arrived on a dusty country road near Las Canoas where U'wa Indians were peacefully protesting Gibraltar One, the site of Occidental Petroleum's proposed oil well in northeast Colombia. The helicopters unloaded 150 riot police who allegedly attacked the group of 450 U'wa men, women and children who were attempting to block the rural highway to Gibraltar One. Without warning, the riot police used heavy machinery and tear gas to charge the blockade forcing the Indian protesters into the dangerous rapids of the nearby Cubujon River. During the confusion three U'wa Indian children drowned, according to a statement from the U'wa Defense Working Group.[41]

In September 1999, the Colombian government granted Occidental the right to conduct exploratory drilling a few miles outside the legal boundaries of the U'wa reserve. "This is our land. We will not leave it," Roberto Pérez, head of the U'wa nation's council of leaders, told the Associated Press.[42] Tribal leaders said they would not give in to the U.S. company's plans to drill for oil in their traditional lands, even after the clash with police. Although the drilling site was outside the officially recognized tribal lands, the U'wa said that oil exploration would bring violence to them and destroy their culture.

"I'm not moving. This is my land, and nobody is taking it from me," said Pastor Bocota, who said his four-month-old daughter died after riot police broke up the protest.[43] The Associated Press reported that communication with the U'wa was difficult because many of them did not speak Spanish, but one Indian girl, nine-year-old Kesiowia Bocota, was able to tell reporters through an interpreter that she had lost Pastor Bocota's baby while trying to cross the Cubujon River.[44] The young girl, who was not related to the man or the baby, said the infant slipped from her arms.

The government denied reports of deaths in the police action to clear the road of protesters. "They can say what they like," said Ebristo Cobaria, the U'wa tribe's legal adviser, "but it's their fault. They will have to pay for these lives,"[45] Occidental could not immediately be reached for comment, according to the Associated Press.

General Alfonso Arellano, the National Police Operations Director, said riot police dispersed the protest outside the U'wa reservation near the eastern border with Venezuela without incident.[46] "If there were any dead, let them show us the bodies," Arellano said.[47]

Within days local television showed the body of one of the alleged victims.[48] Authorities said they were still searching for the bodies of the other two children.

A week after the riot police action, more than 285 soldiers were nestled in foxholes beneath trees for protection against the searing heat. They guarded the road to Gibraltar One. Twenty yards away, leaders of the U'wa Indian community watched helplessly as the outline of the new road took shape. The road was the first part of a multibillion-dollar project by Occidental. Gibraltar One was about a half-mile climb up a mountain and covered a 27-acre drilling area. The site reportedly contained 1.4 billion barrels of oil, enough to satisfy Colombia's need for crude for several years.

"I feel defenseless against 3,000 or 2,000 or even 500 armed men," U'wa Indian Ebaristo Tegria said. "Especially if you don't have any guns to say, I am just as strong as you."[49]

Notes

1. Author's interview with Phil Chicola, Washington, D.C., 21 January 1999.

2. John Otis, *Houston Chronicle*, "Colombia Peacemaker Is the Middleman Both Sides Trust / Former Senator Is Vital Link Between Rebels, Government," 29 November 1998, A, p. 26:1.

3. Douglas Farah, *Washington Post*, "U.S. Officials, Colombian Rebels Meet, Unprecedented Secret Talks Last Month Were Aimed at Salvaging Peace Effort," 5 January 1999, A, p. 8:1.

4. Author's interview with Chicola.

5. Tim Johnson, *Miami Herald*, "State Department Defends Meetings with Colombian Rebel," HERALDLINK, 5 January 1999.

6. The kidnappings of the three U.S. missionaries were an important factor in Secretary Albright's October 1997 decision to designate the FARC a terrorist organization. United States Department of State, Office of the Spokesman, Press Statement by James P. Rubin, 6 February 1998.

7. Author's interview with Chicola.

8. "The American Whiskey Rebellion of 1794 was a protest against a tax on whiskey imposed by Congress. Farmers in western Pennsylvania were accustomed to distilling much of the grain they raised into liquor because corn and rye were too bulky to be transported long distances; the new tax hit them hard in the pocketbook. President George Washington, however, raised an enormous force (larger than any army he had commanded during the Revolution), and the 'rebels' quickly dispersed." *The Reader's Companion to American History* (Boston: Houghton Mifflin, 1991), p. 916.

9. *Bloomberg News*, "U.S., Colombian

Officials Met FARC Rebels, *El Espectador* Says," Bogotá, 4 January 1999.

10. Douglas Farah, *Washington Post,* "House GOP Subpoenas State Dept. on Colombia," 21 May 1999.

11. *Washington Post,* For the Record, 11 February 1999, A, p. 36.

12. Jane Ayers, *San Francisco Chronicle,* "Colombia's U'wa Indians Battling Violence, Oil Interests, Environmental Group Is Calling for Investigation," 30 April 1999, A, p. 1.

13. John Vidal, *Manchester Guardian,* "Indigenous Rights: California Dreamer," England, 10 March 1999, Society, p. 4.

14. *Ibid.*

15. Jared Kotler, Associated Press, "Colombia Rebels Blamed in Deaths," Bogotá, 8 March 1999.

16. *Ibid.*

17. *Ibid.*

18. *Ibid.*

19. Reuters, "U.S. Groups Doubt Rebels Behind Colombia Killings," Washington, 8 March 1999.

20. Colombia is the second richest nation after Brazil in biological diversity. It has the world's greatest variety of birds, with 1,850 species, 66 of which can only be found in Colombia. The nation also has 358 types of mammals and more than 45,000 types of plants.

21. Vivian Sequera, Associated Press, "Slain Americans Were in Risky Area," La Victoria, Venezuela, 6 March 1999.

22. *Ibid.*

23. *Ibid.*

24. Tom Brown, Reuters, "Americans' Killings a Blow to Colombia Peace Bid," Bogotá, 6 March 1999.

25. *Ibid.*

26. *Ibid.*

27. *Ibid.*

28. Jared Kotler, Associated Press, "Colombia Suggests Rebel Cover-up," Bogotá, 11 March 1999.

29. Reuters, "Colombia Ties Top Rebel's Brother to U.S. Murders," Bogotá, 26 March 1999.

30. Newsday, Combined News Services, "Colombia Victim Was Threatened," Bogotá, 8 March 1999, A, p. 15.

31. *Ibid.*

32. Reuters, "Colombia Rebels Deny US Deaths, Peace Bid Teeters," Bogotá, 6 March 1999.

33. Reuters, "U.S. Groups Doubt Rebels Behind Colombia Killings." Washington, 8 March 1999.

34. Matthew Jones, *The Financial Times,* "Gore Attacked Over Colombia Oil Project," London, 20 January, 2000.

35. *Ibid.*

36. *Ibid.*

37. *Ibid.*

38. *Ibid.*

39. *Ibid.*

40. *Ibid.*

41. PRNewswire, "News from U'wa Defense Working Group," Cubara, Colombia, 11 February 2000.

42. Vivian Sequera, Associated Press, "Indians, Police Clash in Colombia," Las Canoas, 13 February 2000.

43. *Ibid.*

44. *Ibid.*

45. *Ibid.*

46. *The Chicago Tribune,* "Cops Disperse Indians Protesting U.S. Oil Firm's Plans for Drilling," Bogotá, 13 February 2000.

47. *Ibid.*

48. Steven Dudley, *Washington Post,* "In Colombia, a Dispute Fueled by Oil," Cubará, 20 February 2000.

49. *Ibid.*

CHAPTER FIVE

The Next Vietnam

Who goes in if this thing blows up? Tell me this is not Vietnam again. — Senator Ted Stevens, Republican from Alaska, Chairman of the Senate Appropriations Committee, in official comment at hearings for emergency U.S. military aid to Colombia.[1]

Colombia's problems are so complex that they make the Balkans look simple.... If shooting people could solve the problems of Colombia, then Colombia would have become a heaven on Earth long ago. — Charley Reese, *Orlando Sentinel*.[2]

Whatever the official spin, it has the scent of yet another Vietnam. Then Eisenhower and Secretary of State John Foster Dulles announced that they were not going to permit Communists to overrun southern Vietnam without a fight. By the time Kennedy was gone he had placed 16,000 American military advisers in Vietnam. Then came Johnson and Nixon and 58,000 American dead, hundreds of thousands wounded, and perhaps a million or more Vietnamese killed. Do we really need another military intervention, a renewed draft, mass protests and yet another war memorial to our boys in Washington? — Murray Poiner, author, "No Victory Parades: The Return of the Vietnam Veteran."[3]

"What are the chances of a coup?" was the urgent question the CIA was ordered to answer by the White House. In other words, Bill Clinton urgently wanted to know if the Colombian armed forces were "enemies of the peace process." The senior officials walking the corridors of the White House needed fresh evidence to determine if the revolt among the military's senior leadership was a deliberate move to loosen Pastrana's grip on power. The Americans were alarmed. The crisis was the biggest clash between civilian and military power in half a century.

The leader of the mutiny was the President's trusted Defense Minister, Rodrigo Lloreda. The soft-spoken Lloreda was a 1990 Conservative Party presidential candidate, a former senator, a former ambassador to Washington and a retired newspaper publisher. He was widely seen as the political heavyweight within the Cabinet.[4] Saying he was at the end of his patience, Lloreda issued an ultimatum to Pastrana on Tuesday evening, May 25, 1999. The minister said he was prepared to resign if the government's chief peace negotiator, Víctor G. Ricardo, did not rescind the decision to give the FARC un-limited access to the demilitarized safe haven. Lloreda was seething over the fact that the FARC had threatened to break off peace talks if the safe haven did not con-tinue, and that guerrilla peace negotiator Raúl Reyes had the audacity to ask the gov-ernment to expand the size of the demili-tarized territory.

The tough-talking Reyes alienated many Colombians when he told the Asso-ciated Press that "If the government con-siders it most profitable to achieve peace and to keep talking in order to cement peace, it will maintain the pullout. And if the pullout doesn't continue, the talks will be canceled." Reyes also enraged Republi-can leaders in Washington when he ad-vised the U.S. that it needed to put behind it the deaths of three American human rights activists killed in March by a rogue FARC unit and resume contacts with the organization.

Lloreda was pointing a gun to the head of President Pastrana. Since the new government's inauguration Lloreda had embarked on an ambitious program to strengthen the beleaguered armed forces and had won intense loyalty from top officers. Lloreda, a civilian, won respect from the Colombian army by working closely with U.S. military experts to help turn around the forces considered among the most poorly motivated in Latin Amer-ica. In the shadows, 47 senior military officers were ready to hand in their resig-nations in support of the Defense Minister. Surely, some of them were hoping Pastrana would step down. Colombian observers in the region said the crisis placed the future of the nation's fragile peace process in doubt.[5]

The following morning, Lloreda at-tempted to telephone Pastrana to explain his position in detail, but was informed by the private secretary that the President could not attend to him because of other pressing obligations. Pastrana was in the seaside resort of Cartagena where Colom-bia was hosting a presidential summit of the oldest trading group in Latin America, the five-nation Andean Bloc, which was celebrating its 30th anniversary with a two-day conference. Unable to speak with Pastrana directly, Lloreda was forced to an-nounce his resignation publicly without consulting the President.

"Too many concessions to insurgents have been made by the government, and that is the perception of an overwhelming majority of Colombians," Lloreda said at a news conference. During the conference, he established that he supported efforts to negotiate a peace with the FARC guerrillas, but had serious doubts about the willing-ness of the FARC to end the conflict. In a letter to the President, Lloreda said he was resigning as defense minister because of differences within the administration over "The gravity of the threats the nation faces and the way the peace process is currently handled. If one looks at the polls over the past three days, it is clear that more than 75 percent of Colombians are not in agree-ment with the indefinite character of the safe haven," the letter stated. At least 16 military generals and 31 colonels submit-ted their resignations in support of Llo-reda. An entire division and one brigade in key conflict zones were left without senior officers. The departures signaled a signifi-cant breach between the government and the military on the issue of tactics for achieving peace.[6]

President Pastrana canceled a work-ing session at the summit and immediately accepted Lloreda's resignation. He then ap-pointed General Fernando Tapias, the armed forces commander, interim Defense Minister and summoned the top military brass to Cartagena. By midafternoon there was an air of political crisis throughout the country as newscasters repeatedly broke into radio and television programs to announce that top military officers had offered to resign.

The nation was held in suspense while the President privately huddled with the branch commanders of the armed forces. Rumors swirled in the streets of Colombia that a coup was taking place. After nearly four hours, Pastrana emerged and read a short statement praising the military for "the support you have expressed to the chief of state and the democratic institutions.[7] The government and the armed forces are deeply united and identified with the national aim of seeking peace."

General Tapias quickly dismissed reports of massive military resignations and pledged support to Pastrana. He added, however, that he and other commanders had spoken "frankly" with the President about their concerns over his decision to remove limits on the amount of time the FARC could occupy the massive safe haven in southern Colombia while peace talks were under way. When asked by the press about the military high command resignations, he said, "For now, no one is leaving. We are aware that the best contribution we can offer the nation is to keep working in difficult times."[8]

The following morning, the reassuring headline "The Storm Is Over" was splashed on the front page of *El Tiempo*. However, the publication's lead editorial stressed that the crisis highlighted structural weaknesses in Colombia's democracy and a lack of "coherence in its peace strategy." The editorial also urged Pastrana to show firmer leadership as he sought to guide the country through "One of the most difficult periods in the nation's history."

"This was an alarm bell," said Liberal Party opposition leader Horacio Serpa, who lost the 1998 presidential election to Pastrana. He added that it was "inconceivable" that Pastrana would refuse to take a call from his own Defense Minister.[9]

Lloreda went on the radio talk show circuit after the President accepted his resignation. Speaking in an interview with one local radio station, Lloreda went beyond asking Pastrana to back down, saying that the territorial concession had triggered "a lot of concern" among senior army commanders and friction between the government and the military.[10] Openly questioning Pastrana's handling of peace talks with the FARC, he also said the President's tactics had little public support. Asked if the armed forces thought the government had given up too much in exchange for little or nothing from the FARC, Lloreda said that was the view shared by most Colombians. "I think there's a large sector of public opinion that has that perception, whether or not it's mistaken, and obviously that takes public support away from a process that needs public backing," he said.[11]

Lloreda's comments drew immediate backing from army commander General Jorge Enrique Mora, who read a statement on behalf of the entire military high command supporting the minister in his showdown with the government. "We totally identify with the minister of defense because the armed forces, and the army, consider him the best minister we've ever had.... A permanent demilitarized zone is inadvisable for the country," the statement said.

In another radio interview, Lloreda said neither he nor armed forces chief Tapias had been consulted about giving rebels unlimited dominion over the area which is bigger than the U.S. state of Maryland. A poll earlier in the week in Bogotá's *El Tiempo* showed nearly 80 percent of Colombians opposed the safe haven; a similar poll in *El Espectador* indicated the opposition was 71 percent.

President Pastrana stoically responded to the growing criticism by saying the peace process would continue undeterred. "My government's peace policy has been carried out within the legal and constitutional framework, and I will stick by it until the end of my term," he said.

The crisis started on May 20, 1999. That was the date Víctor Ricardo announced Colombia would give the FARC the safe haven indefinitely. "The demilitarized zone for negotiations will be established without any time limits and without deadlines, in the same area where the dialogues have taken place," Ricardo said in a speech in Bogotá.[12] "The zone will continue being important." He added that international monitors chosen by the government and the FARC would be invited to oversee activity in the rebel-controlled area, which has about 90,000 civilian residents.

The same evening, the White House threw its weight behind the dramatic peace bid.[13] In a prepared statement released by the White House, President Clinton voiced strong support for the process and praised Pastrana for the "tremendous courage" shown in his efforts to reach a negotiated settlement of a war that had claimed 40,000 lives in the last decade alone. "Successful peace negotiations are the best way to advance our shared goals: economic advancement for all the Colombian people, greater regional security, respect for human rights and justice, and effective curbs on drug trafficking," the statement said. The White House had remained mostly silent about the peace process since early March, when the FARC admitted their role in killing Terry Freitas, Ingrid Washinawatok and Lahe'ena'e Gay. Clinton had said then that the United States was determined to see that those responsible for killing the trio of Americans were brought to justice.

Clinton's statement was welcomed by Foreign Relations Minister Guillermo Fernandez de Sota as a shot in the arm for the peace process, which was facing growing criticism from hard-core rightists and even from some left-leaning critics in Colom-

bia. "It reiterates once again the unconditional support of our nation's peace process," Fernandez said.[14] President Pastrana was counting on the support from his friend in the White House. In addition to the heavy criticism in Colombia, some journalists were now calling him a political lightweight incapable of resolving the nation's conflict.

One of Colombia's prolific political cartoonists, Vladimir Flórez, was now routinely depicting President Pastrana as a comical tiny figure engulfed in an oversized business suit, his head barely sticking out above the shirt collar.

Rafael Santos described the country's situation in an eloquent column in *El Tiempo* earlier in the month. "A day in Colombia is like watching a surreal horror movie.... It's a picture of war and cruelty that most Colombians watch in impotence, without knowing how to keep hope alive for a happy ending."

Adding to the crisis were comments by National Police chief General Rosso José Serrano, acclaimed throughout the world as the man who dismantled the Cali Cartel, who said the demilitarized zone was full of clandestine airstrips and was planted with more that 24,000 acres of coca, the raw material for cocaine. Military sources in the United States and Colombia said they suspected the FARC of using the demilitarized zone as a staging point for drug shipments, and for receiving weapons smuggled back into Colombia from abroad.

However, the most stinging attack on the safe haven came from Roman Catholic church officials. They accused the FARC of running the zone like a fiefdom, with widespread taxation and the forced recruitment of children as young as 13 in the zone. The nation, they concluded, had good reason to suspect that the earnings from drug trafficking was bankrolling arms shipments and preparing the FARC more for war than for peace.

Conservative political commentator Carlos Alberto Montaner referred to the safe haven in an *El Tiempo* column. "As in feudal Europe, no central power is in charge. There are only the lords of war, to whom tributes must be paid, so they don't kidnap or kill their terrified vassals."

On Friday, May 14, 1999, a group of Republicans in the House of Representative's subpoenaed all State Department records on contacts between the Clinton administration and the FARC. The Republicans alleged that United States diplomats had carried on unauthorized negotiations with a terrorist organization. The move reflected growing hostility between the State Department and the group of House Republicans led by Representative Dan Burton, the Chairman of the Committee on Government Reform, over the administration's policy toward Colombia and its fragile peace process.[15]

The subpoena covered all correspondence and e-mail exchanges between State Department official Phil Chicola and the FARC, as well as records of all his telephone conversations since December 1, 1998. It also ordered the State Department to hand over internal correspondence on the matter between Chicola and his boss, acting Assistant Secretary of State for Inter-American Affairs Peter Romero.

The storm clouds began brewing two weeks earlier, when Burton blasted the Clinton Administration's war on drugs while attending a large ceremony at the Sikorsky Aircraft plant in Connecticut. The ceremony was celebrating the first delivery of six new UH-60L Black Hawk helicopters to the Colombian National Police (CNP).

In attendance at Sikorsky were Colombian Ambassador Luis Alberto Moreno, dignitaries from the State Department and the U.S. Army, and Connecticut Democrats Senator Christopher Dodd and Representative Rosa DeLauro. Also present were Republican Representatives Benjamin Gilman of New York and John Mica of Florida. Gilman, who was elected to his 13th term in the House of Representatives on November 5, 1996, was the influential Chairman of the House International Relations Committee (formerly known as the Foreign Affairs Committee) and a strong supporter of CNP chief Rosso José Serrano who also was in attendance.

Burton lamented the loss of 4,000 Colombian police and soldiers murdered by the "narco-guerrillas," and added, "Chairman Ben Gilman and I, almost on our own, have been trying to get a reluctant Clinton Administration to provide these helicopters and other equipment to the CNP for years. We have fought tooth and nail with a misguided Administration, which has let the war on drugs take a back seat to negotiating sessions with Colombian FARC terrorists. It is good to see my Democrat [six] colleagues here today. I encourage Senator Dodd and Representative DeLauro to join Chairman Gilman and myself in our efforts to provide even more Black Hawks and other equipment to our CNP allies. I encourage them to use all of their persuasive powers with the Clinton Administration to fight the war on drugs the way it should have been fought all along ... at the source," Burton said.

The $289 million in aid the Republicans muscled through Congress made Colombia the third-largest recipient of U.S. direct foreign assistance in the world, behind Israel and Egypt. Unfortunately it was not enough. U.S. intelligence sources reported the FARC earned more than $500 million a year from Colombia's cocaine and heroin trade. Moreover, U.S. intelligence sources in Germany indicated the FARC were buying Russian shoulder-held surface-to-air missiles on the international arms black market with their drug-financed war chest.

Chairman Gilman, whose career reflected a lifetime of dedicated service to
helping others, used his remarks in an uplifting fashion. "General Serrano and his
forces have destroyed the Medellín and
Cali drug cartels. Under unforgiving conditions in a mountainous, jungle terrain,
they have eradicated hundreds of thousands of hectares of coca and opium. They
have destroyed massive cocaine labs, seized
tons of drugs and precursor chemicals, as
well as the assets of those criminal cartels,
who target our nation, and the rest of the
world, from Colombia. Only belatedly is the
world starting to recognize what a courageous ally we all have in General Serrano.

"General Serrano, these high-perfor-
mance choppers will be dedicated to all of

The primary mission of the UH-60 Black Hawk squad-carrying assault helicopter is to transport infantry units into combat, re-supply those units while in combat, and perform the associated functions of
aero medical evacuation and repositioning of reserves. *Courtesy of United Technologies Sikorsky Aircraft*
    Congressman Ben Gilman of New York, Chairman of the House of Representive's Committee on
International Relations. *Courtesy of Ben Gilman*

the brave men and women of the CNP, and the far too many widows and orphans your force already experienced in the fight against drugs. Hopefully, these modern helicopters will help save the lives of your men, and avoid many more widows and orphans. With these birds will fly the hopes of many American parents that no more young lives will be lost here to deadly Colombian heroin and cocaine. These helicopters will carry the best of Colombia's young men and women and the equal hopes and prayers of their parents, families, and friends that they too will be safe and return to live in a peaceful and prosperous Colombia."

Deliveries of the new helicopters would bring to 26 the number of Black Hawks serving in Colombia, making it the largest non–U.S. government fleet in the Western Hemisphere, according to Sikorsky Chairman and CEO Eugene Buckley, whose organization inexplicably denied a request from the CBS news organization that its *60 Minutes* producers attend and report the ceremony. (*60 Minutes,* with one of the finest reputations for investigative journalism in the United States, was doing background work on a special report on Colombia.)

Back in Washington, the State Department was scurrying to honor the May 28, 1999, subpoena deadline. A State Department official said, "The documents would support in general terms and in detail what we have said, that we have talked but not negotiated with the FARC and only at the request of the Colombian government." The *Washington Post* reported that

Colombian National Police stand guard before destroying an illicit coca field carved out of the jungle. *Courtesy of Gil Macklin*

Colombian National Police inspect the wreckage of a police Huey helicopter shot down by guerrillas. *Courtesy of Gil Macklin*

while subpoenas were often threatened when Congress wanted information it felt was being withheld, they were seldom served. However, according to State Department officials and congressional aides, the distrust was so deep and the dislike so strong that the subpoena *was* served, and with little warning.[16] Burton and other Republicans charged that the Clinton Administration was negotiating with a terrorist group that kidnapped and executed Americans, that was on the State Department's list of terrorist organizations, and that got hundreds of millions of dollars a year from protecting cocaine and heroin traffickers.[17]

"I think the U.S. … has no business negotiating, talking to, or meeting with

terrorist organizations of any kind," Burton said in a May 13 letter to congressional colleagues. "Ironically, it has been the bedrock principle of the United States not to negotiate with terrorist organizations, and this administration has casually dismissed this policy by sitting down at the table with a group that actively seeks to wantonly kidnap and murder American citizens."[18]

Department spokesman James P. Rubin responded, "We are being fully responsive to the request from Congress for information, and we intend to turn over the relevant documents." He noted the department already offered to make available reports of its meetings with the FARC. However, Rubin would not comment on a

Washington Times report that said a State Department official had e-mail and telephone contact with the FARC.[19] He said Department lawyers advised that it was more important to respond to the legal requirements of the subpoena than to respond to questions on the matter.[20]

Oddly enough, a powerful voice in opposition to the Clinton administration's policy in Colombia was the Heritage Foundation, a Conservative think-tank based in Washington, D.C. In a superb report authored by John P. Sweeney titled, "Tread Cautiously in Colombia's Civil War," the Heritage Foundation stated that the Colombian conflict threatened stability in Latin America and endangered U.S. interests in the region, including the war on drugs.[21]

However, the most significant assessment of the report criticized President Pastrana's peace plan. "Clearly, President Clinton should not have endorsed this plan," it stated.[22] Sweeney found three reasons why Pastrana's peace plan was not likely to succeed. "First, the Colombian government has been unable to counter the growing involvement of Marxist insurgents in drug trafficking, and the Colombian army has been unable to defeat the rebels in battle. Moreover, the rebels have little incentive to abide by a peace agreement because they believe they hold the upper hand. Second, by making major concessions to the narco-rebels, Pastrana is conferring political status and an implicit legitimacy on their efforts. Third, even if the peace talks succeed, the illicit drug trade that funds the rebels' activities is unlikely to be deterred significantly. Even if the rebels decide to curtail drug operations in their areas, the traffickers will simply move their operations."

Sweeney pointed out that the FARC leadership had repeatedly stated that their goal was to establish political control over as much of Colombia as they could capture in order to install a Marxist socialist regime. Furthermore, the FARC would have to fight the paramilitary death squads to do so, he added. Sweeney pointed out the potential for a bitter conflict in a comment by death squad chief Carlos Castaño who had said, "We do not share the concept of peace at any price because we consider it dangerous for the existence of the nation and its institutions."[23]

Sweeney also faulted the unrealistic position of the FARC. "Commander Manuel Marulanda Vélez has demanded that the government recognize the FARC as a military force. The FARC want a new military doctrine based on the defense of Colombia's borders, a reduction in the size of Colombia's armed forces, a greater respect for human rights. The FARC wants a revision of Colombia's military treaties, a ten-year moratorium on Colombia's foreign debt, and a drug solution that targets demand in the United States and other large consumer countries rather than interdiction of supply and production in Colombia." Moreover, Sweeney said, Marulanda intended to pursue a clear socialist agenda that "Combines the best from Soviet socialism, from Chinese socialism, from Vietnamese socialism, and from Cuban socialism.[24]

"Pastrana's peace proposal is little more than a white flag signaling the government's surrender," according to Sweeney.[25] The report described how Colombia's urban centers would remain under the government's control, but most rural territory would fall under guerrilla and paramilitary control under the peace plan. Sweeney made troubling observation made by many other Americans. "To achieve lasting peace, Pastrana must change Colombia's institutions and legitimize and protect private property rights. He also must change the culture of institutionalized corruption, violence and systematic abuse of human rights. Although the involvement of the FARC and ELN rebels in drug trafficking, kidnapping, extortion, and cattle rustling makes them criminals and not revolutionaries, the fact remains that some of their grievances against the Colombian state are valid."[26]

Sweeney outlined how the political actors in Colombia maintained different objectives. He noted how the FARC and ELN rebels had no real intention of negotiating peace and then adhering to an agreement. "They want to establish a Marxist government, nationalizing banks and natural resource industries, redistributing land to millions of peasants, and expel foreign investors." Further, the paramilitary death squads were financed by private landowners and drug traffickers and were determined to wipe out the FARC and ELN, he said.

He also wrote, "the Colombian army's credibility and image have been tarnished by high-level corruption in the chain of command and systematic human rights abuses." Sweeney said that the armed forces hoped to change this image, recover from the humiliation they had suffered from an inability to control the rebels, and finally destroy the guerrillas. He then pointed out that "the Clinton Administration wants peace to help it eliminate illegal drug trafficking and U.S. and Colombian business interests care less about drugs and guerrillas and care more about creating a stable economic environment that is conducive to investment, growth, and profits."

Overall, the Heritage Foundation detailed the complexities of the Colombian peace plan and concluded that Colombia was on the verge of becoming "a no-win situation." "If the Pastrana peace talks fail, which appears increasingly likely, Colombia will sink deeper into a vortex of violence that could spill into neighboring countries, endangering regional stability. The country is a tinderbox awaiting only a careless spark to explode in flames.

"Above all, the Clinton Administration must not lose sight of the fact that the conflict between the government, rebels, drug traffickers, and paramilitary forces in Colombia is fundamentally a Colombian problem that the Colombians themselves must resolve. If the limits of U.S. military involvement are not spelled out clearly at the outset, the risk is great that the Colombian quagmire would swallow up significant numbers of U.S. soldiers. The President and Congress would be wise to remember that America's involvement in Vietnam, a steadily escalating involvement that President Clinton himself opposed as a university student, began with a few dozen U.S. Military advisers and a small investment."[27]

In April 1999, retired U.S. Army Major Andy Messing, a highly regarded counterinsurgency expert with visits to 27 different war zones around the globe, including numerous trips inside Colombia, made an astounding assessment of the conflict. Messing told the *Miami Herald* that the FARC were capable of assuming power.[28] "We're not dealing with a bunch of farmers with pitchforks here," he said.[29]

Earlier in the year, *The Economist* voiced grave concern about the U.S. involvement in Colombia's precarious peace process. "Were the talks to break down, it could well throw Colombia into all-out conflict, and might even drag the United States, however unwillingly, halfway into yet another jungle-based guerrilla war."[30]

The leaders of the 5,000 guerrillas that made up the National Liberation Army (ELN) were fuming. Antonio García and Pablo Beltrán, two senior commanders of the ELN, were tired of playing second fiddle to the FARC. President Pastrana and peace commissioner Víctor Ricardo had put the ELN in the backseat of the peace process and they were extremely unhappy about their second-class status. The ELN had also requested a safe haven during

Comandante Nicolas "Gabino" Rodríguez is head of the National Liberation Army's (ELN) five-man ruling Central Command. *El Tiempo*

peace talks in February 1999, but were emphatically denied by Pastrana and Ricardo.

The President and his peace commissioner appeared to have a double standard in place, using patience with the FARC and a hard line with the ELN. Military sources said the ELN was desperate because of a growing debility.[31] They reported paramilitary death squads had made significant advances in recent months against the ELN units in the north-central region that had been a stronghold, nearly wiping them out in some areas.[32] Moreover, in October 1998, the ELN blew up an oil pipeline near Machuca in northwest Antioquía province, killing 67 villagers and increasing public opposition to the movement.

Consequently, García and Beltrán were resolved to be the "intellectual authors" of a bold new guerrilla campaign designed to enhance the bargaining power of the ELN. After consulting Nicolas Rodríquez, alias

"Gabino," the highest ranking commander of the ELN's five-man ruling Central Command, and getting approval, García and Beltrán set about implementing a campaign that they were convinced would prove that they were a worthy military force and would bring the government to its knees. The new ELN guerrilla campaign would introduce the innocent citizens of Colombia to a new dimension of terror.

The first ELN operation began in the northeast city of Bucaramanga, on the morning of Monday, April 12, 1999, when five well-dressed men carrying briefcases boarded an Avianca airline flight bound for Bogotá. All appeared normal on the airplane, according to witnesses, but shortly after takeoff, the men pulled ski masks over their heads and swiftly took positions around the cabin waving pistols. The Avianca plane, a Fokker 50 turboprop, was carrying 41 passengers and crew in addition to the hijackers. The commandos immediately instructed the crew to land the plane on a clandestine jungle airstrip near the town of Simití, alongside the Magdalena River. Upon landing, the five gunmen were met by a heavily armed column of ELN guerrillas who quickly ushered all 41 passengers down the Magdalena River and away from the makeshift runway. They left the Fokker 50 undamaged.

Within days the ELN released nine of the oldest and weakest captives, including a three-month-old baby. Analysts speculated that the first group was freed as an attempt to keep a promise the ELN made in July 1998 to stop abducting children and the elderly.[33] Colombian authorities reported that three of the captives included an Ecuadorian nun, a Colombian congressman and an American whom the ELN identified only as Daniel Wolman, 33, of Chicago.

The Avianca plane hijacking was only the third in the history of the nation and the first during the 1990s. But the nation was very worried. Up until April 12, air transportation was not a guerrilla objective, so air travel had been considered the safest way of avoiding kidnap at guerrilla roadblocks throughout the country. Now Colombians who needed to move around could only trust the large airports in major cities where security was massive.

As a matter of everyday life, Colombians knew to stay off the roads outside the cities. Abductions by guerrillas and common criminals officially totaled 2,216 in 1998; however, most people knew the count was much higher because many kidnappings were never reported to the authorities. The government maintained that the rebels had generated earnings of $1.8 billion in ransom payments over the previous

An abandoned Avianca Airlines Fokker 50 turboprop airplane sits on a makeshift runway after a successful hijacking by the ELN following take-off from Bucaramanga Airport, April 12, 1999. *El Tiempo*

eight years. The business was so profitable the guerrillas took to calling it "miracle fishing." They cast a wide net over large portions of the country to assure they missed few opportunities for income.

On May 4, the ELN released seven Avianca hostages. Twenty-five hostages, including American Daniel Wolman, remained in guerrilla hands. In a lengthy statement read by a freed hostage, the ELN issued a scathing criticism of successive governments for failing to address Colombia's vast gap between the rich and the poor. It added that rampant corruption and political exclusion justified the ELN guerrilla movement. "Colombia's armed conflict is rooted in a structural crisis caused by bad governments," said the communiqué.[34] They also asked that a swath of land in Bolívar province be cleared of troops as a prelude to peace talks.

President Pastrana branded the Avianca hijacking a blatant act of terrorism and said he would not cede to political demands from the ELN. His office released a statement lashing out at the group, "You are seeking to use the taking of hostages, and violations of the civilian population's rights, as an instrument to formulate peace proposals…. The national government ratifies its rejection of using atrocious crimes like this with the intent of achieving political goals or benefits."[35]

In essence the guerrilla plan backfired. The President rejected the ELN demands and maintained his hard line. Moreover, the hijacking created additional opprobrium for the ELN among the people. Therefore, the ELN started plans to unleash a second guerrilla operation designed to raise the level of terror. The masterminds, García and Beltrán, were about to take on one of the most respected groups in the world. It was a calculated risk, but they appeared hellbent on showing the ruling elite that the conflict in Colombia would not spare anyone, anywhere.

García and Beltrán, the two authors of terror, planned one of the largest abductions in the history of Colombia. The operation took place in La María, a Roman Catholic Church located in a wealthy neighborhood of the southwestern city of Cali. It started during Sunday morning's high mass, near the end of the ceremony. Thirty uniformed ELN commandos posing as soldiers entered the church during the homily, shouting that there was a bomb in the building and that they were going to deactivate it. The ruse allowed the commandos to quickly force the 140 bewildered worshipers out of the wooden pews and into canvas-covered trucks waiting outside. A bodyguard pulled his gun as the hostages were being loaded into the trucks and was immediately dispatched with a fusillade of bullets. The trucks then took off for the southern residential district of Ciudad Jardín.

Within minutes the police and military gave chase. Captain Arnulfo Traslavina, who led the military pursuit, told the Associated Press that his men caught up to a truck carrying six ELN guerrillas but no hostages and killed two commandos in a firefight.[36] Traslavina said homemade mines laid on the ELN escape route hindered the pursuit as his troops were forced to stop and disarm them.[37]

Army General Jorge Enrique Mora told the Carocol Radio Station that helicopter gun ships and waves of troops swarmed over the area, forcing the ELN to frantically abandon 84 worshipers within the first few hours and flee into the nearby mountains with the remaining hostages. The scene was surreal as rash family members reportedly climbed into the mountains in four-wheel drive vehicles to look for relatives they feared had been abandoned by the commandos.

(What Mora didn't say, according to a February 2000 Human Rights Watch report, was that the Cali-based Third Brigade subsequently set up its own "paramilitary" group called the "Calima Front" using "active duty, retired and reserve officers ... along with paramilitaries" taken from the ranks of Carlos Castaño's forces based in northern Colombia in response to the attack on the La María church. According to civilian government investigators, witness accounts and the government-sworn testimony of a former army intelligence agent, the front went on a rampage through southwest Colombian villages, committing targeted assassinations, and massacres of peasants, and forcing the displacement of hundreds of villagers. The Human Rights Watch report said the Third Brigade provided the front with intelligence and logistical support. Working with the army, it says, local drug traffickers also provided the Calima troops with food, supplies and local lodging. "The Calima Front and the Third Brigade are the same thing," the report quotes one government investigator as saying.)

Ultimately, news reached the United States embassy in Bogotá that an American was attending services in the La María church. Roy Howard Saykay of Long Island, New York, would bring the total of United States citizens kidnapped in Colombia in the first five months of the year to 12, twice as many as in all of 1998, the U.S. State Department reported. Saykay would bring the number of Americans in captivity in Colombia to three. Guerrillas in eastern Colombia had abducted Matthew Aaron Burtchell, a U.S. helicopter technician working under contract for British Petroleum on May 14, and the ELN still held Daniel Wolman.

On his way to a State Visit in Canada, President Pastrana said that the ELN abduction was "a crime against humanity." Canadian Prime Minister Jean Chrétien offered to advise Colombia in its peace effort, but Pastrana said the process was still in its infancy and such outside help would be premature.

Colombian Roman Catholic prelate Monsignor Alberto Giraldo was livid that the guerrillas would raid a Mass in the overwhelmingly Catholic country and said church doctrine allowed for the excommunication of people who "Profane the Eucharist."

Acting Defense Minister army General Tapias described the act as demented and sacrilegious. "This is an act of war against the peace process. One can't try to achieve negotiation through blackmail and intimidation of the civilian population," he said.

Juan Gossain, a highly respected commentator for the RCN radio and television networks voiced the horror of the country. "What's ahead? What's next? Will they seize a supermarket and take the shoppers? Will they seize a stadium full of people?"

In the final analysis Colombians knew there were no more sanctuaries left in the nation, and they trembled when the ELN boasted of the ease with which the war could spill from the countryside into the cities. Certainly, this was the prelude to another assault, they thought. Hence, the nation cringed as rumors swirled through the streets that the next ELN operation would take place in the country's largest city ... Bogotá.

The public outcry caused the ELN to beg for forgiveness. "We're not enemies of the Roman Catholic Church.... We beg forgiveness from the church and all the faithful for this act, and we're sure that many will understand what happened," Gabino, the chief commander of the ELN, told Colombia's *Semana* magazine a week later.[38]

In interviews with German news organizations Gabino said he had asked his fighters to carry out a high-profile attack to avenge the killing by paramilitary death squads of at least 25 peasants on May 29 in an ELN stronghold on Colombia's northern border with Venezuela. The ELN commandant alleged he had not authorized the targeting of a church and said roughly 95 percent of the ELN's rank and file were devout Catholics. According to *Semana,* Gabino added that he was troubled by the decision made by Cali's archbishop to excommunicate all rebels involved in the kidnapping during Mass in the La María church, an act which Pope John Paul II condemned as a sacrilege.

However, Gabino told *Semana,* the attack was justified because it showed that Colombia's wealthy urban elite could not escape the ravages of the conflict that had taken the lives of more than 35,000 Colombians in the last decade. "Once in a while rich people have to experience the consequences of war," he declared.[39] In the *Semana* interview, Gabino reiterated the demand for an ELN safe haven, indicating it could prompt the release of the 54 churchgoers, 25 Avianca airline hostages and the nine members of a Colombian sports club who were taken prisoner while fishing on a river near Barranquilla a few days after the church raid.

Gabino was obviously uncomfortable. The ELN had traditionally drawn many of its estimated 5,000 fighters from adherents of Liberation Theology, a socially conscious form of Roman Catholicism that combines Christian and Marxist teachings. Until his death in 1999, Manuel Pérez, a Spanish-born former priest who was one of the leaders of Liberation Theology, led the ELN. Moreover, one of the high-profile members of the ELN was the legendary Colombian socialist, priest and revolutionary, Camilo Torres, who put aside the privileges and duties of the clergy and was killed in battle while leading his band of guerrillas against the army on February 15, 1966. Further complicating the ELN position in the nation was news that the guerrillas were secretly seeking ransoms for some of the wealthiest church captives. Antonio García defended the action with a terse statement, "We have to finance the war."[40]

Back in Washington, D.C., the State Department responded to the brazen act in Cali by upgrading its "Travel Warning" in Colombia, urging Americans to avoid the country at all cost. "There is a greater risk of being kidnapped in Colombia than in any other country in the world," the department said, in one of the strongest statements ever issued to American travelers.[41] "Violence by narcotraffickers, guerrillas, paramilitary groups and other criminal elements continues to affect all parts of the country. Citizens of the United States and other countries have been victims of recent threats, kidnappings, domestic airline hijackings and murders," the travel warning reported. It also explained, "Since it is U.S. policy not to pay ransom or make other concessions to terrorists, the U.S. government's ability to assist kidnapped U.S. citizens is limited."[42]

Sureshot was angry. The Colombian military and police were committing highway robbery, and Carlos Castaño was clandestinely recruiting Contra mercenaries from Nicaragua to join his paramilitary death squads. Sureshot wanted the world to know the enemies of peace were the military and paramilitary death squads. He publicly accused the military and police of systematically stealing food and other supplies to prevent them from being trucked into the guerrilla safe haven. The FARC delivered a statement to the Attorney General and to the Colombian Chief Prosecutor in May 1999 that said members of the army and police were demanding $365 bribes to let trucks pass through roadblocks ringing the demilitarized safe haven.[43]

The FARC also provided an exclusive scoop to *Cambio,* the magazine publication owned by Gabriel García Márquez and directed by the highly regarded journalist Mauricio Vargas, substantiating the presence of Contras in Colombia.[44] The FARC provided information that included clandestine routes, dates, and photographs to substantiate the charge that Carlos Castaño was paying Contras to wage war against the guerrillas.

"All cargo trucks working the routes into the safe haven are stopped and stripped of anything of value," the statement said. Security forces had set up a total blockade, preventing trucks laden with food or any other cargo from entering. "The situation has led to a rapid exhaustion of food supplies and has pushed people to the brink of desperation because of the famine to which they now are being condemned," the FARC charged. The Colombian military refused to comment on the accusations, according to Reuters.

The FARC maintained that three junior army officers, who were posing as members of a right-wing paramilitary group and working under orders from a regional army commander, were responsible for the blockade, certainly, paramilitary commanders had conceded they were seeking to disrupt supplies going into the area. They routinely prevented the Red Cross from entering the safe haven and accused the respected international organization of being infiltrated by guerrillas and of working with the FARC. But they stopped short of saying they were seeking to starve the 90,000 civilians out of the region. Ultimately, Sureshot made it known that he believed there were only two sure ways to stop the covert actions against the FARC—kill Carlos Castaño, and continue to annihilate the army.

The battle plan to destroy Carlos Castaño was a brilliant military strategy, and it was executed to perfection. In June 1999, a FARC reconnaissance team located Castaño's new hideout in the Nudo de Paramillo mountain range. After studying the field intelligence, Sureshot and his military strategists ordered the search and destroy mission with explicit instructions to execute Castaño. There were no plans to take any death squad prisoners. The orders

did include instructions to gather valuable documents and any cash on hand, but the primary objective of the attack was the total destruction of Castaño and his mobile headquarters unit.

The FARC attacked with a fury. Many of the guerrillas had waited a long time to avenge Castaño's reign of terror against unarmed peasants. The 500-strong FARC unit stormed the secret mountain encampment and was very close to crushing the commander-in-chief of the death squads. However, in a moment of desperation, Castaño contacted his allies in the armed forces high command. As a result, just when it appeared that the FARC would complete its objective and destroy the dangerous leader of the Colombian paramilitary death squads, the government's armed forces came to the rescue and saved its principal asset in the "Dirty War."

It was damning proof of the secret alliance between the death squads and the armed forces. Without hesitation, senior military leaders responded to Castaño's frantic pleas and prevented his battlefield destruction at the hands of the FARC. The army immediately dispatched a Russian-made M1 helicopter to the field of combat at Puerto Libertador and dropped 44 soldiers into the fray. The overwhelming superiority of FARC fire compelled the helicopter to immediately abandon the combat, leaving the army troops with no backup. The absence of air support was the equivalent of a death sentence for the 44 soldiers.

The arrival of the army unit provided the cover for Castaño's battered paramilitary group to flee, and they left the Colombian army to fight the 500 FARC guerrillas alone. The subsequent firefight between the FARC and the 44 army soldiers was lopsided and over quickly. The army never had a chance of survival without air support and reinforcements. Although they must have known they were thrown into a deathtrap recklessly, the young army soldiers courageously fought to the very end, but they were no match for the vastly superior FARC force.

Thirty-five of the army soldiers perished in the battle, six were wounded and the rest were missing in action. There was no hiding the truth. The Colombian soldiers were sacrificed, so Carlos Castaño could survive. The army's second in command, General Nestor Ramírez, explained the indifferent mindset of the armed forces senior leadership to the Associated Press. "The latest battlefield losses are not a major setback but more like a soccer game in which there are goals against you."

The dark alliance between the Colombian armed forces and the death squads was no longer a well-kept secret. "The apparent fact that the army always seems to show up when the FARC or other armed opposition group is engaged in fighting with paramilitaries, seems to once again highlight the close nature of the relationship between the Colombian security forces and the paramilitaries," Carlos Salinas, head of the Americas section of Amnesty International, told Reuters by phone from Washington.[45]

The FARC released a statement laced with sarcasm. "Pastrana's promise to crack down on the paramilitary forces sounds strange when government troops arrive on the scene to save them."

In comments to reporters, General Víctor Julio Alvarez, head of the army's First Division, rejected the allegation of collaboration. He said the paramilitary gunmen had fled when the army arrived on the scene while the rebels stood and fought.

The fresh army casualties challenged recent assertions by some U.S. officials that Colombia's military was gradually recovering from a series of stinging defeats since 1996.[46] Earlier in the week, the top U.S. military commander for Latin America,

General Charles Wilhelm, told the U.S. Senate that Colombia's military had "boxed the ears" of the guerrillas on three recent occasions, inflicting tactical defeats.[47] Wilhelm would later tell the *Washington Post* that most of his waking hours "and some of his sleeping hours" would be spent consumed with the conflict in Colombia.

Afterwards, the army reported that it killed 19 FARC guerrillas in the Puerto Libertador skirmish. It was unable to produce the bodies to substantiate its claim.

President Pastrana suffered a political blow in the Colombian Congress in June 1999 when lawmakers narrowly but effectively managed to block his bid to assume extraordinary powers and grab total political control of the peace process. Pastrana was seeking the ability to pardon war criminals in order to increase his leverage in the peace talks, but his request for such sweeping authority was attacked for its "Imperial style" and rejected.

Critics said the bill, which Interior Minister Nestor Humberto Martínez insisted could not be reworded, was tantamount to giving Pastrana "a blank check" for peace.[48] "It would have empowered the President to do anything in the name of peace," said political analyst Hernando Gómez Buendia.[49] The final vote was a cliffhanger: the political reform bill was defeated 10 to 9. In an act of defiance, Martínez accused the Congress of turning its back on the peace process and said the government would seek to win the powers sought through a national referendum.

However, the chance of broad national support for the President's plan was slim. A poll published at the end of June 1999 suggested that three out of four Colombians thought President Pastrana had failed in his election pledge of sweeping political and economic change. *El Espectador* reported the results of a poll, conducted by the National Consultancy Center, which indicated that 79 percent of Colombians believed that

Pastrana had not succeeded in bringing about any real change in the country. Moreover, almost 75 percent said they disapproved of Pastrana's record on economic management. Eighty-nine percent said Pastrana had failed to take effective measures to cut unemployment, which had spiraled to a record high of almost 20 percent, up nearly 5 percentage points since the start of his administration.

In conclusion, the poll found that more than two-thirds of those surveyed said they disapproved of the way the President was handling his peace policy and 86 percent said he should change his negotiating tactics. The two most damaging disclosures of the poll were that almost half of those surveyed feared Pastrana's next three years would be even less productive, and that 55 percent said that in hindsight they should never have voted for him.[50]

The report was a major embarrassment to the Clinton Administration. It confirmed the worst fears of the U.S. drug policy experts—the United States was not only losing the war on drugs, but cocaine and heroin production was going to increase by as much as 50 percent. It was a severe setback for Washington, which was funneling a record $280 million in counternarcotics aid to Colombia in 1999.

The report was issued to Congress by the General Accounting Office (GAO) on July 1, 1999. It said: "Active insurgent groups and their growing involvement in drug-trafficking activities over the past several years are complicating Colombia's ability to reduce drug-trafficking. The cocaine threat from Colombia has worsened since 1996 and could deteriorate even further within the next two years.... Also Colombia is now the primary provider of high-grade heroin to the eastern United States."[51]

The GAO report was also bad news for the FARC and ELN. The dialogue in Washington was starting to become much more belligerent. While everyone still welcomed the peace talks, there was growing discourse about having to take action to smash the alliances between the guerrillas and the drug-traffickers, and the death squads and the drug traffickers. As part of the ongoing effort to stem drug trafficking, the GAO said U.S. officials were now routinely sharing intelligence on guerrilla activities with the Colombian military.

"Recent offensives by the insurgents ... suggest Colombian security forces will be unable to conduct effective anti-drug operations in regions where guerrilla forces dominate and control the area," the GAO said. Moreover, it maintained, an estimated two-thirds of the FARC and one-third of the ELN were now involved in the drug trade. "Despite the demise of the notorious Medellín and Cali drug cartels, the U.S. Drug Enforcement Agency calculates Colombia is still responsible for about 75 percent of world cocaine supply and about two-thirds of the heroin sold on U.S. streets."[52]

A FARC spokesman responded to the criticism in Washington. "Just as we are engaged in talks with the government ... the threats from the Pentagon, Central Intelligence Agency, the Drug Enforcement Agency and the hawks of war in the United States are all the more evident and damaging."[53] Jorge "Mono Jojoy" Briceño, the chief military strategist of the FARC, warned against a broader U.S. role in Colombia's civil war in an exclusive interview with *El Espectador*.[54]

Briceño said the U.S. could get sucked into a Vietnam-style war that it would have no chance of winning. "This isn't Yugoslavia for them to just come in and do whatever they want.... Those kind of troops wouldn't last long here, given all the discomforts and the harshness of the tropical climate," he said. "If they invade they'll have to take the consequences."

Mono Jojoy then went on to attack the

United States. "The North Americans have been intervening here for more than 50 years, but now they want to do it more directly.... Look what happened in Yugoslavia. The North Americans talk about human rights while they bomb a nation and destroy it. They're the world's worst terrorists," he claimed.

Mono Jojoy admitted that the killing of the three Americans by FARC guerrillas was an error, but he was anything but contrite about it. "The tricky thing is that three gringos die and they make a whole damn song and dance about it, but 200 Colombians are killed on orders from them [the U.S.] and it's as if nothing happened here."

Other FARC leaders continued to remind the world that the peace talks in Ireland did not include the surrender of arms. They also reiterated the demand that the Pastrana government dismantle the paramilitary death squads.

Despite whatever the guerrillas said, the man who potentially would be given the military assignment to wipe out the FARC, General Charles Wilhelm, commander of the Miami-based Southern Joint Task Force, took a hard line when he spoke with Reuters. The rebels, he insisted, were endangering regional stability and warned that the Pentagon could intervene unilaterally, particularly in Panama, if the rebels persisted in making cross-border raids.

Andrés Pastrana was no longer the golden boy. The thinking in Washington was shifting. He had captured the hearts of the White House during the state visit, but his decline in popularity was so great that the *Washington Post* wrote of his failures on the front page of its July 6, 1999, edition.

"Andrés Pastrana became President of Colombia last year amid high hopes that he could bring an end to years of violence, drug trafficking and government red ink.... But by most measures, things only have gotten worse.... For the Clinton administration, Pastrana's leading foreign backer, the belief that peace was achievable and would provide a victory in Washington's drug war has descended into gloomy uncertainty. International organizations estimate that as many as a million Colombians—a number exceeding the exodus from Kosovo—have left their homes, fleeing the fighting or fearing reprisals."[55]

The policymakers in Washington had wanted to give the peace talks a chance but Pastrana's waning popularity forced them to change gears. Ultimately, they were forced to concede that the President's peace process had only catered to the guerrillas and failed to win any concessions. The absence of tangible results hurt Pastrana. Moreover, the President was weakened by the poor relationship he maintained with the Colombian Liberal Party. He relied heavily on his Conservative Party allies for crucial support and unwisely kept the opposition in the dark on strategic national decisions. This partisan policy reduced the chance of cooperation with Liberal leaders who controlled the Colombian Congress.

To some in Washington it appeared that the FARC had outsmarted the Colombian government. They had managed to reduce the government's credibility abroad and they continued to enhance their appeal to the poor inside the country. There was concern that Sureshot and his band of leaders were upgrading the "blueprint" and reaching out to new sources of cooperation in Colombia. For the most part, Sureshot and the FARC controlled the countryside, but lacked punch in urban areas. However, political observers in Colombia were alarmed by how the FARC was infiltrating the flow of displaced peasants entering the miserable poor sectors of the big cities, particularly the southern neighborhoods of Bogotá.

The observers also voiced concern

that communist sectors of the highly organized workers unions were in deep discussions with the FARC. The talks allegedly focused on forming a coalition government to run the country after Sureshot wrested control from the oligarchy. Another dangerous development in Colombia was the alliance between the FARC and ELN.[56] Colombians realized that a full integration of the military might of the 20,000 strong FARC army and the 5,000 ELN guerrillas would change the nature of the threat in Colombia considerably.

As a consequence of all these developments, observers of Colombian affairs in the United States worried about the FARC's military and political capabilities, and conceded it was capable of victory in Colombia. It all depended on the thousands of disenchanted poor pouring into the cities, the radical elements of the nation's unions, and disenchanted left-wing students. However, with Colombia experiencing its worst recession since 1931, the government was not in a position to immediately satisfy the demands of the poor or the workers. In fact, Pastrana's government lacked the resources to introduce any fresh social reforms. Under these circumstances, Sureshot's propaganda had greater appeal than the government's belt-tightening and measures of fiscal austerity.

The debate intensified as to how far the United States should go in smashing the alliances between the guerrillas and the drug traffickers. On one side of the open-ended debate were the hawks, who said only U.S. troops were capable of going in and wiping out the guerrillas. They predicted the campaign could be completed with little "collateral damage," a euphemistic phrase used by the Pentagon that generally meant there would be civilian casualties but relatively few. On the other side, the doves in the U.S. urged patience and said it was much too early to

abandon the peace process. They warned that world opinion would turn against Washington if the White House acted in haste. In the middle of the argument were the influential moderates who were quietly working behind the scenes to try and form an international peacekeeping force to send into Colombia, made up of units from Canada, Brazil, Argentina and Chile. However, early prospects for such a force were not encouraging. The Americans found that very few countries wanted anything to do with the Colombian civil war.

Ultimately, it was decided to tilt the odds. The Colombian armed forces outnumbered the FARC, had more sophisticated weapons, and were being trained by the best and brightest of the U.S. military establishment. All that wasn't enough to help them overpower the insurgents, so it was decided to increase the assistance. The White House ordered, for the very first time, the sharing of sensitive real-time intelligence on the movement of the guerrillas with the Colombian military.[57] The intelligence included satellite images, communications intercepts and other sensitive data.

The Clinton administration had always feared getting involved in counterinsurgency operations because it loathed the army's long history of human rights abuses. However, this new arrangement did not entangle the U.S. with the Colombian military, at least not immediately; it was designed to slow down the progress of the guerrillas until more powerful measures were put into effect later in the year. The White House hoped the tide would turn for the better when the Black Hawks arrived in September and when the new U.S. funded army-police intelligence center at Tres Esquinas, in southwestern Colombia, was completed.[58] Additionally, the U.S. military Southern Command was training human rights-vetted troops in Colombia and hoped to have a 950-soldier elite counternarcotics army battalion ready to enter the war by the end of the year. The setup cost of the rapid reaction battalion was estimated at $70 million.[59]

The new intelligence sharing assistance troubled human rights groups. They feared the Colombian military would pass U.S. information on to the paramilitary death squads who would target human rights activists, labor leaders, and other civilians suspected of being leftists. "As far as we know, there have been no reforms instituted that would guarantee that does not happen again," said Winifred Tate of the Washington Office on Latin America.[60]

Notes

1. Murray Poiner, IntellectualCapital.com, 9 March 2000.

2. *Ibid.*

3. *Ibid.*

4. Tod Robberson, *Dallas Morning News,* "Colombian Defense Minister, Officers Quit to Protest Rebel Haven," Caracas, 27 May 1999.

5. Tim Johnson, *Miami Herald,* "Defense Minister's Resignation Sparks Exodus of Colombian Generals," Bogotá, 26 May 1999.

6. Ruth Morris, *Los Angeles Times,* "Colombia Minister Quits Over Concessions," Bogotá, 27 May 1999.

7. Tim Johnson, *Miami Herald,* "Bitterness Lingers in Colombian Forces Over Peace," Bogotá, 28 May 1999.

8. *Ibid.*

9. Tim Johnson, *Miami Herald,* "Pastrana Rejects Mass Resignation by Generals," Bogotá, 27 May 1999.

10. Reuters, "Colombia Defense Chief Slams Concessions to Rebels," Bogotá, 25 May 1999.

11. *Ibid.*

12. Reuters, "Colombia to Give Rebels Safe Haven Indefinitely," Bogotá, 20 May 1999.

13. Reuters, "U.S. Throws Weight Behind Colombia Peace Bid," Bogotá, 21 May 1999.

14. *Ibid.*

15. Douglas Farah, *Washington Post,* "House GOP Subpoenas State Dept. on Colombia," Washington, D.C., 21 May 1999.

16. *Ibid.*

17. *Ibid.*

18. *Ibid.*

19. Associated Press, "U.S. to Provide Colombia Documents," Washington, 21 May 1999.

20. *Ibid.*

21. John P. Sweeney, Heritage Foundation, "Tread Cautiously in Colombia's Civil War," 25 March 1999.

22. *Ibid.,* p. 3.

23. *Ibid.,* p. 4.

24. *Ibid.,* p. 5.

25. *Ibid.,* p. 7.

26. *Ibid.*

27. *Ibid.,* p. 18.

28. Tim Johnson, *Miami Herald,* "With the Rebels in Colombia: What Makes Them Keep Fighting?" El Carbonal, Colombia, 25 April 1999.

29. *Ibid.*

30. *The Economist,* "Colombia Talks Peace in the Long Shadow of War," San Vicente del Caguán, 9 January 1999, p. 31.

31. Larry Rohter, *New York Times,* "A Colombian Rebel Group Gains Notice, Loses Sympathy," Bogotá, 21 June 1999.

32. *Ibid.*

33. Suzanne Timmons, *Los Angeles Times,* "Air Passengers Latest Victims of Colombian Unrest," Bogotá, 15 April 1999.

34. Ricardo Mazalan, Associated Press, "Colombian Rebels Free More Hostages," Monterrey, Colombia, 7 May 1999.

35. Reuters, "Colombia Rejects Any Deal for Release of Hostages," Bogotá, 26 April 1999.

36. Jared Kotler, Associated Press, "Colombian Gov't Won't Talk to Rebels," Bogotá, 31 May 1999.

37. *Ibid.*

38. *Semana,* "Habla el ELN. *Semana* entrevistó a Gabino, el No. 1 del Ejército de Liberación Nacional, responsable de los secuestros de la iglesia en Cali y del avión en Bucaramanga," Bogotá, 7 Junio de 1999.

39. *Ibid.*

40. *Semana,* "Antonio García: Hay que financiar la guerra," Bogotá, 21 Junio de 1999.

41. Colombia — Travel Warning, United States Department of State, 10 June 1999.

42. *Ibid.*

43. Reuters, "Rebels Accuse Colombian

Army of Highway Robbery," Bogotá, 19 May 1999.

44. *Cambio,* "¿Contras en Colombia? Investigan la llegada al país de ex militantes de la Resistencia Nicaraguense. La guerrilla asegura que están a órdenes del jefe paramilitar Carlos Castaño," Bogotá, 7 Junio 1999.

45. Karl Penhaul, Reuters, "Colombian Army Helps Death Squads—Amnesty," Bogotá, 24 June 1999.

46. Jared Kotler, Associated Press, "Colombian Army Says 35 Soldiers Dead," Bogotá, 23 June 1999.

47. *Ibid.*

48. Tom Brown, Reuters, "Colombian Lawmakers Block Presidential Power grab," Bogotá, 8 June 1999.

49. *Ibid.*

50. Reuters, "POLL—Colombians Say President Is Floundering," Bogotá, 27 June 1999

51. Karl Penhaul, Reuters, "U.S. Seen Losing War on Colombia Cocaine, Heroin," Bogotá, 1 July 1999.

52. *Ibid.*

53. Karl Penhaul, Reuters, "New Colombian Peace Talks as US Warns on Rebel Drugs," Bogotá, 4 July 1999.

54. Luis Fernando Ospina y Rafael Baena, *El Espectador,* "Que la oligarquía haga los cambios," Enviados especiales Serranía de La Marcarena, 5 de Julio de 1999.

55. Karen DeYoung, *Washington Post,* "Colombia's U.S. Connection Not Winning Drug War," Bogotá, 6 July 1999.

56. *El Espectador,* "Alianzas entre Eln y Farc, En zonas tales como Montes de Maria (Bolívar), el llamado corredor de Frontino (Antioquia), el nudo del Paramillo, y la región d e Arauca, se han evidenciado acciones conjuntas del Eln y las Farc," Bogotá, 8 de Abril de 1999.

57. Douglas Farah, *Washington Post,* "U.S. Widens Colombia Counter-Drug Efforts," 10 July 1999.

58. *Ibid.*

59. Karl Penhaul, Reuters, "U.S. plane wreck seen in rebel-held Colombia jungle," Bogotá, 25 July 1999.

60. Tom Brown, Reuters, "U.S. Report Highlights Abuse by Colombian Army," Washington, 28 July 1999.

CHAPTER SIX

Guerrillas at the Door

MESSAGE TO THE OLIGARCHY

As a last cry of alarm I want to tell you: Gentlemen of the oligarchy: the people no longer believe in you. They do not want to vote for you. They are fed up and desperate. They do not want to go to the elections you arrange for them. The people are suffering and they will do anything for relief. The people also know that you will do anything to save yourselves. This is why I ask you to be realistic: if you want to mock the people with new political ideas you must know that they no longer have faith in you. You know that the fight will be carried out to its ultimate end. Existence has been so bitter that the people will stop at nothing. Unfortunately, the isolated, blind, and proud oligarchs seem not to want to realize that the revolution of the Colombian masses will not stop until the people have attained power. — Camilo Torres, priest and revolutionary, December 9, 1965[1]

After the Bogotazo in April of 1948, President Mariano Ospina's government trusted few Liberals. Fearing further chaos from the *pueblo,* Ospina banned public meetings in March 1949, in May, he fired all Liberal governors; in November, he prohibited any opposition to his rule and ordered the army to forcibly close Congress. All the while, rural police forces, under the control of the extreme Conservatives, heightened the effort against belligerent Liberals. Unfortunately, moderate Conservatives failed to protest the government's political viciousness; they realized that blind loyalty to their party bosses was what kept them on the government payroll. Soon the motto of the Conserva-

tive era was "the Party over and above the country." As a result, unimagined horrors were inflicted on the *pueblo.*

All Liberals, from ministerial to the local level, resigned in protest at Ospina's nondemocratic actions. When the 1949 presidential election arrived, the Liberals refused to present a candidate, and as a result Laureano Gómez, the Conservative and only candidate, took office by default in August 1950. Gómez ignored the needs of the poor. Instead, the new President worked feverishly to enhance the authority and autonomy of the presidency beyond the limits Ospina had established, and expanded the powers of Conservative governors. Like Ospina, Gómez feared opposition and firmly incorporated broad measures into the system that curtailed civil liberties. Overall, he took strong steps with an eye to limiting the possibility that the Liberals could ever regain influence in Colombian decision making.

Colombian democracy was going backwards. The ultraconservative President dismantled pro-labor laws passed in the 1930s and eliminated independent labor unions with an executive decree. Moreover, his Conservative government held congressional elections without opposition and censored the press. Gómez administered justice through courts controlled by the executive branch, and limited the freedom of worship by getting Conservative thugs to attack Protestant chapels and other non–Catholic places of worship. The Protestants established themselves in Colombia in the 19th century but were never able to attract many converts. By 1950 they made up less than 1 percent of the population. Nevertheless, Gómez wanted to intimidate all Colombians who practiced a faith other than Catholic.

As President, Gómez took every opportunity to label Liberal opposition Communist. To Gómez, anyone who differed from his ultra right-wing political views was the enemy, and his handpicked police and army enforcers would go on rampages to stamp out any opposition. Consequently, the number of violent deaths in Colombia, a nation of 11 million, climbed to 1,000 per month. Within a short period of time, Gómez tolerated no opposition whatsoever and lost the support of many moderate members of the Conservative Party and the armed forces.

His fatal mistake was alienating the oligarchy. Therefore, in November 1951, when Gómez became ill, the oligarchy seized the opportunity and plotted against him. The illness obliged Gómez to name his deputy, Roberto Urdaneta Arbeláez, acting President until he was fit to return

to office. Urdaneta followed most of Gómez's policies but refused to dismiss General Gustavo Rojas Pinilla who had led the Colombian forces in Korea and whom Gómez suspected of conspiring against his government. When Gómez regained his health in June 1953, a strongly unified coalition comprising elite Conservative and Liberal moderates disapproved of his resumption of power; they instead supported General Rojas Pinilla who blocked the dictator's return with a bloodless military coup.

Few lamented the downfall of Gómez, whose erratic tyranny had alienated most of his countrymen, including former President Ospina. Gómez, therefore, became the first President to be toppled in a coup since Vice-President José Manuel Marroquín replaced the aging Manuel Antonio Sanclemente in 1900.

The mandate of General Rojas Pinilla was to end the violence, and to that end he immediately offered amnesty and government aid to belligerents who would lay down their arms. Initially, there was widespread support for the peace program and thousands accepted the offer of amnesty. Moreover, Rojas Pinilla was applauded nationally when he neutralized Gómez's thugs by forcing the entire National Police into the orbit of the armed forces. Moderates in the nation also welcomed his relaxation of press censorship and authorization to release hundreds of political prisoners. The measures brought a relative calm to the country during the first few months of the coup. Unfortunately, the tranquillity did not last.

Rojas Pinilla feared the oligarchy, and attempted to circumvent their power by recruiting political support from nontraditional sources. The new President trumpeted a "Bolivarian" view of government that supposedly represented the patriotic, brave, loyal and true character of his administration. He also seduced the military by raising salaries and constructing lavish officers' clubs, and courted the church by espousing a "Christian" doctrine as the foundation of his government. In many ways, Rojas Pinilla used Gaitán-flavored rhetoric to attempt to fuse the *pueblo* and urban workers into a movement that would counter the oligarchy's traditional domination of the country's politics. Interestingly enough, Rojas Pinilla did indeed attempt to attend to some of the needs of the obedient poor. However, his overall programs only succeeded in angering the ruling class.

As a result, support for the Rojas Pinilla regime faded within the first year of his government. Toward the end of 1953, rural violence was renewed and he quickly undertook strict measures to counter it. Following a substantial increase in police and military budgets, the government assumed a dictatorial and demagogic character. It continued to reverse reform measures and tighten press censorship. The former general deliberately antagonized the ruling class when he closed a number of the country's leading newspapers, both Liberal and Conservative. Finally, under a new law implemented to ensure the legitimacy of his rule, anyone who spoke disrespectfully of the President would be jailed or fined.

Politically, Rojas Pinilla held on to power by allowing a handpicked assembly of supporters to elect him to a full four-year term beginning in 1954. The same assembly implemented constitutional changes, which included women's suffrage, a long overdue measure that no longer raised much opposition in Colombia. However, since Rojas Pinilla never allowed a popular election to endorse him, Colombian women would have to wait years to vote. Therefore, Colombia barely escaped the dishonor, which went to Paraguay, of being the last Latin American nation in which women were able to vote.[2]

Colombia's cancer — extreme poverty — continued unabated under the Conservatives and provided the impetus for the guerrilla movement in Colombia. However, it was the assassination of the beloved Jorge Eliécer Gaitán on April 9, 1948, that marked the official era of armed resistance in the Republic of Colombia. The brutal police state implemented by President Mariano Ospina after the death of Gaitán and the ruthless dictatorships introduced by President Laureano Gómez and President Gustavo Rojas Pinilla legitimized the guerrilla movement in the eyes of the *pueblo*. From the time of Gaitán's murder, guerrillas were no longer considered bandits by the ordinary people. To the contrary, they were considered the credible opposition to a series of corrupt and brutal governments.

With time, the guerrillas became folk legends among the poor. They included colorful characters like the gallant Guadalupe Salcedo Unda — a tall, dark, Creole horseman who roamed the Plains of Colombia with 5,000 armed cavalry and was christened "the Centaur of the Plains."[3] They also included the likes of the dashing but extremely dangerous Capitán Dumar Aljure, who carved out a well developed role in Colombia's Meta province as a political, economic, and socially prestigious figure.[4]

Other well-known guerrilla heroes of that era included Eliseo Velásquez, the Fonseca brothers, Rafael Parra, the Bautista brothers, Jorge González Olmos, and Eduardo Franco Isaza, who would go on to write the classic exposé of the insurrection on the Plains titled, "Las guerrillas del Llano." In due course, the lone survivor of the first generation of guerrillas, the only individual continuing the armed struggle against the state into the next century, was Pedro Antonio Marín, better known by his nom de guerre, Manuel "Sureshot" Marulanda, the supreme commandante of the FARC.

Folk legend Guadalupe Salcedo Unda, a tall, dark, Creole guerrilla who roamed the plains of Colombia with a cavalry of 5,000 armed horsemen, was called "The Centaur of the Plains." *El Tiempo*

The greatest of the guerrilla folk legends Guadalupe Salcedo Unda, was born in Surimena in 1922, the son of Antonio Salcedo from Boyacá, and Tomasa Unda, a Creole born on what Colombians called the Llanos (Plains). The family had strong family ties on the Plains that run up as far north as the province of Arauca, on the border of Venezuela, and all the way down to the province of Meta, which extends about 200 kilometers southeast of Bogotá. When Guadalupe reached adolescence he took off on his horse to roam the immense savannas that covered the Llanos.

Young Guadalupe was tall and lean, with dark eyes, dark skin and curly hair, which gave him the striking beauty of a Moor.[5] He barely went to school, but after years of roaming about on horseback, exploring the natural secrets of the Plains, he became a brilliant equestrian and an expert pathfinder in the vast rims and savannas of Casanare, Arauca, Cravo and Meta. Sometime after the assassination of Gaitán, Guadalupe was arrested by the army while sleeping out on the Plains with a group of fellow horsemen. He was accused of being a Liberal Party sympathizer, put on a truck and transported to prison. He fled jail in 1949, during an uprising on the Apiay military base, and immediately decided to take vengeance against the conservatives for denying him his freedom. At first, it was a life on the run for Guadalupe and his stallion. They jumped walls, negotiated deep rivers, and managed to escape several army and police ambushes. Eventually, he enlisted with Eliseo Velásquez, a lumberjack who had assembled a small band of about 100 Plainsmen who were joining the bitter uprising against the Conservatives.

His parents said Guadalupe was rebellious by birth and that he was a son of destiny. Shortly after joining Velásquez's guerrillas the prognostication came true. Guadalupe racked up an amazing string of daring conquests against the Conservatives. His horseback exploits against the Conservative militia were the talk of the Plains and inspired other men to join the armed resistance. Guadalupe confronted soldiers and government airplanes but still managed to outfox the enemy with his cunning strategies and intimate knowledge of the Plains. Day after day, his name inspired strength, and as his legend grew, herd after herd of horsemen joined the ranks, and soon songs were written to tell the tales of the Centaur of the Plains. In due time, he was named the supreme leader of the Liberal guerrillas of the Plains and had 5,000 armed horsemen under his command willing to follow his every order. The horsemen from the Plains had a legendary ability to fight; from their ranks the Liberator Simón Bolívar recruited his most intrepid warriors a century and a half earlier in the war of independence against the Spanish. During *La Violencia,* Guadalupe and his men proved to be just as daring and fearsome fighters.

The Liberal guerrillas fought the Conservative government over the course of four years. They established control of the Plains and protected Liberal liberties for the *pueblo.* However, when General Rojas Pinilla assumed power the guerrilla horsemen were enticed by the offer of amnesty to all belligerents. Historically, the Colombian military was nonpartisan, so an amnesty offered by Rojas Pinilla, a military man, was one Guadalupe and his men could trust. They would never have trusted an offer of amnesty from the Conservatives.

The Centaur of the Plains and his intrepid cavalry were ready to consider the surrender of their weapons to a neutral party and return to a life of peace. President Rojas Pinilla flew to the historic meeting in Yopal to personally negotiate with Guadalupe. To the President's displeasure, the proud guerrilla declined to come down from his horse to shake hands with him. However, after studying the terms of the government's proposal Guadalupe agreed to the offer of amnesty for himself and his 5,000 horseback warriors.

A few years later, Guadalupe was invited to Bogotá to receive homage from Liberal dignitary Juan Lozano for his work on behalf of the Party during the period of *La Violencia.* A Liberal Party official reportedly bought him a new wool suit to ward off the cooler high-altitude climate of Bogotá. The ceremony was to take place in the northern section of the city. Somehow, though, Guadalupe was duped into going to the southern section of the city where a squad of Conservative policemen was eagerly waiting to avenge his years of insurgency. He was trapped, far away from the Plains, and the Conservative assassins had little trouble murdering him. Thousands of Colombians attended his funeral. His legend grew. In the end, Guadalupe fell victim to the treason of President Rojas Pinilla. The former General had arrived at the sinister conclusion that as long as Guadalupe Salcedo Unda was alive, he was free to rebel, and that threat was too great to leave unattended.

Rojas Pinilla would capitalize on Laureano Gómez's decision to be the lone Latin American President to send troops to Korea. Gómez's decision to join ranks alongside the United States and confirm the American-inspired concept of collective security under the United Nations won Colombia strong allies in Washington. Consequently, Gómez and Rojas Pinilla escaped the condemnation they deserved from American officials.

The former American diplomat and accomplished historian, Robert W. Drexler, offered a pragmatic explanation of Colombia's participation in Korea. "The

Colombian venture in Korea becomes even darker when one examines the once-secret diplomatic record and perceives how Gómez and Rojas Pinilla were enabled to manipulate the United States government. Indeed, when the sending of Colombian troops to Korea is viewed in this deeper perspective, the troop deployment must inevitably be judged in political terms since such a small force had no weight in the military balance."[6]

Gómez shrewdly used the Korean War to reduce Liberal military opposition to his rule and to win powerful support from the American government. Moreover, as commander of the lone Colombian battalion in Korea until 1953, General Rojas Pinilla picked up a first-class political understanding of anti–Communist rhetoric, an education he would use with enormous skill afterwards when dealing with an American government obsessed with the Cold War.

When the calm of his first few months in office expired, President Rojas Pinilla unleashed his military forces in campaigns of merciless repression with the full knowledge that it would escape the attention of the United States. The President understood the Cold War politicians in Washington favored an iron-fisted leader in Colombia and were willing to overlook human rights violations as long as they were conducted against alleged Communists.

Therefore, the Cold War played a critical role in the American passiveness towards the violence in Colombia. Rojas Pinilla, like Gómez before him, played the Communist card brilliantly. He fully understood that powerful American officials feared a Communist takeover in Colombia. However, not all Americans sided with the former general. On January 20, 1954, the State Department's intelligence staff reported to Secretary of State John Foster Dulles that Rojas Pinilla, far from returning to "Democratic paths," was determined to perpetuate his stay in office through increasingly authoritarian measures and a growing militarization of the government.[7]

Fortunately for Rojas Pinilla, Dulles' track record in Latin America was deplorable. Dulles' and the Eisenhower administration's use of the CIA in the 1954 intervention in Guatemala to overthrow the government of Jacobo Arbenz confirmed Rojas Pinilla's Cold War strategy. He understood, just as Gómez did before him, that as long as he continued to maintain an extremely high voltage of anti–Communist rhetoric that the decision makers in Washington would turn a blind eye to his thirst for power and supply him with the arms to maintain public order. Unfortunately for the Colombians who sought the return of democracy, Dulles would overindulge the dictator. To the U.S. Secretary of State, the threat of Communism superseded America's deep commitment to democracy.

As a result, the Rojas Pinilla government became the first in Latin America to acquire U.S. built jet aircraft when six Lockheed T-33A training planes were delivered in 1954. Later that year, Colombia received 19 B-26 bombers, four helicopters and a substantial number of M2A1, 105mm Howitzer artillery pieces from the U.S. In addition, in 1955, the U.S. Army provided special instructors so that the armed forces could establish the Escuela de Lanceros (Lancers School), a training facility created to instruct Colombian troops in state-of-the-art counterinsurgency techniques.[8]

Just like Gómez before him, Rojas Pinilla used the power of the presidency to eliminate democratic rule. When he, too, became a shameful dictator, the ruling class banded together to prevent a complete destruction of the nation. The beginning of the end took place on Sunday, January 29, 1956, when Alberto Lleras

Camargo, one of the best and brightest Liberal Party leaders in Colombia, invited Phillip Bonsal, the U.S. Ambassador to Colombia, to attend the first bullfights of the season with him in his private box. Lleras Camargo had been out of Colombia during most of *La Violencia* attending to his duties as Secretary General of the OAS, so the sight of the respected Colombian alongside the American Ambassador prompted the large Bogotá crowd to ecstatically cheer. However, when Rojas Pinilla's daughter and son-in-law arrived at the bullfights, the crowd turned on them, whistling, booing, and catcalling them out of the Plaza de Toros.

The following Sunday, the infamous, "Bullfight Massacre" took place. Rojas Pinilla reportedly took tremendous offense to the disrespect shown his daughter and son-in-law the previous Sunday by the people of Bogotá and wanted revenge. So his intimate circle of government supporters launched a plan to win the pleasure of the President. The conspiracy included the purchase of $15,000 worth of bullfight tickets[9] which were then distributed to the President's loyal enforcers who were instructed to arrive at the bullfights out of uniform and in civilian plainclothes. The plan then called for the thugs to strategically spread out throughout the amphitheatre with the other regular Bogotá spectators before the first toreador strutted into the arena.

On signal, and according to plan, the Rojas Pinilla thugs started shouting "vivas" for the Rojas Pinilla government. But when the crowd failed to cheer Rojas Pinilla sufficiently and even booed him sparingly, the government's goons took matters into their own hands and beat the crowd into bloody submission. Witnesses reported seeing spectators dragged down the steps, heads banging all the way down. The political violence was devastating. *Time* magazine reported the bloody incident. "Whip-

ping out blackjacks, knives and guns, they attacked in milling fury. Victims were tossed screaming over guardrails above the exit passageways; hundreds of others were toppled into the arena. Pistols banged away. The toll: at least eight dead, fifty hurt."[10] The needless bloodshed and tragic loss of life was a typical act of brutal repression by the proud and ruthless tyrant.

The Bullfight Massacre prompted traditional party adversaries to finally stop feuding and join forces—the masquerading democracy was at risk. Rojas Pinilla and his corrupt government lost the support of the people. Weeks prior to the Bullfight Massacre, Conservative and Liberal leaders had quietly negotiated the beginning of an alliance. By July 1956, former President Laureano Gómez and Liberal leader Alberto Lleras Camargo had signed the Declaration of Benidorm, a document that laid the foundation for the future institutionalization of a coalition government. The move politically crippled Rojas Pinilla and left him clinging to power with brute force and widespread corruption. The coalition against him panicked the President and he instituted a scorched-earth policy to annihilate opposition to his rule.

Old-timers in Bogotá still live with the haunted memories of repression.[11] They remember the brutality of the Rojas Pinilla government vividly. Some gave eyewitness accounts of Bogotá police and soldiers kicking down doors of innocent families in the middle of the night, barging in to intimidate and steal anything of value. Others told details of how parents back then took the precaution of hiding daughters in obscure places during raids for fear the police would rape them. More frightening were the accounts of how citizens who protested mistreatment or thefts to the proper authorities would be severely beaten or, in some cases, simply disappear, and later be found dead in remote parts of the city.

Life in the rural areas was an even greater nightmare. Bandit gangs and guerrillas roamed the countryside creating havoc at will. It was this mounting anarchy that finally forced traditional elite Liberals and moderate elite Conservatives to overcome their political differences and join forces to remove Rojas Pinilla. However, initial attempts were opposed by ultra right-wing Conservatives, who wanted to hold onto valuable government posts. The scant support allowed Rojas Pinilla to make one last desperate move on May 1, 1957. He defiantly had his handpicked assembly confirm him as President until 1962. The blatant grab for power backfired and triggered far-reaching opposition, particularly from prominent Conservative Party moderate Guillermo León Valencia. The subsequent arrest of León Valencia by Rojas Pinilla ignited widespread street demonstrations which the dictator ordered the armed forces to step in and smash.

The results were tragic. Over 100 demonstrators were beaten to death and scores were ruthlessly bludgeoned. The oligarchy rushed to organize a replacement government under the banner of the "National Front." The country's business and professional establishment hastened to do its part against Rojas Pinilla by orchestrating a general strike. It was not a strike by workers so much as a lockout by owners who simply closed the doors of their businesses and factories to employees.

Although some factionalism still existed among moderate Liberals and Conservatives, they agreed to sign a final agreement stipulating the procedures for a new coalition government in San Carlos in 1957. The accord was based on the Sitges Agreement signed by Conservatives and Liberals in Sitges, Spain, in 1957. Under the pact, a Conservative would be the first President of the National Front, and he was to be selected by a National Congress previously elected by popular vote. The Sitges and San Carlos agreements, which sought to reduce interparty tensions and provide a basis for power sharing by the parties, called for the alternation of the presidency between the two parties every four years. Thus, on May 10, a military junta led by General Gabriel Paris, who promised the free election of a civilian president in 1958, overthrew the dictator. The coup forced Rojas Pinilla to seek exile in Spain.

In December 1957, Colombians voted in a national plebiscite to approve the Sitges and San Carlos agreements as amendments to the Constitution of 1886. Congressional elections were held soon thereafter and the right-wing Conservatives emerged as the largest faction of the Conservatives in Congress. This empowered Laureano Gómez to toss his considerable political weight around and veto the proposed presidential candidacy of Valencia, who until then was the strongest candidate among the Conservatives. As a result of the division within the Conservative Party, faction leaders agreed to allow a Liberal to be the first President under the National Front, and to extend the provision of the coalition government from 12 to 16 years. The agreements were ratified by Congress as constitutional amendments in 1958 and shortly afterwards, Alberto Lleras Camargo was elected as the first President of the National Front.

President Eisenhower worked hard to patch things up with Colombia. He invited President Lleras Camargo to a state visit in April 1960 and gave him the red carpet treatment. During the state visit Lleras Camargo spoke at the National Press Club where he emphasized his country's urgent need for economic development assistance to keep new dictatorships, revolts and anarchy at bay, and called for a reappraisal of American policies toward the Latin American region so as to put development rather than military goals foremost. Lleras was positive and optimistic in his stance, but he showed lingering pain over Dulles's policy toward Rojas Pinilla when he warned Americans against the passiveness with which he said some in the United States viewed Latin American dictatorships.[12] The Eisenhower Administration also arranged for Lleras Camargo to address a joint session of Congress, visit Camp David, and be honored with a parade in New York City.[13]

To its credit, the Eisenhower administration examined its role in Latin America and came to the conclusion that its policy had flaws.[14] Eisenhower had, in the precious decade, provided military assistance to Rojas Pinilla and other Latin American governments to strengthen the region's defense against external Communist attack. However, in 1959, a Congressional Committee report reviewed the U.S. foreign military assistance program and favored dropping the promotion of defenses against external threat and recommended a training of Latin American military leaders so that they would acquire a stronger sense of the values and policies of the United States. The focus on the democratic and moral education of military officers was extended during the Kennedy administration, which was inclined to view the Latin American military caste as nationbuilders, forces for social change, instruments for civic action, and, above all, as a bulwark against Communist-inspired insurgency.[15]

After Rojas Pinilla's downfall the ruling class took control of the country and the military reverted to its subordinate role in Colombian society. Unfortunately, there was no formidable judicial accounting from the National Front leaders of the five years of oppressive actions under Rojas Pinilla, or of the military and police atrocities of *La Violencia*. Moreover, with no session of Congress held between 1949 and 1957, the people had no voice in the administration of justice during a period when hundreds of thousands of Colombians perished. After the restoration of congressional activity at the beginning of the National Front era, a substantial majority was still required to enact legislation, and this dampened any dynamism and discouraged the *pueblo* from seeking justice.

Rojas Pinilla was brought before the Colombian Senate in 1958 to be tried for wrongdoing he committed in office. However, he was treated leniently. The Senate, acting as a special jury for ex-presidents, merely deprived Rojas Pinilla of his right to hold office and to vote, but the Supreme Court later overturned even this sentence. There was a general political unwillingness to press matters too far with the former dictator. The major reason was that many people in the upper echelons of the newly formed National Front government had been collaborators of Rojas Pinilla in the earlier phases of his regime and did not want to be subjected to ridicule as they would if the dirty linen of those times was exposed in public.[16]

Thus, the pattern of nonaccountability for the military and police started by President Ospina in 1946 became an unofficial practice in Colombia under the National Front. The military did lose esteem throughout the country for its ineptitude in confronting the guerrillas but was able to dodge a close review of its behavior during *La Violencia*. The military leaders knew that they were safe enough — the National Front needed them to battle Colombia's insurgents. They realized the oligarchy wanted to exterminate the guerrillas and that they were the only force that was capable of completing the assignment, their incompetence notwithstanding. Realistically, the armed forces knew they could never completely wipe out the guerrillas, but they were confident they could contain them. As a result, the military leaders developed a new sense of national pride in knowing the oligarchy would always need them by their side.

The National Front was created to stop the partisan violence, rehabilitate the economic sector, dramatically improve education levels and unite the nation. Inspired by this promise, Colombians turned out in record numbers on December 1, 1957, to approve the new government of unity and participate in the first popular vote since 1949.

However, to the peasants in the countryside, the National Front was an "invitation only" political system. Gaitán's Colombia had included the poor. He preached to the *pueblo* that the state was obliged to protect those with less in society and to provide equally for all. So, the *pueblo* lost faith in the system when, as they saw it, the oligarchy assembled the elite families in the nation and legislated their exclusive rule for the next 16 years. In the view of the lower classes, the ruling elite had ignored the lessons taught by Gaitán: they still owned the Presidency and the *pueblo* still had exclusivity over appalling poverty.

Thus, a new political era started in Colombia. The National Front made it compulsory to share all elective and appointive positions on an equal basis between the Liberals and Conservatives, and guaranteed the alternation of the two parties in the Colombian presidency. The downside was that it also formally excluded any third party from participating in the political decision making in the country or in the share of power. A new voice would have to masquerade as a Liberal or Conservative in order to join the political mainstream. The system represented a clear denial of democratic principles.

One of the prime consequences of the new system of government was a dramatic shift in Colombia's traditional hereditary hatreds. Previously, those hatreds were political, between the Conservative and Liberal Parties. The National Front gave birth to something different. It rid the nation of its political stripes and created a ruling class based on wealth, power and influence. Its leaders had one thing in common — they were the oligarchy. Therefore, politics no longer generated the resentment of years past; now hereditary hatred was better defined as a class issue. The National Front was a reaction to the existence of a wider sociopolitical dysfunction; effectively, it was a case of the rich uniting for reasons of self-preservation. However, that unity spawned a society of haves and have nots like never before, and the hatred in the country became that of the poor for the rich.

President Lleras Camargo adopted vigorous measures to improve economic conditions, with the result that in 1958 Colombia recorded its most favorable balance of trade in 20 years. He also made sure that Protestants and those of other faiths were no longer mishandled for either political or religious reasons. Moreover, the government ambitiously instituted a series of programs to improve the living conditions of the masses, including expansion of the water supply, sewers, housing, and education. Advances in transportation and communication also served to lessen the differences among regions, and bring a common national culture closer to realization. But the advances also made the glaring problem of poverty in Colombia more difficult to overlook.

One of the greatest shortcomings of the National Front was the inability to carry out viable land reform. Rich landowners rigidly considered agrarian reform Communist and blocked efforts to introduce government change. Nonetheless, Lleras Camargo made serious attempts to improve the quality of life in Colombia, but it simply was not enough to reverse years of neglect and overcome the distrust of the poor towards the oligarchy.

A man of good deeds in the early days of the National Front was Major General Alberto Ruíz Novoa, who had been the second in command of the Colombian battalion in Korea. Unlike Rojas Pinilla who cynically manipulated America's Cold War fears, Ruíz Novoa was a great advocate of America's altruistic military doctrine of civic action. He was impressed with the U.S. government's theory that the Latin American armed forces had great potential for helping the people.

As a result, General Ruíz Novoa helped develop ambitious programs of civic military action whereby military detachments were deployed to build needed roads and schools and clinics in violence-afflicted areas. He also played a role in ordering army dentists to fill cavities free of charge in peasant mouths. The military civic action took place with a view to gaining the confidence of the rural population, without which true pacification would not come.[17]

However, as Ruíz Novoa's popularity rose he became more of a maverick and presented a challenge to the rule of the National Front. With time he ruined his career and made the historic misjudgment of joining the military pioneers in Colombia who took part in the catastrophic formation of paramilitary self-defense units.

In January 1959, Fidel Castro's victorious rebel army was driving through Santa Clara, Cuba, on their way to Havana to seize power. The poor throughout Latin America cheered Castro's victory. In 1960, Che Guevara published his manual on guerrilla warfare, *La Guerra de Guerrillas,* and many regional experts predicted it would be gospel for young revolutionaries. Shortly afterwards, Radio Havana broadcast nightly shortwave appeals to the masses to "Turn the Andes into the Sierra Maestre of the continent."

Communism in Cuba heightened the anxiety of the oligarchy in Colombia. They feared a chain of popular explosions that would resound throughout the hemisphere. Some Americans in Colombia at that time privately hoped that the fear of Castro might improve the social consciousness of the National Front and oblige them to relieve the grinding poverty of the majority of the population.[18] However, when it became clear that the U.S. government could be relied upon to contain Castro if not overthrow him, the Colombian oligarchy's concerns about Communist insurgency were reduced, along with some of the impetus for drastic social reform.[19]

Accordingly, the National Front leaders increased the budget to the military and raised troop strength so that the Colombian armed forces and their American advisors could search for and destroy the insurgents through large military operations. The ruling class concluded it was much smarter to exterminate the guerrillas; it was extremely suspicious of a civic-minded military that could easily turn into a social-working army.

Marquetalia looms large in FARC mythology. On June 14, 1964, at exactly 8:02 A.M., the Colombian government finished assembling a massive military force in preparation for an attack. It included 20,000 soldiers and the Air Force's entire fleet of Iroquois helicopters, backed by an elite group of American military advisors.[20] The Colombian government was confident of success. The troops were going to stage a mammoth offensive against the tiny village of Marquetalia, about 200 kilometers southwest of Bogotá.

The village of less than 100 farming cooperative families had tired of the poverty and lack of political inclusion within Colombia and had declared themselves an independent republic. They were protected by a small self-defense group of men and women guerrillas. The target of the Colombian military invasion was the commander of the guerrillas, Manuel

Marulanda Vélez, alias Sureshot, and his two principal lieutenants, Jacobo Arenas and Ciro Trujillo Castaño, alias Mayor Ciro. Other guerrillas with Sureshot marked for execution by the armed forces were Rigoberto Losada, Isauro Yosa, Isaías Pardo, Luis Pardo, Jesús M. Medina, Darío Lozano, Tarcisio *Guaracas, Parménides* Cuenca, Roberto López, Miriam Narváez and Judith Grisales.

The mission called for the annihilation of the guerrillas. To ensure success, the Air Force conducted an intense bombardment of Marquetalia in advance of the ground troop invasion.[21] The plan to terminate Sureshot was called, "*Operación Cabeza,*"[22] and was part of a major five-phase government offensive to root out Communism in Marquetalia and four other independent republics established in El Pato, Guyabero, Sumapaz, and Tequendama. The offensive, given the title "Soberanía," (Supremacy), would go on for the entire year.

The escape was inexplicable. The 2,000 Colombian soldiers selected to stage the initial attack on the village after the bombing found no signs of the guerrillas. Sureshot and his small band of 50 slipped out of Marquetalia through a narrow path the Indians had constructed for them in the event of an attack. The escape route was covered with heavy jungle canopy and was completely undetectable from the air. Afterwards, Colonel José Joaquín Matallana, the army commandant of the operation, grudgingly admitted admiration for the stealthy manner in which the guerrillas had evaded certain destruction.[23]

Sureshot and his band regrouped in the nearby village of Riochiquito, where five months later the FARC would hold the landmark conference that created the Southern Bloc of guerrilla fighters. It was at that same conference that Sureshot and his lieutenants mapped out and defined the military-political role of the FARC. The well-respected Colombian historian, Arturo Alape, offered a concise commentary of the importance of the episode: "With Operation Marquetalia, the directing class of the country created the FARC movement in Colombia."[24]

By 1965, it looked like Conservative Party President Guillermo León Valencia was going to fall. He had assumed the presidency in August of 1962, and had not been able to generate political or economic support for his policies. As a result, the National Front was facing a stiff challenge despite the constitutional amendment stipulating that only the Liberal and Conservative Parties were authorized to participate in elections. The major problem for the National Front was the strong dissident groups, which had formed movements to challenge the establishment. The movements were presenting candidates under the Liberal and Conservative labels, circumventing the strictures of the constitution.

One spirited opposition group was called the Liberal Revolutionary Movement (Movimiento Revolucionario Liberal). Its leader, Alfonso López Michelsen, the son of ex–President López Pumarejo, was pressing the government for significant economic reforms. López Michelsen, a rising star on the Colombian political stage, was reportedly working closely with the CIA station in Bogotá, according to the later statements of an ex–U.S. secret agent. Philip Agee left the CIA after 12 years of service and wrote a book which was the most comprehensive and unglamorous inside look at CIA activities in Latin America in the history of the agency. *Inside the Company: CIA Diary* included critical accounts of the dubious CIA role in the Bay of Pigs, the death of Che Guevara, and the fall of Salvador Allende.[25] The book covered the 1960s in depth and included names of agents and details of covert American operations ongoing throughout Latin America during the height of the Cold War.[26]

Another dissident group attempting to loosen the President's grip on power was the populist political organization, Anapo, the National Popular Alliance (Allianza Nacional Popular). Former President Rojas Pinilla, who had miraculously resurrected his political career, had founded the organization. The former dictator was building credibility among the lower classes by demanding significant social reforms. Rojas Pinilla and his daughter María Eugenia Rojas were also attracting widespread support with the poor because of their hatred of the oligarchy and for the skillful use of Gaitán-like political rhetoric. Anapo was quickly becoming a force to be reckoned with.

On another front, León Valencia also faced a challenge from his War Minister, Alberto Ruíz Novoa, who was attempting to convince the ruling class that he was more capable of handling the nation's problems than the President. Complicating matters further was the fact that León Valencia continued to receive criticism from the ultra right-wing faction of the Conservative Party lead by Laureano Gómez.

However, a subtler and yet serious provocation confronting President Valencia was growing opposition from Roman Catholic priest Father Camilo Torres, an intellectual fluent in English, French, German and Spanish. Winds of reform were blowing through the Latin American Roman Catholic Church in the 1960s. The church had always been considered a traditionally strong force — well-disciplined and conservatively oriented — but young priests in various parts of Latin America were seizing the banner of social reform and were leading their "flocks" into a series of confrontations with the "power structure."

Officially, the Roman Catholic Church was slow to enter the fight for social reform. However, this small group of "rebel priests" were, individually or in loose association with one another, energetically pressing the struggle against oppression among the vast numbers of Latin America's poor. The rebel priests caused strains with the Vatican, which attempted to discipline them and encouraged them to act in a more moderate manner.

On June 25, 1965, Father Camilo Torres attended a private meeting at the U.S. embassy in Bogotá with political attaché Stephan Comiskey. Comiskey had granted Father Torres's request for an interview because of the Roman Catholic priest's growing popularity among the underprivileged and university students. Torres informed the American that Colombia needed a revolution.[27] He explained to Comiskey that Colombia was ruled by an oligarchy and that the only way to achieve social and economic equality in the nation was to seize it in an uprising.[28] "Violent" asked Comiskey? "Not necessarily," responded Father Torres.[29]

Comiskey was not surprised by the announcement. It was well known in Colombia that Torres was a revolutionary. At a 1963 National Congress of Sociology in Bogotá, he had bewildered the nation when he declared, "Violence has released a social process unforeseen by the ruling class. It has awakened the peasant's consciousness, it has given him group solidarity, a feeling of superiority and sureness in action.... It has opened possibilities for social improvement and it has institutionalized his aggressiveness.... We can say that the violence has constituted for Colombia the most important socio-cultural change in the peasant areas since the Spanish Conquest."[30] During this era ex–U.S. Vice President Richard Nixon predicted that Colombia would be the next Latin American country to "go red."

Camilo Torres was a priest and a revolutionary. He preached a gospel of hope to the poor and hungry. His name was a symbol of Christian commitment to the

Priest and revolutionary Camilo Torres (center) stands with Fabio Vásquez (left) and Víctor Medina, founders of the ELN, in January 1966. *El Tiempo*

cause of social justice in Colombia. For most of his life Camilo was convinced that the Christian faith was "a force capable of humanizing any system," and that "the Church could become again what it had once been, the spiritual center of the world."

Torres was born on February 3, 1929, to parents who were members of the oligarchic class. His father, Calixto Torres Umaña, was one of the most respected doctors in Bogotá. His mother, Isabel Restrepo, a woman of considerable beauty and strong independent mind, was left a fortune when her first husband, German businessman Karl Westendorp, suddenly died. Calixto was an intellectual and anticleric enamored with Isabel. He was in Hamburg when Isabel settled there with her two young children shortly after the death of her husband. Calixto realized Isabel was ahead of her time. Her indomitable spirit bucked the cultural tradition that women be subordinate to men. However, Calixto convinced Isabel that he was a freethinker and she agreed to marry him. Afterwards Isabel would remark, "I've always done everything upside down … I married a German in Colombia and a Colombian in Germany."[31]

The couple returned to Bogotá where Fernando and his younger brother Camilo were born. Isabel and Calixto bought the Hotel Ritz on Seventh Avenue (Bogotá's main street) and, shortly after Camilo's birth in 1929, the family moved into a spacious apartment which adjoined it.[32] The Ritz was an enormous social success but a financial failure, and the family returned to Europe. Isabel used her considerable influence to get newly elected Liberal President Enrique Olaya Herrera to give Calixto a post with the League of Nations in Geneva.[33] (In the thirties, Isabel was political on a social basis— 20 years later, older and more fiery, she reportedly led a demonstration of a few thousand women through the streets of Bogotá that was broken up by the police with water hoses."[34]

In 1934, after nearly three years in Europe, the husband-wife relationship began to unravel. Isabel and Calixto decided to return to Bogotá to make one last effort to achieve stability and a happy marriage.[35] It didn't work out, and in 1937 the couple decided to separate once and for all.[36] Upon the family's return from Berlin, Camilo attended the German School in Bogotá, but when the school was closed in 1941, he continued his studies at Lycée Cervantes, an elite Catholic high school in Bogotá. Although everyone acknowledged Camilo was bright, his behavior in those early years was spontaneous and haphazard. Nevertheless, upon graduation from high school in 1947, he enrolled in the National University where he studied law and first started to get involved with other students in works for social betterment.

"Camilo was not leading at all a good life. He was running around with a wild set, and had no interest whatever in religion," according to his brother Fernando, who would go on to become a neurologist at the University Hospital in Minneapolis, Minnesota.[37] With time, young Camilo matured and came under the sway of two cultured French priests, Fathers Blanchet and Nielly, who were in Colombia as members of the Dominican order. Fathers Blanchet and Nielly introduced Camilo to a "rational expression of belief" and convinced him to abandon the fun crowd and make the dramatic decision to become a priest.

Afraid that Isabel would explode with disapproval, Camilo decided not to tell his mother of his decision to join the priesthood. Instead he left her a note and

planned to depart Bogotá on the railroad. Upon hearing the news, Isabel reportedly stormed down to the railroad station and dragged her son off the car. She then held him prisoner in his room, incommunicado, for several days.[38] In due time, Isabel and Calixto, who rushed to Bogotá from a medical conference in Washington, were persuaded to support their son's decision. Subsequently, Camilo's devotion to the priesthood led him to seven years of study at the Archdiocese Seminary in El Chicó a few miles north of Bogotá. It was there, from September 1947, that he was exposed to clerics from varied economic backgrounds and developed a genuine concern for the moral welfare of the poor. Soon Camilo was committed to following the Dominican motto "contemplata aliis tradere," which translated, means, "pass on to others the truths which you have contemplated."

Camilo was ordained in the seminary chapel on August 29, 1954. The next day he went to the chapel of his old school, the Lycée Cervantes, where family and friends celebrated the ritual of his first Mass. In October, Father Torres went to Belgium to obtain a master's degree in social science at the Catholic University of Louvain. Shortly afterwards Isabel joined her son there and to set up house for him outside the dorms. Within a short period of time the house became a vibrant meeting place for the Latin American colony in Louvain.

Upon graduation in June of 1955, his superiors were so impressed with Father Torres that they appointed him vice-rector of the Latin American College, a seminary founded by Belgian bishops to train priests for service in Latin America. With Isabel's return to Bogotá after graduation, Torres had more time to attend lectures, participate more fully in student life, and spend weekends with famous European priests who devoted their lives to working with the poor. In due course, altruism, ethics, and the suppression of the motivation of personal advantage became "ever-recurring leitmotifs" in the writing of Father Torres.[39] Christianity manifested a "purity of intention" in the young priest. It was at this time in his life that Camilo intellectually decided to nurture social reforms within political and administrative organizations. He also studied and compared the serious dedication of his Marxist friends with that of the frivolous carousings of the many Colombian students in Europe he kept in touch with.

Father Torres returned to Colombia in 1959, and was appointed chaplain at the National University. The transition from a modern and democratic-thinking Europe to a quasi-democratic, poverty-stricken Colombia was climactic. The 30-year-old priest was appalled by the miserable conditions of the poor in the slums of Bogotá and devastated by the plight of the ordinary citizen, and he could not contain his bitter disappointment. He shared his critical views of conditions in the barrios of Colombia with the students of the university and started to train them to join with peasants and workers in a communal effort to attack poverty.

Impatient with the lack of effort from the government, Torres started to aggressively combine his religious duties with participation in student strikes and progressive political movements in order to speed up change. At the time, the most attractive and passionate student leader in Bogotá was Antonio Larrotta. Within two years the super charismatic Father Torres would surpass his popularity and become the most fashionable cult figure among both rich and poor in all of Colombia.

Torres would defend his actions by saying he was working on behalf of the poor. "When we choose the poor, we are always sure, doubly sure, of having made a good choice. We have chosen like Jesus. And we have chosen Jesus." Still the Church hierarchy in Colombia was not swayed. Father Torres was removed as university chaplain in February 1961. However, his supporters helped him secure an appointment to the faculty of Sociology and the School of Economic Sciences. He soon wore out his welcome there with his radical rhetoric, and in September 1962 settled for a position with the School of Public Administration as a Dean of the Institute of Social Administration.

Camilo Torres was a strong advocate of women's rights in Colombia. Perhaps because of his mother's "extraordinary personality," he felt the pressures exerted on women in the Latin male culture. Moved by the lack of equality, he authored a compassionate message to the women of Colombia. "Within the popular class, the woman has many duties of a material nature and almost none of a spiritual nature. The highest degree of illiteracy is found among the women of the popular class. They must work very hard in the hidden but quite arduous domestic tasks (kitchen-gardens-chickens, etc.) to say nothing of the difficulties and responsibilities of motherhood. The woman of the working class enjoys no social or legal protection. When, in a country like ours, a man is harassed by misery, unemployment, and the weighty responsibilities of a numerous family, he sometimes takes refuge, mistakenly, in vices: he abandons the home and his wife must assume responsibilities. How often we see the home of a working parent locked during the day and filled with half-naked and hungry children awaiting the return of their mother from her daily job. Nevertheless, the Colombian woman has values as a human person and is not simply an instrument. The Colombian woman realizes that she is exploited not only by the society, as are the majority of Colombians, but by the men."[40]

Ultimately, Father Torres could not

tolerate the indifference of the government. He was deeply offended by the ruling elite's lack of compassion for the lower classes. He concluded that the oligarchy would prohibit change, so he embraced the revolutionary rhetoric of Fabio Vásquez and Víctor Medina, the two guerrillas who founded the National Liberation Army (ELN) on July 4, 1964. Torres made the radical decision to abandon his Christian vocation and forsake its nonviolent teachings. He reasoned that as a Catholic and a priest, he had an obligation to live the life of a Christian with integrity. To him, that meant being concerned with the needs of his neighbors and doing something about them.

The ruling elite attempted to deter Father Torres. Alfonso López, one of the most distinguished political figures in Colombia and heir apparent to the Liberal throne, reached out to him. He attempted to explain to Torres that he was committing political suicide. "The papers will wipe you off the map, Camilo," López said. "That's their technique, you know. They give you loads of publicity today, in order to overwork your image and discard you tomorrow. I don't know if you are familiar with the story of what the ancient Aztecs used to do with their leading warriors. It was like this: when a warrior won a battle, they promoted him to commander; if he won another, they appointed him to govern a province; but if he won a third, they cut off his head. That's what they're planning to do with you, Camilo. I'm warning you. I have it on the best authority."[41]

Father Torres was fearless. Intellectually, he realized the oligarchy did not consider the poor a part of legitimate society and therefore did not protect or provide for them. However, unlike the beloved Gaitán, who put his faith in the honesty of the Colombian political system, Torres turned his back on the oligarchy. Catholic leaders considered any word association with revolution or Communism deserving of excommunication. Well aware of this thinking, Torres decided to sacrifice his vocation anyway, and in May 1965, joined the struggle of the poor for equality and became a guerrilla liberator. "I have taken off my cassock in order to be a truer priest. I have put aside the privileges and duties of the clergy, but I have not stopped being a priest. I think I have given myself to the revolution out of my love for my neighbor. I have stopped offering mass to live out the love for my neighbor. When the revolution has been completed, then I will offer mass again, if God so wills it. I believe that in this way I am following Christ's injunction."[42]

On that note, Camilo Torres, one of the best and brightest minds in Colombia, joined the ELN guerrillas. He entered into a life in the mountains and jungles in the hope of revolutionizing his country. Living outside the city would allow him to break bread with the *pueblo,* and according to tradition, he would become the "compañero," the one who breaks bread, the companion.[43] As a revolutionary, Torres treated the poor with scrupulous honesty and respect, but his life as a guerrilla liberator was short. He was killed in a poorly prepared ambush of a small army patrol at Patio Cemento, Corregimiento El Carmen, Municipio San Vicente de Chucurí, on February 15, 1966. He foolishly dashed out to collect a dead army soldier's rifle as a trophy of his first guerrilla combat. Torres was 37 years old.

LAST PROCLAMATION OF
CAMILO TORRES TO THE
COLOMBIAN PEOPLE

All genuine revolutionaries must see force as the only means left. The people are waiting for the leaders to give the battle cry by their example and presence. I want to tell the Colombian people that this is the moment, that I have not betrayed them, that I have walked through the streets and parks of our towns and cities in an effort to unite and organize the popular class for the take-over of power. I have asked that, if necessary, we even give up our lives for these objectives. Now all is ready. The oligarchy wants to organize another farcical election, with candidates who resign and then accept again, with bipartisan committees, with movements for renewal which group [together] not only old persons with old ideas, but persons who have betrayed the people. What else are we waiting for, Colombians?

I am joining the armed struggle. From the Colombian Mountains I mean to continue the fight with a gun in my hand until power is won for the people. I have joined the Army of National Liberation because I have found the desire for and the realization of unity at the base, the peasant base, without religious or traditional differences, without antagonism toward the revolutionary principles of other sectors, movement[s] or parties, without Caudillism. The Army of National Liberation seeks to free the people from imperialism and from exploitation by the oligarchs and will not lay down its arms as long as power is not entirely in the hands of the people. Its accepted objectives are those of the United Front. Let us not be deaf to the call of the people and of the revolution! — Camilo Torres, from the Mountains, January 1966.[44]

The following year, a 23-year-old Spanish-born priest named Manuel Pérez Martínez was expelled from the Dominican Republic and arrived in the slums of Cartagena to work with the poor. In 1968, Colombia hosted the Latin American Catholic Bishops conference in Medellín. In a historical development, Pope John XXIII stressed the need for the worldwide reduction of socioeconomic inequalities and cast the Church in the role of promoting reforms. The bishops applauded the call for social action by the Vatican but rejected calls by radical young priests to confront brutal rulers.

So like the legendary Camilo Torres, Father Manuel Pérez would grow frustrated with the absence of significant advances for the underprivileged, and, despite the Vatican's altruistic position, after one year in the barrios, Father Pérez would come to the frightening conclusion that Colombia needed a revolution to break the chains of the ruling class. Consequently, he accepted an invitation to travel to Bogotá to attend a clandestine meeting in a nunnery with 15 men of the religious community to discuss whether they should follow the steps of Camilo Torres, and leave the priesthood to join the armed struggle.[45] After a long examination of the duties of the church and the needs of the poor, Father Pérez and two others decided to enlist in the ELN.

Pérez showed little early promise as a soldier in 1969. He was said to be undisciplined and prone both to getting lost in the jungle, and falling asleep while on guard duty.[46] At that time, the ELN was not noted for its sympathetic treatment of the disorganized, and Perez may well have been executed had he not been a man of the cloth. But he managed to escape both the firing squad, and the fate of the ELN's most famous guerrilla-priest, Camilo Torres, who was killed in action. In fact, he excelled after the rough start, so much so that by his death at the age of 54, in 1998, Manuel Pérez, priest and revolutionary, had become the ideological force and key military strategist of the ELN guerrilla organization. The two other priests who joined the ELN with Pérez died in action shortly after entering the war.[47]

In August 1966, Liberal candidate Carlos Lleras Restrepo assumed the presidency of Colombia. Conservative President Guillermo León Valencia had completed his four-year term and left the new President a nation with strong reservations about the National Front arrangement. Nearly a year later, on July 18, 1967, Stephen

Comiskey, the American political attaché in the embassy, filed a down-to-earth confidential report explaining the realities of the Colombian political system.[48]

In the report, Comiskey examined the allegations that a ruling class governed Colombia and pragmatically concluded that, "There is some justice in these charges, but it must be a rare country indeed where the management of politics and the affairs of state are not confined to a relatively small group which is interested in its self-perpetuation."

He also observed that the President was described by some as the "Father" of the concept of community action in Colombia because of his attempt to set up a system of primary elections for the selection of Liberal candidates for the March elections of 1964. However, Comiskey noted, the attempt was a dismal failure with only very small numbers of party stalwarts showing up at the polls, and the concept was abandoned.

The confidential report concluded, "While it may be argued that the Colombian government is not as responsive as it might be to the aspirations of the people, we must remember that the population is in may respects asking an impoverished patron for largesse the government of Colombia does not have."[49]

A major problem was that the Colombian government had ignored the needs of the countryside. Since the days of Bolívar, the government had never nurtured a strong presence outside of the big cities. Therefore, as the guerrillas grew in strength, they in effect, became the rural government. By 1968, most guerrillas in Colombia had abandoned the affiliation with the Liberal Party and joined the ranks of the FARC, ELN, or the Maoist EPL, Ejército Popular de Liberación (Popular Liberation Army). However, there was one major guerrilla fighter in 1968 who refused to join the revolutionaries trying to over-

Former Roman Catholic priest Manuel Pérez Martínez was the ideological force and key military strategist of the ELN until his death in 1998. *El Tiempo*

throw the government. The Liberal Party guerrilla was still loyal to the political bosses in Bogotá. His name was Capitán Dumar Aljure.

In January 1968, Capitán Dumar Aljure, the dashing fighter who sported a finely trimmed thin mustache, was in a Llanos bar toasting his 18-year career as a bandit, guerrilla chief, and political leader of the Liberal Party. Having resisted Sureshot's 1964 attempt to recruit him into the ranks of the FARC, Aljure remained fiercely loyal to his party bosses in Bogotá, and enjoyed his status as an official Liberal Party warrior. Over the years, he had carefully constructed a delicate balance of popular support and physical coercion that allowed him to enjoy immunity from the law in the Province of Meta. By most accounts, he rose to power as a local warlord because of his courageous acts of political vengeance against the Conservative governments of Presidents Ospina, Gómez and Rojas Pinilla. Socially, at least to the old-timers of Meta, he was part of the larger family making up the region's rough and removed frontier mentality.

Aljure's armed action against the brutal governments in Bogotá was legendary. He maintained important political relationships that posed major problems for the army, especially for the military commanders who wanted to impose law and order in portions of the countryside now that the politicians in Bogotá had formed the National Front to restore peace to the nation. Armed forces leaders were increasingly reluctant to accept the political restrictions on military operations in Aljure's backyard. They detested the modus vivendi Aljure was granted, and wanted to crush the defiant guerrilla leader once and for all.[50]

The alcohol in the Llanos bar was flowing for hours. Capitán Aljure was drunk and took offense at the manner with which the bartender was serving him drinks. Perhaps the bartender felt comfortable enough with the presence of an army sergeant inside the bar to be offhand. Regardless, in an act of intoxicated arrogance, Aljure pulled out his revolver and killed the bartender for not showing him proper respect. After finishing his drink, he leisurely walked out of the bar unhindered. "It's not just for nothing that I'm the Liberal Chief around here!" he boasted.[51]

Aljure's domain fell within the jurisdiction of the VII Brigade. A component of the Brigade, the 21st, or Vargas Battalion, was stationed in Granada and was directly responsible for the section of Meta run by Aljure and his Liberal Party guerrillas. Army commander Major General Guillermo Pinzón Caicedo, found Aljure's senseless murder particularly galling and was not going to accept any political considerations in his pursuit of the Liberal Party guerrilla chief. General Pinzón was determined to put an end to Aljure's immunity from the law.

The day of reckoning took place three months later, on the morning of Thursday, April 5, 1968. Capitán Aljure, along with his wife and 13 of his guerrillas, was on horseback en route to a meeting when he was ambushed. Aljure lived up to his dangerous reputation. He and his men killed six soldiers before they were overrun. When the gunsmoke cleared, Aljure's entire group has been wiped out in the bloody skirmish by a vastly superior army force.

Thus concluded the career of a notable Colombian Liberal Party guerrilla leader. The significance of Aljure's death was that it put an end to one of the last guerrilla fighters from the period of *La Violencia* who maintained a loyalty to the political establishment. (During his life, he could even be seen with prominent members of the Liberal Party when he visited Bogotá.) The death of Capitán Dumar Aljure prompted many of his followers who fought by his side against the Conservative forces to abandon their loyalties to Bogotá, and join other guerrillas in the region.

The Central Intelligence Agency was obsessed with Fidel Castro and in 1968 completed a comprehensive secret report on the Cuban leader which contained chilling details. The CIA went into considerable depth on the dangers Cuba posed to Latin America as a whole, and specifically to Colombia.[52] The report assembled impressive information on Castro's formation of the Cuban foreign espionage and subversion agency called the General Directorate of Intelligence (DGI), which was established within the Ministry of Interior. Moreover, it studied the role of Manuel Pineiro, the infamous "Red Beard," who was Castro's handpicked Director General of the DGI, and who was closely associated with Raúl Castro (Fidel's brother). But most importantly, the report examined how Fidel Castro spread revolution in Colombia.

The CIA secret report explained that Cuba's DGI methods of selecting, training, and assigning foreign agents contained a high degree of professionalism. "There are two basic categories of these agents; one is a deep-cover clandestine group — recruited, trained, and subsequently run by the department charged with collecting information as well as penetrating local governments. The second group is recruited and directed by the department of national liberation to guide and support revolutionary activities. At least 2,500 Latin Americans are known to have gone to Cuba for such training since 1961."

Many of Castro's Latin American trainees returned to their home countries to train others, and they were assisted by DGI's sophisticated capability to correspond clandestinely with its agents abroad. The CIA report said: "Other support and propaganda mechanisms included Radio Havana, which is beaming approximately 170 hours a week in Portuguese, Spanish, and even Creole, Quechua, and Guarani to Latin America. It also transmits open code messages to Cuban intelligence agents. In addition to the construction of this support mechanism and the growth and improvement of its clandestine service and propaganda machine, Cuba has been able to bring about limited international cooperation of national movements and parties in some areas. Two groups providing such support to the Venezuelan movements were uncovered in Colombia in 1966, and one of the Colombian movements has chosen the Venezuelan border region as its area of guerrilla operations.

"In Colombia, there was renewed and intensified guerrilla activity during 1967. The Cubans are giving assistance and training to several groups, some of which are remnants of bandit gangs that have operated in the country for years. The group which has received by far the most Cuban aid is the ELN. Some of its members were recently arrested while trying to slip back into the country carrying small arms, ammunition, and radio transmitters. They reportedly told Colombian intelligence officers that they and a number of other Colombians had just completed a guerilla warfare course in Cuba and that the weapons had been given to them there.

"The pro–Soviet Communist Party (PCC) is reportedly trying to convert its guerrilla arm, the FARC, into inactive self-defense groups. This follows a request from the Soviet Union to avoid any incidents that might complicate its newly established diplomatic relations with the Colombian government.... Cuba has given ample notice that it intends to continue its propaganda, training, and financial support to selected revolutionary groups, especially those in Colombia, Guatemala, and Venezuela. Given Castro's goal of developing and exploiting opportunities for further armed violence, plus the vulnerabilities that exist in many Latin American countries, new outbreaks of Castro-sponsored rural-oriented violence in Latin America can be expected."

Finally, the 1968 CIA secret document identified the key to revolution in Colombia. "Such ventures (guerrilla) will have little chance of success, however, unless they exploit genuinely popular antigovernment causes and develop a broad peasant base and a charismatic indigenous leader.... The danger increases, however, in those countries where political and economic development has been marginal ... that what has been minor disturbances in the countryside could suddenly mushroom into a political force out of proportion."[53]

Complicating matters further in Bogotá was the government's inability to assemble an intelligence operation to deal with the guerrillas. Another secret report, out of the U.S. embassy in Bogotá, explained the intelligence problems the government of Colombia was encountering in combating the growing insurgency.[54] The report said that neither Colombian civilian nor military intelligence operations were very effective, and both suffered from a lack of trained manpower, inter-agency rivalries, unavailability of funds, poor organization and overlapping jurisdictions. The American embassy concluded that while the guerrillas inside Colombia were getting considerable assistance from the Cubans, Soviets and Chinese, Colombia's main intelligence agency, The Administrative Department of Security (DAS), which had about 3,000 employees and was subject to political patronage, would never become a professional corps of intelligence operatives as long as the ground rules for administering the agency remained unchanged.[55] The embassy said that the best raw intelligence in Colombia was coming from the National Police. "However, the National Police officers often complain that nothing is done with the information which they pass ... that it is not acted upon ... and that the agencies to which they pass it hold police intelligence in rather lower esteem."[56]

Meanwhile, the Colombian military was the recipient of some of the largest amounts of economic development assistance which the U.S. granted to Latin America. This was because the U.S. was promoting the "Alliance for Progress," and considered Colombia a model country. However, the military officers in Colombia that dedicated their careers to the American sponsored practice of military civic action were overwhelmed by a hierarchy that opted to combat the guerrillas the old-fashioned way: by hunting them down and killing them. As a result, Colombian soldiers would continue killing Colombians and being killed by them,

with the full approval and official blessings of the oligarchy.

However, there was one military officer who attempted to change the self-serving culture of the Colombian armed forces. His name was Lieutenant Colonel Alvaro Valencia Tovar. He was close to many American embassy officials and was admired for advocating the enlightened civic-minded principles of the Alliance for Progress.[57] Valencia Tovar was one of the most effective, intrepid, intelligent and well-known antiguerrilla fighters in Colombia, according to embassy officials.[58] Among his many credentials, he was responsible for overseeing the army victory over the ELN in which Camilo Torres was killed. He was headquartered in Bucaramanga some 60 miles away when his well-deployed troops counterattacked the amateur ELN ambush and killed Torres.

Valencia Tovar was also special because he understood the long-term consequences of the Colombian ruling class's indifference to social reforms. The well-educated man authored a best-selling novel in Colombia, published in 1970, in which the hero was an army officer who advocated social reform as the best means of putting down the Communist insurgency.[59] Like the hero protagonist in the novel, the real life Valencia Tovar argued with his colleagues in the armed forces that while the guerrillas could be contained militarily, they could not be defeated politically. He maintained that the civilian government of Colombia had to do much more to remedy the social and economic ills of the vast majority of the population.

The lieutenant colonel was well liked by Americans in the embassy, but his uncommonly high social consciousness and his insightful analyses of Colombia's problems won him little respect among the ruling class. In due course, his rising popularity was despised by the oligarchy. Certain corrupt members of the ruling class and military hierarchy feared they were going to lose their grip on power as a result of the officer's growing power, so they devised a plan to rid themselves of him. They wouldn't kill him, but they would conduct a campaign of character assassination by releasing damaging rumors that he was planning a coup. The vicious misinformation eventually ruined his career. The ray of hope that Colombia would rehabilitate its dysfunctional political character was extinguished, and Valencia Tovar was forced to accept an early retirement.[60]

Voter apathy in Colombia worried the United States. Voters stayed away from the polls in massive numbers for the Colombian congressional elections of March 17, 1968. Only a scant 31 percent of the eligible voters participated: the lowest turnout in Colombian history. In the wake of the election many Colombian leaders attempted to analyze the reasons behind the large-scale abstention and proposed remedial courses of action. Most of the analyses tended to make Colombia's archaic electoral system the primary object of criticism while ignoring a more fundamental cause of abstention, according to the embassy in Bogotá.[61] Americans believed that the traditional political structure which, by and large, excluded the masses from active participation was to blame for the mass apathy.

The National Civil Registry reported that 7,668,894 persons were eligible to vote in March 1968. According to unofficial tallies the actual vote was around 2,400,000, approximately 31 percent compared with 72.3 percent that turned out for the 1957 national plebiscite that created the National Front. Colombian observers theorized that the small turnout in the more recent election was due to a fundamental lack of respect on the part of the general public for a "do nothing" Congress. President Lleras himself contributed to the climate of disdain for the legislature by re-

peatedly criticizing Congress for not showing up at sessions, for petty politicking, and, more than anything, for failing to act promptly and affirmatively on his programs.[62]

According to the U.S. embassy the problem was, "Symptomatic of the apathy of a majority of Colombians toward the political process ... an apathy that is growing constantly.... A small number of wealthy, powerful men have controlled the traditional parties for more than a generation. The recent observance of the twentieth anniversary of the Bogotazo, (April 9, 1948) brought home to some observers the realization that most of the names in the news on that infamous day still dominate Colombian politics ... Ospina, Lleras, Gómez, and Lopez. New blood, fresh faces in the traditional parties are a rarity, not because the 'Grand Old Men' of the parties have won out against challenges to their leadership, but because such challenges have not been mounted, except in rare cases. The traditional parties have no mechanism for training and pushing ahead promising young leaders. This tends to drain the parties of their vitality and reduce their appeal to younger voters."[63]

During the 11 years of the National Front, the Liberal and Conservative Parties shared in the spoils of power. The outcome of the 1968 elections was that the two traditional parties lost much importance; their fortunes no longer assumed as much significance to the average voter. The inescapable conclusion of the vote was that the Colombian people had little faith the government would do anything to reverse the miserable conditions of the poor. More importantly, the immediate danger for the oligarchy was that the disgruntled populace was seeking support in nontraditional political arenas.

As a result, knowledgeable American observers of the 1968 political situation admitted that the guerrillas in the countryside understood the problems inside rural Colombia better than the elite politicians in Bogotá. The Americans thought that there was not yet a revolutionary climate in Colombia among the poor, but rather a desire or hope that under a peaceful process, their way of life and standard of living could be improved. The National Front managed the economy in a responsible fashion but that was of little comfort to the lower classes. The fruits of economic development were not reaching the poor quickly enough. Therefore, when Rojas Pinilla and his Anapo organization appeared with promises of a better life for the lower class, the poor flocked to him.

The nation was bubbling with political discontent in 1970. The National Front had worn out its welcome and the guerrillas were a small but organized threat to the existing political order. Nonetheless, the oligarchy clung to the 1957 national plebiscite that created the National Front and refused to relinquish control of political power. It was the Conservative Party's turn to assume the presidency in 1970 but leaders were unable to field one candidate only. So four contestants stepped forward for the elections: Misael Pastrana, Rojas Pinilla, Belisario Betancur, and Evaristo Sourdis. They were all vying for the presidency on the Conservative ticket but only one would be the official handpicked candidate of the oligarchy. That honor went to Misael Pastrana.

The oligarchy was confident of a Pastrana victory, and failed to notice the considerable political momentum of Anapo candidate Rojas Pinilla. The former general was a whirling dervish who advocated strong social reforms. As a result, Anapo was attracting massive urban support. Rojas Pinilla's promise of dramatic labor and land reforms prompted former president Ospina to enter the fray. Ospina quickly became the driving force behind Pastrana's support among the ruling elite.

Ospina worked hard to hail the virtues of Pastrana and portrayed him as the "Candidate of Youth." He also skillfully negotiated a political arrangement with former President Alberto Lleras to secure a Liberal Party endorsement for Pastrana. However, a confidential report written by an American embassy official who accompanied the Pastrana campaign on a trip to Medellín December 13–15, 1969, gave important insights into Pastrana's shortcomings.[64] The report described the Pastrana campaign and made it quite clear that Pastrana, although he was the "Official Candidate" and had the ruling elite political machine behind him, lacked strong national recognition.

The report said: "Following all the preliminary ballyhoo, it was surprising to the reporting officer that only a handful of people were present at the airport to receive Dr. Pastrana at the time of his scheduled arrival. Several buses of school children were on hand with blue flags, but they did not seem to be very well posted as to the reason for their presence since many of them were shouting slogans on behalf of Belisario Betancur and of General Rojas Pinilla. Due to the slowdown strike of Avianca, the flight bringing Dr. Pastrana, Dr. Ospina, and other members of the group from Bogotá was almost three hours late in arriving. During this lengthy process a number of other Pastrana supporters materialized at the airport, but not more than 75 persons were present at the actual time of arrival and press photographers (who had evidently been instructed to make it appear as though the reception was a jubilant and tumultuous one) were obliged to take pictures very close to the airplane to avoid pointing up the smallness of the reception committee."

Marinilla was the pièce de résistance of the trip, according to the report. The town of about 25,000 was well known as a citadel of conservatism in Colombia, and in past years, it had always given a rousing send-off to the national Conservative candidate. "Arriving sometime ahead of the politicians in order to observe proceedings discreetly, the reporting officer was astounded to see that the whole central square of Marinilla, as well as the approaches thereto, were plastered with red posters proclaiming the virtues of Belisario Betancur and others, hailing Senator 'Nacho' Vives as the candidate of the 'Revolution.' They were soon covered up with Pastrana signs."

When the Pastrana caravan finally arrived in Marinilla, there were a number of cut and dried speeches by local politicians before Ospina appeared and spoke forcefully. "He hearkened [*sic*] initially more to the past than a younger man might have done and he stressed his ties, and those of all his family, with the area and the like, but following these reminiscences he proceeded, to deliver slashing attacks on General Rojas Pinilla and Belisario Betancur," according to the report. Ospina said he witnessed a small attempt to sabotage the meeting but did not think Dr. Belisario Betancur sponsored it. "You must realize that as far as Rojas Pinillismo is concerned, Ospina is the enemy, Ospina is the oligarch. I accept this challenge," said Ospina.

In hailing Pastrana as the "Candidate of Youth" and in closing his address, Dr. Ospina said that the National Front was scheduled to end within four years but "Liberals and Conservatives will insist that it continue on, stronger and more vigorous than ever." Ospina obviously loved his role as powerbroker but his final remark was a dud, according to the report: "the crowd did not seem to be as interested in this last comment," it dryly commented.

Pastrana followed the former President with a fairly run-of-the-mill speech, which referred to the "multitudes" who had greeted him at the airport and else-where on his travels, and he paid tribute to the nature of the area. The only somewhat substantive part of his speech was directed at the country people and their need for economic help and, most particularly, for education.

The embassy report also provided a glimpse of insiders' expectations about how the election would go. "John Gómez, Editor and owner of the daily *El Diario* and usually a realistic (pro–Pastrana) Liberal, said privately after the visit that his candidate should amass a minimum of 1,200,000 votes. Similarly, most political pundits in the area continue to feel Dr. Pastrana will eventually find himself and acquire the mystique of a winning candidate; ultimately going on to victory at the polls, although hitherto the campaign has definitely dragged. The same observers feel that Belisario (an attractive and popular candidate), can conceivably win, but lacked the organization as well as the strong personal backing, which the establishment was giving Pastrana.

"Dr. Pastrana's host Sunday night (Diego Villegas, a wealthy and aggressive young Conservative politician) tells us he thinks [of] the numbers game in the following terms, approximately 2,600,000 people voted in the last Presidential election. Probably less than 10 percent more will vote this time and, in his thinking, the vote now shapes up as follows: Belisario 950,000, Rojas 600,000, Sourdis 200,000, and Pastrana one million plus. Villegas says that he told Pastrana confidentially that the race is currently much to[o] close for comfort."

The confidential report concluded: "One obvious aspect of the visit, to the reporting officer, was the importance of Dr. Ospina's activities on behalf of the National Front candidate, both in the public meetings and seemingly in the private ones as well; Dr. Ospina gave the appearance of really carrying the ball and providing the needed 'arrastre' or drag, which is so strongly needed if the campaign is to get off the ground."[65]

Ospina was not the only political heavyweight in Pastrana's corner — there was also Alberto Lleras Camargo. Lleras was so much for Pastrana that he went to the U.S. embassy and emphatically told American officials there that he regarded Misael Pastrana as "The only candidate who was sufficiently well prepared and motivated to carry on with the transformation-development program that the present administration had begun."[66] Alberto Lleras was heavily involved in National Front politics and appeared to be the major factor in the Liberal Party decision to endorse Pastrana.[67] Consequently, Pastrana looked like a sure winner. He had the official blessing of the "Magic Names" like Ospina and Alberto Lleras, the two political titans largely responsible for orchestrating the transition of power during the National Front years. The only problem with the cozy ruling elite arrangement was the maverick ... Rojas Pinilla. His Anapo organization was growing teeth and was demanding an end to National Front rule. Moreover, workers, university students, and the poor in the big cities, typical Liberal voters, were marching to the Anapo banner.

Under close inspection, the 1966 presidential elections won by Liberal Party candidate Carlos Lleras Restrepo indicated that the Anapo organization was no longer a political toddler. José Jaramillo Giraldo, the Anapo presidential candidate, was a virtual unknown political commodity in 1966, with little national support. However, he and the Anapo party machine managed to collect over 28 percent of the national vote. Breaking down the turnout, Anapo ran strongly in big cities: 40 percent of the vote in Bogotá, 35 percent in Barranquilla, 28 percent in Cali, and 27 percent in Medellín. The final tally was

1,891,175 votes for Carlos Lleras and 742,133 for José Jaramillo.[68] The results were extremely impressive because José Jaramillo only campaigned for one month. Therefore, Rojas Pinilla was quite optimistic about the Anapo Party prospects in 1970. Given the 1966 results, the leaders of the Anapo organization, who preached a greater social equality and protested the lack of popular participation in the political system, truly believed they could knock out the National Front.

In March 1970, with little more than one month to go before the vote, the National Front leaders knew they were in trouble. Anapo presidential candidate Rojas Pinilla was gaining ground fast. Evidence of his growing popularity was a poll conducted by Monsignor Salcedo of Radio Sutatenza, which gave Pastrana 36 percent of a national vote and Rojas Pinilla 32.5 percent. The poll worried the oligarchy. They could see that while Rojas Pinilla was gaining valuable momentum going into Election Day, the Pastrana campaign was still not producing the desired results. Consequently, National Front leaders were no longer speaking confidently of a Pastrana victory. They could see the poor were giving Anapo massive support and they cringed at the political heavy-handedness of President Carlos Lleras in trying to tilt the election towards Pastrana.

Over in the Anapo camp, Rojas Pinilla really was gaining momentum. The presidential election was coming up on April 19 and Rojas Pinilla was preparing for the final campaign sprint. On March 6, he used his considerable influence with the armed forces to assemble 10,000 to 12,000 military reservists at Bogotá's Plaza Bolivar for a mass demonstration. President Carlos Lleras's Defense Minister lamely responded by issuing a declaration that calling out the reserves was the sole prerogative of the government.

Rojas Pinilla followed up his success

at the demonstration with a television address where he openly challenged the integrity of the government and charged that the Foreign Trade Institute (INCOMEX) was guilty of irregularities in granting import licenses. The television appearance generated massive appeal among the poor, but brought against him charges by his enemies in the government that he was making false accusations. In turn, a large group of Anapo allies demanded that the Attorney General bring charges against the President for violation of the law prohibiting government officials from engaging in politics.

A subsequent confidential U.S. embassy report provided another strong insight into the true condition of the Colombian political situation.[69] "A decision against the President by the Attorney General, a punctilious Conservative, would embarrass not only the administration but also damage Pastrana. A revelation of actual irregularities in INCOMEX, which observers consider possible, would do the same. Thus even Pastrana supporters say if Lleras opens his mouth again another 100,000 votes will be lost for Pastrana, whereas when Rojas speaks nation-wide he gains 100,000. Perhaps someone will have the courage to get the word to Lleras, who feels more fight of his kind is needed, and now that the boys have failed to make a show, the men (he and his cousin, Ex-President Alberto Lleras) must step in. Carlos Lleras would do better to leave the fight to Alberto, in spite of the belief of some Pastranistas (and most editorialists in the nation's press) that the President provided the type of fire needed to get Pastrana off dead center."[70]

On March 11, five weeks before the presidential election, Alberto Lleras took to the airwaves on behalf of Pastrana. He demanded that his television audience come out of their lethargy and apathy to vote against the return of dictatorship in Colombia. The ex–President urged them to endorse the National Front democratic system. Alberto Lleras carelessly showed his ruling elite bias on the airwaves when he warned Colombians against obligatory suffrage and defiantly stated that it was not right for the uneducated masses to decide the nation's problems only because they were obliged to vote.[71]

The statement was a stunning admission of how great the oligarchy feared Rojas Pinilla. The National Front leaders were using every political stunt possible to defeat Anapo. The hatred and distrust between the National Front and Anapo party bosses was immense. Anapo insiders suspected the possibility of foul play. They feared President Carlos Lleras would manipulate unrest in order to declare a state of siege, empowering him to implement crowd control measures to prohibit the lower classes from getting to the polls to vote for Rojas Pinilla. Anapo leaders publicly called Pastrana a ruling class puppet. To them, Pastrana was unknown and had little national political punch. Moreover, they were aware that Pastrana had lost a bid for the Senate in 1966 to Independent Conservative Felio Andrade and that Pastrana's hometown of Neiva, the capital of Huila Province, only had a total voting population of 50,000 of which only 12,000 to 14,000 were likely to actually cast their ballots in the presidential elections.[72]

Rojas Pinilla and the rest of the Anapo organization realized that the real power in Colombia was Mariano Ospina, Laureano Gómez, Alberto Lleras, and President Carlos Lleras. They were certain National Front leaders selected Pastrana to run for President because he was a fresh face and obedient to the demands of the oligarchy that would pull the strings once Pastrana was in power. The Anapo leadership concluded that the oligarchy had made a big mistake to assume that they could simply carry a candidate with little national appeal all the way to victory on the shoulders of the National Front political machine. To Anapo, Pastrana was the "Imposition Candidate" and they would conduct a campaign heavily communicating that message.

On April 17, two days prior to the presidential elections a confidential embassy report was sent directly to the head of the National Security Council, Henry Kissinger, in the White House.[73] It said the vote in Bogotá on April 19 was the most crucial presidential election in Colombia in 20 years and that an extremely close race was predicted. The report explained that the Rojas Pinilla challenge was deliberately modeled on that of Juan Perón in Argentina. It went on to describe how Rojas Pinilla wanted to force all organized labor into a single organization under state control and hoped to set up a social welfare agency headed by his daughter, María Eugenia, and that he wanted to give his daughter the funds and the influence to play the role of Eva Perón in Colombia. María Eugenia was a member of the Colombian Senate and an astute politician who would undoubtedly play a key role in a Rojas Pinilla administration, the report added.

"Rojas has developed his own mass political organization, Anapo, which, like Perón, Odria in Peru, and Pérez Jiménez in Venezuela, appeals most strongly to the urban lower class. The leadership of organized labor (only a third of the urban labor force is organized) is anti–Rojas, but they admit growing defections to Rojas among the rank and file. Rojas, although a 70-year-old diabetic, has conducted a tireless and well-organized campaign which has consistently attracted larger crowds than any other candidate," the embassy reported to Kissinger. A target of ridicule was Rojas Pinilla's economic ideas, which the embassy said "were insufficiently developed."

Regarding Pastrana, Kissinger was informed he was middle-of-the-road and unexciting. However, the report said Pastrana was the front-runner in the estimate of most politicians and "primitive" public opinion polls. In concluding, the report openly questioned whether Liberal voters would turn out in sufficient numbers to support a Conservative candidate, and whether enough Conservative voters would support a candidate they felt was closely linked with the Liberals.

The weather on Election Day was perfect and Colombian voters headed to the polls in large numbers all over the country. The voter participation exceeded the expectations of the National Front leaders. Colombian observers said it looked like close to four million voters decided to cast a ballot for the country's next president. American observers said it was one of the most peaceful elections in the nation's history. All observers noted a festive atmosphere in the big cities, with hardly any incidents to tarnish the election proceedings.

The excitement in the country heightened when the initial radio reports from political commentators reported that Rojas Pinilla had the advantage over the National Front candidate Misael Pastrana.[74] The radio reports quoted the government's National Registry and unofficial field reports from Colombian journalists. The nation was jubilant. Change was in the air. For the first time in history it appeared as though the people had voted for themselves, and soundly rejected the candidate of the ruling class.

The people of Colombia were euphoric that the 12-year National Front arrangement was about to come to an end. They knew the economy was managed in a responsible fashion, but they didn't care, they were more concerned with the feeble standard of living and turned out in massive numbers to elect a president who represented their interests, not those of the oligarchy.

The last politician to answer the needs of the lower class was the beloved Gaitán, but he had been plucked from the *pueblo* in a mysterious fashion. Still and all, Colombia was a democracy, and as the day progressed the nation's major radio stations were reporting results from polls all over the country describing in great detail the substantial lead that Rojas Pinilla had over Pastrana. Some radio stations were reporting a landslide victory for Rojas Pinilla. The Anapo camp was thrilled; they knew that the oligarchy owned every major radio station in the country and considered the reports a "White Flag" from the ruling elite.

As the sun went down on election day, political transparency disappeared. Late that evening, President Carlos Lleras Restrepo's Minister of Government, Carlos Augusto Noriega, appeared on radio and television and accused the press throughout the country of gross irresponsibility and threatened them with government sanctions if they did not stop describing their unofficial returns as products of the government's National Registry[75]: only the National Registry returns were valid, he insisted. The Lleras Restrepo government's forceful announcement almost had the intended chilling effect; some radio stations discontinued reporting all unofficial results. But many radio and television journalists across Colombia refused to be intimidated. They ignored the government warning and defiantly continued to report that reliable sources indicated a Rojas Pinilla victory.

Just before midnight, at 11:45 P.M., the government released National Registry Bulletin No. 3. It reported that Rojas Pinilla commanded a small lead over Pastrana — the numbers were 1,117,902 for Rojas Pinilla and 1,096,140 for Pastrana.[76] The people didn't believe the government. The information was contrary to what they had seen on the streets, heard on the radio, and seen on television.

In the early hours of April 20, at 2:50 A.M., the government released National Registry Bulletin No. 4. It reported that Pastrana was ahead of Rojas Pinilla. The new numbers were 1,368,981 for Pastrana and 1,366,364 for Rojas Pinilla.[77] As the nation slept, National Front operatives continued to count votes and Pastrana continued to widen his lead.

When the sun rose to waken the nation to the election results on the morning of April 20, the people of Colombia felt violated. They suspected someone stole the election under the cover of darkness. The sense of wonder and infinite strangeness generated by the National Registry was a tragic reflection of the complex realities that dominated the Colombian experience. The absence of transparency blemished democracy in Colombia. The irregular reporting of the vote forced many people in the country to lose faith in the political process. To many who recalled how the poor were denied a voice in Colombia with the murder of Gaitán in 1948, the results of the 1970 election meant that all Colombians were free to cast a vote but that no one would count them.

The American embassy explained the questionable Colombian vote to Washington in this manner.[78] "The day following the election, April 20, Anapo followers took to the streets to demonstrate their support for Rojas and their rejection of the vote advantage that Pastrana had finally gained early that morning. There was widespread belief among Anapo supporters that Pastrana and the oligarchy were trying to steal the election from Rojas. Many others supporting the candidacies of Betancur and Sourdis were of the same opinion (including some Pastrana supporters). The usual reason given for believing there had been fraud was that Rojas was ahead until Noriega's intervention and that Noriega's intention had been to cover up a juggling of the election results by keeping the vote count from the people. The fact that the subsequent official Bulletin after Noriega's intervention showed Pastrana ahead increased this general suspicion.

"On April 21, the demonstrations became more massive, the crowds uglier and the security forces were ordered to dislodge the demonstrators from the central part of Bogotá, and stop groups from marching at will through the city. A few injuries occurred and property damage (mainly broken windows) and looting took place when the demonstrators were dispersed late in the afternoon.

"President Lleras again went on radio and television to the Colombian people at 7:30 P.M. on April 21. He declared a State of Siege and gave as his basis for doing so that a subversive movement was underway [sic] to overthrow the constitutional order. In imposing the State of Siege, the President also imposed a 9:00 P.M. curfew in Bogotá and authorized all the departmental governors and mayors to impose a curfew at an hour deemed appropriate. Subsequent decrees imposed radio and press censorship, authorized government authorities to take appropriate measures in regard to the sale of alcoholic beverages and established military councils to judge crimes against the state under military law.... Almost the entire Anapo National Command, some secondary Anapo leaders, two rebel priests and a number of Communists were arrested by government security forces during the evening and day following the President's speech. In addition, a strong military cordon was thrown around Rojas' house in Bogotá and it became obvious that Rojas and his daughter, Maria Eugenia, were under virtual house arrest.

"Almost every politician in the country has been writing letters, making declarations and signing petitions in regard to what went wrong with the elections. Every possible explanation has been offered by the writers for the revolution that took place on April 19 and there is no lack of scapegoats, ranging from the archaic organization of the traditional political parties to the dislike of an Imposition candidate like Pastrana.... The events of the past few weeks have shaken Colombia throughout its social and political structure. The unexpected strength of Rojas came as a shock to those Colombians, Conservative and Liberal, who had previously explained away Rojas' strength and had confidently expected an easy Pastrana victory."[79]

To his credit, Pastrana was never accused of any involvement in the election scandal. Once in office, he dedicated his administration to the "Social Front," and proved to be extremely independent of the oligarchy. The new President turned his back on traditional party politics and angered certain segments of the ruling class by formally committing himself to strong socially conscious programs. Pastrana's new government aggressively called for universal education through the ninth grade, and increasing the rate of land redistribution.

Moreover, Pastrana personally ushered programs through Congress that vastly expanded low-cost housing and urban services for the lower classes. President Pastrana managed to balance the need for social reform with sound economic policies that enabled him to maintain the confidence of a good portion of the business community. The unexciting campaigner and so-called "Imposition Candidate" became a caring President who worked diligently to heal the deep wounds of the election scandal and restore credibility to the democratic process in Colombia.

The strong belief among Rojas Pinilla's followers that the presidency was stolen from them gave birth to the Movimiento 19 de Abril (19th of April

Movement). The group was formed in 1972 and initially called the armed branch of Anapo, but with time that name was abandoned in favor of M-19, and under that name it became one of the most feared and effective urban guerrilla organizations in Colombia. Like the other guerrilla groups in the country, the M-19 was fighting for social justice but with two distinctly different twists.

Its founder, the irreverent Jaime Bateman, was a man who had an eye for the spectacular, and was devoted to the idea that "The Revolution Was a Party!" Under Bateman's guidance the M-19 would soon become one of the most daring and flamboyant guerrilla groups in the world. Inside accounts of the M-19 "school of thought" were published by Darió Villamizar in Jaime Bateman: *Profeta de la Paz* (Prophet of the Peace), and by Angel Becassino in his book *M-19, El Heavy Metal Latino Americano*. The common bond

within the M-19 guerrilla movement was that the struggle against the Colombian government was a crusade for freedom.

The M-19 didn't make its presence felt until January 1974. By then they had incorporated a hardened mentality that revolution was the only means of bringing about change in Colombia. The 1970 elections proved to them the impossibility of bringing about change through the existing political system. What made the M-19 different from the FARC and ELN, was that its urban apparatus included many middle class and well-educated guerrillas. Moreover, the leadership of M-19 was very concerned about its image and nurtured a Robin Hood reputation among the lower classes by regularly stealing food and other materials and giving it away to the poor.

Another unique feature of the M-19 was that they conducted dangerous operations for the sake of symbolism. It burst

Jaime Bateman Cayon (left), the romantic founder of the M-19 guerrilla army, had an eye for the spectacular and was devoted to the concept that "The Revolution Was a Party." *El Tiempo*

on the scene with a sensational break-in of the Quinta de Bolívar and the theft of Simón Bolívar's sword. The nation was surprised when the M-19 organization promised to return the treasure as soon as the Liberator's true ideals were instituted. The M-19 contended that Colombia had failed to free the masses from socioeconomic oppression because selfish local elites had ignored Bolívar's ideas and supported the wishes of the U.S.[80]

In early 1976, the M-19 showed its fangs and repulsed the country when it kidnapped and murdered José Raquel Mercado, the black leader of the Confederation of Colombian Workers (Confederación de Trabajadores Colombianos, CTC). The labor leader had admirably worked his way up the ladder from being a lowly stevedore on the docks of Cartagena to becoming one of the most influential public figures in Colombia. The M-19 defended the execution with a statement that Raquel Mercado "sold out to the establishment."

International acclaim did not arrive until 1979, when the M-19 demonstrated precision timing and absolute daring by tunneling into the major military arsenal in Bogotá to steal 5,000 weapons while Colombians were celebrating New Year's Eve. Within weeks, however, most of the weapons were recovered and many of the participants arrested. In October 1979, the government rounded up more than 200 M-19 guerrillas and brought them to trial in Bogotá. Not to be outdone by the trial, though, the M-19 boldly staged a spectacular raid in February of 1980 that made headlines around the world.

The takeover of the Dominican Republic embassy was spectacular. The M-19 seized control of the Embassy while it was hosting a celebration of its national holiday, and held 14 diplomats hostage for two months. Included in the group was the U.S. Ambassador to Colombia, Diego Asencio, who won fame for the heroic manner in which he conducted himself during the captivity. Fortunately the seizure ended peacefully when the kidnappers received safe conduct to Cuba and the Inter-American Human Rights Commission promised to investigate charges of human rights abuses by the Colombian military. However, the raid on the embassy made it obvious—the M-19 had the gift for the spectacular, and took high-profile risks that the FARC and ELN might only dream of.

The political assassination of Gaitán, the oppressive Ospina, Gómez and Rojas Pinilla governments, the sterile National Front arrangement, and the religious devotion of Camilo Torres, they all played large roles in the establishment of the guerrilla movement in Colombia. However, it was the strong appearance of fraud in the 1970 presidential elections that gave the movement such dramatic impetus, just as it permanently stained the credibility of the ruling elite and altered the course of Colombia's democracy.

The absence of credible election transparency distanced the lower classes from the ruling elite. The mentality of the oligarchy was that they knew what was best for the nation; the rich thought they were acting in a fatherly fashion and merely attempting to properly guide the uneducated masses. However, when the poor witnessed the government indifference to their misery, when they observed the steadfast glorification of the capitalist system, when they looked at the growth of huge fortunes for the elite families many decided that war was better than servitude. Consequently, from 1970 onwards the guerrilla revolutionary was an expanding segment of the Colombian population.

Germán Archiniegas, the Colombian writer and diplomat, died in December 1999 at the age of 99. For many years Americans considered him the finest mind in Colombia. During the span of his long life,

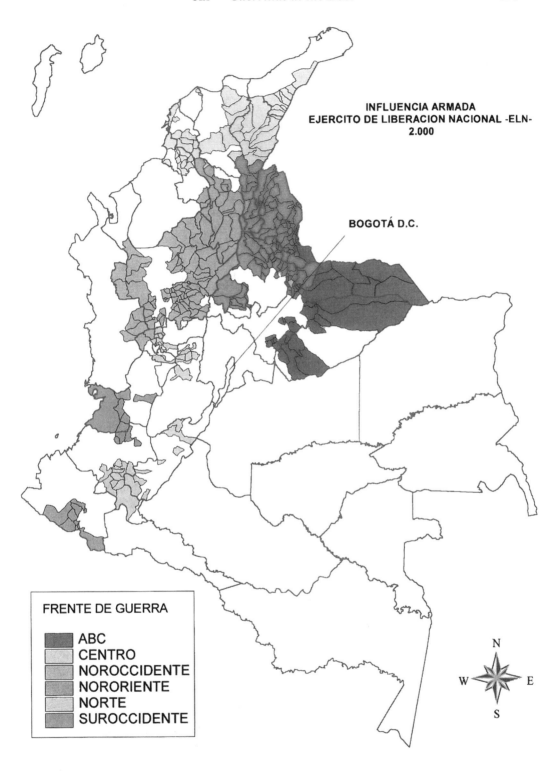

Armed Influence of the National Liberation Army–ELN (2000). From *Defense of the Pueblo, Republic of Colombia*

Archiniegas wrote 70 books, mostly histories and biographies, and an estimated 15,000 essays and newspaper articles. Born in Bogotá, his childhood memories were haunted by the story of his grandfather's barbaric death during the War of One Thousand Days. A victim of Colombian political violence, his grandfather was tied naked to the iron bars of a window, castrated, then pulled apart by four horses.

Some Colombians considered Archiniegas a radical. Nearly 30 years ago, he wrote that there were two Latin Americas: the visible and the invisible. The visible Latin America was the Latin America of presidents, generals, embassies, newspapers, business houses, universities, and cathedrals; the invisible Latin America was mute, repressed, and a vast reservoir of revolution.

Archiniegas's vision not only depicted Latin America but suitably described Colombia, except visible Colombia in the year 2001 was impotent, unable to produce change and the ruling elite was clinging to the United States for survival. Invisible Colombia, on the other hand, was still a vast reservoir of revolution but with a veteran force of menacing guerrilla warriors determined to unite millions of poor *campesinos* and show the world how well they had learned their history lessons.

Notes

1. Virginia M. O'Grady, John Alvarez Garcia, and Christian Restrepo Calle, *Camilo Torres: Priest and Revolutionary, Political Programme and Message to the Colombian People, With a preface by Dorothy Day* (London: Sheed and Ward, 1968), pp. 113–117.

2. David Bushnell, *The Making of Modern Colombia, A Nation in Spite of Itself* (Berkeley: University of California Press, 1993), pp. 216–217.

3. *El Tiempo, Lecturas Dominicales,* "100 Personajes del Siglo XX en Colombia," 6 de Diciembre de 1998.

4. Richard L. Maullin, *The Fall of Dumar Aljure, A Colombian Guerrilla and Bandit* (The Rand Corporation, Santa Monica, 1969).

5. *El Tiempo, Lecturas Dominicales,* 6 de Diciembre de 1998.

6. Robert W. Drexler, *Colombia and the United States: Narcotics Traffic and a Failed Foreign Policy* (Jefferson, N.C.: McFarland & Company, 1997) pp. 67–68.

7. *Ibid.,* p. 72.

8. *Ibid.,* p. 74.

9. *Ibid.,* p. 75.

10. *Time* magazine, "The Bull Ring Massacre," 20 February 1956.

11. Author interviews with Colombian senior citizens, Bogotá, May 1998.

12. Drexler, p. 80.

13. *Ibid.,* p. 81.

14. *Ibid.*

15. *Ibid.*

16. Bushnell, p. 228.

17. *Ibid.,* p. 226.

18. Drexler, p. 83.

19. *Ibid.*

20. *The Economist,* "War and Jaw," Bogotá, 14 November 1998.

21. *Ibid.*

22. *Semana,* "Marquetalia, 35 años después," Bogotá, 31 de Mayo 1999.

23. *Ibid.*

24. *Ibid.*

25. Philip Agee, *Inside the Company: CIA Diary* (London: Penguin Books, 1975), p. 192.

26. *Ibid.*

27. *Semana,* "El archivo secreto," Bogotá, 7 de Junio 1999.

28. *Ibid.*

29. *Ibid.*

30. O'Grady, Garcia, and Calle, pp. 17–18.

31. Walter J. Broderick, *Camilo Torres: A Biography of the Priest-Guerrillero,* (New York: Doubleday & Company, 1975), p. 12.

32. *Ibid.,* p. 14.

33. *Ibid.*

34. O'Grady, Garcia, and Calle, p. 9.

35. Broderick, p. 15.

36. *Ibid.,* p. 17.

37. O'Grady, Garcia, and Calle, p. 10.

38. Broderick, p. 32.

39. *Ibid.,* p. 79.

40. O'Grady, Garcia, and Calle, p. 10.

41. Broderick, p. 280.

42. O'Grady, Garcia, and Calle, p. 1.

43. *Ibid.*, p. 21.

44. *Ibid.*, pp. 125–126.

45. Phil Gunson, *The Manchester Guardian,* "Obituary: Manuel Pérez: The Priest Who Went to War," England, 15 April 1998.

46. *Ibid.*

47. *Ibid.*

48. Stephen Comiskey, Confidential U.S. Embassy Report, Department of State, "Some Observations on Democracy, the Political Environment and Local Government in Colombia," Bogotá, 18 July 1967, reproduced by author with permission of National Archives, 2 February 1999.

49. *Ibid.*

50. Maullin.

51. *Ibid.*

52. Secret Report, U.S. Central Intelligence Agency, Directorate of Intelligence, "Cuban Subversive Activities in Latin America: 1959–1968," 16 February 1968, declassified 1 February 1997, reproduced by author with permission of LBJ Library, 26 February 1999.

53. *Ibid.*

54. Secret Report, U.S. Embassy, Department of State, "Internal Security: Alertness to Potential Insurgency," Bogotá, 18 August 1967, reproduced by author with permission of the National Archives, 2 February 1999.

55. *Ibid.*

56. *Ibid.*

57. Drexler, p. 84.

58. *Ibid.*, p. 85.

59. *Ibid.*, p. 87.

60. *Ibid.*, p. 88.

61. Official U.S. Embassy Report, Department of State, "Voter Abstention in Colombia," Bogotá, 3 May 1968, reproduced by author with permission of the National Archives, 2 February 1999.

62. *Ibid.*

63. *Ibid.*

64. C. Sedgwick, Confidential U.S. Embassy Report, Department of State, "Initial Visit of Dr. Pastrana as Official Candidate to Medellín, Marinilla and the Hinterland: Assessment of the Visit," Bogotá, 16 December 1969, reproduced by author with permission of the National Archives, 2 February 1999.

65. *Ibid.*

66. Official U.S. Embassy Report, Department of State, "Lengthy Conversation with Alberto Lleras Camargo," Bogotá, 21 November 1969, reproduced by author with permission of the National Archives, 2 February 1999.

67. *Ibid.*

68. Official U.S. Embassy Report, Department of State, "Analysis of Election Statistics," Bogotá, 4 December 1969, reproduced by author with permission of the National Archives, 2 February 1999.

69. Confidential U.S. Embassy Report, Department of State, "Political Biweekly," Bogotá, 13 March 1970, reproduced by author with permission of the National Archives, 2 February 1999.

70. *Ibid.*

71. *Ibid.*

72. Official U.S. Embassy Report, Department of State, "Visit to Department of Huila," Bogotá, 20 March 1970, reproduced by author with permission of the National Archives, 2 February 1999.

73. Confidential U.S. Department of State Special Memorandum for Mr. Henry A. Kissinger, the White House, "Colombia to Hold Presidential and Congressional Elections, Sunday, April 19," Washington D.C., 17 April 1970, reproduced by author with permission of the National Archives, 2 February 1999.

74. Confidential U.S. Embassy Report, Department of State, "Political Roundup, Events following the general elections in Colombia on April 19," Bogotá, 8 May 1970, reproduced by author with permission of National Archives, 2 February 1999.

75. *Ibid.*

76. *Ibid.*

77. *Ibid.*

78. *Ibid.*

79. *Ibid.*

80. Bushnell, p 246.

CHAPTER SEVEN

The War on Drugs

Andrés Pastrana could barely hide his humiliation. A Colombian Air Force plane carrying 1,639 pounds of cocaine was seized by U.S. Customs at Fort Lauderdale Hollywood International Airport in Florida after inspectors boarded the C-130 Hercules on Monday, November 10, 1998. Less than two weeks before, President Pastrana had been in the White House with President Bill Clinton and pledged his full commitment to trying to rid his country of cocaine and heroin production. Moreover, he received $289 million of American aid for anti-drug efforts and economic development.

Raymond Kelly, Commissioner of the U.S. Customs Service, called the case "disturbing" and said investigators were trying to sort out who loaded the plane in Colombia and who had access to it before it arrived at 2:30 P.M. with a crew of six, and five passengers. (Family members of air force personnel are allowed to buy tickets on cargo flights.) Kelly said that foreign military airplanes regularly flew into the United States with supplies and personnel for embassies and consulates, or for specific missions, and that his agency routinely asked permission for random searches. Monday was the first time that the searches had discovered drugs on a Colombian government plane, he said. Kelly was appar-

ently unaware that three former Colombian Air Force mechanics were convicted on November 3, 1998, of transporting eight pounds of heroin in 1996, stashed in the nose and luggage compartment of then President Ernesto Samper's official airplane. Kelly also failed to note that 22 pounds of cocaine was discovered on board an identical Colombian Air Force C-130 Hercules aircraft during a stopover in Fort Lauderdale in 1991 or that a 1984 U.S. military intelligence report alleged that 95 Colombian Air Force personnel were actively involved in drug running.[1]

Customs officials said inspectors found the 700 packages of cocaine after noticing that several pallets in the cargo bays had unusual rivets and smelled of fresh glue. A drug-sniffing dog confirmed the inspector's suspicions. After drilling the pallets and extracting white powder that tested positive for cocaine, the inspectors dismantled the pallets and found 1,639 pounds of the drug. Customs officials questioned the crew and the passengers, a family of five they said included an unidentified retired Colombian Air Force officer, but no arrests were immediately made. Kelly said it was possible that the cocaine was placed on the plane without the involvement of anyone in the military, but added that the case was still troubling: "It's disturbing a military aircraft was used. We're talking something close to a ton of cocaine on an official aircraft." A U.S. Customs spokesman said that the wholesale value of the cocaine was $12.7 million.

Late that afternoon, in Bogotá, Colombian Air Force Commander General José Manuel Sandoval announced that the drug seizure "damaged the image of our Air Force and ... Colombia as well," and then offered his resignation to President Pastrana. It was immediately accepted, ending a 36-year career in the air force. At a news conference the next day, Sandoval said that the C-130 went to Florida to pick up airplane replacement parts and night visors and that it had been searched by drug-sniffing dogs before it left a military air base in Bogotá. He also said that as Commander of the air force, he had to take responsibility for the incident but denied any widespread involvement of the military in the drug trade. However, he acknowledged the possibility that a small number of people were committing crimes inside the service.

In a separate local radio interview later that day, Sandoval elaborated further and said there was no question that there were "people dedicated to drug trafficking within the military institution." Sandoval was careful—he stopped short of mentioning anyone by name—but he deliberately noted that 19 Colombian Air Force personnel worked out of an office at the Fort Lauderdale airport, and would have been on the receiving end of Monday's lucrative shipment.

The Colombian press attacked the corruption in the armed forces unmercifully. They officially dubbed the Colombian Air Force the "Blue Cartel." The influential *Semana* magazine openly speculated that the large quantity of drugs found on the plane in Fort Lauderdale indicated that the shipment did not come from a small organization and suggested that the air force

link had to be with large narcotraffickers. On Thursday, five members of the air force were arrested in Colombia. Colombian agents from the federal prosecutor's office detained the intelligence chief of the military airport in Bogotá, Major Gonzalo Noguera, and four aviation technicians. The investigation also led to the retirement of the airport commander, Colonel Arturo Dueñas, and his second in command.

* * *

A child sat on a dirt street in the Colombian jungle town on Monday playing with the discarded firing pin of a hand grenade and surrounded by the rubble of ruined buildings. Army helicopters (Russian-made MI-17's and U.S. Black Hawks) clattered overhead ferrying the bodies of scores of dead Marxist guerrillas to a nearby military base. Puerto Lleras, a small river port in the jungles of eastern Meta Province, was the scene of some of the worst clashes during a nationwide rebel offensive over the weekend. Reuters, July 12, 1999[2]

The objective of the FARC attack was thought to be the principal highway connecting Bogotá to southern Colombia. Causing further alarm among the Colombian military hierarchy was that the bearded FARC commander, Romaña, was spearheading the offensive on Thursday, July 8, 1999: it added tremendous significance to the battle. Sureshot and military strategist Jorge "Mono Jojoy" Briceño were sending one of their best combat commanders into action.

The military feared the worst. The fighting started at dawn near the small town of Gutiérrez, only 15 miles south of Bogotá. The Colombian army rushed in troops and roughly 600 soldiers squared off with 500 guerrillas. There was no official estimate of casualties early that morning. The army press office would only say that the fighting was intense and that the FARC was trying to show its strength before the next round of peace talks scheduled for July 20, Colombian Independence Day.[3]

As the day wore on, the army reported 52 deaths in heavy fighting that was spreading into the mountains. The army also sent fear into the hearts of the seven million-plus inhabitants of Bogotá when they said the FARC was preparing a spectacular attack on the capital.[4] They added that the casualties included 15 crack counterinsurgency troops and 37 FARC guerrillas. Moreover, bad weather prevented rushing reinforcements into the battle. Colonel Paulino Coronado, stationed in Bogotá, described the situation as very serious and said there were heavy losses on both sides. He was unable to say what targets the FARC unit was preparing to strike in Bogotá but said he also thought the rebels were aiming to carry out a high-profile show of force to strengthen their hand at the upcoming peace talks. The battle was now raging 8,500 feet above sea level in the rain-soaked plateau and mountain area outside Bogotá, he explained. There was some speculation in the capital that Romaña was headed to Bogotá's high-security La Picota penitentiary to break out the hundreds of FARC guerrillas held there. However, military intelligence officials discounted such talk, saying that it was a guerrilla ruse to confuse the deployment of the armed forces. By 10:30 Thursday evening, there were 78 confirmed deaths so far. An army intercept of a coded radio conversation between Romaña and Mono Jojoy released to the press alluded to a battle plan. "Congratulations. Take all necessary measures. Block the main routes to Bogotá and then advance." The army was wary of the underground network the FARC had in the poor southern section of the city. Although the army officially said there were no more than 500 guerrillas in the city, the FARC belittled the estimate and indicated the real count was in the thousands.[5] Regardless of the exact count, the army wanted to prevent Romaña from possibly hooking up with any of the trained urban guerrillas spread out in the poor southern neighborhoods of Bogotá. The government attempted to calm the residents of the capital by reporting that there was little chance the battle would spread to the traditional hotbeds of FARC support.[6]

Colombians in the capital were on edge. On July 3, *El Espectator* published an article that quoted military intelligence sources as saying that the FARC had mobilized several hundred guerrillas for a "Gigantic Plan" to attack southern Bogotá. Many of the approximately 28,000 U.S. citizens in Colombia were frightened. They knew most of the middle class was fully behind the government but they had deep reservations about the convictions of the poor. The Americans understood the underprivileged had nothing to lose and dreaded the thought of the lower classes taking up arms, and perhaps going door to door, fighting to take control of the city. Consequently, some Americans working in Colombia gave serious thought to abandoning Bogotá and heading back to the states. One American sadly observed that virtually no facet of life was left untouched by Colombia's chaotic state of insecurity. The sense of helplessness in the nation was severe, he said.

The fighting was fierce. The offensive was considered the worst since the peace talks were officially launched in January. A midranking FARC commander in the combat zone explained to reporters that the guerrilla offensive was "homage" to regional FARC commander Miller Perdomo, killed by the army close to Bogotá earlier in the year.[7] Before his death, Perdomo told Reuters that the FARC, had 17,000 fighters nationwide and was planning a series of hit-and-run guerrilla attacks in Bogotá in an attempt to bring the civil war uprising "To the doorsteps of the rich."[8]

Armed forces chief General Fernando Tapias said, "This is not a disaster for the army. There have been heavy losses on both sides." An army spokesman said 40 crack insurgency troops were dead, along with 38 FARC guerrillas. There were no reports that the FARC had in fact succeeded in blocking any of the major routes in or out of Bogotá. However, the army was on a full-scale alert; its brass had canceled all leave across the country and recalled all troops to barracks to prepare for a massive counteroffensive.

Two days later, as the battle raged on, the Colombian government took drastic measures and declared a curfew across more than 30 percent of the nation, including the outskirts of Bogotá. The rare wartime decree was made in an effort to contain what was now a nationwide offensive. The curfew prohibited all highway and river travel from dusk to dawn and gave mayors in the southeastern part of the country authorization to extend the ban to daylight hours. Interior Minister Nestor Humberto Martínez made the announcement as the FARC attacked security forces, raided towns and bombed energy infrastructures across the country. Government sources said the armed forces had lost all contact with several army and police units after they came under attack by the FARC. Additionally, reliable Colombian sources were privately advising the U.S. that they feared the FARC was preparing to storm regional capitals and was going to stage a fresh offensive on Bogotá. The White House was informed of the situation and was prepared for the worst ... the evacuation of Americans in Bogotá.

That night the army reported that 64 guerrillas taking part in a nationwide offensive had been killed in fighting with government security forces across Colombia during the past 24 hours. It added that security forces reported only three police killed and six civilians murdered after

guerrillas attacked 15 towns, bombed banks and destroyed key energy facilities. The FARC reportedly suffered 38 losses near the town of Hato Corozal, in oil-rich eastern Casanare Province, and another 19 killed as they tried to overrun a police barracks in the town of Doncello, in southern Caquetá Province.[9] Minister Martínez said heavy fighting was continuing after nightfall in the jungle towns of Puerto Lleras and Puerto Lopez in eastern Meta Province.[10]

On Sunday, 1,000 FARC guerrillas were using armor-plated trucks and homemade missiles to attack Puerto Lleras, a town 110 miles southeast of Bogotá.[11] However, at this point it appeared the tide was turning and the armed forces were stopping the FARC advances. The army reported a running total of 55 soldiers and police killed along with over 200 guerrillas since the nationwide offensive started on Thursday. Colombian government officials said guerrilla deaths could not be confirmed because the FARC rarely left their dead behind when retreating. General Tapias addressed reporters in Bogotá after attending a funeral of 22 soldiers who died in combat Thursday, and said the FARC had swarmed out of the demilitarized zone to launch its attacks. He added that four army battalions were responding to the attack on Puerto Lleras.[12]

That same day, the *Los Angeles Times* reported that the Colombian Air Force had conducted an aerial attack against the FARC destroying four trucks carrying guerrillas out of the demilitarized zone into battle.[13] The report was one of the first American indications of how the Colombian armed forces were inflicting such heavy casualties on the FARC and confirmed growing rumors in the capital that the government had struck several heavy blows against the guerrillas.

El Tiempo disclosed the full details of the aerial victories on July 12. It reported that the Colombian Air Force used U.S.

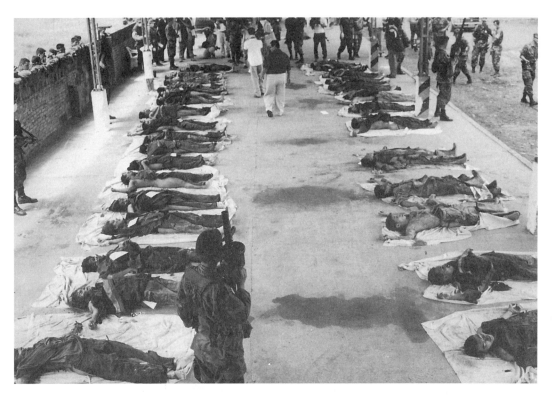

Reportedly guided by super secret U.S. intelligence data, the Colombian Air Force used U.S. helicopter gun ships and Vietnam-era AC-47 "Phantom" aircraft to turn the tide of battle and inflict heavy casualties on FARC guerrillas at Puerto Lleras in July 1999. Here the Colombian Army shows off prized trophies to journalists. *El Tiempo*

helicopter gun ships and Vietnam-era AC-47 "Phantom" aircraft to destroy seven FARC trucks in Hato Corozal and a truck and two armored vehicles in Puerto Rico. *El Tiempo* added that at least 17 police officers and four soldiers were killed during 22 attacks across the country. The leading newspaper in Colombia put FARC fatalities at 202. Reuters reported that guerrillas were engaged in hand-to-hand combat with security forces in the streets of at least three communities and that the FARC put the death toll at 68 security force members killed and 32 guerrillas dead.[14] Reuters also confirmed that the armed forces were neutralizing the FARC offensive.

The newly appointed Defense Minister, Luis Fernando Ramírez, President Pastrana's close ally and former vice-presi-

dential candidate in the failed 1994 presidential elections, maintained a high profile during the offensive. He informed the nation that "People who persist in terrorism, kidnapping and drug trafficking will feel all the weight of the state security apparatus." He also told Reuters that he did not believe the FARC had any chance of seizing power in Colombia.[15] "Taking power is one thing, but committing terrorist acts is another matter entirely. The guerrillas cannot take power without political backing, and right now their popularity is at its lowest level," he explained. Ramírez was referring to a poll in a local newspaper that showed 70 percent of respondents believed the FARC was a terrorist organization without ideology, while 61 percent believed the group was fighting to achieve economic, not political, goals.[16]

The United States expressed outrage at the FARC violence. However, the Clinton administration stopped short of joining Republicans in Congress criticizing the peace plan. "While we expect that the Colombian government and the FARC peace talks will resume as planned on July 20, we are outraged by this latest outbreak of FARC attacks," State Department spokesman James Foley said on Monday, July 12, 1999. "We call upon the FARC to cease these attacks and to engage in substantive peace negotiations ... real peace negotiations."

The *New York Times* reported that FARC leaders warned that they were preparing a "First great offensive," to be carried out if they were not satisfied with the course of the peace efforts.[17] The *Times* article cited an interview published in an Argentine newspaper with FARC representative Javier Calderón saying that the peace talks were the last flame of hope, and if that flame went out there would be total war. "We don't want war. We don't want the Colombian people to continue immersed in this war. But we will wage it if necessary. We are prepared for it," Calderón said.

The *Times* also made reference to the Cali newspaper *El País* which editorialized that the initiation of talks was itself a tactic of war designed to lull the government into complacency and that the guerrillas wanted to intimidate ordinary Colombians into thinking that they were in better condition than the armed forces to produce a military victory.

Finally, on Tuesday, the government reported that the four-day FARC offensive was over. "They showed all of their military capacity, and all of that capacity was no risk for Colombian democracy," boasted General Tapias.[18] "In the rest of the country the offensive is over." Detailing the terrifying severity of the offensive, Tapias said that the FARC had mobilized

between 12,000 and 15,000 guerrillas for the combat, and that it was the largest action by the FARC since they had coordinated with the ELN to terrorize the nation in the last days of the Samper government.

Afterwards the FARC would use that figure to hint that their overall troop strength in Colombia was well above that of all official estimates.[19] "We did not commit all of our forces to the offensive and the army knows this very well," the Senior FARC official explained.[20]

The victory was a shot in the arm for President Pastrana. However, many Colombians said the attacks created enormous psychological damage. Collectively, the people of Colombia were suffering from the destruction of the civil war, and the FARC offensives during the past year were not what they had expected when they voted for Pastrana. They had hoped that the President's jungle meeting with Sureshot prior to the elections was a sign that peace was at hand, but nothing was further from the truth. The Colombian people were trapped in a world filled with violence. They watched with horror as Colombian television stations reported ghastly scenes every night of carnage. The devastation was so great that responsible directors of several television news networks decided to stop showing political violence in color and opted to broadcast the bloodshed in black in white. The initiative was the first in the history of Colombia.

Moreover, many Colombians feared the FARC was merely conducting probes into the defenses of Bogotá and would return and inflict greater damage at a later date. Some mentally devastated Colombians were still expecting doomsday. "The city [Bogotá] will fall if the four million poor in the barrios of Bolivar, Kennedy and Soacha turn against us," predicted one pessimistic coffee exporter. Overall, the nation was a time bomb and Colombians were abandoning their country in unprecedented numbers. The U.S. Consulate in Bogotá said it had a four-month waiting list of visa applications and that applicants were arriving at a rate of 200 to 300 per day.[21] The Canadian Consulate reported a similar increase.

Nonetheless, the military was thrilled with its performance. In a statement, the command declared that more than 200 FARC rebels had been killed in what it now was calling, "The biggest and most demented guerrilla offensive in the past 40 years."[22] General Rafael Hernández, head of the Joint Chiefs of Staff, said, "The guerrillas have demonstrated that politically and militarily they can do nothing. They are living in another epoch."[23] The military dedicated the victory to President Pastrana but behind the scenes they were attributing the triumph to the Americans.

U.S. authorities declined to comment publicly on whether they tipped off Colombia about the impending rebel offensive and helped them pinpoint rebel columns. One U.S. military source, however, told Reuters, it would be an "educated supposition" to suggest that that had been the case.[24]

Colombian army sources denied there had been any cooperation and said U.S. technicians had "fled" back to Bogotá from radar stations in the eastern towns of San José del Guaviare and Marandúa when the first rebel shot was fired.[25] "We were on the alert in the critical points of the country because we knew the offensive was coming. We organized air support which allowed us to give ground troops backing," a senior Colombian officer told Reuters.

The Colombian armed forces' use of air power was the difference between victory and defeat in the four-day offensive. The FARC was annihilated from the air, not on the battlefield. However, Colombian military intelligence was trying to keep it hush-hush that the real-time information for the swift and devastating airborne assault was gleaned from American de havilland RC-7 spy planes flying high above the area of combat. A version of the aircraft was used in Korea to monitor North Korean military activities.

The super-secret planes flying over the mountains and jungles of Colombia were packed with sophisticated intelligence electronics equipment that intercepted radio and mobile phone communications with the use of satellites. Moreover, the equipment allowed the Americans to positively identify the voiceprints of key FARC leaders. The spy planes also contained state-of-the-art computerized infrared imaging systems and sensor equipment that could pierce the dense jungle canopy to determine the size of troop units, their direction, their rate of movement, and the firepower they were carrying.

"This had to do with surveillance.... We're not supposed to be monitoring guerrillas, but that's what they were doing," one source familiar with the flight mission told *Newsweek*.[26] Prior to the FARC offensive, the U.S. aerial surveillance in the jungles and mountains of Colombia was the Pentagon's biggest covert operation in Latin America.[27]

The army was showing off their prized trophies. Helicopters touched down on the sweltering infantry base in Granada and military escorts led a pack of journalists to the human carnage they were brought there to observe.[28] Spread out before them were 30 punctured, torn, and bloated FARC guerrilla corpses that gave off the rancid stench of war. A third of the dead on display were women. Most of the lifeless bodies looked like teenagers. Many had the typical FARC battle flags draped around their chests with the red, yellow and blue national colors. The banners represented the struggle for control of Colombia.

Although the FARC clearly suffered a defeat and failed to inflict heavy casualties during the offensive, many Colombians still thought they were making steady progress. "They've managed to show force, to intimidate [Colombia's] establishment, and without a doubt made it possible to push harder at the negotiating table," said the respected former national security adviser Alfredo Rangel.[29] The offensive had a greater impact on the battlefield — in one rubble-strewn town, shell-shocked civilians had draped homemade white flags from roofs, windows and doors, begging for neutrality and praying to stay out of harm's way in the bloody civil war.[30]

General Charles Wilhelm, commander in chief of the U.S. Southern Command, said the Colombian military did a good job.[31] "I am very confident in saying that government losses in the recent offensive came in double digits. FARC's losses are in the triple digits," he explained.[32] He added that the Southern Command was in constant communication with Colombia's military during the offensive and that they were "not losing" the war with the FARC.

A week later, in Washington, President Clinton praised Colombia's struggle for peace.[33] "In addition to wanting a neighbor and a democracy in Latin America to be free of the kind of violence and heartbreak that the Colombian people have undergone, it is in our national security interest to do what we can if we can be helpful in ending the civil conflict so that Colombia can go about the business of freeing itself from the influence of the narco-traffickers," said the President.[34] He finished his remarks by saying he wasn't prepared to make a dollar commitment (for the year 2000), but he was in close touch with President Pastrana and that he admired the way the Colombian leader was throwing himself into trying to end his nation's civil conflict.

Tod Robberson, of the *Dallas Morning News*, was one of the better American journalists in Colombia. Unlike the wire-service spot reporters, who reported the news with lightning speed and were usually not paid to file in-depth stories, Robberson, together with a handful of other Americans in Bogotá, was an investigative journalist. Robberson's journalistic skills were quite evident in his reports from Colombia. Therefore it was no surprise that he broke the news in the United States that in its quest for victory, the Colombian Air Force had opened fire on innocent civilians during the battle for Puerto Lleras.[35] Moreover, to the organization's credit, the *Dallas Morning News* was the only American newspaper with the conviction to follow up on Colombian eyewitness reports that indicated some of the aircraft involved in the Colombian air war against the FARC guerrillas wore American flags.[36]

The Colombian military took advantage of U.S.-supplied aircraft, logistical support and equipment to open fire on the civilian population of Puerto Lleras, according to Robberson. During the heat of battle, the Colombian Air Force swooped from the sky to bomb and strafe dozens of buildings, including houses, a hospital, a church and a convent killing three civilians and wounding several others.

Robberson spoke with local government officials, residents and rescue workers in Puerto Lleras to document his report. Extremely troubling was that the Colombian Air Force strafed a hospital with a red cross painted on its roof and with a Red Cross flag posted outside. The hospital was providing shelter for 400 civilians trying to escape the combat. The air force also fired on a clearly marked ambulance carrying wounded civilians for evacuation. Witnesses quoted by Colombian newspapers said they identified American flags on the tail fins of some aircraft.

Colombian Air Force General Angel Mario Calle, the commander of the air assault, denied any wrongdoing and insisted that the FARC inflicted the damage on the civilian area. General Calle also denied U.S. participation. He said that at no time did U.S. personnel participate in the attack, nor was U.S. intelligence supplied to help guide military aircraft against the guerrillas.

However, Robberson reported that at the time of the airborne strikes the focus of the FARC attack was the town's police station, defended by 60 police officers and under assault by hundreds of guerrillas. (Inside the police station was a Colombian housewife, who helped her policeman husband and his colleagues defend the jungle village. A week later she would receive the Medal of Valor, one the country's highest military honors.)

Robberson discovered that several blocks away from the scene of the attack on the police station was widespread physical evidence that the military's airborne assault was directed at civilian-occupied areas of Puerto Lleras. The *Dallas Morning News* reporter substantiated his report with consistent eyewitness accounts. Moreover, Robberson examined the dozens of high-caliber rounds embedded in walls and floors of the hospital that had entered from the roof. He also inspected the Catholic convent next door to the hospital that was slammed by a rocket from the air that blasted apart two rooms, and checked the roof of the Catholic Church hit with aerial rounds. Additionally, Robberson confirmed that .50-caliber rounds had raked the roof of the local government building in Puerto Lleras.

General Edgar Alfonso Lesmes, the Colombian Air Force Commandant, contradicted the remarks made by the commander of the air assault, General Calle. Lesmes told reporters shortly after the attack that U.S. aircraft participated in the operation, providing logistical and administrative support and helping transport Colombian ground troops. Moreover, he

went on to say that the Colombian aircraft used in the pursuit operation were U.S. supplied Black Hawk and UH-1H helicopters, and Vietnam-era OV-10 "Broncos," A-37 "Dragonflies" and Hercules C-130 transport planes. Lesmes also said that the aircraft involved in the assault were stationed at the nearby Apiay air base. About 20 American servicemen were stationed at Apiay at the time of the Puerto Lleras assault, according to Colombian air force officers.[37] The Apiay air base provided support for the U.S. Army 204th Military Battalion.

Lieutenant Colonel John Snyder, a spokesman for the U.S. Southern Command, said the Americans based at Apiay, 45 miles southeast of Bogotá in a mountainous region in Meta Province, as well as elsewhere in Colombia, were strictly limited to participation in counternarcotics activities. "Because that was a purely military operation directed at the FARC, we would not have had any troops involved. That's not what we're in the business of doing down there," he said.[38]

General Calle insisted that his airmen followed strict rules of engagement that prohibit them from firing on any area where civilians might be present, even if guerrillas are mixed with the civilians. "We do not shoot when there is a risk whatsoever to the civilian population," he said, suggesting that civilian accounts of the airborne attack were part of a "misinformation" campaign by guerrilla sympathizers. "This is a war of words. The guerrillas' objective is to make us look like murderers before the international media."[39]

Robberson reported that the allegation of an attack on civilians was not the first such charge against the air force. The military was investigating accusations that 17 civilians in the northern town of Narino in Antioquía Province were killed in early August in an airborne military assault aimed at dislodging FARC guerrillas who occupied the town, and that in December, at the town of Santo Domingo, 200 miles northeast of Bogotá, 18 civilians were killed when a U.S.-supplied OV-10 Bronco attack plane and assault helicopters fired on the town in a counternarcotics operation.

Human-rights groups say the incidents underscore the dangers posed by a U.S. policy of sharing intelligence, weaponry, expertise, aircraft and war material with a Colombian military whose record on human rights is checkered. "We are deeply concerned," said Carlos Salinas, who monitors Colombia for the human-rights group Amnesty International.[40] "One of the hallmarks of the conflict in Colombia is the tendency of all sides—including the armed forces—to attack the civilian population without remorse. This would not be the first time the civilian population have been grouped as being with the enemy merely for having lived close to the scene of an attack."[41]

The FARC realized that it needed to considerably upgrade its firepower to counter the sophisticated American weaponry that gave the Colombian armed forces air superiority. The guerrilla leaders were obsessed with neutralizing the military's new assets, so they stepped up plans to buy Russian RPG surface-to-air missiles. The hand-held Russian weapons had downed four U.S. Black Hawks in Mogadishu, Somalia, in October 1993, when soldiers of Task Force Ranger and Delta Force were sent to capture two Habr Gidr clan lieutenants of renegade warlord Mohamed Farrah Aidid. The FARC understood the military and propaganda value of knocking out the U.S.-made Black Hawks. Therefore, they were also secretly buying SAM 7, SAM 14, and SAM 16 hand-held surface-to-air missiles in El Salvador, Guatemala and Nicaragua, according to *Semana* magazine.

Months later the government dis-closed more evidence of guerrilla plans to counter the air war. General Héctor Velasco announced that the FARC had offered its guerrillas a $2,500 reward for every pilot they assassinated.

On Saturday, July 17, the FARC made the surprise announcement that it had failed to agree on the creation of a team of international observers to monitor the talks with the government, and the peace process would be put on hold.[42] President Pastrana responded by saying his patience was running out and accused the FARC of throwing up obstacles to his bid to find a peaceful solution to the civil war. "We must build peace on the basis of seriousness and credibility," Pastrana said in a speech to mark the opening of a new session of Congress.

The U.S. blamed the FARC for the breakdown of the peace talks and accused them of "bloody unprovoked" attacks that killed innocent civilians as well as security forces. "The blame for the failure of the peace talks to proceed rests squarely on the shoulders of FARC leaders Manuel Marulanda and Jorge Briceño. They are personally responsible for this setback," said State Department spokesman James Rubin.[43]

A week earlier Defense Minister Luis Fernando Ramírez was in Washington to ask Congress for $500 million in military aid to fight the FARC, should the peace talks collapse and Colombia entered a full-scale war.[44] However, Rubin explained to the press that despite plans to increase aid to Bogotá, a negotiated settlement remained the most viable way to achieve peace in Colombia.

"This is a difficult time due to everything that is happening to us," Pastrana said. "But we know where we are going, we have international backing, and we will move forward. I insist that presidents should be judged at the end of their term and not at the beginning," he said.

Nonetheless, critics of Pastrana said

the son of a former president was arrogant and out of touch with average Colombians. "One of the most common errors of presidents is that they lose contact with reality," offered Liberal Party leader Juan Manuel Santos, a former presidential candidate. "They are closed off in a glass house and only listen to those they want to hear."

"The situation is very grave," Alfredo Rangel said. "For the first time, the peace process is in serious danger of freezing indefinitely or of being suspended. I think the government is starting to pay for the carelessness with which it has managed the process up to now."

Internationally, the United States was Colombia's best friend. Latin American leaders were extremely reluctant to get directly involved despite concern about the growing anarchy in Colombia. This meant that the U.S. risked getting sucked deeper into the, "narcoguerrilla" war.

In a thoughtful in-depth analysis of the issue,[45] Reuters said that with nationwide rebel offenses exposing the Colombian government's fragile grip on power, U.S. officials were sounding the alarm that the civil war could destabilize the whole region. Reuters reported, moreover, that the region's presidents rarely joined forces to tackle problems, even though they were worried about the worsening crisis in Colombia, particularly the possibility of a spillover of violence, drug trafficking and money laundering into their own nations.

"Colombia's crisis is amazingly complicated and entrenched ... and has no obvious solution," John Crabtree, a visiting fellow of Latin American studies at London University, told Reuters. "It's a no-win situation and it seems Latin American leaders ... with enough worries of their own ... mainly prefer to leave it to the United States."

The exceptions were Cuban leader Fidel Castro and his ally, Hugo Chávez, Venezuela's new and unpredictable president. While both were willing to mediate with the guerrillas in Colombia, however, their antidemocratic credentials made them awkward peace partners for Bogotá and Washington.[46]

"Historically, the Colombian government retained an authority even in the most troubled times. But now there is a perception that many Colombians no longer believe in the capacity of their government to stand above developments," David Scott Palmer, a Latin American expert at Boston University, told Reuters.

Upcoming elections in Argentina, Mexico and other nations, as well as domestic economic turmoil in Brazil and Ecuador, prevented Latin American leaders from summoning more energy for the hemisphere's most volatile crisis, according to political analysts.[47]

"There's a slippery slope of interventionism. The more bodybags that appear in the United States, the louder the calls are for extra people to be sent down to protect their personnel," Crabtree said. "Once involved, there's a tendency to get sucked in."

President Chavez, who had completely redefined the political structure in his country, was upset by the U.S. role in Colombia and warned Latin American leaders of the "Vietnam under our noses."[48] Washington's high-profile coordination with Bogotá was sparking intense media speculation throughout Latin America that the United States was considering direct military intervention, according to Reuters.

American lawmakers were also extremely worried about Colombia, especially Republicans in the House of Representatives. They said advances by "Narcoguerrillas," could lead to a Vietnam type of debacle for the United States and blamed "feeble" Clinton Administration policies for the shortcomings in Colombia.[49]

Dan Burton, the powerful Chairman of the House Committee on Government

Reform, was the loudest critic of the Clinton Administration. Burton, Dennis Hastert of Illinois, Bob Barr of Georgia, Benjamin Gilman, the influential Chairman of the House International Relations Committee, and John Mica, the new Chairman of the House Subcommittee on Criminal Justice, Drug Policy and Human Resources, were arguably the most important supporters of the Colombian government in the House.

Burton's battles with the Clinton administration were legendary and he was using the August 1999 House Government Reform subcommittee hearings to expose deep and often partisan divisions with the White House over the deteriorating

Key Republican congressmen at Colombian Black Hawk hearings in the House of Representatives (left to right): Dan Burton of Indiana, Bob Barr of Georgia, Ben Gilman of New York and Dennis Hastert of Illinois. *Courtesy of Gil Macklin*

situation in Colombia. Burton, who began his first term in Congress in November of 1982, said he had visions of Americans someday fleeing Colombia by helicopter from the roof of the U.S. embassy, duplicating the nightmarish departure from Saigon in April 1975 as the city fell to Communist forces.[50]

Republican Representative Mark Souder added that Colombia was in some ways more of a headache for the U.S. than Vietnam had been, because drugs that originated in Colombia threatened the lives of countless Americans and that had never been an issue in Vietnam.[51]

A letter to President Clinton from the two most important Republicans in Congress, Senate majority leader Trent Lott, from Mississippi, and Speaker of the House Dennis Hastert, from Illinois, was introduced at the hearing. It said recent developments in Colombia threatened democracy and, if unchecked, "Will have severe implications for the United States of America."[52] The Republicans demanded that President Clinton develop a comprehensive plan to deal with the situation.

Subcommittee Chairman Mica, whose responsibilities included oversight of the nation's antinarcotics programs, said, "Our hemisphere and the U.S. are facing one of the greatest challenges to regional and national security as the situation with Colombia continues to deteriorate."

The Associated Press reported that some Democrats expressed doubt whether an expansion in U.S.-backed interdiction efforts would make a difference. They suggested that U.S. resources focus on education of American youth and an expansion of treatment centers. Representative Janice Schakowsky, Democrat of Illinois, said there was no net reduction in drug flows from Colombia despite outlays of $625 million in recent years. "Why should we believe that investing more in this plan will achieve a different result?"[53]

Deeper U.S. involvement in Colombia could aggravate the problem, Representative Edolphus Townes, Republican of New York, suggested. He argued that U.S. resources should be devoted to prevention programs at home, and Representative Elijah Cummings, Democrat of Maryland, agreed. "If you didn't have demand, you wouldn't have to worry about Colombia," he said.[54]

Tempers flared at the hearing when Chairman Gilman disagreed on points of fact with the Clinton Administration's top antinarcotics official, a former general, Barry McCaffrey, Director of the Office of National Drug Control Policy. Gilman charged that only a few of the 30 Black Hawk helicopters authorized by Congress for Colombia in 1996 were actually delivered to Bogotá. McCaffrey, the beleaguered, but extremely dedicated, U.S. drug czar, replied that seven Black Hawks were delivered to the Colombian Army, and another 13 to the Colombian Air Force. Additionally, six more helicopters would be sent to the Colombian National Police, some in October and the balance in March, according to General McCaffrey.

Gilman also charged that ineffective counter narcotics policy in Colombia had resulted in a major heroin epidemic on the East Coast. McCaffrey countered that only a tiny percentage of heroin traffic came from Colombia compared with Burma and Afghanistan. The tension continued unabated when there was a major difference of opinion as to how much guerrillas in Colombia derived from the narcotics trade. Burton said the figure could be as high as $1.2 billion a year. McCaffrey responded that hypothetically the figure could be as low as $215 million a year, and that it was a difficult task to quantify guerrilla narcotics earnings in Colombia.

The quarrel between the Republicans in control of Congress and the Democrats in the White House had been going on for years. Gilman, Hastert, Barr, Burton, and Mica, were at the forefront of the confrontation with the White House on Colombia. During hearings in Congress in 1998, Chairman Gilman took a quote by Vice President Gore and put the Republican spotlight on it. Gore had said that illicit drugs cost the U.S. an astronomical "$67 billion" in societal costs each year.[55] Gilman used Gore's cost of America's devastating drug problem to dramatically argue the point that spending should be increased to "Help the courageous people in Colombia fighting our fight."[56]

At a previous hearing, Burton crystallized his position on the drug war with the succinct warning that, "I can think of no greater threat to our national security than the dangerous drugs entering American streets and schools."[57] The Republican perseverance with the White House paid off. Gilman and Burton, along with other Republican allies combined to bulldoze the Clinton administration into awarding Colombia $289 million in foreign aid for 1999, making Colombia the third-largest recipient of American foreign aid in the world.

On Friday, July 23, 1999, the United States armed forces lost a spy plane in Colombia. At 1:30 A.M. a four-engine, de Havilland RC-7 loaded with secret electronic surveillance equipment and with five Americans and two Colombians aboard took off from the Apiay air base for a seven and one-half hour antidrug reconnaissance mission. The five Americans comprised two officers and three enlisted men based at Fort Bliss in El Paso, Texas, who were in Colombia for a three- to four-week stint.

The last U.S. military spy plane lost in the war on drugs was in May of 1992 when the Peruvian Air Force mistakenly shot down one of Southcom's C-130s on a clandestine reconnaissance mission along the north Peruvian border with Colombia.

(From 1990 to 1992 Peru shot down 124 narcotrafficking aircraft.)

Colombian authorities rushed to conduct a search and rescue mission when contact was lost and the RC-7 failed to return at 9:00 A.M. U.S. State Department helicopters joined them. However, "adverse weather conditions" including lowcloud cover hampered the mission.

On Saturday, special U.S. rescue teams captured a signal from the downed RC-7 but were unable to spot the plane due to thick clouds. "We don't know if there are any survivors," said General Luis Ernesto Gilbert of the Colombian National Police.[58]

Lieutenant Colonel John Snyder of the Southern Command in Miami confirmed, "We still don't have any visual verification. The plane went down near San Miguel in Putamayo Province, along the Colombian-Ecuadorian border, a FARC stronghold."

"It's still a search-and-rescue operation," U.S. Navy lieutenant Jane Campbell told the *Miami Herald*. "They are still attempting to find seven people alive."

"If any of the crew is alive," a U.S. diplomat said, the main task for rescue forces would be to, "keep them away from the FARC."[59] The cause of the high-wing aircraft's downing remained a mystery. "The weather we don't believe was a factor. The weather was not adverse during that time. There was thick cloud cover, but the ceiling was at 4,000 feet," Snyder said. The RC-7 routinely flew at an altitude of between 5,000 and 25,000 feet, out of range of ground fire from guerrillas. The U.S. was using special teams from around Latin America and the Caribbean in the search but rugged terrain and triple jungle canopy slowed the mountain rescue.

The RC-7 was not the first American counternarcotics plane to crash in Colombia. The United States lost two American pilots in 1998, and one in 1997. Wayne

Harley Mulgrew of Napa, California, and Gary Clyde Chestnut of Leesburg, Alabama, both 46, died in July 1998 when their Thrush turboprop crop-dusting aircraft went down near a military base at San José del Guaviare, 200 miles southeast of Bogotá.[60] The U.S. embassy statement termed the deaths an accident and said that there were "No indications of hostile activity during the accident, and that one of the pilots was training the other pilot on how to conduct training exercises when the plane went down." In January 1997, Robert Martin, 35, flew his crop-dusting aircraft into a tree while on an eradication mission only one day after arriving in Colombia.[61] The three American pilots worked for U.S. firms based in Chantilly, Virginia, and Fort Worth, Texas.

Andy Messing and Steve Salisbury checked out the "Pray and Spray" operations in Colombia firsthand. In July 1998, the two military experts reported Colombian crop-spraying casualties in *Soldier of Fortune* magazine.

"From January 1994 to November of 1997, three police light airplanes and five helicopters had been shot down, while planes had been hit by gunfire on 67 separate occasions and helicopters on 74. During the same period, at least five pilots were among the 44 anti-narcotic personnel killed and 72 wounded," according to information Messing and Salisbury accumulated.

On Monday, the five Americans and two Colombians were feared dead. "They have located the wreckage and it's under observation," said General Barry McCaffrey who arrived in Colombia the previous day on a scheduled three-day visit. "The evidence so far would indicate that the five brave American aviators and two Colombian Air Force officers have probably lost their lives in a fatal accident," he explained. The wreckage was located at an altitude of about 7,000 feet in jungle-clad mountains that divide southern Putumayo

and Nariño Provinces, close to the border with Ecuador.

Dense fog prevented ground rescue teams from reaching the site. Lieutenant Jane Campbell said no aircraft could land near the plane and rescuers would have to insert down ropes from helicopters in order to obtain "100 percent confirmation" that the wreckage was indeed the RC-7. There was no sign of FARC guerrillas at the site, she said.

The RC-7 crash heightened American concern about the U.S. role in Colombia. Matthew Baker, a senior analyst at Stratfor Inc., an Austin, Texas-based firm that monitored international military activity, said that U.S. forces in Colombia were performing a wide variety of functions that extended far beyond the mission described by the Clinton Administration as counter narcotics training and support.[62] "They're doing a lot more than just search and rescue and training. They're taking fire. In Colombia we're stretching our definition of providing advice and counter narcotics assistance to the limit," he said. "My impression is that there is a movement to increase the U.S. military involvement in Colombia."

American civilians in Bogotá suspected that the U.S. was doing more than just training troops in Colombia. However, it was the *Dallas Morning News* that first reported the alarming development. The Texas daily said that U.S. intelligence services employed retired American Special Forces personnel to conduct "live" jungle training operations with Colombian troops and police. The object of the operations was to pursue and deliberately engage the guerrillas. "There have been American casualties during such missions," reliable sources told the *Dallas Morning News*.[63]

Hard evidence that U.S. combat troops were fighting in the Colombian jungles came from Sewall H. Menzel, a former colonel in the U.S. Army who served on the staff of Southern Command from 1985 to 1989. In 1998, Menzel was teaching Latin American politics at Florida International University. In one of his academic papers titled "Southcom in the Andes," Menzel affirmed that, "Green Berets, Seal's and Marines are now allowed to accompany Colombian military and police forces on anti-drug training patrols" against the narcoguerrillas.

Winifred Tate, a Colombian monitor for the Washington Office on Latin America, was a critic of the growing U.S. involvement. "I find the escalation of the rhetoric [in Colombia] very disturbing. I find the escalation of the U.S. military involvement very disturbing," he said. "I also find disturbing the fact that the United States is increasingly disingenuous about its involvement."

On Tuesday, rescue forces braved bad weather and pulled some of the dead from the crash site. U.S. officials told the *Washington Post* that a team of American and Colombian personnel were inserted from helicopters onto a peak more than 900 feet above the debris field, and, working in visibility of less than five feet, they took about three hours to descend the ridge.

Colombians were actually the first to arrive at the crash site. An elite unit marched through the jungle the night before, and scaled the mountain with ropes, and hand over hand techniques. When the rescue team was inserted, the Colombians provided a secure perimeter to guard against marauding FARC guerrillas.

"Rescuers have at last managed to reach the crash site and are evacuating the corpses," U.S. Ambassador Curtis Kamman told Reuters. "It seems there were navigation problems and they [the de Havilland crew] did not know there was a mountain [uncharted] in that area."[64] Officials said the crew gave no indication that they were being fired upon before losing contact with controllers. Some FARC guerrillas had been spotted in areas near the wreckage but there were no reports of clashes.

A source in the counternarcotics division of the National Police told Reuters that four corpses were pulled from the wreckage. There were no survivors, he said. Work was continuing to recover the other three bodies and fly them to the large U.S. counternarcotics base at Tres Esquinas in neighboring Caquetá Province.

Navy Rear Admiral Craig Quigley told the *American Forces Press Service* that the RC-7 slammed into the mountain. "The identities of those found were not known ... forensic experts will try to identify them," he said.

Captain Jack Miller, a spokesman for the U.S. Army's Miami-based Southern Command, confirmed that the wreck was that of the de Havilland but was not immediately able to comment on casualties.

While attending an inspection of a specialized Colombian antidrug battalion, trained by U.S. military personnel, former General McCaffrey praised the crew, saying they were the first American military personnel killed while fighting illegal drugs in Colombia. McCaffrey also pledged increased U.S. aid to Colombia to confront what he described as an "emergency situation," but stressed there would be "zero intervention" by U.S. personnel in frontline counterinsurgency operations.[65]

A week after the crash, the army identified the American casualties. The five were listed as: Captain José A. Santiago, Captain Jennifer J. Odom, Chief Warrant Officer Thomas G. Moore, Private First Class (PFC) T. Bruce Cluff, and PFC Ray E. Krueger. They had been assigned to the 204th Military Intelligence Battalion.

In a somber ceremony at Dover Air Force base in Dover, Delaware, at 2:30 A.M., on July 31, 1999, General McCaffrey stood on the tarmac to honor the fallen aviators of the 204th Military Intelligence Battalion as their remains arrived from Colombia. With him were Secretary of the Army Caldera, Congressman Silvestre Reyes representing the people of Texas, Ana Maria Salazar and Brian Sheridan from the Pentagon, and other VIPs.

A stoic McCaffrey said, "The President asked me to state that these dedicated Americans and their Colombian comrades were engaged in the vital work of combating the drug trade, which threatens the welfare and the security of both our nations. It's my view that these soldiers died in the best traditions of the U.S. armed forces. These dedicated soldiers answered the call of duty to protect their country, their loved ones, from the enormous threat to our nation from heroin and cocaine criminal organizations.

"These soldiers gave their lives to safeguard our nation and our children. By their passing … in honor of their devotion to duty … we pledge to never forget their sacrifice and to redouble our own efforts at home and abroad. A grateful nation extends its condolences and thanks to these selfless soldiers and their families."

A U.S. military invasion of Colombia was the buzz in Latin America. At the end of July 1999, a public opinion poll indicated that some of the ruling elite and many ordinary Colombians were prepared to swallow their national pride and were openly welcome to help from U.S. troops. The RCN radio poll indicated that 66.1 percent of 1,963 Colombians in 41 cities and towns favored U.S. intervention in the civil conflict.[66]

"It is desirable through international anti-drug treaties that foreign troops participate to combat narco-trafficking," Fernando Devis head of the Colombian Agricultural Society (SAC), which represents large landowners, told Reuters. "But it's ridiculous to think there could be a U.S. invasion."

"Maybe we won't see the arrival of the U.S. Marines,…" wrote *El Espectador* columnist Luis Cañón. "But U.S. intervention in our conflict began some time ago."

The FARC responded to the expanding U.S. role in a belligerent fashion: "The North Americans have been intervening here for more than 50 years, but now they want to do it more directly…. If they invade they'll have to take the consequences."

Barry McCaffrey rejected the possibility of American military intervention in Colombia. "There will be no intervention, not even a discussion at all," he said.

Seeking to calm Colombian fears that U.S. military intervention was imminent, Undersecretary of State Thomas Pickering, touring Colombia, called such speculation "totally false, totally crazy."[67] Washington, he said, had not given up on President Pastrana's faltering attempts to bring the FARC to successful peace talks.

"It's going to take a sustained, long-term effort," added Pickering, the third-highest ranking U.S. diplomat to visit Colombia in half a decade. "The canard floating around is that the United States is about to introduce a military intervention in Colombia. It is totally false, totally crazy, totally in my view irrelevant to the situation. The stories floating around about a dramatic change in the situation are just not true."

U.S. officials traveling with Pickering took pains to emphasize that the U.S. was not slipping covertly into military involvement in Colombia.

Friday the 13th of August 1999 was a black day in Colombia. The nation was in tears. Jaime Garzón, a beloved comic, whose skits made him one of the most popular political satirists and peace activists in the nation, was gunned down by two motorcycle assassins when he stopped at a red light on his way to work in the morning.[68] Garzón, was shot five times in the head and chest. President Pastrana, who was a friend of Garzón, said in a national radio interview, "It wasn't just that he made us laugh … Jaime in large part identified with the sentiments of Colombians, with what we were thinking."

"They've just killed the most beautiful thing in the world," Javier Saavedra, 30, lamented as he stood at the foot of the Capitol's steps, watching his countrymen wait in a long line snaking across Bolívar Plaza to pay homage to the comedian. "This man was a symbol of honesty, of courage, of truth." Garzón was the most prominent Colombian assassinated in Bogotá since the November 1995 killing of Alvaro Gómez, then leader of the political opposition to the government of President Ernesto Samper.

"I'm confused, I now have to investigate the murder of a great friend," said the sobbing chief of the National Police General Rosso José Serrano on radio. "It could be he [Garzón] was killed for his humanitarian efforts."

Garzón was a threat to the ultra right-wing elements of the Colombian military establishment. They considered him a mouthpiece for the FARC and feared the enormous influence his views had on ordinary Colombian people. Essentially, his dedication to peace and the way he depicted the FARC's social reforms for impoverished peasants, which was in total contradiction to the way the military depicted them, marked him for death. The Colombian military welcomed the sophisticated U.S. weaponry and training that significantly upgraded the capability of the army, air force and navy. They were preparing for war. As a consequence, the ultra right-wing in Colombia was worried Garzón would single-handedly sway millions of Colombians to support urgent reforms and deprive the armed forces of the opportunity to escalate the conflict.

Friends said Garzón was a humanitarian who stood for eliminating war, poverty, and restrictions on individual freedom. He was also known for fostering a spirit of cooperation and concern in the generation growing up. Garzón was not a revolutionary who advocated violence, he simply wanted to live in peace, his friends said.

U.S. military aid in Colombia was based on the "Fair Game Theory." A new Washington policy that maintained that as long as the FARC was engaged in an "unholy alliance" with powerful drug traffickers, the U.S. could funnel nearly $289 million in counternarcotic funds to the Colombian military for counterinsurgency warfare. Garzón, as well as President Pastrana, was of the opinion that the FARC was not involved in drug trafficking. The FARC taxed drug barons for protecting illegal crops, labs and clandestine airstrips, but they were not drug mules.

Pastrana admitted as much when he told an Argentine newspaper on July 28. "I've always said, and I repeat: I would never talk with the drug traffickers. We are trying to find a political solution to the guerrilla problem, and at the same time we are fighting the drugs trade," he said in an interview with *Clarin*, a daily Buenos Aires newspaper.

The FARC was fond of pointing out to international observers that the government has never captured a FARC guerrilla transporting drugs or prosecuted one for narcotrafficking. However, Colombian military intelligence officers said that Josué Eliseo Prieto, the FARC's financial chief, was killed on a raid of a drug installation in July 1999. The intelligence officers said they uncovered evidence at the drug installation that Prieto planned to use $3 million of illicit drug earnings to buy 30,000 AK-47 rifles.

Garzón, a gifted mimic, was considered "an aspirin for the country's pain."

He became a household name with hugely popular television shows "Zoo Society" and "Quac." Weekly from 1993 to 1997, the shows poked fun at Colombia's biggest political corruption scandal: the entry of millions of dollars in drug money into the election campaign of former President Samper.

A former street urchin who rose to become a magazine columnist and small-town mayor, Garzón created personas for his satires that were nearly always lower-class Colombians, revealing a strong affinity for the downtrodden.[69] Garzón's latest persona was Heriberto de la Calle, a toothless, humble, but perceptive shoeshine man whose conversations with the high and mighty were heard and watched by millions. At one point, Garzón outraged the military when he traveled to the Colombian jungles with a camera crew for one of his television skits to shine the combat boots of a FARC guerrilla leader.

In a joint communiqué, the country's human right groups denounced the slaying as a deliberate attempt to silence the voices of peace, force an end to dialogue with armed groups, and plunge Colombia into total war. Colleagues at Radionet cried on the air when they broke the news to the nation. "It's as if, in the United States, they had assassinated Woody Allen. It's the equivalent of killing Charlie Chaplin," said friend and fellow actor Luis Fernando Orozco, explaining Garzón's appeal.

Colonel Germán Jaramillo, head of the Colombian DAS secret police, blamed the nation's ultraright death squads for Garzón's slaying. "Everything points to the fact that Carlos Castaño is responsible," he told Reuters. But Castaño, who managed the dirty war with the aid of corrupt members of the military, strongly denied the charge.

The ultra right-wing in Colombia was a political force. In the 1998 presidential elections retired General Harold Bedoya, who ran as an Independent Party candidate and advocated a war of annihilation against the insurgents, represented them. However, the nation soundly rejected Bedoya's tough military tactics and opted for Pastrana's promise to seek peace.

El Tiempo and *El Espectador* came out swinging. They heroically dared to point a finger at the most powerful institution in Colombia — the military. Francisco Santos of *El Tiempo,* and Rafael Pardo of *El Espectador,* risked the same fate as Garzón when they published scathing articles accusing "the military extreme right" of involvement in the murder of Colombia's beloved comic. Pardo went so far as to insinuate that General Jorge Enrique Mora was a cohort of Castaño. Mora vehemently denied the allegations in an interview that was featured on the front cover of *Semana.*

The military fought back. "It is a crime we reject and repudiate and we are willing to cooperate with State organizations to clarify it," said the commander of the military forces, General Fernando Tapias.

Tapias and other senior members of the military were not completely loyal to Pastrana. They were now regularly contradicting the President in public and parroting the ultraright rhetoric that the FARC was a "narco" organization. Military leaders also reacted angrily when the public suspected them of collusion with the death squads. Overall, the military was seething. Observers were puzzled as to why Pastrana allowed such a blatant schism in the peace process.

The Police also said that they suspected Garzón was slain by gunmen from a right-wing death squad.[70] The comic had received death threats in the past week and was trying to arrange a meeting with the country's death squad top gun, Carlos Castaño, to discuss the warnings.

Garzón was known to have angered the Colombian extreme right by promoting talks between the Pastrana government and guerrillas. Antonio Navarro Wolf, a Colombian Congressman and former M-19 guerrilla, said Garzón had told him about the threats. "I told him, Jaime, this is serious. In this country, they kill people."[71] Wolf feared a "wave of aggression" against the nation's civilian peace activists. As for the peace activists themselves, they were trembling: the political assassination of Garzón conveyed to them a chilling "we can get you anywhere and anytime" message.

It was clear to the citizens of Colombia that the death squads were plotting against Pastrana. Reuters reported the existence of a new ultrafascist death squad created to kill high-profile backers of the peace process. "I've found out that they're organizing an ultra-fascist death squad composed of some 4,000 men," a highly regarded political analyst told the news agency.[72] "It seems they are made up of retired military men indignant at the way Pastrana is making concessions to the guerrillas."

Wealthy groups and individuals in the northern section of Bogotá, the analyst said, were financing the new unit. He added that those close to the secret project told him Garzón was one of about five top peace advocates on the death list. He said government Peace Commissioner Víctor Ricardo could be another likely target.[73]

The *Economist* also reported the existence of the 4,000 member "New ultra-right organization led by retired military officers and financed by wealthy Colombian businessmen."

The National Front was finally over. On August 7, 1974, Liberal Party candidate Alfonso López Michelsen was inaugurated as President. Technically, he was the first freely elected president of Colombia since Laureano Gómez. However, since Conser-vative violence prevented full Liberal participation in the 1950 election, and the National Front selected presidents from 1958 to 1970, López truly was the first freely elected president of Colombia since the elections of 1946.

Thus, the citizens of Colombia finally selected a president in an unhindered election after a dreadfully long wait of 28 years. The oligarchy, though, was still alive and well, as witnessed by the candidates in the election — perhaps the rarest field ever seen in modern electoral history. The top three presidential candidates were all children of former presidents: Alfonso López Michelsen, son of President Alfonso López Pumarejo (1942–46); María Eugenia Rojas de Moreno Díaz, daughter of President Gustavo Rojas Pinilla (1953–57); and Alvaro Gómez Hurtado, son of President Laureano Gómez (1950–53).

In 1974 a new law required power sharing in all administrations. Article 120 was created to provide adequate and equitable participation for the minority party in each government. Hence, from 1974 onwards each administration would include opposition party politicians in the cabinet. The López government, though, would be the first in the history of Colombia to start sharing the nation with a new power broker … drug traffickers. (In Colombian vernacular, they were christened Narcos or Mafia.) The flow of easy money into the country in the early 1970s gave birth to an extremely seductive force that would eventually corrupt the nation.

Colombia's arrival as a major player in the international drug market took place in 1975, during the López government. Two years earlier, the U.S. had established the Drug Enforcement Administration (DEA). Also in 1975, the DEA, in one of its first major international operations, pressured Mexico into launching a massive drug interdiction operation that virtually wiped out the centralized marijuana crop.

Thus, the Colombian Narcos took full advantage of the dearth of supply on the market and quickly took over as the center of marijuana production. Within two years, Colombia was providing 70 percent of the marijuana in the U.S.

The cocaine trade was also expanding, and was using a sophisticated system of planes, boats and human donkeys to bring its precious commodity into the states. As a result, hundreds of millions of dollars were now pouring back into Colombia. The nation was flush with cash and members of the lower classes that rushed into the "trade association" now had the power and riches to rub elbows with the ruling elite.

The López administration failed to recognize the danger of the easy money, and its response to the hundreds of millions of dollars coming into the country was to facilitate it. In a questionable move, López welcomed the Narco dollars by opening the "ventanilla siniestra" or left-hand window, at the nations' Central Bank (Banco de la República) whereby anyone who walked up could exchange dollars for pesos with no questions asked whatsoever. Other dollars entered the economy through the long-flourishing black market for the currency. However, due to the López decision, soon dollars were worth less on the black market than they were in official exchange. Many other dollars were simply not brought into the country but placed in banks and investments in other countries. The importance of the new drug income cannot be understated. Colombia now had the devil in its backyard.

The Narcos played by their own rules, and with time, they wanted nobody to get in their way. They quickly established a tradition of corruption that offered two options, compliance or death. They would soften the selling of one's soul to the devil with enormous bribes. It was a vicious game, and thousands of honest government officials and legitimate businessmen in giant, medium and small enterprises became corrupted; many others and their family members would lose their lives bravely standing up to the ruthless and uncouth Narco criminals.

The first American Narcocasualty in Colombia was Octavio González, the DEA special agent in charge of the Bogotá office. On Monday, December 13, 1976, González, who was seriously trying to combat drug trafficking, was shot to death in his office by a Narco-assassin. The killer committed suicide when he found his escape blocked by U.S. Marines who rushed to the scene from the nearby embassy.

Unfortunately, U.S. attempts to alert López to the dangers of the mushrooming drug trade were complicated by the icy relationship the President maintained with American Ambassador Phillip V. Sanchez. The two men barely spoke to one another. López reportedly could not hide his contempt for Sanchez.

Former diplomat Robert Drexler, who served in the embassy at that time, concluded that the appointment of Sanchez by President Gerald Ford was "the worst ambassadorial appointment to Bogotá since President John Quincy Adams' posting of William Henry Harrison in 1828."[74]

Sanchez reportedly intended on coasting through his assignment with the barest attention to official business and was famous for his lack of propriety and fondness of the nightlife in Bogotá.[75] Therefore, the U.S. must assume some of the blame for the López government's lack of effort combating the growing influence of the Narcos from 1974 to 1978. Sadly, post–Watergate America was a divided country and Washington took its eye off the ball at a critical time, allowing the Narcos to establish an important beachhead in Colombia.

On another important front, the López government was serious about the peace process. López attempted to reach out and broker a peace by sitting down and negotiating an accord with the guerrillas. However, the peace talks were sabotaged by the Colombian military's systematic blocking of any negotiations with the ELN, which the armed forces were convinced they could quickly annihilate.[76] So the López years would be marked with a continuation of the armed struggle by guerrillas in the countryside and the appearance on the national scene of flashy big spenders. The new Narco multimillionaires considered themselves hardworking businessmen and desperately wanted to be accepted into the highest social strata of Colombian society.

President Pastrana was in serious trouble in August 1999. He had just celebrated his one-year anniversary in office and the national polls indicated he had lost the confidence of most of the country. Moreover, the United States was growing increasingly impatient with the lack of progress in the peace process and was pushing him hard to work out a new strategy. It was obvious that Pastrana was losing credibility among the power brokers in Washington.

Intellectually, the lack of support was unfair. When Pastrana was sworn in on August 7, 1998, no one in the world anticipated a peace agreement in one year. The guerrillas had been fighting the government since the death of Gaitán on April 9, 1948, and the drug traffickers had taken 25 years and billions of dollars to organize their sophisticated network. But the truth was, fair or otherwise, with only one year in office, the President's popularity had collapsed, and he now was one of Colombia's most unpopular figures.[77]

Pastrana was a flop in the polls. The numbers were so lopsided against him that influential politicians in Colombia were whispering that he would not complete his four-year term, that he would eventually step down to prevent the disintegration of the Republic. The influential *El Tiempo* said, "The most revealing fact is that President Pastrana now has a higher unfavorable rating than any other personality in national public life, exceeded only by the main actors in the armed conflict."[78]

A survey of 511 adults carried out for *El Tiempo* by the Napoleón Franco polling company in six of the largest cities showed 66 percent had an unfavorable image of Pastrana while 30 percent supported him. By comparison, 67 percent said they had a bad impression of Carlos Castaño, the country's ruthless paramilitary death squad top dog; however, just 9 percent said they had a positive view of him. It was mind-boggling. The man who butchered innocent citizens was only one tiny percentage point less popular than Pastrana. One man was a murderous hawk, the other a dove, and yet the people disliked them nearly equally. It was a frightening statistical phenomenon.

More than half those questioned in the poll said they disagreed with President Pastrana's efforts. Seventy percent of the Colombians in the poll believed the government had no clear strategy in the peace process, reflecting criticism that Pastrana had ceded too much to the rebels for virtually nothing in return. Just one-fifth of the respondents said they backed Pastrana's management of the economy.

The respected *El Espectador* daily also reported the President's unpopularity. It headlined a center spread that said, "Pastrana Flunks the Year." Using findings of a Gallup poll, the paper said that support for Pastrana, who was elected with the biggest vote in Colombian election history, had slumped to 21 percent and was only about half the support that his predecessor Ernesto Samper had enjoyed at the same point in his administration.[79] Citing a poll carried out by the National Consultancy Center in August 1995, the paper said Samper had 41 percent support after a year in office.

Further damage to Pastrana's popularity took place one week later. Moody's Investors Service, the highly regarded grading agency, erased the last vestige of Colombia's reputation for economic stability. Moody's stripped Colombia of its prized investment-grade rating, which guaranteed low-price foreign loans. The rating had provided Colombia with bragging rights on Wall Street. Only two countries in all of Latin America were investment-grade borrowers—now there was only one ... Chile. In simple terms, investment grade meant that a nation's economic fundamentals were healthy.

The *Economist* reported in an article titled "Supermodel angst" that the Colombian economy was in the worst recession in almost 70 years. "This sounds the death knell for Colombia's good economic reputation," Leonardo Bravo, an analyst with the Bogotá-based brokerage Corredores Asociados, told Reuters.[80] The two-notch downgrade in Colombia's long-term foreign currency ceiling for bonds and notes came against the backdrop of the troubling recession and the internal civil conflict. "The last thing we had was our investment grade credit rating and now that's gone," Bravo said. Industry analysts said it would take between two and five years to restore grading agency confidence. The bottom line on the financial rating downgrade was that Colombia would have to spend more to borrow funds abroad.

Initially, Finance Minister Juan Camilo Restrepo blasted the Moody's decision, calling it "Unjust and rash."[81] However, after considerable thought he relented and said Colombia's economy could indeed shrink by as much as 2 percent in that fiscal year, 1999—an admission that made it evident that Colombia was in one of its worst economic recessions ever.[82] The political significance of the recession and the downgrade was that Colombia was not in a financial position to pay for the escalation in the civil conflict or for the implementation of important social reforms, and would have to turn to the United States to secure additional military and economic assistance.

On September 15, 1999, the secret ultra right-wing death squads in Bogotá murdered another major Colombian peace activist. At approximately 6:40 P.M., Jesús Antonio Bejarano, 53, was shot once in the head as he was leaving his classroom where he taught economics in the Universidad Nacional. A student witness who caught a glimpse of the political murder said that there were two assassins and only one took out a gun and fired. The medical examiner that pronounced Bejarano dead said the executioner fired one round directly to the forehead.

Bejarano, an intellectual, who authored masterpieces on the Colombian economy, had been the country's tough peace commissioner in President César Gaviria's government (1990–94), and afterwards had taken part in the historic peace accord that ended the civil war in El Salvador. President Pastrana's peace commissioner, Víctor Ricardo, said the crime attacked a society that was clamoring for an end to the violence and for respect for human rights.

Former President César Gaviria said the criminal act took away from Colombia a man who had devoted his life to the construction of peace. The following evening university students conducted a candlelight vigil in memory of their beloved professor.

Bejarano was a persuasive advocate of social reforms and was respected across the country for his dedication to human rights. As a young man he was politically associated with socialists and maintained friends in the Communist Party. As was the case with Jaime Garzón, the police suspected ultra right-wing death squads, determined to silence a voice for peace, had carried out the assassination. However, unlike with Garzón there were no allegations in the media that the military had played a role in the political assassination. "He was killed right under our noses," read the headline in *El Tiempo* the morning after the murder.

Intellectuals speculated that Bejarano was executed because of his credibility throughout the country with young university students. Therefore, political analysts concluded that the death squads attempted to intimidate the media with the assassination of Garzón, and they wanted to send a warning to the academic community with the murder of Bejarano. The next logical step was the government, according to the analysts. Many influential Colombians thought the next target was Víctor Ricardo and feared for the safety of the peace commissioner. Ricardo publicly responded by criticizing opponents of the peace talks, "Who wanted to win the war from the safety of their own sofas."

The war on drugs was ravaging Colombia and the United States. Experts realized that both nations were fighting a losing battle. The former four-star general, Barry McCaffrey, calculated that 52,000 Americans died every year from drugs and drug-related violence, and he was particularly alarmed by the "new industrial techniques" used in Colombian drug labs for increasing the potency of cocaine and heroin, which could only make matters worse. McCaffrey wanted the Clinton administration and Congress to dramatically increase aid to Colombia to help the government take back parts of their country from guerrillas and paramilitaries in order to destroy coca and poppy fields.

As Director of U.S. drug policy, General McCaffrey was an enormous advocate of investing in prevention and treatment programs at home. At the same time, as a military man, he was deeply disturbed that funds from American drug users were financing guerrillas and paramilitary death squads. It troubled him that drug income was threatening democracy in Colombia, and he knew beyond a shadow of a doubt that Colombia was unlikely to advance in its fight against the drug traffickers unless it received additional drug interdiction aid from the United States. To McCaffrey, the bottom line was that the flow of dollars from U.S. consumers to drug traffickers, guerrillas, and paramilitary death squads meant an increased production in Colombia that would likely result in more drugs shipped to the United States.

All in all, there were many theories on how to fight the war on drugs. The political left, center and right had competing ideas on how to combat drug use in the United States. In 1999, Ron Chepesiuk published *Hard Target; The United States War Against International Drug Trafficking, 1982–1997,*[83] which offered a pragmatic view on how America should approach the drug problem.

"Law enforcement worldwide … should continue to interdict drugs and try to put the drug syndicates out of business, but the ill effects of 15 years of failed anti-drug policy can be reversed only by changing priorities and moving from a punitive law-and-order strategy to one that offers more flexibility and stresses harm reduction, not prohibition; treatment, not punishment; and gets at the economic and social roots of the international drug problem," he said.[84]

Patrick L. Clawson and Rensselaer W. Lee III wrote a clear-eyed analysis of the Latin American cocaine business in their book, *The Andean Cocaine Industry,* and took the drug argument one step further by examining an explosive taboo … the controversial subject of legalization.[85]

"We cannot wipe out drug production in source countries or stop drug exports" Clawson and Rensselaer wrote. "The potential supply of drugs is virtually unlimited; trafficking routes and points of entry into the United States are multitudinous; and once destroyed laboratories, drug shipments, planes, money, chemicals, and other trafficking assets can be replaced easily.... What can the United States do in face of these barriers to controlling the Andean cocaine trade?

"Legalization is too extreme in the other direction. Many proponents of legalization argue that such a step will take most of the profits out of smuggling and distribution. However, legalization is not a panacea for crime. Look at the U.S. history. Prohibition spawned the growth of major criminal enterprises in the United States, but when Prohibition was repealed and alcohol again became legal, these criminal enterprises just expanded into new areas ... drugs, loan sharking, gambling and the like."[86]

The call to legalize drugs in the United States came from the intellectual spark of the conservative movement, Nobel Prize–winning economist Milton Friedman. However, other important Americans such as former Secretary of State George P. Schultz and conservative columnist William F. Buckley also echoed Friedman's call for decriminalization but they failed to convert the political establishment to their viewpoint. However, in a 1991 interview on "America's Drug Forum," a national public affairs talk show that appeared on public television stations, Friedman openly discussed the legalization of drugs in the United States and defended his conclusions.[87]

Friedman was a senior research fellow at the Hoover Institution on War, Revolution, and Peace at Stanford University and was considered the leader of the Chicago School of monetary economics. He won the Nobel Memorial Prize in Economic Science in 1976, and was also the recipient of the National Medal of Science and the Presidential Medal of Freedom from the U.S. government in 1988. *Fortune* magazine went as far as to call Friedman the "economist of the century."

The appearance on the public television station program provided an excellent platform for Friedman's sharp-edged analysis. When the moderator of "America's Drug Forum" asked Friedman how he saw the issue of legalization of drugs changing America for the better, he said, "I see America with half the number of prisons, half the number of prisoners, ten thousand fewer homicides a year, inner cities in which there's a chance for these poor people to live without being afraid for their lives, citizens who might be respectable who are now addicts not being subject to becoming criminals in order to get their drug, being able to get drugs for which they're sure of the quality. Under prohibition of alcohol, deaths from alcohol poisoning, from poisoning by things that were mixed in with the bootleg alcohol, went up sharply. Similarly, under drug prohibition, deaths from overdose, from adulterations, from adulterated substances have gone up."

On the subject of how legalization would adversely affect America, Friedman said, "The one adverse effect that legalization might have is that there very likely would be more people taking drugs. That's not by any means clear. But, if you legalized, you destroy the black market, the price of drugs would go down drastically. And as an economist, lower prices tend to generate more demand."

Friedman continued the legalization discussion by saying, "Prohibition was repealed in 1933 when I was 21 years old, so I was a teenager during most of Prohibition. Alcohol was readily available. Bootlegging was common. Any idea that alcohol prohibition was keeping people from drinking was absurd. There were speakeasies all over the place. But more than that. We had this spectacle of Al Capone, of the hijackings, of the gang wars. Anybody with two eyes could see that this was a bad deal, that you were doing more harm than good. In addition, I became an economist. And as an economist, I came to recognize the importance of markets and of free choice and of consumer sovereignty and came to discover the harm that was done when you interfered with them."

The Nobel economist was then asked, "For us to understand the real root of your beliefs, how about if we just talk a minute about free market economic perspective, and how you see the proper role of government in its dealings with the individual?" Friedman responded by saying, "The proper role of government is exactly what John Stuart Mill said in the middle of the 19th century in *On Liberty*. The proper role of government is to prevent other people from harming an individual. Government, he said, never has any right to interfere with an individual for that individual's own good."

The national public affairs talk show moderator then followed with the observation, "Well, I would bet that former drug czar William Bennett, some other folks along those lines, would probably suggest that the present sale and distribution of illegal drugs is, in fact, an enterprise which harms another person and the government has to step in to protect the vulnerable."

Friedman answered by saying, "It does harm a great many other people, but primarily because it's prohibited. There are an enormous number of innocent victims now. You've got the people whose purses are stolen, who are bashed over the head by people trying to get enough money for their next fix. You've got the people killed in the random drug wars. You've got the corruption of the legal establishment. You've got the innocent victims who are taxpayers who have to pay for more and more prisons, and more and more prisoners, and more and more police. You've got the rest of us who don't get decent law enforcement because all the law enforcement officials are busy trying to do the impossible.

"And, last, but not least, you've got the people of Colombia and Peru and so on. What business do we have destroying and leading to the killing of thousands of people in Colombia because we cannot enforce our own laws? If we could enforce our laws against drugs, there would be no market for these drugs. You wouldn't have Colombia in the state it's in.... But I don't believe that legalization should be viewed primarily as a way to help the poor. Legalization is a way to stop ... in our forum as citizens ... a government from using our power to engage in the immoral behavior of killing people, taking lives away from people in the U.S., in Colombia and elsewhere, which we have no business doing."

Notes

1. *Bloomberg News,* "Colombia Sacks 3 Top Officers, Arrests 6 in Drug Smuggling Case," Bogotá, 13 November 1998.

2. Carlos Linares, Reuters, "Death, Destruction Hang Over Colombian Jungle Town," Puerto Lleras, 12 July 1999.

3. Associated Press, "Fighting Reported South of Bogotá," Bogotá, 8 July 1999.

4. Karl Penhaul, Reuters, "52 Die in Heavy Clashes in Mountains Near Bogotá," Bogotá, 8 July 1999.

5. Bogotá troop strength communicated to author at clandestine meeting in Colombia by Senior FARC commander, September 1999. (Colombian military intelligence says the FARC has only 300 to 400 urban guerrillas in Bogotá.)

6. Karl Penhaul, Reuters, "Colombia Army, Rebels Clash Near Bogotá," Bogotá, 8 July 1999.

7. *Ibid.*

8. *Ibid.*

9. Reuters, "Colombia Army Says Killed 64 Rebels in Clashes," Bogotá, 10 July 1999.

10. *Ibid.*

11. Martin Hodgson, Associated Press, "Colombian Rebel Offensive Continues," Bogotá, 11 July 1999.

12. *Ibid.*

13. Ruth Morris, *Los Angeles Times,* "Colombian Guerrillas Defy Latest Crackdown," Bogotá, 11 July 1999.

14. Karl Penhaul, Reuters, "Colombia Rebel Offensive Rages, Death Toll Unclear," Bogotá, 11 July 1999.

15. *Ibid.*

16. *Ibid.*

17. Larry Rohter, *New York Times,* "As Colombia Declares an Alert, Rebel Offensive Rages On," Rio de Janeiro, 12 July 1999.

18. Jared Kotler, Associated Press, "Colombia Gov't Solidifies Control," Bogotá, 13 July 1999.

19. Author interview with FARC, Colombia, September 1999.

20. *Ibid.*

21. Tod Robberson, *Dallas Morning News,* "More Colombians Elect to Leave Homeland as War With Rebels Rages and Social Woes Mount," Bogotá, 16 July 1999.

22. Tod Robberson, *Dallas Morning News,* "Colombia Says Rebels Repelled," Bogotá, 13 July 1999.

23. Karl Penhaul, Reuters, "Sporadic Clashes, Colombia Says Rebels Routed," Bogotá, 13 July 1999.

24. *Ibid.*

25. *Ibid.*

26. Joshua Hammer and Michael Isikoff, *Newsweek,* "The Narco-Guerrilla War, A mysterious U.S. Army Plane Highlights the Pentagon's Biggest Covert Operation in Latin America," Bogotá, 9 August 1999.

27. *Ibid.*

28. Marko Alvarez, Associated Press, "Colombian Army Displays Dead Rebels," Granada, Colombia, 13 July 1999.

29. *Ibid.*

30. *Ibid.*

31. Patricia Zengerle, Reuters, "Colombian Army Beat Rebels in Fighting — US general," Fort Benning, 15 July 1999.

32. *Ibid.*

33. Reuters, "Clinton Lauds Colombia Peace Efforts," Washington, 21 July 1999.

34. *Ibid.*

35. Tod Robberson, *Dallas Morning News,*

"U.S. Aid Questioned in Colombian Battle. S. American Nation's Military Denies Hitting Civilian Areas," Puerto Lleras, 16 August 1999.

36. *Ibid.*

37. *Ibid.*

38. *Ibid.*

39. *Ibid.*

40. *Ibid.*

41. *Ibid.*

42. Reuters, "US Blames Colombia Rebels for Peace Talks Collapse," Washington, 19 July 1999.

43. *Ibid.*

44. *Ibid.*

45. Saul Hudson, Reuters, "Analysis — Latam Leaves Colombia Crisis to U.S.," Lima, 30 August 1999.

46. *Ibid.*

47. *Ibid.*

48. *Ibid.*

49. Associated Press, "GOP Worries Colombia Could Become Another Vietnam," Washington, 6 August 1999.

50. *Ibid.*

51. *Ibid.*

52. *Ibid.*

53. *Ibid.*

54. *Ibid.*

55. Hearing before the Committee on International Relations, House of Representatives, One Hundred Fifth Congress, second session, "U.S. Counter-Narcotics Policy Toward Colombia," 31 March 1998.

56. Hearing before the Committee on International Relations, House of Representatives, One Hundred Fifth Congress, second session, "U.S. Counter-Narcotics Policy Toward Colombia," 26 February 1998.

57. Tim Johnson, *Miami Herald,* "Signals from downed U.S. Plane Detected, but Clouds Hide Location," Bogotá, 25 July 1999.

58. *Ibid.*

59. Tod Robberson, *Dallas Morning News,* "2 U.S. Pilots Die on Colombian Anti-narcotics Mission," 29 July 1999.

60. *Ibid.*

61. Tod Robberson, *Dallas Morning News,* "Wreckage of Spy Plane on Drug Mission spotted in Colombia," Bogotá, 27 July 1999.

62. *Ibid.*

63. Karl Penhaul, Reuters, "Rescuers pull dead from US plane crash in Colombia," Bogotá, 28 July 1999.

64. *Ibid.*

65. Karl Penhaul, Reuters, "Colombians

See Wider US Role in Rebel War," Bogotá, 30 July 1999.

66. Tim Johnson, *Miami Herald*, "U.S. Diplomat Tries to Allay Invasion Fear in Colombia," Bogotá, 11 August 1999.

67. Frank Bajak, Associated Press, "Colombia Mourns Satirist, Activist," Bogotá, 14 August 1999.

68. *Ibid.*

69. John Otis, *Houston Chronicle*, "Famed Colombian Humorist Slain," Bogotá, 13 August 1999.

70. *Ibid.*

71. Karl Penhaul, Reuters, "Colombian Death Squads Said to Plot Against Peace," Bogotá, 15 August 1999.

72. *Ibid.*

73. Robert W. Drexler, *Colombia and the United States: Narcotics Traffic and a Failed Foreign Policy* (Jefferson, N.C.: McFarland & Company, 1997), p. 92.

74. *Ibid.*, p.94.

75. Harvey F. Kline, *Colombia, Democracy Under Assault*, 2nd ed. (Boulder: Westview Press, 1990), p. 58.

76. *Ibid.*

77. Reuters, "Colombia's Pastrana Deeply Unpopular, Poll Says," Bogotá, 1 August 1999.

78. *Ibid.*

79. *Ibid.*

80. Karl Penhaul, Reuters, "Death Knell Sounds for Colombia Economic Image," Bogotá, 11 August 1999.

81. Javier Mozzo, Reuters, "Interview — Colombia Minister Sees Recession Deepening," Bogotá, 12 August 1999.

82. *Ibid.*

83. Ron Chepesiuk, *Hard Target: The United States War Against International Drug Trafficking, 1982–1997* (Jefferson, N.C.: McFarland & Company, 1999).

84. *Ibid.*, p. 276.

85. Patrick L. Clawson and Rensselaer W. Lee III, *The Andean Cocaine Industry* (New York: St. Martin's Press, 1998).

86. *Ibid.* pp. 239–241.

87. Schaffer Library of Drug Policy, "Interview with Milton Friedman on the Drug War," internet; http:www.druglibrary.org/schaffer/Misc/friedm1.htm.

CHAPTER EIGHT

Death Squads

In reality, paramilitary groups are responsible for twice as many homicides in Colombia than the guerrillas. — President Belisario Betancur, October 1983.

I am against paramilitaries. They are nothing but "Terrorist Organizations." In reality, their victims are not guerrillas. They are men, women, and even children, who have not taken up arms against institutions. They are peaceful Colombians! — President Virgilio Barco, April 1989.

The National Strategy Against Violence acknowledges that one of the most important factors contributing to violence in Colombia is the illegal bearing of arms, and in it, the government will take steps to rid the country of illegally held arms. The measures put forth in the Strategy will be employed rigorously; weapons will be taken out of the hands of paramilitary actors. — President César Gaviria, December 1991.

We took Bedoya out because of human rights. [In 1997, the Colombian government forced the retirement of General Harold Bedoya, whose hostility to human rights and career-long association with joint army-paramilitary operations was notorious, according to Human Rights Watch's "War Without Quarter" report.] — President Ernesto Samper, September 1997.

Colombian witnesses frequently state that massacres are perpetrated by members of the armed forces passing themselves off as paramilitaries, or by paramilitaries enjoying the complicity, support, or acquiescence of the regular forces. — United Nations High Commissioner for Human Rights, March 1998.

No peace can be conceived without silencing the arms [of the paramilitaries], a task which must be carried out as an exclusive responsibility of the state. — President Andrés Pastrana, January 1999.

The [Colombian] Government's human rights record remained poor; there was some improvement in several areas, and the Pastrana administration took measures to initiate structural reform, but serious problems remain. Government forces continued to commit numerous, serious abuses, including extra judicial killings.... Despite some prosecutions and convictions, the authorities rarely brought officers of the security forces and the police charged with human rights offenses to justice, and impunity remains a problem. At times the security forces collaborated with paramilitary groups that committed abuses; in some instances, individual members of the security forces actively collaborated with members of paramilitary groups by passing them through roadblocks, sharing intelligence, and providing them with ammunition. Paramilitary forces find a ready support base within the military and police, as well as local civilian elites in many areas.— United States Department of State, 1999 Colombia Report on Human Rights Practices, February 2000.

Far from moving decisively to sever ties to paramilitaries, Human Rights Watch's evidence strongly suggests that Colombia's military high command has yet to take the necessary steps to accomplish this goal. Human Rights Watch's information implicates Colombian Army Brigades operating in the country's three largest cities, including the capital, Bogotá. If Colombia's leaders cannot or will not halt these units' support for paramilitary groups, the government's resolve to end human rights abuse in units that receive U.S. security assistance must be seriously questioned.— Human Rights Watch, February 2000.

What will change the human rights situation [in Colombia] is political will and that has been largely absent.— Carlos Salinas, Director for Amnesty International, March 2000.

In 1978, Liberal Party candidate, Julio César Turbay narrowly defeated Conservative Belisario Betancur in the race for the presidency and was duly inaugurated President of Colombia. Turbay's family was prominent, prosperous, and politically well-connected, but its Levantine origins caused some Colombians of better pedigree to look down on the new president and treat him as a "Turco."[1]

Turbay inherited a country riven with social unrest. Colombia was suffering from vast rural poverty, widespread insecurity, inadequate health and educational services in the countryside, unbalanced income distribution, unjust taxation practices, and patterns of land ownership that stifled progress. Turbay's solution to the social unrest was repression. His government was the most authoritarian in Colombia since the 1950s.[2]

Diplomatically, however, Turbay was the complete opposite of President López, who was considered an aloof stuffed shirt by most American officials and who maintained a frosty relationship with the United States from 1974 to 1978. Julio César Turbay was a breath of fresh air to the Americans. The President sported a trademark bow tie and had a backslapping, good-old-

boy personality that dramatically improved the diplomatic relationship in Bogotá. Moreover, Turbay readily established rapport with visiting American Congressmen concerned about the narcotics problem, whereas López Michelsen was usually distant in manner and often failed to win their confidence.[3] As a result, Turbay was able to quickly establish a warm relationship with the new U.S. Ambassador to Colombia, Diego Asencio.

Politically, President Turbay was a skilled manipulator whose loyalty was to the Liberal Party organization rather than to any set of theoretical principles.[4] He observed the constitutional requirement to share power, but entered office handicapped. Colombia was a mess. The President sought a nonviolent solution to the guerrilla problem with offers of amnesty to the belligerents in March 1981 and again in 1982. However, the amnesty offer was to all except those who had participated in "atrocious crimes" such as kidnapping, extortion, noncombat-related homicide, arson, the poisoning of water, and "acts of ferocity or barbarism." Few guerrillas were willing to come forward under these terms.

The Americans loved Turbay despite growing rumors that his government was rife with political patronage. His high-priority, "get-tough" attitude towards narcotics trafficking and his eagerness to work with the United States were a welcome relief to López Michelsen's unabashed conviction that America was solely to blame for the drug problem. Intellectually, López made a catastrophic mistake by failing to take effective measures against drug trafficking. In hindsight, Americans thought that at the start of the López presidency, the balance of forces between the Colombian government's enforcement authorities and the Narcos was probably tilted in favor of the government. However, that changed because López purposely gave drug trafficking a low priority and was unwilling to draw closer to the U.S. government in matters regarding internal affairs.

Washington considered Turbay the perfect candidate to wage war against drugs and cared little about anything else he did in Colombia. American officials were confident that the war against drugs could be won with the right partner in place and immediately went to work drawing up a dynamic counternarcotic policy. The desired objective was not that easy to attain, however. By the time Turbay was inaugurated, the narcotics industry had spread so widely and deeply that no Colombian president, no matter how courageous, able, and determined, could prevail against it.

Americans arriving during the Turbay administration would come to the painful conclusion that the war on drugs was already lost. They would learn that the Narcos had completely corrupted the López government. They also found out that in July of 1977, DEA Administrator Peter Bensinger met secretly with President López to warn him about the cancer within his government. Bensinger apparently insisted on meeting with López with no other Colombian officials present in order to deliver a report of about ten pages citing the names and activities of Colombians holding important government positions whom the U.S. strongly suspected of being on the payroll of the Narcos.

Amazingly, López ignored the report and did not act to clean up the widespread corruption. Americans quickly concluded that López cared little that Narcos had crawled into the highest levels of his government. The drug traffickers were entrenched across the country and had established a strategic head start on the DEA during the López Administration. Thanks to López, the Narcos had managed to build a well-organized criminal enterprise and were not going to be easy targets for the DEA during the Turbay government, no matter how cooperative the new President.

By the time Turbay took office, the Narcos had already put dozens of strategic middle-level government bureaucrats on their payroll in order to know every move of the new administration, according to former DEA officials. Moreover, the Narcos were using heavy four-engine planes to transport cocaine, and they owned large vessels, "mother ships," capable of transporting tons of marijuana. In the United States, powerful drug bosses from Medellín muscled into Miami, killing off Cuban rivals and establishing a strong base there. Cali bosses infiltrated New York City (however, with less bloodshed), setting up shop in Jackson Heights in the borough of Queens. In reality, Turbay was not fighting a war against drugs in 1978, he was fighting a war for control of Colombia.

Turbay pacified the Americans with his can-do attitude towards the drug war and then unleashed the armed forces in a bloody campaign to wipe out the guerrillas. He appointed General Luis Camacho Leiva, a hard-liner, the Minister of Defense. Consequently, the military understood that the mission was to annihilate the FARC, ELN and M-19 guerrillas and that the President would turn a blind eye to how they went about doing it. Soon, the

Turbay administration would face charges from human rights activists that the army was engaged in arbitrary arrests, using torture, and causing people to "disappear" in the worst tradition of Latin American military brutality.

Turbay unwittingly had a secret weapon at his disposal: he received considerable help hunting down the insurgents from an unlikely source — Narco death squads. Moreover, the Narcos were taking advantage of a growing Colombian resentment of the United States. For decades there had been a love-hate relationship with the U.S. Colombians admired the U.S. for its economic aid and because a growing number of them had many American personal and family relationships; they respected American scientific and technological achievements. On the other hand, though, they resented the U.S. because they thought Americans were rich, and because they thought Americans exploited them by forcing unfair trade terms on them. The Narcos shrewdly nurtured this resentment.

The guerrillas battled and counterattacked. They also increased kidnappings to finance the bloody war with the Turbay government. In January 1981, the M-19 took out its rage on an American: they kidnapped a linguist and lay missionary, Allen Bitterman, from his office in Bogotá. The M-19 alleged that Bitterman was CIA and his group an agency front company, which, they asserted, was an affront to the cultural integrity of indigenous Colombians. The guerrillas demanded that the group be expelled from the country; when Turbay refused, Bitterman was found murdered, wrapped in an M-19 flag, on a Bogotá street. It was during this era that the normally urban M-19 guerrilla organization participated in rural activities in Chocó and the Nariño-Putumayo areas.

A critical historical benchmark in the evolution of Colombian death squad violence took place at a secret national convention of Narco bosses in December 1981. Prior to that date, Colombian paramilitary death squads were legally set up (Law 48 of 1968) by the armed forces as part of an official antiguerrilla strategy. The Narcos took the strategy one step further. The Narcos were angry and intent on ending the guerrilla practice of kidnapping Colombians for ransom to finance their subversive activities. During the 1981 convention they pledged $7.5 million to create the "Death to Kidnappers" (Muerte a Secuestradores, MAS) death squad.

The drug-financed death squad was to protect "Honest hard-working Narco-gang bosses" and conduct search and destroy missions to eliminate the threat of guerrillas. The Narco bosses would go on to hire British and Israeli mercenaries to train MAS and secretly established firm relationships with senior military officials to coordinate warfare against the guerrillas. However, the Narcos had other sinister intentions. They feared the American aided Turbay war on drugs and engineered a wave of killings in a strategy designed to undermine the entire judicial system and to strike fear into the hearts of ordinary Colombians. Some of those MAS assassinations were even carried out with the cooperation of corrupt army and police officials, according to well-informed Americans.

María Jimena Duzán was a journalist who risked her life investigating the violence in Colombia. She documented her harrowing descent into Colombia's netherworld in her book, *Death Beat: A Colombian Journalist's Life Inside the Cocaine Wars.*[5] In 1982, she traveled into Colombia's rain forest to interview Jaime Bateman, the founding father of the M-19. Publicly, Bateman claimed that Duzán was kidnapped by the M-19, so that she would not be a target of death squads. She stayed with the guerrillas for more than one month. When she returned to Bogotá still stinking of the guerrilla encampment, she wrote an account of her adventure before going home and washing the filth off. When Duzán finally entered her apartment, it blew up. Just after she recovered consciousness and discovered that she was not badly injured, the phone rang. "The bomb was set by MAS, bitch," said a man with a deep voice. "The next time, we'll kill you!" Duzán went into hiding.

Most of the Narco military cooperation was secured with bundles of American dollars. The drug trade was a cash cow. Honest, cash starved, military brass and politicians throughout Colombia soon saw rivals living in the fast lane, with lavish homes, splendid cars, fantastic family vacations to Disney World and questionable investments. Colombians in the countryside initially welcomed the Narco protection and that of other notorious death squad leaders such as Ramón Isaza, but they quickly realized that the ruthless paramilitary guerrilla campaigns often killed indiscriminately and saw human rights violations multiply. Through MAS and groups like it, the Turbay government was able to inflict tremendous losses on the guerrillas; they nearly wiped out the ELN. In that process, however, the government consistently conducted gross violations of human rights across the Colombian countryside and Turbay's severely repressive security measures created the greatest violence in Colombia since the days of *La Violencia,* 30 years earlier.

Father Javier Giraldo, a human rights activist and author of the book *Colombia, The Genocidal Democracy,* recorded a chilling account of the terror in the countryside.[6] With icy precision and passionate prose, Father Giraldo described scenes from the dirty war. "I will never forget the first week I spent in Caquetá in April of 1982. The large number of denunciations of torture, disappearance and murder that

we had been receiving prompted me to travel to the region. When I arrived at midday at the modest dwelling of several members of the religious community and asked them if I could set up a meeting with family members of some of the area's victims, one of them looked at me and smiled. Just take a seat over there Father. There are so many that come to tell us what happened to them and how they have suffered … well, just sit down for a moment, she said.

"She was right. I spent the next four full days taking notes and taping interviews, taking time out only to visit two nearby villages and talk to more victims. When I returned to Bogotá, I took with me a macabre list of 144 murder victims; some of them had been subjected to extreme cruelty, and 240 cases of torture. In those days, there was no doubt as to whom [*sic*]was responsible for these atrocities; soldiers killed and tortured openly in front of numerous witnesses. But it was impossible to identify them because, before committing crimes, they removed the identification they were required to wear by law."

Father Giraldo documented another tragic scene from the dirty war. "Alvaro Ulcué Chocué was an Indian priest. When he was ordained in 1973, the ceremony made the national news because it was so very rare than an Indian entered the priesthood. A theology student at the time, I felt especially happy for him, as I had always been particularly sympathetic to the struggles of the Indians of Cauca department, heroic survivors of five centuries of oppression. I subsequently met Alvaro at different national meetings of Christian groups. Humble and soft-spoken, he was nevertheless totally committed to the liberation of his people.

"It was not long, however, before Alvaro's decision to work and struggle alongside his own people put him directly into conflict with the region's large landowners whose interests were in opposition to those of the Indians. After he suggested that his Indian parishioners stop choosing wealthy white people as godparents for their children, because landowners subsequently felt they had the right to demand their godchildren work for free on their haciendas [country estates], Alvaro became the target of the landowners. The army, too, had him in its sights, accusing him of leading Indian protests and marches in the region and inciting Indians to kill landowners.

"By 1981, Alvaro was in the center of the storm. Landowners continued reporting him to the army, and even to the Archbishop, claiming he was inciting the Indians to violence. Soldiers continued abusing the Indians in order to provoke them, and, when they responded by protesting, increased their harassment. During one of these 'incidents,' Alvaro's sister Gloria was killed and his parents were injured after members of an army patrol attacked them as they were returning from a communal work project.

"A communiqué made public in late 1982 by Christian groups in Cauca announced that landowners have placed a bounty on Alvaro's head and only the love shown by those who surround him has so far prevented him from being disappeared. Two days before he was murdered Alvaro met with three army generals to denounce the constant abuses the Indians were suffering and insist the army present evidence to back up their accusations against him. After listening to him in silence, the generals told him they were as convinced as ever that he was provoking the Indians into illegally occupying lands they had no right to.

"As he was preparing to officiate a baptism in the small town of Santander de Quilichao, Alvaro was shot and killed by two *sicarios* [paid assassins] dressed in civilian clothes. A witness who later identified both killers as members of the F-2, the intelligence service of the police, was subsequently harassed and received death threats. Soon after that, the case file of the investigation disappeared from the prosecutor's office."[7]

In 1982, Conservative Party candidate Belisario Betancur won the presidential election with his campaign slogan, "Sí se puede" (Yes, it can be done). Betancur won by a narrow margin over former president Alfonso López Michelsen and immediately made it known that he had no intention of pursuing Turbay's bloody campaign of violence. Betancur sought to capitalize on his reputation as a typically hardworking, practical-minded Antioqueño, and he did in fact embody many of the traits stereotypically associated with his native Antioquía.[8]

Born to a lower middle class family of over 20 children, most of whom died young, he had become wealthy strictly through his own efforts. Betancur was at one time a die-hard follower of Laureano Gómez, but by the time of his election he was known as a progressive who cultivated contacts with a wide spectrum of cultural and intellectual figures, in part through his work in the publishing business.[9]

Within six weeks of assuming office Betancur announced the formation of a Peace Commission. Law 35 of 1982, signed by the president on November 20, granted amnesty to all those in armed conflict with the government before that date except those who had committed noncombat-related homicides or homicides that had included "cruelty" and in which the victim had been in a position of "inferior strength."[10] Moreover, Betancur decided that guerrillas already in jail for the pardoned crimes, whether convicted or merely indicted, would be released. In the first three months of the initiative, nearly 400 guerrillas accepted the amnesty.[11]

President Betancur was an honest

man, who desperately wanted to bring peace to Colombia. He based his amnesty offer on the assumption that guerrilla violence was the product of the poverty, injustice, and the lack of political inclusion in Colombia. He reached out to the guerrillas and negotiated agreements with the FARC, EPL, and the M-19 based on the concept of a "national dialogue." He genuinely wanted to implement social reforms to reduce violence in the countryside.

The peace initiative and dialogue with the guerrillas was not popular with the military. Still and all, most remained loyal to the president despite their preference for a "total war" against the insurgents. However, dissident members of the military circumvented the president's efforts by secretly increasing assistance to the death squads. Members of the army and police started to conceal their identities, frequently wearing civilian clothes and hoods. They also drove around in unmarked cars to grab victims and take them to clandestine torture centers. The dirty war generals wanted to forego the legal formalities of arrests and strike fear into the hearts of innocent Colombians.

Despite the dirty war, Betancur announced a groundbreaking agreement with the FARC on April 1, 1984. The pact called for a one-year cease-fire, and the creation of a "High-level Commission" to verify the terms of the accord. Betancur also provided for a series of juridical, political, and social guarantees to facilitate the return of the guerrillas to "Democratic Life."[12] The FARC even supported the formation and organization of the Patriotic Union political party (UP). The M-19 and EPL agreed to a similar truce the following month.

All the while, the government was taking a hard line with the Narcos. Justice Minister Rodrigo Lara Bonilla was Betancur's point man. Lara stepped up attacks on the Narcos and their centers of operation. Moreover, he warned that drug money was being invested in legitimate enterprises, including professional soccer and bicycle racing, and accused several members of Congress of having received drug money for their political campaigns.

The Narcos tried to seduce Lara with bribes; when he refused, they decided to silence him. The assassination of Lara on April 30, 1984, by Narco assassins triggered an official "State of Siege" by the government. Raids were directed against the property of suspected Narco kingpins, including 80 in the city of Medellín alone. Betancur also started a program of aerial spraying of marijuana crops and began enforcing an extradition treaty with the United States. The Narcos knew the government wanted their heads, so they reached out to an old ally, former president Alfonso López.

The Narco bosses met López in Panama, and persuaded him to broker a truce with Betancur similar to the ones being signed with the guerrillas. The Narcos promised López they would desist from future drug trafficking and sweetened the deal with an offer of $2 billion to pay off the national debt if they were allowed to return to Colombia in peace. Betancur wasn't impressed and vehemently rejected the offer. During the crisis, a handful of legitimate politicians were calling for tough measures against the Narcos. Liberal dissident Luis Carlos Galán was by far the most outspoken. Galán, a Colombian Senator, was bravely articulating a reformist agenda that limited the influence of the Narcos in Colombia. The young populist was warned on several occasions to modify his defiant rhetoric, but he refused to be intimidated.

The peace pact collapsed when Betancur was unable to control the enemies of peace. By the end of 1985, two of the three truces were broken, with leaders of the M-19 accusing the government of causing the rupture. The government countered that the guerrillas had broken the peace agreement. In reality, the insidious military–death squad partnership had ruptured the pact.

Complicating matters further, in October of 1985, the Roman Catholic Church retreated from its position of standing with the continent's poor. The Catholic Church restored conservative discipline and subordinated theological concerns to politics when Ronald Reagan became the first American president to officially recognize the Vatican. However, many Latin American priests refused to retreat, and faithfully continued to work with the poor.

The M-19 announced its decision to return to combat on June 20, 1985. "The problem is that the oligarchy does not want to give up anything because they think that the solution for this country comes from [the] submission and silencing not only of the guerrilla movement but also of the democratic sectors and of the new forces that want a different life," declared Alvaro Fayad, one of the M-19 leaders who emerged after the death of Jaime Bateman.[13]

Father Giraldo tallied the victims of the Betancur peace agreement. "During the Betancur administration, an Amnesty Law for guerrillas renouncing the armed struggle was passed. Almost immediately, however, it became clear just how risky a proposition it was to depend on this law for protection as scores of amnestied guerrillas were murdered, frequently only hours after legalizing their situation. The Patriotic Union political party, another fruit of the Betancur peace process, was founded in November 1985. Since then, a UP party member or supporter has been murdered every 53 hours. In the party's first four years of existence, this persecution was even more intense with a murder every 39 hours, and, in the run-up elections, even more chilling, one UP party member was murdered every 26 hours."[14]

November 6, 1985, was a dramatic day in the history of Colombia. It was a typical Bogotá rainy morning, when about 40 heavily armed young M-19 male and female guerrillas invaded the capital and took possession of the Palace of Justice. The guerrillas managed to immediately take more than 100 hostages, including 11 of the 24 Supreme Court Justices in the first hour of the surprise attack. The M-19 declared that they sought to "hold a public trial" of the government for betraying the hope of the nation. The hulking block square Palace of Justice was on the north side of the spacious Plaza Bolívar, the historic seat of the Colombian government, and three blocks south of the Casa de Nariño (the Colombian White House), the President's office and home.

President Betancur instructed the Colombian Army to "restore order and above all to avoid bloodshed." The army generals flagrantly refused to follow the President's explicit orders: they obeyed "restore order" but ignored "avoid bloodshed." Ana Carrigan, a Colombian-Irish journalist who worked for the *New York Times,* studied the disaster and wrote a gripping tale of the episode in her book, *The Palace of Justice: A Colombian Tragedy.*[15] Carrigan explained the Byzantine nature of the tragedy extremely well, but despite her breathtaking account, no one will ever know for sure what truly took place that day. Considering the bloodshed that followed, however, many Colombian intellectuals concluded that, "The army staged a mini-coup and instructed President Betancur to backoff while they detonated the crisis."

After the secret army huddle, Betancur took to the phones in an effort to bolster his support. He called five of Colombia's living former presidents, including one who at that moment was dining in Paris with Gabriel García Márquez. The plot thickened, though, when he inexplicably refused,

Government tanks and troops take positions outside the Palace of Justice after a November 6, 1985, M-19 guerrilla occupation. *El Tiempo*

or was not permitted, to take calls from Andrés Almarales, the M-19 commandant in the Palace, or answer the desperate pleas from the Supreme Court Justices held hostage there. The army attacked with tanks and started directing "massive and indiscriminate" fire into the Palace of Justice. The 2,000 troops showed no regard whatsoever for the safety of the hostages inside. Over the next 27 hours the army would systematically turn the Palace into an inferno and reduce the building to rubble.

Colombian Minister of Justice Enrique Parejo rushed to the scene. The hot-tempered intellectual went straight to the Casa de Nariño and desperately lobbied the army for a cease-fire. Carrigan explained that Almarales and Parejo grew up together in the little town of Ciénega, well known to every Colombian school child as the place where in 1928 the army slaughtered hundreds of banana workers to break

a strike. (See Chapter Three: The Genesis of Violence.") The strike was a galvanizing historical episode fabled in the fiction of García Márquez, whom Almarales and Parejo both knew.[16]

Alfonso Reyes, the Chief Justice of the Colombian Supreme Court, an authentic national hero, never lost his composure as bullets and flames ate away at his office where he was trapped.[17] Reyes' dignified telephone interview live on national radio in the late afternoon brought the country to a halt. The Army attempted to cut him off by shutting off the electricity, but the phone line still worked and Reyes told the nation, "We are on the point of death."

Ultimately, the fighting stopped and the army reported there were no M-19 survivors. But voluminous documentary sources, videotapes of the battle, and audiotapes of telephone conversations and military communications recorded by amateur radio operators indicated otherwise. Moreover, it appeared that many M-19 survivors were massacred in a bathroom inside the Palace. It came as no surprise; Colombians knew the army was intent on the complete annihilation of the M-19 and had no plans to permit any of them inside the Palace to live. The few court-employed survivors who were hiding inside the Palace of Justice challenged the official army story that they tried to prevent the needless loss of human live.

Carrigan's investigation was thorough. She managed to secure a clandestine interview with a pathologist who examined bodies as they were brought to a morgue from the ruins of the Palace. The information she discovered was horrid. She found that the Chief Justice was burned alive inside the Palace and that somebody nonetheless poured gasoline on his body and incinerated it. She also reported that other bodies were dumped into a mass grave and soaked with acid so identification would be difficult.

The army cover-up continued five days later when a volcano erupted outside Bogotá; hundreds of bodies from this natural disaster were dumped into the same mass grave as those from the Palace of Justice, sealing the forensic secrets. (In 1998 experts began excavating the mass grave in a grim bid to discover how many of the hostages and rebels who died in the 1985 incident were in fact dragged alive from the building and summarily executed by the Colombian army.) All together, 105 Colombians died, including rebels, civilians and 11 senior judges. Despite numerous investigations and lawsuits, no one has ever been punished for the carnage at the Palace of Justice, and no responsibility fixed. To this day the army asserts that it patriotically defended the nation's honor.

The Liberals regained control of the presidency in 1986 with Virgilio Barco, an MIT trained engineer and former Ambas-

sador to the United States. The Liberal handily defeated the Conservative Party candidate Alvaro Gómez Hurtado. The victory prompted Barco to conclude that the National Front inspired idea of power sharing diluted the responsibility of government initiatives and contributed to the decline of public confidence in the political system.[18] Consequently, he ended the collaboration with the Conservatives and returned Colombia to rule by one party at a time. However, the return of one-party governance, with the Conservatives reduced to the role of opposition, did not result in the nation's ills being conquered.

Jésus A. Bejarano, Barco's "Presidential Adviser for Reconciliation, Normalization and Rehabilitation," outlined the administration's plans for the restoration of peace and for maintaining social harmony.[19] However, on the diplomatic front, Barco was not winning many points in the U.S. Washington was of the opinion that the Colombian authorities were not fully carrying out the U.S. prescription against narcotics trafficking.[20] Few Americans wanted to hear Barco's argument that Americans should share more of the responsibility for the drug problem.[21]

Of more importance to Colombians was that Barco, like Betancur before him, could not control the activities of the death squads. In October 1987 assassins on a highway near Bogotá murdered Jaime Pardo Leal, the first presidential candidate for the Patriotic Union (UP). Between 1985 and 1989, 614 UP members were murdered and 36 disappeared. Additionally, 88 cases of arbitrary arrest, torture, threats or attempted murder took place against UP members.[22] Moreover, Narcos in Medellín were employing large contingents of hired gunmen (*sicarios*) and death squad armies to settle conflicts in the countryside now that they were investing heavily in large landholdings. With the huge infusion of Narco dollars, paramilitary death squads raised political violence to the highest levels of the 1980s.

During Barco's government the number of death squads rose to over 140. A partial list given by one Colombian sociologist included, in addition to the MAS, the Group (El Grupo), Death to Rustlers (Muerte a Abiegos), Punishment to Swindling Intermediaries (Castigo a Firmantes e Intermediarios Estafadores), The Embryo (El Embrión), Alfa 83, Pro-Cleanup of the Magdalena Valley (Pro Limpieza del Valle del Magdalena), the Soot-Faced (Los Tiznados), the Colombian Anticommunist Movement (Movimiento Anticommunista Colombiano), the Crickets (Los Grillos), the Machete Squadron (El Escuadrón Machete), Falange, Death to Land Invaders and Their Collaborators and Supporters (Muerte a Invasores, Colaboradores y Patrocinadores), and the Green Rangers (Los Commandos Verdes).[23]

One of the most notorious paramilitary leaders was Fidel "Rambo" Castaño, the older brother of Carlos Castaño. Rambo apparently made his fortune in the emerald and drug trade and bought vast expanses of cattle-breeding land in northwestern Colombia. He swore his own war to the death with guerrillas after some of them kidnapped his father in a rural section of northeastern Antioquía. Ransom was paid but his father was never surrendered. Rambo then launched a violent anti–Communist crusade in which armed men massacred whole groups of peasant suspects, often after torturing them in a hope of gaining information about the hated guerrillas.

Rambo was named as one of the intellectual authors of the November 1988 massacre in the town of Segovia, Antioquía, and of the mass murder of peasants in the hamlet of La Mejor Esquina also in 1988. Because of his connections to multiple atrocities, Rambo was one of Colombia's "Most Wanted" criminals. However,

the death squad leader considered his work honorable, craved respectability, and wanted acceptance into legitimate Colombian society. Therefore, he created and endowed the Foundation for the Peace of Córdoba (FUNPAZCOR), and donated extensive tracts of land to peasants in the area. But the charity was tainted because most of the peasant families benefiting from his largesse were members or former members of his death squads. The donations never earned Rambo the legitimacy he yearned but it did shield him from justice.

Americas Watch, the human rights organization, interviewed Colombians who visited Rambo in Córdoba and reported that high-ranking military officers on active duty in Montería, the departmental capital, were directly in charge of Rambo's security. According to many eyewitnesses, Rambo regularly appeared in Montería at events to highlight his land donations and other philanthropy, in the presence of civil and military authorities, and church and civic leaders.

The Narcos, guerrillas, death squads, and ordinary criminals took advantage of the breakdown in law and order. The Colombian sociologist, Alvaro Camacho, calculated that 75 percent to 80 percent of the violence in Cali was "private," and that the violence was not political but the private settling of accounts relating to such matters as debt, property, sexual and marital issues, robberies, barroom brawls, and family problems. As a result, homicides in 1986 ballooned in the two major drug centers, averaging between 2.17 and 6.46 per-day in Cali and between 5.77 and 9.70 in Medellín.[24] According to the Colombian government, at least 80 percent of the crimes in the country went unreported, and of those reported only 10 percent led to indictments and convictions.

Under Barco the breakdown of law and order in Colombia was utter. In March 1989, the UP was hit again. Death squad killers murdered Communist leader José Antequera at Bogotá's Dorado airport. Antequera was a member of the UP political coalition that was attempting to join the political mainstream and give the left a voice in Colombian politics. Liberal Party politician Ernesto Samper and his wife Jacky had the misfortune of standing behind Antequera when the airport attack took place. The 38-year-old Samper was shot at least seven times and almost lost his life. His wife was not injured.

The violence in Colombia touched all segments of society. That year, Colombia's emerald king, Gilberto Molina, and 17 other people were assassinated. A death squad fighting for control of the world's richest emerald mines was blamed for the murders. Police said about 50 men stormed the mine owner's luxury ranch, El Eden, in the early hours as Molina and his guests swayed to the music of two bands. The attackers took over the ranch at Sasaima, 45 miles west of Bogotá, without a fight. The death squad then handcuffed and shot Molina, 16 bodyguards and a friend, but did not harm women and children. Molina was suspected of involvement in drug dealing, and had managed to escape three other attempts on his life. He headed the big Tecnominas emerald firm and had been battling for control of another big enterprise, the Coscuéz mines. Additionally, with the 1989 average of 77 murders per every 100,000 citizens, Colombia was officially the murder capital of the world.

Defenseless, poverty-stricken children were also big targets of violence in Colombia. Casualties of the war zones, runaways, prostitutes or children abandoned by their families and the state faced constant danger throughout the nation. Human Rights Watch described the grisly details in "Generation Under Fire, Children and Violence in Colombia.[25]

The report said, "It is unusual for Human Rights Watch to focus on a partic-ular group. Yet [because of this collapse of law and order] we believe this focus is merited. Children face special risks, since they lack the knowledge or skills to defend themselves. Often, their families and the state, which does little to protect them from violence, have abandoned them. It is ironic that children face such threats in a country that purports to honor the rights of children.... On paper, they are the country's most protected citizens, while in practice, they are more prone to murder than children in any other country in the world.

"Official investigations have repeatedly uncovered the link between government forces and the murder of children. The police in particular have participated in hundreds of killings of children since 1980, including the so-called 'Social Cleansing' by selling weapons on the illegal market to men who then kill children with police complicity. The torture of children detained by the police and military continues to be the norm in Colombia. We received testimony about beatings, rape, electrical shocks, near-drownings in filthy water, ugly reality for children in detention in Colombia. Children are also murdered because the government forces pledged to maintaining order refuse to intervene when others break the law. Throughout Colombia, extra-legal forces, guerrillas, paramilitaries, social cleansing squads, militias and gangs have carved out territories that they rule with minimal government interference, whether because government agents fear intervening, are inefficient, or are corrupt.

"Human Rights Watch/Americas found that the few investigations carried out of official involvement in the murders of children rarely resulted in more than dismissal for implicated officers. Despite numerous police purges, officers continue to be implicated in the murder of children. While we support the dismissals of officers who commit violations, we believe that they should be prosecuted in civilian courts for these crimes. Promises to restrain the military have yet to bear tangible fruit.

"Measuring impunity presents some difficulties, since many children refuse to testify against their attackers out of fear or a conviction that state agents will not be punished. In addition, forensic investigations into murders are often incomplete. For instance, in one city, the authorities charged with collecting evidence in a series of 'Social Cleansing' murders did not gather forensic evidence, but instead washed, shaved, and cut the hair of the victims, making identification nearly impossible. This report would not be complete without recognition of the fact that children are also among Colombia's most prominent killers. Children belong to the gangs that prowl urban centers, assaulting pedestrians and hijacking cars. Recruited and trained by drug traffickers, children make excellent assassins, since they learn quickly and according to law cannot be punished as severely as adults.

"To be a child is to be at risk in Colombia. To be a poor child, a runaway, a child prostitute, or a child in a war zone is to live with the threat of murder in daily intimacy. At an average of six per day, 2,190 children were murdered in 1993, according to Colombia's national statistical bureau. In some regions, the murder of children has reached epidemic proportions. In the city of Cali, for instance, the murder of children increased by more than 70% between 1991 and 1992. Per capita killings of children in Colombia exceed those in Brazil, where the killing of black street youth has captured world headlines. Like most Third World countries, Colombia is a nation of youth, so to speak of children is to include close to half its population."

On May 25, 1989, the Colombian Supreme Court overturned the provisions in Law 48 that allowed the Army to distribute restricted weapons to civilians. Decree 1194 issued in June 1989 established criminal penalties for civilians and members of the armed forces who recruit, train, promote, finance, organize, lead, or belong to "the armed groups, misnamed paramilitary groups, or groups that carry out their own justice." Unfortunately, the decree failed to do anything about the arms already in the possession of the death squads.

By decade's end, Colombia had more paramilitaries than ever. In the 1970s human rights groups recorded 1,053 political killings; in the 1980s, that figure leapt to 12,859. The Supreme Court decision, although a step in the right direction, was too late to eliminate the paramilitaries. The death squads were too strong and had powerful forces dictating their activities. The anti–Communist Narcos supplied the death notices and the military unlawfully orchestrated the logistics. The combination was too great to overcome.

In August 1989, a death squad assassinated Luis Carlos Galán, the courageous Liberal Party presidential candidate, who was an outspoken critic of the Narco bosses. Galán was one of the few politicians in Colombia brave enough to warn of the corruptive role that the Narco bosses played in the nation. Galán, an honest and sincere populist, was well on his way to the presidency with a platform of ambitious reforms and a strong nontraditional view of party politics. He assembled a dedicated political team, which included his cousin, "Mr. Clean," Alfonso Valdivieso, and was attracting the support of respectable members of the Colombian business community.

The death of Galán prompted the Barco government to declare (with the enthusiastic support of the Bush administration) a "War on Drugs." Police and military forces arrested more than 11,000 people in raids on ranches, homes, companies, soccer academies, and even discotheques owned by the Narcos. "There has never been a raid like this in the history of Colombia. All of the properties of the Narcos are occupied by government troops," a Defense ministry spokesman told the *Christian Science Monitor*.[26]

The *Los Angeles Times* reported, "The assassination of Luis Carlos Galán hit a nerve in Colombian society, and the courageous response of the people and the government deserves applause. For it is political will, not military might, that ultimately will determine whether Colombia will rid itself of the cocaine cartel."[27]

Meanwhile, a continent away, President Bush called on Americans to stand together in a war on illegal drugs. It was the "toughest domestic challenge we've faced in decades," he said in an address to the nation on September 5, 1989, in which he outlined a $7.9 billion a year strategy to help the U.S. kick its drug habit. "It will take a national strategy, one that reaches into every school, every workplace, involving every family."

The author of Galán's murder was Pablo Escobar, the powerful Medellín Narco boss who was singled out by *Forbes* magazine as the wealthiest man in all of Latin America.[28] *Forbes* called Escobar a world-class billionaire. His immense wealth permitted him to single-handedly paralyze the Colombian justice system with a combination of deaths, threats and bribes. Moreover, he was the keystone of the "Extraditables," a Narco group that was fighting extradition to the U.S.

The Extraditables published a deadly message to the judge responsible for Escobar's persecution. It read: "We are friends of Pablo Escobar Gaviria and we are ready to do anything for him…. We know perfectly well that not even the slightest evidence exists against Mr. Escobar. We have also heard rumors that after the trial you will be given a foreign diplomatic position. But we want to remind you that, in addition to perpetrating a judicial infamy, you are making a big mistake…. We are capable of executing you at any place on this planet…. In the meantime you will see the fall, one by one, of all of the members of your family. We advise you to rethink it, for later you will have no time for regrets…. For calling Mr. Escobar to trial you will remain without forebears [*sic*] or descendants in your genealogical tree."[29]

The Narcos reacted violently to the Galán-inspired government crackdown. On September 2, 1989, a 120-pound bomb ripped through *El Espectador*, the oldest daily newspaper in Colombia. That same day, the headquarters of both of Colombia's establishment political parties and three banks were blown up, and three ranches belonging to wealthy Colombians were burned down.

Amid the panic, María Jimena Duzán, an *El Espectador* reporter who had heard the bomb explode some way away, made some calls, and knew what to expect. Even so, when she arrived, the glass, dust and blood shocked her. But as she stared into the wreckage — at the huge crater the bomb had created, at downed walls and obliterated offices — in an odd way, she was almost happy. "I felt some sense of relief," she wrote in her book. "I knew that at this moment, at least, nothing more could happen to us."

El Espectador's manager, Alfonso Cano, insisted that his newspaper, known for its principled stand against drug traffickers, would not be silenced by the violence of the powerful Narco warlords. "They hit us hard, but we will go on," Cano said. "Tomorrow the paper will be published." The newspaperman went on to recall the assassination of his brother in December 1986, a man whose defiance of the Narco bosses led to his execution by a death squad.

In the midst of all the fear and uncertainty, there were daily acts of courage. A month after the bombing, reporters and editors worked in crowded makeshift offices to put out *El Espectador*. "The newspaper and reporters receive continuous death threats, even against their families," Pablo Augusto Torres, who worked at the paper for 27 years, told the *Washington Post*. "To protect the reporters we would need an army of bodyguards, and even that would not work." But, Torres added proudly, no one on the editorial staff had quit because of the bombing and subsequent threats.

Political analysts said the bombing of *El Espectador* was not only a blow to freedom of the press, but to the stability of Colombia's shaky democratic system. "Upholding a free press in Colombia is a key element of upholding democracy," said former presidential advisor Rodrigo Pardo. "Despite incidents like the bombing of *El Espectador,* the press has to keep publishing. Despite assassinations like Galán's, the candidates must continue campaigning."

The government crackdown included a cleansing of the police. On October 4, *El Tiempo* reported that the National Police Chief, General Miguel Gómez Padilla, dismissed or forced to resign 2,075 policemen for taking bribes from drug traffickers. The paper said that Gómez had started a scrub of the 80,000-strong police force in February and found that the infiltration by drug rings made the dismissals necessary. The General somberly noted "the drug traffickers' great capacity to bribe at all levels of national life."

In an appeal to the citizens of Colombia, the State Security Council — which comprised President Barco, five Cabinet members, and the Attorney General — urged the people to resist pressure from the Narcos. The council's statement asserted that with their bombings, assassinations and other terrorist acts, the Narcos

were intending to turn the people against the government by trying to create the impression that, in refusing to negotiate with them, it was indirectly responsible for the violence. Barco and the others said they would not yield to threats. The Extraditables responded by vowing to kill government officials and their families, and said that they would kill ten judges for each suspected drug trafficker sent to the U.S. to stand trial.

In September 1989, Coletta Youngers, a dedicated and experienced human rights associate who worked with the Washington Office on Latin America, spoke out about the Colombian military's link with drug dealers. Youngers had traveled to Colombia twice in 1989. "The U.S. government is sliding down a slippery slope of intervention in a war it is destined to lose," she wrote. "Combating the Colombian drug traffickers is not a question of military might but of political will. Arresting suspected traffickers and expropriating property, are important moves. However, the Colombian security forces have yet to confront the military arm of the traffickers: the paramilitary structure which underlies political and drug-related violence in Colombia. Until the military shows the political will to do so, U.S. aid is meaningless and may even end up in the hands of the very people we are trying to combat.

"Joining the alliance are members of the Colombian security forces, military and police, who resort to paramilitary activity for profit or out of frustration with the inability to win the battle against the guerrilla insurgencies. In fact, the paramilitary death squads have displaced guerrillas from areas where they have enjoyed substantial popular support. But more often than not, the targets of violence are Colombia's growing nonviolent progressive forces, such as civic movements, peasant and labor unions, and a newly formed political party, the Patriotic Union. Last year there were 2,738

Armed Forces Chief General Fernando Tapias and Army Chief General Jorge Enrique Mora: The two senior Colombian military officers were unable to control the slaughterhouse activities of paramilitary death squads. *El Tiempo*

political assassinations, including 82 massacres of four or more civilians.

"Thus, it should come as no surprise that Colombian security forces have yet to show the political will to confront the paramilitary arm. U.S. military aid only serves to exacerbate internal political conflict. At best, it will not impact on narcotics trafficking, and at worst, some may end up in the hands of the drug lords themselves. Sending U.S. troops, even in a technical role, unnecessarily risks American lives and entangles them in domestic political turmoil. Perhaps of greater concern, the history of U.S. intervention in the third world leads one to question where our involvement will end. Out of frustration with a battle that cannot be won, will the U.S. withdraw or escalate its presence? Unfortunately, our legacy ... particularly in Vietnam ... portends the latter."[30]

President Barco's war on drugs was losing public support in October of 1989. Many Colombians were openly questioning the economic and political costs of the war. The *Christian Science Monitor* reported, "Despite his leaden oratorical style, the iron-willed Colombian president was accorded a standing ovation by the United Nations General Assembly last month. He has been received by President Bush in the private apartments of the White House, and praised by other world leaders, including British Prime Minister Margaret Thatcher and French President François Mitterand. But at home in Colombia, Mr. Barco's war on drugs is getting a more mixed reception. In the wake of the murder of Senator Galán, the man most likely to have succeeded him as president next year, Barco received overwhelming public support for his declaration of war on the traffickers. That is waning. At the beginning there was an emotional identification with the government's measures. Now there is a debate over what this war is for and over its costs."[31]

In December 1989, President Barco defied all odds and negotiated a peace with the M-19. Law-abiding Colombians rejoiced. The peace agreement called for guerrillas to turn in their weapons and join the political mainstream. The accord was a surprise — few Colombians thought the M-19's would ever truly abandon violent action and attempt to rejoin society. However, the Barco government's promise to help the M-19 urban and rural guerrillas form their own political party, the Alianza Democrática M-19 (Democratic Alliance M-19) convinced Carlos Pizarro and Antonio Navarro Wolf, the two top leaders, to give up the revolution and to seek reforms within the political establishment. The new political party quickly organized and fielded candidates for the 1990 elections.

Once again, though, Barco could not stop the death squads. In March 1990, the UP's new presidential candidate, Bernardo Jaramillo, was murdered by a 15-year-old hired gun at the El Dorado airport in Bogotá. The government accused Jaramillo's killer, Andrés Arturo Gutiérrez Maya, of carrying out the assassination on orders of Medellín Narcos, but the evidence was not substantial. Held as a minor under Colombian law, Gutiérrez Maya was allowed to leave the detention center and visit his family in November 1991. The trip was fatal. During the visit, young Gutiérrez Maya was stabbed and shot to death along with his father. The bodies were found in Medellín on January 2, 1992.

In May 1990, the death squads continued the bloody string of assassinations. Carlos Pizarro, the Democratic Alliance M-19 presidential candidate, was shot to death on an Avianca commercial flight. The government blamed Pablo Escobar, but offered little evidence to support its claim. The M-19 then put forth Antonio Navarro Wolf, Pizarro's successor. The UP refused to field a presidential candidate at all in the 1990 elections.

Colombia was shell-shocked going into the presidential elections of 1990. The Narcos terrorized the nation with their vicious campaign of urban violence. The citizens of Bogotá desperately wanted a return of peace. They wanted a president that could make the streets of the capital safe again. They feared for their children, and the future of the nation, and trembled at the thought that the Narco-inspired terrorism would escalate. Colombians in Medellín and Cali were of the same opinion. They were afraid to venture out of their homes for fear they would become victims of a bombing. A simple trip to a shopping center or to a bank was dangerous.

The violence in the countryside was secondary to Colombians in the cities. For decades, the rural territories had been consigned to the periphery, excluded from programs of public investment and development, which would answer the basic necessities of the rural population. Moreover, the citizens in the cities outnumbered those in the countryside. Therefore, public priority number one was restoring peace in the cities: the countryside would have to wait. The out-of-sight, out-of-mind mentality dominated political thinking.

On August 7, 1990, Liberal Party candidate César Gaviria was sworn in as president of Colombia. Gaviria, a low-key but tremendously gifted technocrat, was ushered into office with the considerable support of the Galán political machine. After graduating at the top of his class in economics, he became director of planning for his native Risaralda at the age of 22. Within ten years he was named Deputy Minister of Development in Bogotá, and in 1986 at the age of 39 President Barco named him Minister of Finance. Gaviria thoughtfully returned to the spirit of Article 120 and invited opposition party members into his government. Admirably, he included the M-19 presidential candidate Antonio Navarro Wolf, whom he named Minister of Agriculture.

Inclusion was a critical element of the Gaviria administration. The new president was a pioneer, and introduced vibrant political reforms that sought greater participation from all sectors of Colombian society. Gaviria also surrounded himself with the best and brightest young talent in the country. However, he skipped a generation with many of his appointments and the press in Bogotá affectionately called the young talent in his government the "Kindergarten." Wall Street nicknamed the Gaviria whiz kids "The Kiddi-Corps." The veteran on Gaviria's team was Rudy Hommes, the brilliant Minister of Finance. Together they would revolutionize Colombia's international economic competitiveness with a daring new program called "Apertura" (the Opening).

Gaviria and Hommes were a powerful combination and assaulted the bastions of backwardness in Colombia. However, the pair's rush for a more progressive and efficient Colombian economy angered the oligarchy and left-wing politicians alike. The opposition blasted away at the new government, saying that the Apertura would be at the expense of the poor and that certain sectors of the Colombian economy needed government protection. On the flip side of the coin, Wall Street loved Gaviria and Hommes, and soon armies of investment bankers swooped into Colombia to join the emerging Latin American market's frenzy of privatizations.

Gaviria also attacked Pablo Escobar. However, his scorecard was not as impressive on the drug front as on the economy. Gaviria unveiled a program of negotiation for dealing with the drug problem that was favorably compared to Bentancur's overtures to the guerrillas. The new president proposed that any drug trafficker who voluntarily surrendered to the Colombian authorities and pleaded guilty to one or more charges would not be extradited to the United States but instead would be tried in Colombia. The Gaviria gambit was not looked upon favorably in the United States. To that end, some American drug enforcement officials in Colombia and the U.S. howled disapproval.

The new president was also instrumental in leading the country to the establishment of a constituent assembly to write a new constitution that among other things officially provided for an independent central bank. However, the prestigious constituent assembly comprised strange bedfellows. Legitimate politicians who desperately wanted to end the narcoterrorism in Colombia joined hands with corrupt members of the assembly who were on the Narcos' payroll exclusively to eliminate extradition. Together they struck extradition down.

Some American law enforcement critics said Gaviria was not forceful enough and did not provide the needed leadership to prevent the termination of extradition. Others, who by now were seeing red, were less generous. They said, "Gaviria sold out." However, the truth was Colombians were tired of the bloodshed. Extradition collapsed after Escobar's hired assassins had killed 500 policemen in Medellín alone collecting $2,000 for every kill. Shortly after the elimination of extradition, on June 19, 1991, Pablo Escobar turned himself in to the Colombian authorities under a special plea bargain designed by President Gaviria to end the violent war between the government and the Narcos.

Escobar was allowed to enter a custom-made jail dubbed the "Cathedral" where he would secretly continue to run his drug empire. American critics felt that the government had in effect surrendered to its adversaries. Moreover, Gaviria turned a blind eye to the special luxury accommodations in the Escobar jail despite sharp verbal reminders from the DEA in Bogotá.

Eventually Gaviria's lenient treatment of Escobar backfired. On July 22, 1992, a little over a year after his surrender to Colombian authorities, Escobar defied a government order that he be transferred to another prison and walked out of the Cathedral. The day of the transfer, Escobar took National Prison Director Colonel Hernando Navas Rubio and Assistant Justice Minister Eduardo Mendoza hostage and slipped away with nine fellow prisoners. His escape was made possible by corrupt prison guards and army soldiers working at the Cathedral, and marked a serious defeat for the government's policy of negotiating the surrender of drug traffickers.[32] Subsequent revelations—that Escobar's posh jail was equipped with a bar, kitchenette, big-screen television, Jacuzzi, fax machines, computers, cellular telephones and that the conditions of his confinement were known to government officials—further humiliated the Gaviria government.

Moreover, the fact that Escobar continued to direct drug trafficking operations and order assassinations from the Cathedral caused many DEA officials to question the Gaviria government's commitment to the war on drugs. Backed into a corner by American law enforcement officials, the president mounted an intense manhunt to track Escobar down.

U.S. Ambassador Morris Busby took off the kid gloves after the Escobar escape. Busby asked for covert special operations assistance and received a six-man Delta Force team and a similar Team 6 Navy SEAL unit, according to the *Washington Post*.[33]

On November 9, 1992, Gaviria declared war on the guerrillas. The President lashed out at "the terrorists, murderers, and kidnappers,... the handful of deranged fanatics who have not read in the newspapers the sorry story of the end of communist totalitarianism." Gaviria was disgusted with the breakdown of peace talks between the guerrillas and the government in mid–1992 amidst a sea of mutual recriminations. By late August 1993, the government's confidence in the military strategy and lack of faith in the guerrillas' desire for peace was so complete that Defense Minister Rafael Pardo ruled out future peace talks with the FARC and ELN.

"We do not believe there is need to modify the strategy and policy to restore public order," Pardo said following the funeral for 13 policemen killed in an August 1993 attack by the FARC. "Instead, we must strengthen and intensify them."[34] The honeymoon was definitely over for Gaviria in Colombia. In January 1993, *Semana* magazine reported that the President's approval rating had dropped to 22 percent, a dramatic decline from his 79 percent approval rating a year earlier.

By 1990, the United States Southern Command, responsible for all U.S. military activities in Latin America and the Caribbean, declared counterdrug efforts its "Number one priority." James S. Roach, Jr., then the U.S. Military Attaché and the Defense Intelligence Agency (DIA) country liaison in Bogotá, said, "There was a very big debate going on (about how to best allocate) money for counter-narcotics operations in Colombia. The U.S. was looking for a way to try to help. But if you're not going to be combatants [yourselves], you have to find something to do."[35]

One area where U.S. officials decided they could help was in intelligence gathering. According to Colonel Roach, in the fall of 1990, the United States formed a team that included representatives of the U.S. embassy's Military Group, U.S.

Southern Command, the DIA, and the CIA, The 14-member group was led by a U.S. Navy captain, and made recommendations to the Colombian Defense Ministry for the reorganization of their military intelligence networks. A March 17, 1996, Defense Department letter to Senator Patrick J. Leahy, Democrat of Vermont, confirmed the American team's visit and explained they were there to make Colombia's intelligence networks "more efficient and effective."[36]

On face value, the trip looked innocent. However, certain members who collaborated with the American team were well aware of the Colombian military's long record of human rights violations and its ongoing relations with paramilitary death squads. Colonel Roach admitted as much: "We knew from Colombian news reports and (even) from Colombian military reports that they were working with paramilitaries."[37] Defense Minister Rafael Pardo said that in addition to recommendations received from the United States, the Defense Ministry solicited opinions from British and Israeli military intelligence.[38] Pardo noted that Colombia favored the U.S. plan because it had the most points of convergence with what the Colombian military wanted.[39]

Eventually, the Colombian Defense Ministry issued Order 200-05/91 in May 1991. The stated objectives of the order had little if anything to do with combating drugs. Indeed, throughout its 16 pages and corresponding appendices, the Order, marked "Reserved," made no mention of drugs.[40] Instead, the Colombian military, "Based on the recommendations made by a commission of advisors from the U.S. Armed Forces," presented a plan to better combat what they called "escalating terrorism by armed subversion."[41]

So, the Colombian Defense Ministry took the American team's counternarcotics advice and U.S. dollars and turned them around for use against insurgents. The significance of Order 200-05/91 cannot be overlooked. What started out as a joint U.S.-Colombian counternarcotic effort turned into an illegal, covert partnership between the Colombian military and paramilitary death squads. Although the order carefully avoided using the term "paramilitary," the document explicitly laid out a system similar to that of the MAS and its military patrons in the Middle Magdalena region.

Moreover, Order 200-05/91 was authorized by the military high command in direct violation of the May 25, 1989, Colombian Supreme Court decision to strike down Law 48, which concerned the distribution of arms to civilians. The order violated Colombian Supreme Court Decree 1194 of June 1989 that "established criminal penalties for civilians and members of the armed forces who recruit, train, promote, finance, organize, lead, or belong to" paramilitary groups. Obviously, the military high command considered their role above the law. They knew what was best for Colombia and they were not going to allow the highest court in the nation to stop them. The hatred of the guerrillas among the high command was so great it blinded the hierarchy's sense of justice.

Additionally, from that day forward a pattern was in place, whereby most military commanders would say paramilitaries did not exist. They would say that human rights activists were guerrilla proxies. When military commanders did acknowledge paramilitaries they would say that they simply were people exercising their constitutional right to defend themselves. The cover-up was official. The military was determined to kill guerrillas and didn't care who knew. The military high command now determined all potential guerrilla targets, and that unfortunately meant many innocent Colombians would be victims.

Pardo told Human Rights Watch that the new structure was not intended to incorporate illegal groups or to carry out illegal activities.[42] Regardless of his assurance, the order provided a blueprint for just that: a top-secret network that relied on paramilitaries, not only for intelligence, but also to carry out murder.

Order 200-05/91 authorized the army to set up 30 networks divided evenly between urban and rural areas. The navy was to establish four networks in and around the country's major sea and river ports. The order provided for the air force to set up seven networks. Each network was expected not only to supply the high command with intelligence and act on its orders, but also coordinate closely with other military units in its region. Each network was to be supplied with a staff and administered by "an active-duty officer with great knowledge of the region and its problems, who can easily interact with people of the zone in order to maintain his front."[43] In turn, this officer was to be assisted by "an officer or non-commissioned officer, retired or in active service, who has resources including a false identity and history, a vehicle, and a pre-established system of communications. He should have easy access to the target area…. He may also be a trustworthy civilian with training and influence."[44]

Order 200-05/91 also provided for each network to hire from 25 to 50 "intelligence agents," who, "must be, if possible, retired non-commissioned officers, trained to handle informants and process information."[45] The informants, the order stressed, should be required to "maintain the highest degree of reserve before the people with whom they live."[46]

The order included, however, an urgent warning. "The entire chain of command as well as the networks themselves must remain secret: The study, selection, instruction, training, location and organization of these networks, urban as well as rural, will be covert and under the responsibility of the Division and Brigade Commanders, or their equivalents in other forces, and the Network Commanders."[47]

All written material for the death squads was to be removed once the process was completed, and open contacts and interaction with military installations were to be avoided, according to the order. There "must be no written contracts with informants or civilian members of the networks; everything must be agreed to orally."[48] And the handling of the networks themselves "will be covert and compartmentalized, allowing for the necessary flexibility to cover targets of interest." Thus everything was in place — the order, the organization, the formation: all that was lacking was the execution.

The navy based one of its networks in Barrancabermeja, a port on the Magdalena River and the site of one of Colombia's largest oil refineries. Barrancabermeja was of strategic importance both to the Colombian military and to the ELN. Coincidentally, there was also a history of naval intelligence coordination with MAS murder in Barrancabermeja prior to 1991. On January 15, 1988, former Navy serviceman Pablo Francisco Pérez Cabrera gunned down trade unionist Manuel Gustavo Chacón. Pérez received a 16-year sentence for the murder. However, no officers were investigated for the crime. Witnesses who wanted to testify subsequently vanished, according to El Espectador.[49]

On September 21, 1999, the world-famous Spanish prosecutor Baltasar Garzón Real visited Colombia for a few days as the head of an International Human Rights Commission. Prior to leaving Bogotá, Garzón Real declared that Colombia was not a threat to the region but called on the government to formalize guarantees for the protection of human rights in Colombia. Moreover, Garzón Real forcefully stated

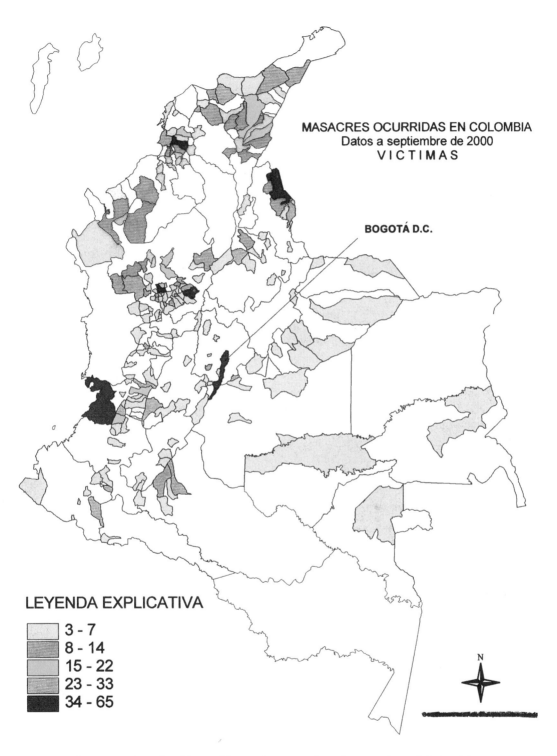

Victims of massacres in Colombia as of September 2000. (Key gives number of victims.) From *Defense of the Pueblo, Republic of Columbia*

that the armed forces military courts restricted investigations and that military human rights violations should be tried before civilian courts. His comments were widely applauded in the press.

"It is definitely clear that a grave situation exists (in Colombia), that is the product of actions by paramilitaries and guerrillas. The violation of human rights principally against civilian victims puts the integrity of the government at risk, particularly when evidence indicates a relationship between the armed forces and paramilitary groups. During this visit I have seen a government commitment to stop the violation of human rights in Colombia. However, it is quite clear that the government must do more to combat the paramilitary groups," he said.

Garzón Real also importantly commented that he hoped U.S. aid did not go into the hands of those committing human rights violations and lamented the fact that he could not personally deliver the conclusions of the International Commission directly to the President of the Republic of Colombia, Andrés Pastrana.[50]

In February 2000, the murderous death squads showed the world their savage indifference to human life. Shockingly, paramilitary death squad killers danced and drank as they tortured and beheaded at least 28 unarmed villagers on a table set on a basketball court during a four-day raid in northern Colombia from February 16 to 19.[51]

In its hunt for suspected FARC and ELN guerrilla sympathizers, a 200-man death squad murdered one of its victims in the Roman Catholic Church of El Salado village, according to Pablo Elías González, the lead investigator with Colombia's Chief Prosecutor's office. "They killed others on the basketball court and there was even a table where these people were sacrificed. They were tortured and then beheaded," he added.[52] He said investigators

were still working to identify the victims in the community in Bolívar province, a region hotly disputed by paramilitary death squads and guerrillas.

Colombian military officials said they were unable to enter the village between Wednesday and Saturday, alleging that paramilitary fighters were locked in combat with rival guerrillas. But González dismissed reports of the battle and said all the dead were civilians. "There was simply no (military) presence and the (paramilitaries) were there from Wednesday to Saturday during which they massacred all these people," he said.[53]

International human rights organizations, including Americas Watch and Amnesty International said additional U.S. aid would inflame Colombia's long-running civil war. The groups once again accused the Colombian armed forces of backing the paramilitary death squads in their "Dirty War" against leftist guerrillas and their supporters, a charge the military continued to vehemently deny. The human rights organizations predicted some of the U.S. aid would be funneled to the illegal paramilitary groups and fuel a rise in attacks on civilians. "As long as Colombian paramilitary groups allied with the Colombian Army continue to commit massacres and other serious human rights violations, U.S. military aid is tantamount to underwriting the Colombian "Dirty War," Amnesty International said in a statement.[54]

In February 2000, Human Rights Watch released an updated report on paramilitary death squad and Colombian Army collaboration. In the report, José Miguel Vivanco, the Latin America director of Human Rights Watch, said that Colombian federal prosecutors were frustrated by their inability to apply civilian justice to military officials. Although President Pastrana and U.S. officials frequently noted that 15 senior army officials had lost

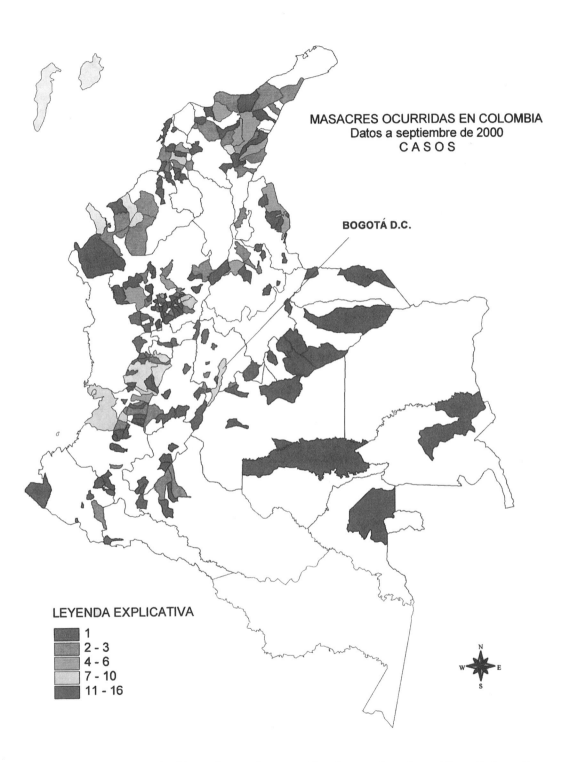

MASACRES OCURRIDAS EN COLOMBIA
Datos a septiembre de 2000
C A S O S

BOGOTÁ D.C.

LEYENDA EXPLICATIVA

- 1
- 2 - 3
- 4 - 6
- 7 - 10
- 11 - 16

Cases of massacres in Colombia as of September 2000. (Key gives number of cases.) From *Defense of the Pueblo, Republic of Columbia* their jobs because of alleged paramilitary ties, Vivanco said none of them had been prosecuted. However, prosecutors and human rights officials, he said, lived in constant fear for their lives, and many had fled the country under threat.[55]

On February 28, 2000, the *Miami Herald* published an editorial titled "Colombia's Deadly Ties, Training in Human Rights Not Enough," that acknowledged the findings of the new Human Rights Watch report on paramilitary death squad activities in Colombia.[56]

The editorial said, "President Pastrana rightly vowed to crack down on the paramilitaries and to punish high-ranking military officers found to be associated with them. Yet Mr. Pastrana's record in controlling the military is shaky. Last year he only went as far as firing three accused generals and promising to bring another to trial — a promise he's yet to keep.

"Mr. Pastrana can begin restoring his government's credibility by directing Colombia's attorney general to indict rogue military officers and bring them to trial. Only if such an effort is undertaken should the United States show its support by pass-ing aid that is now before Congress. That money is earmarked for the fight against drug traffickers, who often form alliances with both the leftist guerrillas and the paramilitary groups. Yet the focus of U.S. attention falls mainly on the guerrillas and the narco-traffickers.

"The paramilitary groups are no less disruptive to Colombia's stability. In its report [February 2000] Human Rights Watch cites compelling evidence showing that army officers have worked intimately with paramilitaries. They shared intelligence, planned and carried out joint operations, provided weapons and munitions, supported raids with helicopters and medical aid, and coordinated on a day-to-day basis. Some of the Colombian army units work side by side with the paramilitaries in areas where those units are receiving, or are scheduled to receive, U.S. military aid.

"Mr. Pastrana deserves Washington's support in his fight against drug traffickers. They're a scourge to the people of Colombia and the United States. But so are the paramilitaries and the army units that aid them. They certainly deserve equal condemnation."[57]

Notes

1. Robert W. Drexler, *Colombia and the United States: Narcotics Traffic and a Failed Foreign Policy* (Jefferson, N.C.: McFarland & Company, 1997), p. 107.

2. Harvey F. Kline, *Colombia, Democracy Under Assault.* 2nd ed. (Boulder: Westview Press, 1990), p. 55.

3. Drexler, p. 133.

4. Kline, p. 60.

5. Maria Jimena Duzán, *Death Beat: A Colombian Journalist's Life Inside the Cocaine Wars* (New York: Harper's Bazaar, 1994).

6. Javier Giraldo, *Colombia, The Genocidal Democracy* (Monroe: Common Courage Press, 1996), pp. 26–27.

7. *Ibid.*, pp. 29–31.

8. David Bushnell, *The Making of Modern Colombia: A Nation in Spite of Itself* (Berkeley: University of California Press, 1993), p. 250.

9. *Ibid.*

10. Kline, p. 58.

11. *Ibid.*

12. *Ibid.*

13. *Ibid.*, pp. 58–59.

14. Giraldo, p. 68.

15. Ana Carrigan, *The Palace of Justice: A Colombian Tragedy* (New York: Four Walls Eight Windows, 1993).

16. *Ibid.*

17. *Ibid.*

18. Bushnell, p. 250.

19. Drexler, p. 127.

20. *Ibid.*, p. 139.

21. *Ibid.*

22. Guido Bonilla, "La Violencia contra la Unión Patriótica: Un Crimen de Lesa Humanidad," Centro de Estudios e Investigaciones Sociales (CEIS), Bogotá, 1990.

23. Kline, p. 63.

24. *Ibid.*

25. Human Rights Watch/Americas Human Rights Watch Children's Rights Project, "Generation Under Fire, Children and Violence in Colombia," New York: Human Rights Watch, 1994.

26. Leslie Wirpsa, *Christian Science Monitor,* "Bogotá Tackles Drug Trafficking Threat," Bogotá, 23 August 1989.

27. Coletta Youngers, *Los Angeles Times,* "Will Colombia Stand Up to Paramilitary?" 31 August 1989.

28. *Forbes,* "The World's Billionaires," 5 October 1987, p. 153.

29. Kline, p. 61.

30. Coletta Youngers, *Washington Post,* "Colombia Military's Link with Drug Dealers," 11 September 1989.

31. Michael Reid, *Christian Science Monitor,* "Colombia's War Against Drugs, Public Support for Barco Wanes," Bogotá, 11 October 1989.

32. Human Rights Watch/Americas, "State of War, Political Violence and Counterinsurgency in Colombia," New York: Humans Rights Watch, 1993.

33. Douglas Farah and Dana Priest, *Washington Post,* "A Tutor to Every Army in Latin America," Washington, 13 July 1998.

34. Humans Rights Watch, "State of War, Political Violence and Counterinsurgency in Colombia."

35. Human Rights Watch/Americas, "Colombia's Killer Networks, The Military-Paramilitary Partnership and the United States," New York: Human Rights Watch, 1996.

36. *Ibid.*

37. *Ibid.*

38. *Ibid.*

39. *Ibid.*

40. *Ibid.*

41. *Ibid.*

42. *Ibid.*

43. *Ibid.*

44. *Ibid.*

45. *Ibid.*

46. *Ibid.*

47. *Ibid.*

48. *Ibid.*

49. *El Espectador,* "USO pide garantías para testigos contra la Armada," Bogotá, 6 de Enero de 1999.

50. *El Espectador,* "El español Baltasar Garzón no pudo entrevistarse con el Presidente. Colombia no es amenaza regional," 24 de Septiembre de 1999.

51. Reuters, "Colombia Death Squad Said to Dance During Torture," Bogotá, 23 February 2000.

52. *Ibid.*

53. *Ibid.*

54. *Ibid.*

55. Karen DeYoung, *Washington Post,* "Colombian Army Tied to Abuses," Washington, 24 February 2000.

56. *Miami Herald,* Editorial, "Colombia's Deadly Ties, Training in Human Rights Not Enough," Miami, 28 February 2000.

57. *Ibid.*

CHAPTER NINE

Northern Brothers

Is America a weakling, to shrink from the work of the great world powers? No! The young giant of the West stands on a continent and clasps the crest of an ocean in either hand. Our nation, glorious in youth and strength, looks into the future with eager eyes and rejoices as a strong man to run a race. — Theodore Roosevelt, letter to John Milton Hay, American Ambassador to the Court of St. James's, London, England, June 7, 1897.

The first American soldiers to ever fight in Colombia arrived during the War of Jenkins' Ear. The conflict between Spain and England broke out in 1739 over commercial and territorial differences but was largely remembered because of Spanish mistreatment of British sailors. One Englishman, named Captain Robert Jenkins, accused the Spanish of cutting his ear off.

Consequently, England was determined to defend British naval honor and avenge the mistreatment of Jenkins with its New World rival. The British commissioned a large fleet under the command of Admiral Edward Vernon with orders to raise troops in the American Colonies and then attack Spanish possessions in the West Indies. Sir William Gooch, the governor of Virginia, assembled 3,600 English-American Colonialists for the expedition. The force was large enough to form 36 companies of foot soldiers, four of which were all Virginians. One was led by Captain Lawrence Washington, the half-brother of George — Lawrence was 14 years

older than the future president of the United States.

After a series of delays, Admiral Vernon's fleet set sail for the West Indies amid high expectations and attacked the Spanish fortress of Cartagena in March 1741, but they were unable to immediately seize control of the well-defended Colombian port. Instead, the English-American siege was prolonged and the battle for the coastal city continued for weeks. Cartagena was extremely fortunate. Veteran commander Blas de Lezo, a one-eyed, one-armed and one-legged Spanish General, designed a domineering defense of the fortress. Subsequently, after two months and heavy losses the English-American expedition abandoned the siege and withdrew to the Colonies. The Americans reportedly fought bravely but were no match for the peg-legged, patch-eyed Spaniard. After the campaign, Captain Washington returned to Virginia and named his estate Mount Vernon in loyal admiration of the British Admiral who commanded the failed Cartagena expedition.

Seventy-one years later, in 1812, a 29-year-old Colonel named Simón José Antonio de la Santísima Trinidad Bolívar y Palacios, better known as Simón Bolívar, the idealistic future liberator of South America, used the "Heroic City" of Cartagena to issue his famous *Cartagena Manifesto*. The *Manifesto* gave Bolívar the instant status of a leading political thinker as well as establishing him as a dangerous foe of Spain's vast colonial empire. The young revolutionary used Cartagena to start his military campaign to end King Ferdinand's Spanish rule in Colombia. Shortly thereafter, he was respectfully called the "Liberator."

Bolívar, the dignified and well-educated son of an immensely wealthy Caracas aristocrat, was only 16 when George Washington passed away in 1799. However, he idolized the former general for valiantly leading a Revolutionary Army against the forces of the British crown and defeating them. Bolívar was inspired by the courageous American struggle for independence and was uniquely determined to defeat the Spanish and be elected president, just like his idol, George Washington.

Bolívar's faith in the American philosophy of freedom was reinforced during an 1807 trip from France to the United States. Bolívar traveled to Boston, New York, Philadelphia, Washington and Charleston and when the young Venezuelan exhausted his travel funds, a Charleston businessman he befriended on the voyage from Paris assisted him. The American hospitality left a strong impression on the young traveler.

Bolívar's romantic vision of American history made him unduly confident of U.S. military and economic assistance. The young General and future founding father to six South American nations was convinced the fledgling United States government would aid his struggle for independence just as the French assisted the revolutionary Americans during their fight for independence. However, Bolívar underestimated the political consequences of intervention for American leaders and failed to understand the full scope of Washington's reluctance to get involved with his South American struggle.

By 1815, Bolívar was completely frustrated by the lack of foreign support and expressed his displeasure in a letter to a friend. "We have had reason to hope that the civilized nations would hasten to our aid in order that we might achieve that which must prove advantageous to both hemispheres. How vain has been this hope! Not only the Europeans but even our brothers to the north have been apathetic bystanders in this struggle."[1]

Henry Clay, the "Coonskin Congressman" from Kentucky, and Speaker of the House of Representatives in 1818, was an important American voice that spoke out for the "People struggling to burst their chains and to be free." Clay was the eloquent orator of his generation and was flattered to think that Bolívar was emulating the United States example. "Of us they constantly speak of as brothers, having a similar origin. They adopt our principles, copy our institutions and … employ the very language of our revolutionary papers."[2] The frontier Kentuckian warmly defended Bolívar's crusade for freedom and condemned President James Monroe's overly cautious policy in South America.

President Monroe and his Secretary of State John Quincy Adams did not disapprove of Bolívar's exploits in South America. Both American leaders admired Bolívar's courageous military campaigns and intellectually agreed with his revolutionary rhetoric. However, Monroe and Adams feared the might of the Europeans and purposely steered clear of any possible diplomatic relationship that could antagonize the powers across the Atlantic. The dilemma that confronted Adams was one of the greatest challenges of his career.[3] If the United States waited too long before recognizing the new South American republics, it could incur their ill will, and a loss of trade to British rivals. If, on the other hand, Washington acted too hastily, Spain would be fully justified in declaring war, and a clash with Spain opened the possibility that all the European monarchies (Russia, Austria, and Prussia) unfriendly to democracy might come to her aid and declare war against the United States of America.[4]

Complicating matters further for Bolívar and his revolutionary forces, President Monroe was privately seeking to negotiate other "high-priority" affairs with the Spanish government. Secretary Adams was adroitly attempting to negotiate favorable terms for the renunciation of Florida, and was secretly preparing the documentation of the Adams-Onís Treaty of February 22, 1819, with Spanish Ambassador Luis de Onís. The treaty also extended the American northwest territory of the Louisiana Purchase to the Pacific Coast. Monroe and Adams were well aware that embracing Bolívar would imperil the delicate negotiations with the Spanish government in Washington and Madrid. Therefore, they avoided siding with Bolívar's war for independence in order to avoid a confrontation with Spain and also to fulfill strong territorial ambitions.

Impatient with the absence of American aid and frustrated with the pace of the long conflict with King Ferdinand's royalist forces in the Americas, Bolívar became invigorated with the arrival of English and Irish volunteers in 1819. The General wanted to use the small legion of volunteers alongside his army to strike a decisive blow against the Spanish occupation army and decided to take the biggest gamble of the war. The risky strategy allowed Bolívar to accomplish one of the greatest feats in South American military history—crossing the treacherous snow-capped Andes Mountains to crush the unsuspecting enemy camp in Boyacá, Colombia.

The 31-year-old Colombian patriot General Francisco de Paula Santander commented that "Even thinking of crossing the Andes with an army in June was sheer madness." But knowing that Bolívar's troops would "Follow him to the end of the world," Santander, who would go on to be Bolívar's Vice President after independence, reluctantly joined the General's frozen march into history. Upon reaching the other side Santander reportedly limped to Bolívar's side and pointed back at the massive mountains behind them. After a moment he said, "There's no going back, is there? We have only two choices now. Either we win ... or we die." The survivors of the march through the Andes Mountains used the element of surprise to defeat the occupation troops on August 7, 1819. Bolívar's bold military tactic paid off handsomely. The Battle of Boyacá formally liberated Colombia from Spanish rule.

The following year a victorious General Bolívar signed an Armistice with Spain prompting Spanish Marshal Pablo Morillo to leave the new republic and sail back to Madrid. However, the Armistice did not last long; it was broken in 1821, and a vastly outnumbered Bolívar managed to defeat the Spanish Army once and for all at the Battle of Carabobo. Later that same year, Venezuela and Colombia officially formed the Republic of Gran Colombia and General Simón Bolívar finally fulfilled a teenage dream when the citizens of the new nation elected him President. Panama and Ecuador would also quickly join Bolívar's Gran Colombia. On June 19, 1822, President Monroe ceremonially received President Bolívar's diplomatic envoy Manuel Torres.

In 1823, President James Monroe, a

disciple of the gifted philosopher-states-man Thomas Jefferson, lectured the European powers with his world famous Monroe Doctrine. The President left no doubt about American intentions in the hemisphere, when he declared, "The political [monarchical] system of the allied powers is essentially different from that of America ... we owe it, therefore, to candor and to the amicable relations existing between the United States and those powers to declare that we should consider any attempt on their part to extend their system to any portion of this hemisphere as dangerous to our peace and safety."

Monroe officially served notice on any nation that doubted the resolve of the U.S. "With the existing colonies or dependencies of any European power we have not interfered and shall not interfere. But with the Governments who have declared their independence ... we could not view any interposition for the purpose of oppressing them, or controlling in any other manner their destiny, by any European power in any other light than as the manifestation of an unfriendly disposition toward the United States."

Americans generally cheered the principled position by Monroe, and South American diplomats congratulated the President's Secretary John Quincy Adams. In Bogotá, the government was thrilled by the act of its northern brother. However, in Continental Europe the aristocrats viewed President Monroe's message with contempt. Many gave vent to such epithets as "haughty," "arrogant," "blustering," and "monstrous."[5] The doctrine of "America for the Americans," came as a shock to nations, which for centuries had looked upon the Western hemisphere as their own private hunting grounds.[6] Even the British, who were on good terms with the U.S., did not relish the U.S. setting itself up as the protector of South America.[7] Nonetheless, the Monroe Doctrine officially instructed the European powers to keep their hands off the remaining Latin American wars for independence and prohibited the extension of European control or influence in the Western Hemisphere.

On May 8, 1830, Simón Bolívar was leaving Bogotá. He was 47 years old, and suffering from tuberculosis and pneumonia. He was no longer President of the new republic. New leaders no longer shared his political vision and anxiously awaited his dignified departure. The rejected General, who liberated the entire northwest of South America — Venezuela, Colombia, Ecuador, Peru, Bolivia and Panama — from Spanish rule accepted the invitation of Joaquín de Mier to stay at his house, Quinta de San Pedro Alejandrino, in Santa Marta, Colombia. Bolívar, who always admired the United States as the land of freedom, was going into exile dressed in plain dark civilian clothes. The only military decoration he carried was George Washington's Yorktown Medal, which he always wore around his neck.

Simón Bolívar died on December 17, 1830. One of his final remarks in his diary was, "My name now belongs to history." In 1832, the United States officially established diplomatic representation in Bogotá, earlier than in any other South America nation.[8]

Ever since the day when news traveled around the world that the great Spanish explorer Vasco Núñez de Balboa crossed the Isthmus and became the first European to see the Pacific Ocean in 1513, leaders dreamed of building a passageway through North and South America. Spanish conquistador Hernán Cortés realized the importance of the Isthmus and suggested that a path across Panama would "be worth more than the conquest of Mexico." In 1534, Charles V of Spain ordered a survey of a possible canal route across "Panama," a Cueva Indian word meaning "a place where many fishes are taken.'"[9] Nevertheless, it would be more than 300 years before a world power would actually start work on a canal.

American isthmian involvement in Panama was spurred by its vast western expansion to the Pacific coast and the 1825 completion of the New York Erie Canal (at that time the longest canal in the world). The United States took its first step toward establishing a presence in the Colombian territory of Panama on December 12, 1846. American Ambassador Benjamin Alden Bidlack, acting on his own initiative, signed a treaty in Bogotá with Colombian Foreign Minister Manuel M. Mallarino granting the United States valuable transit rights in Panama. Under Article XXXV of the treaty, the U.S. was bound to guarantee Colombia's sovereignty over Panama for 20 years and also legally bound to limit itself to "perfect neutrality" of the route so that "free transit of traffic might not be interrupted."[10] The Colombians feared isthmian involvement by France or England and preferred a treaty with the Northern Brothers. Unfortunately, the right-of-way Bidlack-Mallarino Treaty was not approved by a bickering Senate until June of 1848. Shortly after ratification, the Panama Railroad Company (PRC) was chartered in New York. PRC subsequently signed a contract with the Colombian government for the construction of the Isthmus railway. The contract gave PRC a 49-year period to manage the Panama operation in return for 3 percent of its annual profits.

The construction of PRC was opportune. In 1845, journalist John Louis O'-Sullivan authored the jingoistic tenet "Manifest Destiny," editorializing that territorial expansion of the United States was not only inevitable but also divinely ordered. In addition, the California gold rush in 1849 had triggered one of the largest population migrations in the history of the United States. Thus, leaders in Washington needed a quicker route to coordinate the explosion of growth in the Pacific territories. To that end, the Bidlack-Mallarino Treaty allowed the American construction of the transcontinental Panama railway line, but because the 48 mile stretch was built in punishing tropical heat, and carved out of immense jungle thickets, PRC did not finish the project until 1855. However, once completed, the new railway permitted U.S merchants competitive access to the Pacific Ocean and also increased America's growing belief in Manifest Destiny.

The British, on the other hand, considered the southward push of the American eagle bad for business. As Britain was the number one mercantile nation in the world, its powerful British commercial interests were alarmed by the plans for a Yankee nerve center on the Isthmus. English leaders wanted to protect their territorial stake in the Caribbean, which included Jamaica, Belize, and other smaller colonies. In anticipation of American competition, the major naval, commercial and industrial nation in the world disregarded the Monroe Doctrine in 1848, and started a campaign to create a British Isthmus in Nicaragua. The British planned the Atlantic terminus for their canal at the end of the San Juan River on the Mosquito Coast and designated the Gulf of Fonseca as the Pacific outlet. In order to accelerate the canal plans, British forces seized Nicaragua's Mosquito Coast and English naval officers invaded Tigre Island to establish control of the Gulf of Fonseca. When news of the British moves arrived in Washington officials expressed strong disapproval. Furthermore, the British aggression touched off a wave of Anglophobia by the American press. President James K. Polk's Secretary of State, John M. Clayton, wrote of the danger: "A collision will become inevitable if great prudence is not exercised on both sides."[11]

The strong American protest forced the London Foreign Office to retreat. Towards the end of 1849, England sent a new minister to the United States. Henry Lytton Bulwer, brother of the famous author of *The Last Days of Pompeii,* arrived in Washington and revealed a willingness to enter into negotiations with Secretary Clayton.[12] However, the isthmian negotiations stalled over the issue of control. Neither the United States nor England was willing to allow either nation sole control of a future canal. This forced Clayton to play hardball and bluntly inform Bulwer, "There is not one of these five Central American states [Guatemala, Honduras, Nicaragua, Salvador and Costa Rica] that would not annex themselves to us tomorrow, if they could, and if it is any secret worth knowing you are welcome to it. Some of them have offered and asked to be annexed to the United States already."[13]

On that note, the British abandoned the Nicaragua project and signed the Clayton-Bulwer Treaty on April 19, 1850, whereby England and the United States agreed to co-operate in facilitating the construction of an isthmian canal and to never fortifying or exercising exclusive control over any future canal. Most Americans applauded the accord. The treaty was of little cost to the United States and averted a crisis that could have escalated into war. Critics on the other hand said Clayton was "bamboozled by slippery British diplomats."[14]

The critics pointed out that the U.S. was now legally forced to abandon its plans for an exclusive American waterway Isthmus. Supporters said Clayton produced an excellent pact. They said the U.S. was still only a second-rate power and miraculously managed to avert wars in large part because of the immense breadth of the Atlantic Ocean. Moreover, the emergence of other more pressing conflicts kept the European powers preoccupied, they added. More importantly, the Clayton-Bulwer Treaty safeguarded the U.S. while leaders in Washington attempted to deal with the explosive issue of slavery, the supporters concluded.

The Panama Railroad Company provided the fastest route to the gold in the streambeds of northern California. As a result, many rowdy, whiskey-drinking prospectors flocked to Panama and paid the $25 one-way fare for passage to the gold rush. The majority of the crude, rough and tumble Americans found Panama inhospitable. Tropical heat, jungle insects, primitive accommodations and squalid conditions caused most visitors to Panama to develop short tempers. As such, the unruly behavior of the prospectors quickly alienated the natives and the small garrison of Colombian troops stationed in Panama.

One of the first incidents of trouble took place in 1850, before the Isthmus railway was completed, when a mob of agitated Americans defied the local authorities and stormed a local jail to free a fellow countryman. The sympathetic intervention of the U.S. consul on behalf of the rambunctious Americans complicated matters. Afterwards, the Colombian government protested the behavior of the lawless Americans and demanded that the U.S. consul be recalled for his "Wayward and ungovernable character."[15]

The climate created enormous problems for Panamanian travelers. Rains averaging 140 inches a year made passage across the railway a dangerous venture. In July 1852, army captain Ulysses S. Grant led the American Fourth Infantry over the Isthmus of Panama en route to garrison duty in California. The military detachment of several hundred men, together with their dependents, became victims of a raging cholera epidemic that claimed the lives of 150 men, women and children. Grant later wrote of the tragic incident, "The horrors of the road in the rainy season are beyond description." Years afterwards, then President Grant commented on the importance of the Isthmus: "To Europeans the benefits of and advantages of the proposed canal are great. To Americans they are incalculable."

Trouble with the locals returned in 1856, after the Panama Railway Company was up and running. The incident reportedly was triggered by a quarrel over a piece of watermelon that cost ten cents. Apparently a drunken American who arrived in Panama City with several hundred other of his countrymen purchased the fruit. For some unknown reason, the vendor and the intoxicated American argued over the sale of the watermelon and when the Panamanian unsheathed a knife, the American drew his revolver.[16] Nearby Americans attempted to step in to pacify the situation but another Panamanian grabbed the revolver, fired at the Americans and ran for help. He returned with an enraged mob, which went on a rampage that laid waste to the hotels that housed the Americans, and attacked the railroad station where many Americans retreated for safety. When the police arrived, years of foulmouthed abuse by the Americans prompted them to desert their obligation to uphold law and order. They joined the incensed mob attacking the railroad station.

When peace was finally restored, 18 Americans and two Panamanians were found dead.[17] Colombian authorities in Panama and in Bogotá blamed American arrogance for the violence. Washington and PRC officials charged that authorities in Panama instigated the riot in order to share in the looting of American property and to vent hostility toward vulgar prospectors. The dispute would drag on for years, but the immediate consequence of the Watermelon Massacre was Washington's spirited deployment of armed forces to Panama to guarantee the protection of Americans citizens. Two warships, the U.S.S. *Independence* and the U.S.S. *St.*

Mary's, were dispatched to the Isthmus and deposited 160 Marines in Panama City. Four years later, in 1860, the *St. Mary's* returned and stationed more troops with PRC after clashes outside Panama City led to the death of six civilians.

Ultimately Washington considered Colombia too meek and disinterested to maintain law and order in Panama and insisted on U.S. troop deployments. Furthermore, Colombians were in no financial position to provide adequate troop enforcements and welcomed the relief the American military presence provided for its treasury. Eventually, politicians in Bogotá would treat Panama like a cash cow. In 1867, the Republic of Colombia extended the contract with PRC for 99 years in return for a lump sum payment of $1 million and an annual stipend of $250,000.[18]

Evidence of Colombia's neglect of Panama was the parsimonious annual sum of $25,000 it allocated to the maintenance of its Panama territory after signing the lucrative contract with PRC. Subsequently, American military minds would soon assert that they were better positioned to determine how best to discharge Panama's obligation to uphold Colombian sovereignty. Within a short period of time the only significant consideration keeping the Panamanian people loyal to the seat of government in Bogotá was the American military presence providing security for the PRC Isthmus railway.

However, the longer the U.S. maintained troops in Panama the greater the call by politicians in Washington that Manifest Destiny (which had spread across the country and taken on almost biblical proportions) called for American exclusivity in the waterway isthmus. Remarkably, Colombians did not anticipate the danger of Panamanian secessionists conveniently providing the U.S. with a more dynamic foothold in Panama and took an out-of-sight, out-of-mind approach to its northwest territory. Colombian leaders were convinced American decision makers were infatuated with building a canal in Nicaragua and had no designs on using Panama to fulfill Manifest Destiny.

On May 15, 1879, American dreams of being the first nation to build a canal were shattered when the builder of the Suez Canal, the gifted, but aging, Ferdinand de Lesseps announced in Paris that he headed a French syndicate than planned to sever North America from South America. Americans found the French group's "*La Grande" Enterprise*[19] disturbing and calculated that the government in Paris would do everything possible to see that the 75-year-old national hero, de Lesseps, was successful.

President Rutherford Birchard Hayes, the former Congressman and Governor of Ohio, vehemently protested the French plans in March 1880, when he informed the Senate that the proposed canal would "virtually be part of the American coastline," and that "the policy of this country is a canal under American control." The press attacked the French plans and reported that the Monroe Doctrine prohibited a canal under the control of a European nation. Within a year both houses of Congress formally protested against a canal built by foreign capital or controlled by foreign regulations. At the time many Americans were still suspicious of French intentions in the Western Hemisphere. The distrust dated back to 1863 when Napoleon III persuaded Maximilian, the Archduke of Austria to accept the crown of Mexico with the backing of French troops. (Maximilian was court-martialed and shot by Mexican forces in 1867.)

Nevertheless, the French syndicate managed to overcome American opposition to the Isthmus project with the lavish use of $1.5 million in lobbying funds. De Lesseps, who was not a trained engineer, but was a charming and expert promoter, judiciously spent money winning the support of editors, politicians, bankers, lobbyists and allegedly even Congressmen. Lobbying by Americans on behalf of the French syndicate was so great that the *New York Nation* embarrassed many political actors involved in the affair when it editorialized, "Are we never to know how much it cost to draw the fangs of the Monroe Doctrine during those critical years, or who were the men superintending the operation? Such dentistry not only comes high, but also requires great skill, and the public is entitled to know who the expert operators were." The Spanish speaking de Lesseps did not secure the concession with Colombia that authorized the construction of the Panama Canal in February 1881. A subordinate, French Lieutenant Lucien Napoleon-Bonaparte Wyse, negotiated the initial agreement with Liberal Party President Aquileo Parra in Bogotá on March 23, 1878.[20] The Colombian Senate formally ratified the Wyse accord in mid–May.

Americans were relieved when the French syndicate failed. Ultimately, it turned out that the experience of the Suez Canal was of little help to the French. Engineers would soon learn that the fundamental construction requirements of Egypt were completely alien to the tropical climate of Panama, which was often described as "a hell upon earth."[21] Moreover, corruption, financial incompetence, extravagance, engineering problems, torrential rains, tropical heat, thick jungle brush, poisonous snakes, disease, and poor management all combined to force the now 84-year-old de Lesseps and his French syndicate to file bankruptcy in December 1888. (The official end of the syndicate was February 4, 1889, but liquidators did not order the end of construction on the Isthmus until May 15, 1889.)

The failure to complete the "Great Trench–*La Grande Tranchée*" led to the biggest financial collapse in history and ruined hundreds of thousands of small French investors. The syndicate managed to complete just two-fifths of the canal. The cost in human terms was monstrous. Thousands of workers died on the project, prompting some Northern Brothers to call de Lesseps "The Great Undertaker."[22] In hindsight, de Lesseps, who was one of France's chosen of chosen, or "Immortals,"[23] blundered badly. His downfall was rigidity and a nation's blind faith that he could not fail. De Lesseps insisted on building an open-cut canal down to sea level from ocean to ocean, through the rugged Panama terrain despite warnings that the feat was virtually impossible without building locks to control water levels. His iron will and lack of scientific training in the skills of engineering doomed the project from the start. The financial loss was estimated at an astounding $287 million.[24]

The French misfortunes in Panama strengthened American interest in Nicaragua. Many Americans considered Nicaragua a more suitable site than Panama, but debate continued, and proponents of both routes had strong supporters in political circles. However, the Clayton-Bulwer Treaty was still on the books in 1888 and posed an enormous diplomatic barrier to American dreams of unilaterally building, operating and protecting a canal connecting the Pacific and Atlantic Oceans.

The United States was a great power at the turn of the century. The Spanish-American War from 1898 to 1900 showed Europe that America desired a larger role on the world stage. In addition to being a force in the Caribbean, the U.S. was now also a Pacific power. Those who favored "the rising sap of imperialism" and demanded strong overseas expansion soon outnumbered those Americans who favored a diplomatic tradition of isolationism. The traditionalists declared that the annexation of populations against their will violated the spirit of the Declaration of Independence, as well as the vitality of the Constitution. Moreover, the isolationists argued that the United States was not in need of more land and that colonies were too expensive to maintain. It was a turning point in the history of the country.

American diplomatic achievement was no longer relegated solely to the Western Hemisphere. A fiery young imperialist orator named Albert J. Beveridge captured the warmonger philosophy of the era in a speech. "The Ocean does not separate us from the lands of our duty and desire ... the ocean joins us, a river never to be dredged, a canal never to be repaired. Steam joins us, electricity joins us ... the very elements are in league with our destiny. Cuba not contiguous? The Philippines not contiguous? Our navy will make them contiguous!"[25]

Throughout the preceding century the United States had gained what it wanted quickly and cheaply. It had freed the Mississippi Valley frontier of British and Spanish intrigue; taken the Mediterranean pirates off the backs of American seaman; and driven the Spaniards out of Florida, the French out of Louisiana, the Mexicans out of Texas and New Mexico, and the Spaniards out of Cuba, Puerto Rico, and the Philippines. No nation in modern times got its way more often, more completely, or at less expense than the United States of America.[26] However, going into the next century the new American steel navy required a convenient passageway for its battleships to access the Pacific Ocean. Consequently, the United States needed to overcome an important diplomatic obstacle with the British to fulfill its dream of building and maintaining exclusive control of a canal in Central America.

In January 1900, the Senate defied the American signature on the Clayton-Bulwer Treaty and introduced legislation that would provide for the construction of a canal in Nicaragua. The mood of Congress was so nasty that Secretary of State John Hay reported some of the Senators were saying, "Dishonor be damned!" Seeking to avoid a diplomatic confrontation with England, President William McKinley ordered Hay to secure a modification of the Treaty. To that end, Lord Pauncefote, the British Ambassador in Washington, and Hay signed the first Hay-Pauncefote Treaty on February 5, 1900.

The results were less than spectacular and Congress was not happy with the accord. Hay's agreement provided for the construction and ownership of a neutral isthmian waterway but failed to obtain recognition of the right of the United States to fortify the prospective canal. Thus, the expansionists rejected the pact. An outraged Senate, doubly incensed because Hay had not conferred with its Committee on Foreign Relations, proceeded to amend the treaty so drastically that Great Britain refused to ratify it.[27] Hay didn't care for the congressional interference. He attributed Senate opposition to anti–English prejudice and wrote angrily to one correspondent: "When I sent in the Canal Convention I felt sure that no one out of a mad house could fail to see that the advantages were all on our side. But I underrated the power of ignorance and spite, acting upon cowardice."[28] Only wiser counsels persuaded him not to resign in protest.[29]

On September 13, 1901, Vice President Theodore Roosevelt — one-time governor of New York, former Assistant Secretary of the Navy, and ex–lieutenant colonel of the "Rough Riders," the 1st U.S. Volunteer Cavalry which he led on a charge at the battle of San Juan Hill — became the 26th President of the United States. Shots from the anarchist, Leon Czolgosz, at the Pan-American Exposition in Buffalo, New York, had assassinated President McKin-

ley. Roosevelt, not quite 43, became the youngest President in the nation's history. The Harvard-educated Roosevelt took the view that the President as a "steward of the people" should take whatever action necessary for the public good unless expressly forbidden by law or the Constitution. "I did not usurp power," he wrote later in his memoirs, "but I did greatly broaden the use of executive power."

Shortly after Roosevelt assumed office, Hay negotiated a second accord with Lord Pauncefote. The second treaty gave the Senate everything it wanted and the pact was signed on November 18, 1901. Great Britain's surrender of its interests in the canal was a result of its awkward world position in the midst of the Boer War and its consequent willingness to accept the extension of the power of a friendly United States.[30] Certainly, Hay's diplomacy made negotiations with the British easier. But in the final analysis, Theodore Roosevelt, and to a much greater extent, the 77-year-old Senate Chairman of the Committee on Interoceanic Canals, Democrat John Tyler Morgan of Alabama, were the forces behind the changes incorporated into the second Hay-Pauncefote Treaty. Morgan favored a fresh start and advocated the construction of a canal in Nicaragua. He also considered a canal a bonanza for commerce in the Southern United States.

Not relishing the satiric title "His Accidency," Roosevelt set out to prove to the American people that he was entitled to be President in his own right. Nothing, he believed, would impress the country more than the construction of the long-talked about canal after what he called "centuries of conversation." The new President then proceeded to "make the dirt fly" and accelerated America into the future. Roosevelt, a naval expert who believed in military strength, was convinced the Isthmus was the key to American supremacy at sea. The Caribbean was the U.S. Mediterranean, and like the Mediterranean, it demanded a canal, according to American naval scholars. Senators who favored expansionism, chipped in that America would need Hawaii if Roosevelt built a canal. From that point onward, the highly diplomatic and conciliatory Hay would fervently carry out the formal aspects of Roosevelt's ambitions. With the Clayton-Bulwer Treaty no longer an obstacle, the next step for Roosevelt was to decide where the canal would be constructed. The two obvious choices were Nicaragua and Panama.

The new Panama Canal Company, the successor to the failed de Lesseps French syndicate, was asking the astronomical figure of $109 million for the complete rights to its holdings in Panama and was aggressively lobbying influential Americans to abandon plans for a canal in Nicaragua. In November of 1901, the Walker Commission, a group of engineers appointed by President McKinley to study the issue, recommended the Nicaragua route for the canal based on its lower costs and existing franchises. The French panicked when William Randolph Hearst in the *New York Journal* made the results of the secret Walker Commission public. Accordingly the French frantically lowered their asking price by $69 million and offered a distress sale of the Panama concession for $40 million.

Of major importance, the Colombian Minister in Washington, Dr. Carlos Martínez Silva, assured the State Department and the press that his government was ready to deal liberally with the United States concerning Colombia's isthmian province.[31] The government in Bogotá he said would show "No mean nor grasping spirit. Everything in the way of a concession the United States needs to warrant it in undertaking to build the Panama Canal, Colombia is willing to grant."[32] The discounted concession, the better harbors, the fact Panama would be 134.5 miles shorter

and passage would only be 12 hours as opposed to 33 hours in Nicaragua, impressed Roosevelt. Counting on the promise of cooperation from Colombian Minister Martínez Silva, Roosevelt, who had accumulated just over 100 days in office, decided to take the biggest risk of his presidency. The young President, who lived by the motto "never show fear," took on the powerful members of Congress who favored Nicaragua and urged the Walker Commission to reverse its earlier decision and vote in favor of Panama.

The House of Representatives voted for the Nicaraguan waterway, 308 to 2, on January 9, 1902.[33] Nevertheless, nine days later, the Walker Commission would heed the advice of the President and issue a reversal endorsing the Panama Canal. The House vote in favor of Nicaragua shook the Panama Canal Company. Under pressure of losing everything, the new French concern increased its lobbying efforts. They had already hired the most powerful and talented American lobbyists money could buy and were bombarding influential decision makers with pro–Panama rhetoric. Conspicuous among them was William Nelson Cromwell, the partner of the New York law firm of Sullivan and Cromwell that resided at 49 Wall Street. Cromwell was a sophisticated corporate attorney whose area of expertise was "the practice of influence."

One of Cromwell's early measures was to contribute $60,000 to the Republican campaign chest in an attempt to prevent Congressional party members from going on record in favor of the Nicaraguan route.[34] Cromwell reportedly charged the contribution to the new Panama Canal Company and later presented them with another bill in the staggering amount of $800,000 for professional services rendered.[35] The French firm paid him without hesitation. The dapper Wall Street attorney was so good at what he did that one irate congressman called him "the most dangerous man the country has produced since the days of Aaron Burr."[36] Senator John Tyler Morgan would also detest Cromwell for his role in derailing the Nicaragua canal.

One of the authors of the pro–Panama campaign was Philippe Bunau-Varilla, a wily French engineer of the original de Lesseps company who was a large shareholder of the new concern. Bunau-Varilla was a patriot with an excellent command of English, and carried the flag for France after the Walker Commission was published. Bunau-Varilla targeted Roosevelt, Hay and Mark Hanna, the chairman of the Republican National Committee, and advocated Panama as the superior site for the canal. Activity at Nicaragua's Momotombo Volcano in May 1902 prompted Bunau-Varilla to inform American officials that Nicaragua had over a dozen volcanoes and that Panama had none.

The Panama lobby was well-financed, determined, and ingenious. At one point, Bunau-Varilla went so far as to purchase 90 Nicaraguan one centavo postage stamps from local dealers in Washington with a picture of a volcano "belching forth" volcanic activity and "took steps to place one of these stamps in the hands of each Senator."[37] After a difficult debate in Congress, Roosevelt and the new French concern prevailed; the Senate modified the canal legislation and approved Panama by a vote of 42 to 34. The amended measure, which the House accepted, became law on June 28, 1902. Under the new legislation, called the Spooner Act, President Roosevelt was authorized to secure a right of way for the waterway canal in Panama with the Republic of Colombia "within a reasonable amount of time and on reasonable terms."

However, not everything went according to plan. For the next six months President Roosevelt would find a trouble-some roadblock in Bogotá. Negotiations were hampered by a revolving door of Colombian diplomats and a Bogotá government that shifted positions. Minister Martínez Silva retired "in a state of complete exhaustion" and would die a year or so after returning from Washington.[38] Dr. José Vicente Concha, his replacement, spoke no English and had never been abroad except to fulfill his duties in Washington. He "suffered a physical and emotional collapse upon resigning his post and reportedly was put on a ship in New York in a straitjacket."[39] Despite the strain, Concha stood fast and refused to budge from the principle that Colombia was within its rights to ask what it wanted for its most valuable asset. Concha argued that the Wyse Concession explicitly prohibited the sale of the franchise "to any foreign power," and as such Colombia warranted financial compensation for approving the sale.[40]

Complicating matters for Roosevelt and Hay was that Colombia was in the middle of the devastating "War of One Thousand Days." The war started in 1899 and would not end until 1903. During the span of hostilities a staggering 100,000 lives would be lost. (At the turn of the century Colombia had a population of only four million citizens.) Another obstacle for the U.S. was that Colombia was upset with Washington because American troops in Panama restricted the movement of the Colombian armed forces on the Panama Company railway. In 1903, Americans antagonized the Colombians when U.S. troops in Panama required that combatants in the civil war not come within 50 miles of the railroad. The domineering American actions restricting Colombian access to the Panamanian railroad infuriated government leaders in Bogotá.

The President and his Secretary of State were wary of the Spooner Act's mandate to negotiate a treaty "within a reasonable amount of time," and were losing patience with Colombia. Thus, when the Georgetown educated Dr. Tomás Herrán arrived in Washington to replace Concha there was hope in the White House that a treaty was at hand. However, Herrán developed a fear of Roosevelt's "impetuous and violent disposition," and proved to be an extremely cautious negotiator.[41] Moreover, Herrán suspected that President Roosevelt's intentions included the possibility of an outright seizure of Panama by the U.S. "in the name of universal public utility."[42] Therefore Herrán rigidly followed his diplomatic instructions and continued to maintain Bogotá's position that the financial terms of the proposed treaty were inequitable and that Colombia deserved better compensation for their prized territory.

With time running out, the President and his Secretary of State resorted to aggressive tactics. Hay approached Herrán on January 21, 1903, and issued an ultimatum on behalf of the President. Hay threatened to break off all negotiations for Panama and immediately offer American canal construction to Nicaragua unless he fixed his signature on a new Isthmus Treaty giving U.S. what it wanted. After a difficult night contemplating President Roosevelt's domineering unpredictability, Herrán signed the accord the following day. Within 72 hours he received a cable from Bogotá instructing him not to sign and to await further instructions. However, it was too late. Hay provided Roosevelt the signature he needed. The terms of the Hay-Herrán Treaty called for Colombia to transfer the former French canal concession to the United States. In return, the U.S. was to obtain rights to a canal zone ten kilometers wide (6.2 miles) for a cash payment of $10 million and an annual payment of $250,000, beginning in nine years. The leasehold was renewable in perpetuity.

Colombians protested Hay's heavy-handed diplomacy. The entire nation ob-jected to the financial terms, to the impingement upon the nation's sovereignty, and to the unconstitutionality of disposing of Colombian territory in perpetuity.[43] The widespread opposition to the treaty allowed President Marroquín to summon Congress, which he had dispensed with for several years. The Colombian Senate, although favoring a renewal of the negotiations with the United States, voted unanimously against ratification of the Hay-Herrán Treaty on August 12, 1903. Finally, Colombia indicated it was willing to accept the pact for an additional $15 million.[44] However, when that condition was rejected by Washington, leaders in Bogotá decided to wait until October of 1904, when the French concession expired, to legally circumvent American intentions.

Upon the expiration of the French rights, Colombia could dispose of the physical assets of the company to the United States for the coveted $40 million.[45] Colombia thereby elected to play the waiting game and in doing so, made President Roosevelt furious. He declared that the situation "was exactly as if a road agent had tried to hold up a man," and insisted that the "cut throats" and "blackmailers of Bogotá" should not be permitted "permanently to bar one of the future highways of civilization."[46] The President went so far as to draft a message, which fortunately he did not send to Congress, suggesting that the canal strip be taken by force.[47]

Meanwhile, Bunau-Varilla was facing financial disaster if the Colombians waited until the French concession expired. Knowing that the Colombian rejection of the Hay-Herrán Treaty aroused secessionist fervor in Panama, Bunau-Varilla therefore made plans for a revolution. The plan was hatched in Room 1162 of the Hotel Waldorf-Astoria in New York City, where Bunau-Varilla worked out many of the necessary details and raised funds for bribery.[48] The revolutionaries in Room 1162 managed to muster a patriotic army in Panama City that consisted of approximately 500 "bought" Colombian troops and members of the local fire department.[49] The next step was a trip to Washington where Bunau-Varilla met with key figures in Washington, including Roosevelt and Hay, to see what type of cooperation the patriotic army would receive from the United States. Although there was no explicit approval from President Roosevelt, Bunau-Varilla left Washington confident the revolution would not be permitted to fail.

Acting on valuable "insider information," Bunau-Varilla signaled his conspirators in Panama that the U.S. warship, the U.S.S. *Nashville,* would reach Colón on November 2, 1903. The following day, the patriotic army revolted. As expected, the American naval forces prevented Colombian troops loyal to Bogotá from dispersing the patriotic army, thus assuring that the revolution was a success. Moreover, approximately 400 Marines under the command of John A. Lejeune (the future 13th Commandant of the Marine Corps) also landed ashore shortly after the revolution to start the long tradition of American combat troops on duty inside Panama.[50]

A little more than an hour after receiving the news, Roosevelt authorized de facto recognition, which was officially granted on November 6, only three days after the revolution.[51] The patriotic army then formed a provisional government and sent Bunau-Varilla to Washington, as an official envoy, where Roosevelt received him without hesitation on November 13th. The President officially recognized Panama's independence at the meeting with Bunau-Varilla.[52] Five days later, Ambassador Bunau-Varilla and Secretary of State Hay signed a treaty under which the United States was given extraordinary sovereign rights and a wider ten-mile zone to build the Panama Canal.[53]

The Colombian government filed a "Solemn protest" against the United States government's actions and sought to have the Panama dispute submitted to the Hague Tribunal for arbitration. However, Hay rejected the protest and took the position that Panama's independence nullified U.S. obligations in the Bidlack Treaty of 1846. Additionally, Hay warned leaders in Bogotá that after recognizing the independence of Panama, the United States became treaty-bound to guard the new country against aggression by any foreign nation, including Colombia.[54]

Roosevelt steered the United States aggressively. His admonition to "Speak softly and carry a big stick" was now famous. But some Americans protested Roosevelt's actions. The *Springfield Republican* branded the Panama incident as one of the "Most discreditable in our history." The *New York American* editorialized it would "Rather forego forever the advantage of an inter-ocean waterway than gain one by such means as this." Nevertheless, on February 23, 1904, the United States Senate, after another bitter flurry of opposition, approved the treaty by a vote of 66 to 14. Years later, Roosevelt, who was extremely proud of launching the United States on a role of global involvement, would confess to the American betrayal of Colombia. "I took the Isthmus," he boasted to a laughing and applauding audience at the University of California.[55]

Roosevelt, who won the Nobel Peace Prize in 1906 for mediating the Russo-Japanese War, would later defend his actions and offer his version of events in his impressive 1913 autobiography. The athletic former Rough Rider who held that "over or under but never around" was the only way to proceed during nature hikes, obviously was quite proud of his role in building the canal and coated his behavior in strong patriotic terms. Roosevelt wrote: "By far the most important action I took in foreign affairs during the time I was President related to the Panama Canal. Here again there was much accusation about my having acted in an unconstitutional manner ... a position which can be upheld only if Jefferson's action in acquiring Louisiana be also treated as unconstitutional; and at different stages of the affair believers in a do-nothing policy denounced me as having usurped authority ... which meant, that when nobody else could or would exercise efficient authority, I exercised it.

"When we submitted to Colombia the Hay-Herrán Treaty, it had been settled that the time for delay, the time for permitting any government of anti-social character, or of imperfect development, to bar the work, had passed. The United States had assumed in connection with the canal certain responsibilities not only to its own people but to the civilized world, which imperatively demanded that there should be no further delay in beginning the work. The Hay-Herrán Treaty, if it erred at all, erred in being overgenerous toward Colombia."

Theodore Roosevelt offered no regrets for the dismemberment of Panama from Colombia. There's no doubt the world benefited greatly from the marvelous American engineering genius that created the man-made canal. Unfortunately, Roosevelt's determination to see the canal constructed trampled Colombia's sovereign rights. To that end, the President's actions were an assertive demonstration of American Manifest Destiny at the dawn of the new century and for the most part, the nation applauded Roosevelt's behavior.

Picking up in 1904 from the bankrupt French effort, Americans triumphed in a heroic ten-year campaign against the elements. By the time the 50-mile chain of locks and channels opened on August 15, 1914, approximately 5,600 people had died constructing the man-made waterway, many of them black laborers imported from the Caribbean, according to David McCullough's brilliant epic *The Path Between the Seas*. With time, the ten-mile-wide zone along the canal would become an English-speaking enclave under American laws. Additionally, the Americans would call themselves "Zonians" and Panamanians would need permission to enter the enclave. The zone would become the center of United States military activity in Latin America for years and hundreds of thousands of U.S. soldiers would serve there.

Over time Roosevelt's questionable moves made it untenable for the U.S. to retain control of the waterway it built. Fair-minded Americans led by President Jimmy Carter corrected Roosevelt's overzealous diplomacy. In reality the dynamic Roosevelt simply followed the brash will of the American people at the turn of the century. If anything, Manifest Destiny was to blame for the heavy-handed American behavior. The new treaty, replacing the Bunau-Varilla–Hay Treaty of November 13, 1903, was signed by Carter and Panamanian leader Omar Torrijos in 1977 and officially allowed Panama to have complete control of its territory at the conclusion of 1999. Thereafter, the citizens of Panama would be in the unique position of celebrating three different independence days (from Spain, Colombia and the United States) each year.

Joe Toft thrived on stress. He was a fearless, no-nonsense cop, and went about his business in an aggressive fashion. This meant, on occasion, that he would step on toes. Toft was tireless, and dedicated long hours to getting the bad guys. He wasn't Hollywood handsome, but had rugged good looks and an athletic frame that he pushed to the limit on the tennis court. He dressed young, with denim shirts and the top couple of buttons open to show the T-shirt collar. He once posed in *Semana* wearing a bush hat, with one side pinned

Joe Toft (left) and friends appear at a Christmas party in Bogotá in December 1993. From January 1988 to September 1994 Toft managed and directed the U.S. Drug Enforcement Administration's Bogotá station, the largest and most important DEA foreign office in the world. *Courtesy of Joe Toft*

up, which appropriately gave him the look of a big-game hunter. Toft had style and considerable charm to go with this 28 years of experience in busting drug traffickers. To many Americans in law enforcement, Toft was the "Golden Boy." And his assignment to Colombia in January 1988 to manage and direct the Drug Enforcement Administration's (DEA's) station in Bogotá, its largest and most important foreign office, was bad news for anyone that profited from the drug trade … including politicians.

Many powerful Colombians hated him. The honest cops in the Colombian National Police loved him. His problems with certain members of the ruling elite stemmed from his crusade against the flow of drugs. Many elites failed Toft's smell test. His DEA investigators discovered that some less scrupulous members of the rul-

ing elite maintained extremely cozy relationships with drug traffickers. The DEA agents also unveiled glaring cases of official corruption which provided a security ring around the most powerful drug traffickers.

Consequently, influential members of Colombian society and dishonest government officials quickly learned to fear Toft because he frequently used his superb press and television relationships with precision to expose corruption. Toft did such a good job beating up on drug traffickers in Colombia he was honored with the prestigious "United States Presidential Meritorious Service Award" in 1992. In 1993 and again in 1994 he was honored with the acclaimed Colombian National Police Distinguished Service Award.

Therefore when word got out that his tour was up, that he was leaving the country in September of 1994, the bad guys were thrilled. For the most part, his mission was accomplished. Toft spent six years and nine months in Colombia as Chief of the United States Justice Department's DEA office in Bogotá and did a magnificent job. Senior officials in Washington were pleased with his work and offered him the DEA office in San Francisco as his next assignment. It was a tempting location given Toft's fondness for the University of California at Berkeley and its glamorous Golden Bears sports program. But Toft decided to retire. He had had enough of the DEA and was going to join the private sector.

Toft served four different American Ambassadors in Colombia. During most of his time there, he was "obsessed" with hunting public enemy number one, Pablo Escobar, the deadliest drug trafficker on the face of the earth. Escobar's violent reach was immense, allowing him to spill more blood in Colombia and around the world than any criminal in the history of the nation.

Toft shared the nation's joy when Escobar was killed on the afternoon of December 3, 1993. One of his best DEA men was on the Medellín rooftop seconds after the Colombian National Police killed Escobar. The agent immediately called Toft in the U.S. embassy and confirmed the kill. "We got Escobar!" the agent exclaimed. Toft jolted out of his chair when he heard the news. He quickly collected the details, hung up the phone, and shouted into the hall for everyone to hear, "We got Escobar!" Toft then raced to see Ambassador Morris Busby and shared the big news with him. In the end, Escobar was alone, he had no organization to protect him. Ultimately, his downfall was his family. An unnecessarily long call to check the safety of his family allowed authorities to pinpoint his hideout.

"I'm glad we got Escobar," Toft would say afterwards.[56] "I was afraid to leave Co-lombia with him [Escobar] on the loose.... However, at the Escobar celebration I realized in the bottom of my stomach that the battle was not over. To me, the victory was spoiled by the role the Cali Cartel had in the kill and the contamination of the National Police by the Cali Cartel.[57] Escobar was about money and violence.... He brought Colombia to its knees."

Toft then confirmed what insiders long suspected but never made public. "Escobar's death sentence was orchestrated by the Cali Cartel.... They financed the deadly behind the scenes illegal operations to limit Escobar's reach and pulled the strings for the destruction of Escobar's powerful infrastructure. The Cali Cartel was well organized, they knew what they were doing, they established an expensive price list on the heads of Escobar's key people ... then sent Carlos Castaño and his brother Fidel, the founders of People Persecuted by Pablo Escobar, to hunt them down, one by one, murder them, and collect the cash bounty. We wanted Escobar so bad we actually rooted for them. They didn't have the constraints we had. They were ruthless, just like Escobar. We knew the Castaño brothers could do more damage than we could. The Cali Cartel was smart, they disassembled Escobar's empire and made him vulnerable. Without a doubt, the Cali Cartel was responsible for the destruction of Escobar.... We killed him ... but they set it up."[58]

Finally, it was time to leave Bogotá. He had officially resigned from the DEA. He was on his own, a private U.S. citizen. He knew he would miss Colombia a great deal. He had developed many friendships in and around the country, particularly with Rosso José Serrano, of the Colombian National Police, who was a regular tennis partner. Toft fell in love with Colombia and a large part of him wanted to stay despite several death threats. He had learned to appreciate the wonderful qualities of the many good people in the nation.

Toft said the downside of working in Bogotá was attending the funerals of soldiers and police killed in the war on drugs. Overall he worried for the honest citizens of Colombia. The government had a weak judicial system that lacked transparency. Through bribery and intimidation, the Cali Cartel altered and reversed policy decisions by the country's government and banking regulators that interfered with its business, according to Toft.

He would also miss the day-to-day danger in Colombia. He didn't drink; he primarily got his kicks from the chase. Toft's entire professional life was spent putting away the bad guys. His dedication to his job was absolute. He was married to his job—a pattern he had maintained throughout his career and the primary reason why his own marriage had dissolved prior to coming to Colombia. He had strong regrets leaving Bogotá; Colombia was the most dangerous assignment in the world for DEA agents; the private sector job he was about to take provided financial security but lacked thrills.

Deep down he was disappointed because he knew the job was only half done. He realized that the good guys managed to kill Escobar, but there was a far more deadly enemy out there. The Cali Cartel was alive and well. They had helped the Colombian government hunt down Escobar and had acquired powerful friends at the highest level of government in doing so. Somewhere, somehow a deal was struck, Toft was sure of it.[59] Unfortunately, though, he couldn't prove it. But in his heart he knew that the Gaviria government gave the Cali Cartel immunity. To Toft, who saw the damning evidence of government cooperation with Cali Cartel drug traffickers, this was the only explanation for the government's amazing reluctance to investigate, vigorously build a case, prosecute, and jail the powerful drug lords in Cali.[60]

"Escobar always left his calling card. He intimidated Colombia with acts of violence. The Cali Cartel was different, they were sophisticated ... they didn't want to attract needless attention ... they knew violence was a dead end. The Cali Cartel seduced you with money or intimidated you with lawyers, and if that didn't work, then they killed you. They had a meticulous penetration of the Gaviria government and of the Colombian economy. Gaviria was always informed of their position on matters of importance. They used to send him a wish list. The Cali drug organization had well-placed and well-paid members of the Gaviria government advising them and advocating for them at all times. Basically, they were more powerful than the state and the government knew it. So they worked out a secret arrangement so they could coexist without getting in each other's way."[61]

On his way out of the country on September 28, 1994, Toft decided to break his long silence and speak to the press, "on the record." For years the press had hounded Toft for interviews but he always declined. He saved his personal opinion of Colombia for the end of his tour. When he finally agreed to speak, he did so for Colombian television on the condition that it be aired the day after he flew out. Toft jolted Colombia and electrified the world with his perspective. At the time of his departure, Toft was the leading expert on the drug situation in Colombia, so he was supremely qualified to blast the corrupting influence of the Cali Cartel in Colombian politics.

Toft did so by calling Colombia a "narcodemocracy," and said that narcodollars entered the Samper campaign and that narcodollars toppled the Extradition Treaty. "I can't think of a single institution in Colombia that I know of, with any judicial, legal or political influence, which does not have problems of penetration by the narcotics traffickers. The Attorney General's office has serious problems.

Congress is also very infiltrated by narco-traffickers…. Everything favors the Cali Cartel. They got rid of extradition, which was the only thing they truly feared. And now the situation is very favorable for the drug kingpins." Toft was not a politician; he was an honest observer who wanted the world to know the truth about what was taking place behind the scenes in the Republic of Colombia.

The Colombian press was digging into allegations that tapes existed that would prove that Ernesto Samper's presidential campaign received contributions from the Cali Cartel. One television journalist who heard the tapes would optimistically proclaim to friends, "Samper will never govern one day." To Toft, too many Colombians had died in the war on drugs and he wanted to make sure they did not die in vain. He did not share the journalist's enthusiasm that the tapes would prevent Samper from assuming the presidency. Thus he took it upon himself to blow the whistle on the Cali Cartel. Toft was truly afraid the tapes would be swept under a rug and forgotten, and that American officials would join the Colombian government and look the other way, allowing the Cali Cartel to grow in power. Toft was upset that Colombia was led by a president (the newly inaugurated Samper) whose campaign accepted millions of dollars in illegal contributions from the drug lords in Cali. He was also disappointed that the secret tapes that incriminated Samper were kept under wraps by Gaviria, so that Samper could win the elections and keep the Liberals in power.

One of the tapes recorded corrupt Colombian journalist Alberto Giraldo and Cali Cartel boss Gilberto Rodríquez discussing the transfer of funds to the Samper campaign. "What a funny thing … the presidency is in your hands," Giraldo said to Rodríquez. The telephone conversation was reportedly recorded in March 1994,

and then after some unexplained delay the tape were mysteriously given to Andrés Pastrana who, along with Luis Alberto Moreno, delivered it to President Gaviria on June 16, three days prior to the second-round presidential vote. But the tapes were not made public. Therefore, when the nearly eight million Colombian voters went to the polls to select the next president they had no knowledge of the Cali Cartel corruption of the Samper campaign. Toft who quietly managed to get a copy of the tapes from Ambassador Busby shortly after Luis Alberto Moreno dropped them at the embassy, attempted to make the tapes public. He secretly passed copies to a major U.S. publication that got "cold feet" and declined to go public with the explosive information.[62]

Toft's "narcodemocracy" statement created a diplomatic uproar. American officials in Bogotá and Washington immediately disavowed his comments and stressed that Toft was speaking for himself and was no longer on the government payroll. Some of Toft's friends defended him, saying he was burnt out. His remarks reflected years of frustration trying to stop the endless flow of drugs produced in Colombia, they said. Privately many friends cheered his courage. Toft slapped the Colombian ruling elite in the face with his comment. The oligarchy prided itself on its sophisticated culture and bristled at the scathing indictment of their democracy.

Behind the scenes there were many American officials who shared Toft's view and were frustrated with Colombia's reluctance to wage total war against the Cali Cartel. Consequently, Toft's parting narcodemocracy cannonade accelerated a campaign by an influential political actor in Washington to increase the pressure to get tough with the Colombian government. The ringleader of the new crusade was Robert S. Gelbard, the Assistant Secretary of State for International Narcotics and Law Enforcement Affairs and former American Ambassador to Bolivia.

Gelbard was responsible for implementing parts of President Clinton's National Drug Control Strategy. The President's policy involved demand reduction and drug awareness at home, law enforcement and interdiction at home and abroad, and a variety of law enforcement, diplomatic, and alternative development initiatives designed to get other countries to take more aggressive actions on their own. Gelbard was the point man for Colombia. When Toft made his narcodemocracy statement Gelbard was judiciously drafting a shrewd new strategy to attack the Cali Cartel. More importantly Gelbard managed to skillfully navigate the strategy through the most important corridors of power in Washington. The Gelbard blueprint was studied and approved at the highest levels of the American chain of command: President Clinton, Attorney General Reno and Secretary of State Warren Christopher.[63] The most important objective of the strategy was to insist that Colombia sign an extradition treaty with the U.S.

Gelbard, a polished can-do Brooklyn-born career State Department official, graduated from Colby College in 1964, studied economics at the Massachusetts Institute of Technology, and then went on to receive an M.P.A. in economics at Harvard. The former New Yorker and big fan of the Los Angeles Dodgers had all the makings of a white-shoe investment banker and conceivably could have crossed the East River and enjoyed a lucrative career on Wall Street. But instead he took the high road, went to Washington and dedicated himself to a professional life in the State Department. In some ways Gelbard had the wholesome sincerity of a Boy Scout. But his personality also had a tough side, which he used to play hardball with the enemies of the United States.

Gelbard was troubled with the Cali Cartel's untouchable status in Colombia and single-handedly spearheaded an aggressive strategy of high-stakes pressure towards Bogotá. The new "antinarcodemocracy" strategy was introduced with a "holier-than-thou" attitude and included a deafening "megaphone diplomacy." The messenger of Gelbard's hard-hitting diplomacy was the brand-new American Ambassador in Bogotá, Myles R.R. Frechette, a sophisticated State Department veteran and trade expert with little experience in international narcotics and law enforcement but with impressive credentials in Latin America. The official target of the Gelbard-inspired strategy was the Cali Cartel, but the political protagonist that Gelbard wanted to manipulate in order to destroy the drug traffickers was Ernesto Samper. Hence, the Chilean-born Frechette, whose only previous ambassadorship was in Cameroon, was given responsibility for one of the most difficult assignments in the Foreign Service.

Gelbard distrusted Samper well before Toft's narcodemocracy farewell. He was not alone in his assessment of Samper. The White House, the Justice Department, the State Department, the DEA and the FBI shared Gelbard's view. The U.S. had a thick pile of intelligence reports on Samper that dated back to the late 1970s. The reports linked Samper to unsavory characters. Samper hit the U.S. intelligence radar screen in 1979, during his early days in politics, when he advocated the legalization of marijuana cultivation in Colombia. However, as his political career advanced moderates in the Foreign Service advocated a low-key approach to him. The moderates wanted to encourage strong economic ties with Colombia and thought it was in the U.S.'s better interest to maintain good relations with Bogotá. The moderates were confident that if elected president, Samper would conform to U.S. needs and provide strong Colombian leadership against transnational crime.

Hard-liners in the State Department were not sure Samper could be trusted, but they were willing to try to reach a reasonable accord with the Liberal Party candidate for the sake of maintaining strong U.S.-Colombian relations. Therefore when Samper came to Washington in the spring of 1994 the State Department devised a unique strategy. State Department officials decided that they would publicly greet Samper in a cordial manner but they would also take advantage of his visit to take him aside and issue a strong warning to him in a private "one on one" chat.[64]

Thus, when Samper arrived in Washington with his two top aides, Fernando Botero and Rodrigo Pardo, hard-liners in the State Department were waiting to rain on his parade. Ambassador Alexander Watson, the State Department's top official for inter–American affairs, chaired the meeting. Watson was a highly regarded diplomat with many admirers in Bogotá. After a round of political and socioeconomic talks, Samper was invited to meet with Gelbard. Once he was alone with Samper, Gelbard wasted no time on small talk. The message was succinct, and the delivery was straightforward. Gelbard informed Samper that the U.S. had already developed an "extraordinary" amount of information that he and his representatives were "actively" soliciting funds from narcotraffickers.[65] Samper was stunned. He had no idea there was going to be a showdown. "Stop it now!" Gelbard told Samper. "If you take these funds ... we will know about it. You still have time to save this relationship. Stop it now!" Gelbard repeated.[66]

Samper managed to keep his cool. He was known throughout Colombia for having a strong sense of humor, but he instinctively knew that this was no time for jokes. Samper innocently responded to

Gelbard that illegal funds were prohibited from entering his campaign. He also calmly assured Gelbard that a "fail-safe mechanism" had been created by his election team to prevent the corruption of his campaign. Gelbard looked Samper in the eye and simply accepted his answer. As far as he was concerned, his mission was completed. On the other hand, Samper was vividly aware Washington was troubled. He had officially been put on notice. He now knew for certain the U.S. was not convinced of his political purity and took the flagrant measure of warning him that surveillance operatives were going to watch his every move.

The meeting was a turning point in Colombian-American affairs. It was an open secret in Washington that drug traffickers had been buying political influence in Colombia ever since Alfonso López became President in 1974. Insiders also knew that there were serious allegations that Samper accepted a $1 million campaign contribution from Pablo Escobar in 1981. Samper reportedly accepted the funds on behalf of former president Alfonso López who was attempting a presidential comeback in 1982 and needed the funds to bankroll his campaign.[67] In the past, Americans looked the other way when drug traffickers bought political favors. U.S. officials preferred to overlook campaign irregularities to preserve the bilateral relationship.

Not any more, however. The Cali Cartel had grown too dangerous. They were winning the war on drugs and manipulating Colombia's weak political and judicial institutions. The U.S. could barely dent the Cali Cartel protective armor. Moreover, with billions of dollars of holdings in Colombia, and with blue-chip European and American asset management firms placing hundreds of millions of narcodollars into the major financial centers of the world, the Cali Cartel was practically invincible. Their purchasing power was great. They could easily retain the most unscrupulous minds in the world, and they were also capable of acquiring the most sophisticated technology available to fine-tune their criminal enterprises and stay two steps ahead of U.S. law enforcement officials. In reality, the war on drugs was a rout. The United States was not even 5 percent of the global population of 6 billion but it consumed 50 percent of the cocaine produced in the world. Consequently, Gelbard raised the intensity of the war on drugs. After the toe-to-toe meeting with Samper, the hard-liners in Washington were certain that only a desperate person would doubt the resolve of the U.S. and allow the contamination of the campaign by the Cali Cartel.

A few months later, on June 19, 1994, 44-year-old Samper won the presidential election by a bare 2.1 percent margin over Andrés Pastrana.[68] News of the tapes and the fact that the campaign was tainted by Cali Cartel drug money was quickly buzzing among senior Clinton Administration officials. It was the first major piece of evidence that corruption had reached the highest levels of government in Bogotá. White House officials privately expressed dismay that Samper would actually take the oath of office on August 7, 1994. Gelbard told *Time* magazine the corruption of the campaign was the "Worst information we could receive. If these accusations are true, it will definitely affect bilateral relations."[69]

Publicly, Samper vehemently denied he took the drug money and demanded a full Congressional investigation of the allegations. Privately, he cursed his luck. The rapidly escalating Bogotá drugs and politics hullabaloo was taking on a life of its own. So much so, that towards the end of June, president-elect Samper decided to go on a working vacation in New York. The trip was scheduled to allow him to relax, to see old friends, and to enjoy a feast at

one of his favorite New York restaurants, Peter Luger's Steak House across the Williamsburg Bridge in Brooklyn. Samper would also fine-tune new social programs he had promised to the people of Colombia and make last minute preparations for his new administration. Samper's enemies in the Pastrana camp said he went to New York to escape the media frenzy in Bogotá.

When the White House got wind of Samper's plans to be in the United States, officials jumped into action. They immediately contacted the Colombian Ambassador in Washington, Gabriel Silva, and formally requested a meeting with the president-elect. Silva realized the seriousness of the request and called President Gaviria to establish the meeting. Samper dreaded meeting with American officials before he took office and said he had no intentions of visiting Washington during his trip. Samper was haunted by Gelbard's "stop it now" warning and wanted to meet with American leaders as President of the Republic of Colombia. However, when the State Department responded that they would be willing to meet with him in New York, he had no choice but to acquiesce.

On June 29, 1994, Samper reluctantly met in New York with three State Department officials. The trio comprised Deputy Assistant Secretaries Michael Skol and Cresencio Arcos, and Ann M. Wells, the Colombian Desk Officer in the Office of Andean Affairs. The composition of the U.S. delegation was balanced. Skol was the moderate, Arcos was the hard-liner, and Wells was the skilled neutral observer. Skol, a polished diplomat with years of experience in Bogotá, was known to be sympathetic to Colombia. His presence was a comfort to Samper. Arcos on the other hand made Samper nervous. The president-elect knew if he was going to get verbally hammered in the meeting the blows would come from Arcos, who worked for Gelbard. Samper was convinced Arcos was an advocate of Toft's growing "narco-democracy" school of thought — that politicians ran the government in Colombia and drug lords pulled the strings.

Skol and Arcos were ordered to New York by Clinton heavyweights Deputy Secretary of State Strobe Talbott and Tony Lake of the National Security Council. The agenda for the Samper meeting was approved at the highest levels of government. The meeting took place in midtown Manhattan, at the 57th Street office of Colombian Ambassador to the United Nations, Luis Fernando Jaramillo. Samper attended the meeting with Rodrigo Pardo, Néstor Humberto Martínez and Ambassadors Jaramillo and Silva.

The purpose of the meeting was to send another strong warning to Samper. Skol and Arcos were to make sure Samper knew that the Colombian-American relationship was at risk. Skol would patiently explain to Samper that the relationship could be saved, and that the U.S. was willing to give the president-elect the benefit of the doubt, and look to the future. Arcos bluntly said meet our demands or else.

Arcos told Samper that in order to avoid a serious rift with the United States he would have to take a hard line with the Cali Cartel. Specifically, he was told the U.S. wanted the Cali Cartel drug lords arrested and that Colombia must put an end to President Gaviria's soft plea bargains and short jail terms for drug traffickers. The meeting was somewhat contentious. Samper denied the allegations against him and protested the heavy-handed fashion in which he was treated. Samper reiterated his defense that his campaign had a mechanism to prevent the entry of illegal contributions and underlined his commitment to the war against drug traffickers.

The meeting basically was a standoff. Samper stated his innocence, insisted on being treated in a presidential fashion, and promised diligence in the war on drugs.

Skol, who attempted to reason with Samper, was certain the president-elect was well aware of the diplomatic dangers ahead. Arcos, who used forceful terms, was not convinced Samper was going to declare war on the Cali Cartel. Years later, Skol would observe that Samper was given every opportunity to preserve his reputation, and avoid a destructive schism with the Clinton White House.[70]

American law enforcement officials were cynical of Colombia's intentions. "There is evidence that the Colombian government has lost its stomach for the contest ... Colombia is tired of fighting drug traffickers and is willing to let the Cali families launder their money, legitimize their wealth and their names so their sons and grandchildren can someday run for President," a DEA agent in Bogotá told *Time* magazine.[71] The most dramatic indication of rising Washington-Bogotá tensions in July 1994 came when Thomas Constantine, the head of the DEA, abruptly canceled a planned courtesy meeting with General Octavio Vargas Silva, the Chief of Colombia's National Police.

Snubbed, the police chief flew back to Colombia and in a press conference indignantly defended his integrity against published reports that he had taken drug money. "I swear on my honor as a policeman, I swear to God, I swear on my family's honor, I have never broken my oath to serve my country," he insisted.[72] President Gaviria was outraged by the U.S. smear campaign directed at Vargas, who as head of the National Police, was credited with hunting down Pablo Escobar.

In Bogotá, Colombians were dumbfounded with the American behavior. Many Colombians considered the American statements slanderous. At the early stages of the Samper campaign investigation, Colombians rallied around the flag. "The only thing the tapes prove," columnist Enrique Santos wrote in *El Tiempo,* "is that the Cali Cartel was interested in financing campaigns ... not that it succeeded." Samper had modified his statements and conceded that the Cali Cartel had indeed offered his campaign money but that it was not accepted.

Samper wasted little time acting on the U.S. warnings. Upon his return to Bogotá he started a campaign to change Washington's perception that he was in hock to the Cali Cartel. He promised a final push, "one last great battle," against the narcothreat. Within days of his return to Colombia, the president-elect responded with a broadside of pronouncements underlining his strong commitment to the war against drugtraffickers. Samper planned to introduce legislation that would strengthen Colombia's anemic attitude toward money laundering and pledged to increase criminal penalties for drug traffickers. He also wanted to establish an "Elite corps" of investigators to track down drug-related corruption in the government. Samper also wrote a letter to Jesse Helms, the Conservative North Carolina Senator, who was one of his American critics, saying, "We know who the bosses of the Cali Cartel are and we will capture them."[73] Overall, the president-elect was desperate to show Washington that his government would get tough with the Cali Cartel.

Samper had four years to break the grip of the drug traffickers in Colombia and shifted funds earmarked for social programs to fight the war on drugs. Unlike President Gaviria, who argued that the drug-trafficking problem represented only a small aspect of the Colombian reality, Samper reluctantly conceded that the drug barons yielded tremendous political influence in the nation. Samper also attempted to reform Colombian Congress. He was aware of U.S. alarm over corruption in the Congress. Americans were very suspicious of the 263 lawmakers who made up the Colombian Senate and National Assembly during Gaviria's government. The DEA ran the names of the 263 members of Congress into Naddis (the DEA's computerized list of suspects) and scores showed up on the list. Seven of Colombia's 32 governors also appeared on the Naddis list.

The U.S. was still smarting from the elimination of the Extradition Treaty in 1991, and was demoralized by a series of slippery legal initiatives passed by Congress over the years called "narco-micos" that were beneficial to drugtraffickers. Samper went to work to try to clean up the unlawful practice of selling votes to the drug traffickers. However, he downplayed the amount of corruption and asserted that there were no more than 20 dishonest lawmakers in the entire Colombia Congress. A DEA spokesman in Bogotá disagreed. The DEA countered that "from 50% to 70% of Congress is influenced in one way or another by the Cali Cartel."[74] The U.S. was also concerned about the lack of dedication of the Colombian National Police and wanted to weed out members of the security forces on the Cali Cartel payroll. Nonetheless, Samper's quick reflexes won praise in Washington and officials urged the president-elect to continue his diligence. The job to root out Narco corruption was massive. The Cali Cartel's influence within the borders of the nation even decided the outcome of the Miss Colombia beauty contest.[75]

President Gaviria received worldwide credit for eliminating Pablo Escobar and the Medellín Cartel, but in 1994 few observers of Colombian affairs were aware that the Cali Cartel served Gaviria Escobar's head on a silver platter. Samper's job was much more difficult than Gaviria's. The Cali Cartel's lavish use of bribes managed to seduce hundreds of important armed forces officers, police officials, judges and political actors in Gaviria's government. Colombia was an abyss and Samper's duty was immense. He needed someone in law enforcement to ride in on a white horse to clean up the mess in Colombia. Samper also needed the ruling elite to come out of the closet and admit that narcotraffickers had corrupted the nation. It was a strenuous task. Construction was booming with the help of surplus narcodollars, and few Colombians cared to admit that new malls and many of the splendid architectural achievements in the nation's rich skyline were the result of insightful investments made by the sophisticated heads of the Cali Cartel.

Despite the obvious dedication to please Washington, Samper made one fatal mistake. He ignored the wishes of senior American narcotics law enforcement officials. Fernando Botero, Samper's nominee for Defense Minister, had already informed Gelbard during a trip to Washington that he could "have anyone you want," as Chief of the Colombian National Police. The U.S. appreciated Botero's consideration and recommended General Rosso José Serrano for the position. Serrano, a highly organized, honest police officer, was highly recommended for the position by Ambassador Busby and Toft. Gelbard had never met Serrano but after studying his file, was confident he was capable of sanitizing the Colombian National Police.

However, when Samper decided to send Serrano to Washington as an attaché to the Colombian embassy against the explicit wishes of the U.S., and instead nominated General Guillermo Diettes to head the National Police, trouble started. The decision had major ramifications. In the post–Cold War era, international crime was a major threat to world stability and American national security. Diettes was a key Colombian law enforcement official in the downfall of Pablo Escobar, but U.S. intelligence reports indicated he was closely aligned with the bosses of the Cali Cartel. As a result, Diettes did not pass U.S. drug law enforcement inspection. Some Americans suspected Diettes was on the Cali payroll. Subsequently, the selection of Diettes by Samper was considered bad faith and an indication he was not truly committed to attacking the Cali Cartel.

"He [Diettes] did not have a strong track record fighting drugs and his appointment was a sign that Samper was playing games in the war on drugs," according to Gelbard.[76] American officials were astounded that Samper would not cooperate on such an important appointment given the two strong warnings (in Washington and New York) that the U.S. would judge him on his actions, not on his words. Hence, the designation of Diettes was ultimately considered a move to afford protection to the Cali Cartel and a harbinger that Samper could not be trusted. The U.S. was not prepared to completely write off the Samper government as a partner in the war against drugs but they would not longer give him the benefit of the doubt.

President Samper, riding high after almost a year in office, ultimately caved in to American pressure in late 1994 and appointed General Serrano the Chief of the Colombian National Police. The White House did unnerve Samper with a presidential national interest waiver during the March 1, 1995, annual certification ritual, but the nation was content that the U.S. did not decertify Bogotá and announce to the world that Colombia was not a reliable ally in the war on drugs. However, with General

Opposite top: General Rosso José Serrano, Colombian National Police Chief, is surrounded by security and staff while signing a document in front of a village cathedral outside of Bogotá.

Bottom: General Serrano inspects elite Colombian National Police anti-narcotics troops at a landing zone prior to their departure on a search and destroy mission. *Both photographs courtesy of Gil Macklin*

Serrano's remarkable arrests of Cali Cartel chiefs (Gilberto Rodríquez, who said, "Don't kill me. I am a man of peace," when he was captured; and Miguel Rodríquez, who proclaimed, "The President is an honest man," when he was put in jail), Samper was feeling secure about his situation. Moreover, the arrests of other major Cali kingpins, Henry Loaiza alias "El Alcarán" and José Santacruz Londono quieted the talk of illegal campaign contributions.

A few weeks prior to the one-year mark, a poll released by *Semana* magazine indicated that 63 percent of Colombians gave Samper a favorable approval rating despite allegations that his election campaign pocketed $6 million from the Cali Cartel. However, the President suffered a major political setback on July 29, 1995, when his former campaign treasurer Santiago Medina was arrested and made damaging accusations under questioning from prosecutors in the office of Colombia's independent chief prosecutor, Alfonso Valdivieso.

The first victim of the political storm was Fernando Botero, the refined 39-year-old Defense Minister and former Samper campaign manager who many Colombians assumed would be the next president of the Republic of Colombia. Medina confessed to prosecutors that Botero plotted to accept $6.1 million from the Cali Cartel. Botero immediately resigned his position as Defense Minister so he could devote time to his defense. He also declared his innocence, and surrendered to police on August 15. Overall, Medina's revelations stained the nation. The people of Colombia were sick that the world now had hard evidence that they were indeed a "narcodemocracy." In addition to implicating Botero, Medina also claimed the dirty money was raised with Samper's full knowledge and he was told by the President through Botero to thank the Cali Cartel for their generosity.

Damage control was impossible. Samper said he would answer, one by one, the falsities and defamatory remarks to justice authorities and labeled Medina a "Dubious character."[77] The President's office released a statement supporting the prosecutor's actions and also expressed confidence that Botero would be able to prove his innocence. Samper was already under investigation by the Accusations Committee of the House of Representatives (the Colombian lower house) which was made up of many of his Liberal Party cronies, but he was now facing the strongest scrutiny of his presidency. In an attempt to answer his mounting critics in the country, the President declared that if any drug money was used by his campaign it happened "behind his back."[78]

Medina told prosecutors he was approached twice in the spring of 1994 by representatives of the Cali Cartel with offers of money. Initially, Botero rejected the illegal contributions, he said. However, on April 29, 1994, Botero called him into his office and said it was necessary to receive the support that the Cali Cartel was offering, according to Medina. He was then instructed to travel to Cali to meet with the Rodríquez brothers to ask for two billion pesos ($2.4 million) to finance the first round of the two-stage election, set for May 30.

On May 2, 1994, Medina said, "I had a chance to talk with Mr. Samper and told him Mr. Botero had asked me to get these funds."[79] By Medina's account, Samper "told me very nervously that he wanted to be on the margin of this and that I should coordinate it with Fernando Botero."[80] When Medina traveled to Cali to solicit the money, he took with him "five points" that Botero said that Samper wanted to impress on the Cali bosses. He also said that Samper appreciated their backing and valued their help to gain the presidency. Medina added that Samper backed Gaviria's surrender policy and the policy of negotiation to overcome drug trafficking and violence. (The policy would allow for short sentences and enable the Rodríquez brothers to keep their vast property and assets.)

Ultimately, Medina was given only one billion pesos ($1.2 million) for the first election round. With the cash-strapped campaign facing a June 19 runoff, Botero reportedly sent Medina back to Cali to ask for an additional $4.7 million. The drug lords agreed to the request but only if they were given an accounting of how it was spent, according to Medina. After receiving a list of expenditures, signed, Medina said, by Botero, Miguel Rodríquez said (in reference to Botero's famous father, the artist Fernando Botero, Sr.), "This is the smallest but most expensive Botero I own."[81]

At 7:00 A.M., on September 28, 1995, Colombia's death squads got involved in the scandal. Heavily armed assassins fired machine guns at cars carrying President Samper's lawyer and bodyguards, killing two bodyguards and injuring the lawyer. The Bogotá attack on Antonio José Cancino, who was on his way to a nearby university to teach law, complicated the Samper inquiry. However, U.S.-Colombian diplomatic relations sizzled when Samper's loyal political ally, Interior Minister Horacio Serpa stopped short of blaming American officials but suggested to the press that U.S. drug agents were behind a conspiracy to topple Samper and destabilize Colombia.[82]

A group called the Movement for a Dignified Colombia claimed responsibility for the attack and said Samper, his wife and other government leaders would be targeted next.[83] Cancino was present when the head of the Congressional Committee questioned Samper about the illegal campaign allegations a few days before the attempt on his life. The attack took place when five gunmen jumped from a van and fired automatic rifles at Cancino's Mercedes Benz and his bodyguards' car, a witness told Colombia's RCN radio. Cancino, 55, was taken to a military hospital, where doctors treated wounds in his right arm and hand. A third bodyguard was also injured.

Hours later, a telephone caller told radio stations that the group claiming responsibility wanted Samper to resign and criticized the President for trying to "undermine" the probe of the campaign, according to the Associated Press. Cancino publicly attacked the efforts of Prosecutor General Alfonso Valdivieso, who was in charge of the investigation into the influence of drug corruption on Colombian politics. The Valdivieso inquiry, which was named the *Proceso 8.000,* was gathering momentum, and many Colombians were convinced Samper would be impeached. Without providing details, the caller said the group was made up of people, "Who are accused of deeds they did not commit."

Serpa raised diplomatic tensions in Washington when he said officials in the U.S. embassy and the DEA, "Are part of a conspiracy against the President ... I know that in social gatherings, top embassy officials make all kinds of conjecture and speculation about whether President Samper is going to fall, and that to me is extremely serious."[84]

The moves by Serpa to protect Samper were some of many to discredit the work of the U.S. embassy and the start of a war of words with Ambassador Myles Frechette in Bogotá. In a statement from the President's office, the attack was blamed on "dark forces that are trying to create a climate of confusion," and prevent the President from proving his innocence. It also said government prosecutors investigating Samper contributed to the unrest.[85]

Botero abandoned the defense of President Samper on January 21, 1996. The former presidential campaign manager and crucial actor in the acceptance of Cali Cartel narco-dollars told Colombian television program CMI, "He [Samper] knew. It's the truth. He knew…. It's a central fact. He is very severely compromised." Botero's admission left President Samper fighting for his political life. In a television and radio address after Botero's charges, an angry Samper described his former campaign manager's accusations as monstrous lies and adamantly ruled out any move to resign from the presidency. However, an emotional Samper admitted to the nation, "For the first time in many years, the institutional stability of the country is threatened."

The only thing saving Samper's credibility was General Serrano. Since assuming command in the fall of 1994, the Chief of the Colombian National Police had demolished the Cali Cartel by hunting down and jailing the kingpins of the criminal organization. DEA Administrator Thomas Constantine, who spent his entire professional life as a policeman, admiringly called Serrano's work "The most important arrests in the annals of law enforcement." Years later Constantine would say, "When they write the history of Colombia, it will say Serrano saved the nation."[86]

As a result, Samper was arguing that if illegal contributions were accepted in his campaign, it was done without his knowledge and that his government was doing more against drug traffickers than any other administration in the history of Colombia.

"It was one of my biggest personal frustrations," Samper said. "There was no Chief of State in any country who fought drug trafficking as much as I did … and in return I was treated very badly. It will be said that the dismantling of the Cali Cartel was the job of the Colombian Police exclusively, but do you think that an operation of such magnitude, that involved a dozen state agencies, could have taken place without the express will of the President? It would be perverse and ridiculous to think so."[87]

Samper and Serrano were compiling an impressive list of accomplishments. The Colombian government had passed some of the toughest anti-money laundering legislation in the world and the National Police had eradicated 35,000 hectares of illegal crops. Moreover, Samper and Serrano militarized the nation's seven main airports, captured the biggest shipments in the world of precursor chemicals to process coca, and attempted to stamp out narcocorruption in government. Clearly, Samper was arguing, Colombia was shouldering more of its responsibility for fighting the global threat of narcotics trafficking and international organized crime. However, Samper and Serrano were still unable to stop the heavy flow of cocaine and heroin into the United States as a glut of new small local cartels of drug traffickers, much harder to infiltrate and deter, stepped in to fill the void created with the breakup of the Cali Cartel. Ultimately, the natural laws of supply and demand continued to circumvent the best efforts of law enforcement officials allowing the drug trade to remain firmly entrenched in Colombia.

On March 1, 1996, President Clinton placed Colombia with the group of pariah nations (Burma and Afghanistan) that were not cooperating in the war on drugs. Mexico on the other hand received a passing grade and was certified. The move to decertify Bogotá in accordance with the Foreign Assistance Act of 1986 was based on increased coca production in Colombia and a lack of faith in President Ernesto Samper. The decertification of Colombia without economic sanctions was an abrupt turnaround from the business as usual approach afforded the Gaviria government by the Clinton administration.

During the first term of the Clinton administration, the President certified Colombia and Mexico's participation in the war on drugs, worked to pass NAFTA, convened the first Summit of the Americas in Miami, reversed the Mexican peso crisis, restored democracy to Haiti, and brought peace to Guatemala. Now, with the decertification of Colombia, the White House was rolling up its sleeves to teach Bogotá a lesson on how it wanted the war on drugs to be played. Unfortunately, President Clinton lacked the conviction to include Mexico in the diplomatic parenting Colombia was about to get.

Samper was indignant and protested the decertification. No nation in the world matched General Serrano's success breaking up and jailing the top six criminal members of the Cali Cartel, according to the President. Samper thought the highly acclaimed arrests were ample proof of Colombia's commitment to the war on drugs. The Colombian press was upset with the glaring double standard used by President Clinton. They resented the fact that Mexico was given a passing grade and was certified under the powers of the Foreign Assistance Act despite the rapid expansion of Mexican drug syndicates across the United States. The lack of consistency on behalf of the White House generated conflict and bred resentment in Bogotá, particularly among the front-line police and soldiers risking their lives to stop the supply that fed America's destructive appetite for drugs.

For the most part, Latin Americans considered the certification process a sham. Mexican President Ernesto Zedillo called the certification process "offensive" and proposed that the United States be subject to the same review. Other Latin American leaders disapproved of the unilateral, scorecard approach by the United States, the world's largest consumer of illicit drugs.

The Colombian press pointed out that the Mexican government had consistently failed to meet antidrug targets established by Washington and that with the absence of high-profile arrests, official corruption in Mexico was probably much greater than that in Bogotá. Therefore, Colombians understood they were subjected to a higher standard than Mexico and concluded that the White House considered the trade benefits of NAFTA much more important than the war on drugs. In the end, Colombians knew they were now the new whipping boy of American drug policy hard-liners. Former U.S. diplomats and moderates in the State Department agreed. They privately admitted that the certification process was "bad foreign policy," and lamented the isolation of Colombia by the Clinton Administration.

The State Department moderates were hoping the White House would shape the character of the hemisphere so that it could become "A cornerstone of our prosperity and security for the 21st century." Instead, Clinton, a man of extraordinary intellectual powers, a President with a slavish obedience to public opinion polls, decided to use Colombia as a political pawn to counter criticism that he wasn't tough on drugs. In doing so, the White House crippled the Samper government internationally, increased anti–American hatred in Colombia, and unwittingly provided the FARC leadership with valuable propaganda legitimizing their plans to overthrow the government.

Senator J. William Fulbright, one of President Clinton's heroes, once said, "If America has a service to perform in the world, it is in large part the service of our own example." The double standard applied on the decertification of Colombia was a black eye for U.S. foreign policy and failed to live up to Fulbright's criterion. One of the most powerful men in the White House admitted that "Samper's complications made Colombia hard to certify."[88] The statement confirmed what Colombians feared ... that they were not decertified because they did not fight the war on drugs, but because the White House did not trust who was running the country. Colombians would not receive the credit that they well deserved because the distrust of Samper by State Department hard-liners blinded them from the cold reality that the Republic of Colombia was indeed the strongest ally the U.S. had ever known in the war on drugs.

One theory as to why the White House took such a tough stance with Samper had to do with the critical information of a former Cali Cartel financial wizard, Guillermo Pallomari, the well-paid accountant for Miguel Rodríquez, who surrendered to the U.S. witness protection program with his children on September 18, 1995. (Cali Cartel assassins had murdered his wife and best friend.) Pallomari, who was a citizen of Chile, reportedly provided the codes that allowed law enforcement officials to decipher the vast financial network of the Cali Cartel. Robert Gelbard went as far as to say that the information Pallomari provided to the United States was the "Rosetta Stone" of narcotrafficking.[89] Gelbard also said the information related to many countries and explained that it was "tremendously frustrating to see democracy battered" by narcotraffickers.[90] Law enforcement officials in Colombia, Mexico, Switzerland and the United States benefited from Pallomari's information.[91] As Rodríquez's accountant, Pallomari knew what public officials received Cali Cartel payoffs and where the organization's money was laundered.[92]

The Pallomari disclosures were never made public. However, law enforcement insiders said that if Miguel and Gilberto Rodríquez were ever extradited to the United States, the Pallomari information would provide the evidence to keep them in American jails for the rest of their lives.

In what was dubbed "the trial of the century" by the local media, Colombian lawmakers absolved President Samper of drug-corruption charges on June 12, 1996. Samper was the first sitting Colombian president to go through an impeachment trial and was cleared of wrongdoing when the Colombian House of Representatives voted 111–43. American hard-liners considered the vote further proof that the Colombian Congress was corrupt. The hearings included two weeks of rowdy debate, 14 congressional sessions, and nearly 80 speakers. However, there was no doubt the one individual who saved the day for Samper — his loyal Interior Minister, Horacio Serpa. The tireless Liberal Party strongman with tremendous influence along the Atlantic coast of Colombia single-handedly maintained support for Samper. With the political demise of Fernando Botero, Serpa was the obvious Liberal Party front-runner for the presidential elections in 1998 and he took to the airwaves with passionate speeches pleading that Colombians stand behind the man they elected president in 1994.

The Clinton administration reacted with displeasure to the absolution. "The decision to clear Mr. Samper leaves unanswered many questions regarding pervasive narco-trafficker influence on Colombia's institutions and it will not resolve the resultant crisis of confidence," the State Department said in a brief statement. However, critics of Samper in the U.S. Senate called for stepped-up sanctions against Colombia. "If the Clinton Administration does nothing, I think there will be a movement in Congress to take action," a Senate source told the *Dallas Morning News.*[93]

Critics of Samper in Colombia, were hoping the President would "fall on his sword for the good of the nation," before the U.S.-Colombian relationship deteriorated further. However, President Samper's spin on the vote was that the process "demonstrated the strength of Colombian institutions."[94] In the political parlors of Bogotá, the President's supporters were whispering that the DEA, CIA, and other U.S. agencies were plotting to overthrow the Samper government. The President's critics in Colombia complained that Samper's strong Liberal Party loyalty was nurtured by political favors.

The congressional decision marked a major victory for the embattled Samper. The Colombian Congress could not try him again on charges of illicit enrichment, falsifying documents, electoral fraud or cover-up despite the sworn testimony of his former finance manager Santiago Medina, and his former campaign manager Fernando Botero. However it did not quiet opposition to his government. Colombian Senator Jaime Arias, president of the Conservative Party, called the 90 hours of debate before the vote "a comedy."[95] One anti–Samper group called the Colombians for a Referendum, was pushing for a vote to decide whether the people wanted the president to remain in office. "We hope to help create new guarantees that will allow for a real opposition and real alternatives," said Pablo Bustos, a member of the group's coordinating board.[96] Colombians for a Referendum collected 90,000 signatures, far short of the 1.8 million required to force new elections.[97]

Pedro Rubiano, a Catholic bishop in Colombia, was the author of the most famous quote on the more than $6 million narcodollars that entered the Samper campaign for president. "The likelihood the President did not know about the contributions was the same as someone not realizing that an elephant was sitting in his living room," Bishop Rubiano said.[98]

Nearly a month after the lower house vote clearing the president, on July 11, 1996, the U.S. State Department threw what hard-liners hoped would be the punch to knock Samper out of power. Citing the "substantial evidence" that the campaign "solicited and received something over $6.5 million" from known drug traffickers the State Department revoked Samper's U.S. visa. "Our message is clear and it is simple: People who knowingly assist narco-traffickers are not welcome in the United States," said State Department spokesman Nicholas Burns. The decision was approved by President Clinton and supposed to be announced to Samper by Ambassador Frechette. However, due to schedule conflicts, Samper was already aware of the White House decision from news reports by the time Frechette arrived at the Casa de Nariño to officially announce the revocation.[99] Not surprisingly, the initiative to pull the plug on Samper's visa, which was approved by Secretary of State Christopher before being sent to the White House, was drafted by none other than Robert Gelbard.[100]

State Department officials explained that Samper failed to show his commitment to antidrug efforts after his absolution by Congress, by failing to honor U.S. extradition requests on June 24. The extradition requests were for, among others, the jailed brothers, Gilberto and Miguel Rodríquez. Colombian Justice Minister Carlos Medellín responded to the U.S. request with a letter to Attorney General Janet Reno explaining that extraditions were banned by the Colombian constitution. In essence the U.S. was asking Samper to do what President Gaviria was unable to accomplish during his four-year term in office. Nonetheless, the hard-liners in the State Department were pushing Samper hard despite the fact that he was forbidden under Colombian law to fulfill the American extradition requests. Also complicating matters at the time was U.S. anger over the early release from jail of Jorge Luis Ochoa, a founder of the Medellín Cartel, after serving only five and a half years for drug trafficking.[101] The U.S. tried to extradite Ochoa for drug and murder charges as early as 1984 and was extremely unhappy with the generous surrender agreement given to him.[102] Jorge Luis Ochoa's brother, Juan Ochoa Vásquez, was released from prison in July 1996 after serving five months of a six-year sentence. Juan Ochoa was wanted in the U.S. for the 1986 slaying of a DEA informant. A third brother, Fabio, was due to be released from a Colombian prison in August of 1996. All three brothers surrendered to President Gaviria's government and were offered early releases in return for aiding Colombian law enforcement authorities in apprehending other drug traffickers.

Samper addressed the General Assembly at the United Nations in New York on September 23, 1996.[103] The Colombian President asked the world community not to "demonize" his nation, saying his homeland was more a victim than a villain in the war on drugs. "Colombia wants to be part of the solution. We don't want to continue being satanized in the face of the world because of the problem of which we, like all of you, are victims," he said.[104]

Samper proposed a plan against "narcoterrorism," saying drugs and terrorism were inextricably linked. He asked the U.N. for economic aid to replace illegal crops with legal ones; for controls on the sale of chemicals and weapons to drug traffickers and producers; for worldwide application of a European agreement against money-laundering; for an international intelligence center for narcotics information and eventually an international tribunal for drug cases; and for better programs to stop consumption.[105] "One cannot place the entire burden of drug fighting on drug-producing countries, which are the weakest link," he concluded.[106]

In March 1997, Colombia was optimistic about certification. President Samper's Minister of Foreign Affairs María Emma Mejía and Colombian Ambassador to the United States Juan Carlos Esguerra had conducted an exhausting campaign to open American eyes to the "Herculean" effort Colombia had made in the war on drugs. Colombia had accumulated an impressive record. The Samper government authorized tougher 30-year sentences for crimes, implemented rigorous money laundering legislation, pushed through some of the strictest asset forfeiture laws in the world and approved a new maritime treaty with the United States making it easier to nab drug traffickers at sea.

Even Ambassador Myles Frechette was positive. "Despite strained political relations, cooperation between Colombia and the United States has improved. Clearly, in some areas there has been considerable progress," he said.[107] Moreover, Frechette broke ranks with the hard-liners in Washington and officially recommended that Colombia be certified. Unfortunately his expert opinion was ignored.

Colombians were aware that the decertification process did little to curb the supply of drugs entering the United States. They also realized that the certification process was demeaning, and they had little respect for the U.S. policy. "The policy has not worked. Instead, it has provoked an anti-gringo feeling among the vast majority of Colombians.... By making certification a political trial, the United States has ignored [the fact] that the war on drugs is a universal problem.... No other country in Latin America has done so much so effectively as Colombia in counternarcotics related issues, no other country has shepherded antinarcotics laws such as ours," Minister Mejía said.[108]

Despite the outstanding record fighting against all drug traffic related issues, the State Department hard-liners won again. The United States decided to decertify

Colombia for the second year in a row and again give Mexico a passing grade. (The decision to certify Mexico again was a highly questionable move, given the embarrassing news that General Jesús Gutiérrez Rebollo, the nation's top drug law enforcement official, was arrested for secretly working for drug traffickers two weeks earlier, on February 18, 1997.)

President Samper called the Clinton Administration's decision to label Colombia an untrustworthy ally in the war on drugs "demoralizing and unjust.... It is a unilateral decision for Colombia that is totally unacceptable," he said.[109] "Decertification fails to recognize the work of thousands of police, soldiers, prosecutors and fumigation pilots who risk their lives every day on the front lines.... This is profoundly unjust."[110]

Morris Busby, the former U.S. Ambassador in Bogotá who served from 1991 to 1994, didn't like the certification process. Busby, who was also formerly the U.S. government's senior counterterrorism official for three years and directed the U.S. counterterrorism efforts during the Persian Gulf War, was careful not to criticize the Clinton administration but said, "It could have been handled more delicately so that Colombia would not be treated in a harsh fashion."[111] Busby said that what was happening in Colombia was a big challenge for the United States. "We have a mutual interest in the war on drugs and the question that should be addressed is how do we express our unhappiness in some reasonably strong way without destroying the interest we're trying to promote."[112]

Busby was a naval officer for 15 years before entering the Foreign Service. He received a number of military decorations, including the Navy Commendation Medal with the "V" for valor and a Bronze Star for combat action in Vietnam. His military background made him keenly sympathetic to the daily dangers Colombia's combat troops were encountering in the war on drugs. Busby privately questioned the wisdom of announcing the decertification of Colombia and then asking its young men to go into the jungle and risk their lives blowing up labs that were protected by well-armed guerrillas and paramilitary death squads.

Colombians were infuriated with the White House decision. In a surprise move, President Samper announced that he was temporarily suspending Colombia's drug crop eradication program in a direct response to Washington's decision to decertify his nation and lump it with the outlaw drug countries of Iran, Nigeria, and Burma.[113] In Washington, State Department spokesman Nicholas Burns said the U.S. embassy in Bogotá was informed of the decision but received no explanation. "We hope this decision has been taken for technical reasons only and not policy reasons. We certainly urge a resumption of the eradication operations as soon as possible," he said.[114] Samper's international affairs adviser, Diego Cardona, said Colombia was taking a "temporary break" in antidrug cooperation with the United States to evaluate priorities, but denied reports that Colombia might retaliate for the decertification by expelling U.S. drug and CIA agents within its borders.[115]

Colombians were exasperated. One official, Labor Minister Orlando Obregón crabbed, "The marijuana U.S. officials smoke isn't allowing them to see things objectively."[116]

The State Department hard-liners wanted an extradition treaty, and they were going to pressure Samper until he gave it to them. In that regard, Samper was in a quagmire. He was clinging to power by doling out political favors. Consequently, he wasn't politically strong enough to deliver an extradition treaty on U.S. terms.

But Samper realized that Luis Carlos Galán was right. An extradition treaty would give law enforcement officials in Bogotá the teeth to fight drug traffickers, although, he realized, Colombia was not ready to approve a treaty that was retroactive. However, in a last-ditch attempt to show the world his commitment to the war on drugs he lobbied for the extradition treaty aggressively.

It was a long and difficult process. Finally, after weeks of back-room arm-twisting, in December 1997, Samper achieved his greatest contribution to the war on drugs. The President and his loyal political ally, Minister Horacio Serpa, skillfully navigated groundbreaking legislation through the Colombian Congress that overturned the 1991 decision to eliminate the extradition treaty with the United States. It was a crowning achievement for Colombia. The new law, lifting the six-year ban on extradition, was not retroactive, but did provide overwhelming evidence that Colombia did not belong in the Clinton doghouse. As a result of this impressive legislative victory, the U.S. conditionally certified Colombia in March 1998, ending two years in decertification purgatory as a pariah nation.

Looking back on the era, there was never a U.S. ambassador in Bogotá who played such a public role in Colombia as Myles Frechette. The American Ambassador was the country's second most recognized figure, after President Samper.[117]

"My charter was pressure, and I applied it, and obviously it had the desired results," said Frechette in an interview before his departure from Colombia.[118] On October 8, 1997, Ambassador Frechette received the Secretary of State's Distinguished Honor Award for his accomplishments as President Clinton's personal representative and for "performing superbly in an area of critical importance to the United States."

Historically, Theodore Roosevelt and William Jefferson Clinton were the only two Presidents in the chronicles of the United States to publicly belittle Colombia for the entire world to see. Both American Presidents pursued policies that scandalized Bogotá. In addition, Roosevelt and Clinton had no respect for the leaders in Bogotá and took assertive actions to advance self-serving American objectives. The major difference between the two Presidents was that Roosevelt had the Panama Canal to show for his deeds and Clinton ended up empty-handed. The former Governor of Arkansas supported a failed U.S. drug policy that inadvertently nurtured a new generation of guerrilla warriors in Colombia that were prepared to destabilize the region.

Although President Roosevelt undoubtedly inflicted the greatest damage to the Republic of Colombia with the severing of Panama from it, President Clinton would be remembered for taking a wrong turn and abandoning Colombia during a crucial time in its civil conflict. By placing Colombia in the decertification doghouse and by regularly bashing Ernesto Samper, President Clinton created a schism in Bogotá that ruptured the credibility of the government and unconsciously allowed the armed groups in the civil conflict to multiply their presence inside the borders of the nation.

Upon his retirement in May 1999, DEA Administrator Constantine said that the most important achievement of his five-year tenure was working with the Colombian National Police to dismantle the Cali Cartel.[119]

Constantine also warned that Mexican drug trafficking gangs posed a growing threat to the United States.[120] Interestingly, Constantine confessed that he never sat down with President Clinton to discuss drug policy, that he was never called to brief the President on a major enforcement issue, and that he was frequently frustrated as Administrator of the DEA by "the policy-makers from the National Security Council, and the State Department who started with the premise that they were going to certify Mexico."[121]

Overall, President Clinton was the first president since Herbert Hoover (1929–1933) not to visit Latin America during his first term in office. Moreover, unlike President Franklin Delano Roosevelt who established the "Good Neighbor Policy," President John F. Kennedy who introduced the "Alliance for Progress," and President George Bush who implemented the "Enterprise for the Americas Initiative," the Clinton White House virtually ignored the big picture in Latin America until Mack McLarty took over as Special Envoy to the Americas in December 1996. In regard to the U.S. counternarcotics campaign, President Clinton's hard-line policy piled up considerable achievements in the war on drugs but all in a losing effort. Statistically, the production of cocaine in Colombia never decreased; it increased, according to the CIA.[122]

Subsequently, anything gained in the war on drugs by the White House subtracted from Colombia's efforts to find a solution to their complicated civil conflict. In reality, the bullying of Bogotá and the inexcusable neglect of the peace process by the Clinton White House during the Samper government aided the guerrillas. Fortunately, Republicans in Congress, particularly Representatives Benjamin Gilman, and Dan Burton recognized the danger to democracy in Colombia and championed critical support to Bogotá in its time of need. Unfortunately, after all the efforts of both nations, survival for most honest hard-working countryside Colombians today is reduced to four simple choices: a. join the guerrillas; b. join the paramilitary death squads; c. leave the countryside for the safety of the big cities; or d. die a violent death.

Notes

1. Robert W. Drexler, *Colombia and the United States: Narcotics Traffic and a Failed Foreign Policy* (Jefferson, N.C.: McFarland & Company, 1997), p. 7.
2. *Ibid.*, p. 9.
3. Thomas A. Baily, *A Diplomatic History of the American People*, 8th ed. (New York: Appleton-Century-Crofts, 1969), p. 168.
4. *Ibid.*
5. *Ibid.*, p. 187.
6. *Ibid.*
7. Drexler, p. 27.
8. *Ibid.*, p. 4.
9. David McCullough, *The Path Between the Seas: The Creation of the Panama Canal 1870–1914* (New York: Simon & Schuster, 1977), p. 112.
10. Baily, p. 273.
11. *Ibid.*, p. 274.
12. *Ibid.*
13. *Ibid.*, p. 275.
14. *Ibid.*, p. 276.
15. Drexler, p. 40.
16. *Ibid.*
17. *Ibid.*
18. *Ibid.*, p. 39.
19. McCullough, p. 70.
20. *Ibid.*, p 65.
21. *Ibid.*, p. 135.
22. *Ibid.*, p. 145.
23. *Ibid.*, p. 182.
24. *Ibid.*, p. 235.
25. Baily, pp. 475–476.
26. Norman A. Graebner, *An Uncertain Tradition: American Secretaries of State in the Twentieth Century* (New York: McGraw-Hill, 1961), p. 2.
27. *Ibid.*, p. 33.
28. *Ibid.*
29. *Ibid.*, pp. 34–35.
30. *Ibid.*, p. 35.
31. McCullough, pp. 268–269.
32. *Ibid.*, p. 269.
33. Baily, p. 489.

34. *Ibid.*
35. *Ibid.*
36. McCullough, p. 271.
37. Baily, pp. 489–490.
38. McCullough, p 329.
39. *Ibid.*, pp. 329–330.
40. *Ibid.*, p. 331.
41. *Ibid.*, p. 332.
42. *Ibid.*
43. Baily, p. 490.
44. *Ibid.*
45. *Ibid.*, p. 491.
46. *Ibid.*
47. *Ibid.*
48. *Ibid.*, p. 492.
49. *Ibid.*
50. *Marine Corps Gazette,* "Marines Depart Panama," Quantico, Virginia, January 2000.
51. Baily, p. 493.
52. Drexler, p. 46.
53. *Ibid.*
54. *Ibid.*, p. 47.
55. *Ibid.*, p. 46.
56. Author interview with Joe Toft, 16 March 1999, at secret site in the Rocky Mountains of the United States.
57. *Ibid.*
58. *Ibid.*
59. *Ibid.*
60. *Ibid.*
61. *Ibid.*
62. *Ibid.*
63. Author interview with Robert S. Gelbard, 20 October 1998, the State Department, Washington, D.C.
64. *Ibid.*
65. *Ibid.*
66. *Ibid.*
67. Liberal Party candidate Alfonso López received 2,797,627 votes (41 percent) and lost the 1982 Colombian presidential election to Conservative Party candidate Belisario Betancur who received 3,189,278 votes (47 percent).
68. Liberal Party candidate Ernesto Samper defeated Andrés Pastrana by the narrow margin of 3,696,745 votes to 3,563,445.
69. *Time International Inc.,* "Colombia: The Electronic Eavesdropper Was Taping an Explosive Conversation," 4 July 1994, p. 20.
70. Author interview with Michael Skol, Washington, D.C., July 1998.
71. *Time International Inc.,* p. 20.
72. *Time International Inc.,* "The Skirmishing Between the U.S. and Colombia Over Charges That Drug Money reached into Presidential Politics," 25 July 1994, p. 16.
73. *Time International Inc.,* "Colombia: Something Was Afoot in Washington," 8 August 1994, p. 10.
74. *Ibid.*
75. *Ibid.*
76. Author interview with Robert S. Gelbard, 20 October 1998.
77. *Time International Inc.,* "Rocked by Scandal Samper's Presidency Is in Peril as an Aide Claims His Boss Knew of Campaign Gifts from Cali Drug Kingpins," 14 August 1994, p. 20.
78. *Ibid.*
79. *Ibid.*
80. *Ibid.*
81. *Ibid.*
82. Associated Press, "Lawyer for Colombia's President Wounded in Attack, Two Bodyguards Killed," Bogotá, 28 September 1995.
83. *Ibid.*
84. *Ibid.*
85. *Ibid.*
86. Author interview with DEA Administrator Thomas A. Constantine, Arlington, Virginia, 16 February 1999.
87. Author interview with Ernesto Samper, Madrid, Spain, 1 December 1998.
88. Author interview with Thomas F. "Mack" McLarty III, Washington, D.C., 30 October 1998.
89. Author interview with Robert Gelbard, 20 October 1998.
90. *Ibid.*
91. The Associated Press, "Ex-Cali Cartel Accountant Sentenced," Miami, 16 December 1998.
92. *Ibid.*
93. *Dallas Morning News,* "Samper's clearing prompts questions: Action puts pressure on U.S. drug policy," Washington, 14 June 1996.
94. *Ibid.*
95. *Dallas Morning News,* "Colombia leader cleared of Accepting Drug Funds: Vote Does Not End Samper's Troubles," Bogotá, 13 June 1996.
96. *Ibid.*
97. *Ibid.*
98. *Ibid.*
99. Author interview with Myles Frechette, Bethesda, Maryland, 16 October 1998.
100. Author interview with Robert Gelbard, 20 October 1998.

101. Richard Bashor, *Chicago Tribune,* "U.S. Angry as Medellin Cartel Founder Is Freed from Prison," Washington, 6 July 1996.

102. Reuters, "Colombia Says It Can't Extradite Drug Lords," Bogotá, 30 June 1996.

103. Because of its international charter, President Samper did not need a U.S. visa to speak at the United Nations.

104. Barbara Crossette, *New York Times,* "Colombian (Yes, Samper) Lectures U.N. About Drugs," New York, 24 September 1996.

105. *Ibid.*

106. *Ibid.*

107. *Washington Times,* "Recertification of Colombia?" Washington, 1 March 1999.

108. *Ibid.*

109. *Dallas Morning News,* "Samper Calls Move to Decertify Colombia for 2nd Year Demoralizing," Bogotá, 1 March 1997.

110. *Ibid.*

111. Author interview with Morris B. Busby, the Ritz-Carlton, Pentagon City, 30 October 1998.

112. *Ibid.*

113. The Associated Press, "Colombia Suspends Drug Eradication Program," Bogotá, 6 March 1997.

114. *Ibid.*

115. *Ibid.*

116. Tim Padgett, *Time,* "Colombia: Still in Washington's Drug Doghouse," Bogotá, 10 March 1997.

117. *Minneapolis–St. Paul Star Tribune,* "Ambassador to Colombia Ends Tough Assignment," Bogotá, 9 November 1997.

118. *Ibid.*

119. Douglas Farah, *Washington Post,* "DEA Director Retiring After 5 Years at Post," Washington, 25 May 1999.

120. Tim Golden, *New York Times,* "Retired Drug-Enforcement Chief Says Hands Were Tied on Mexico," Albany, New York, 26 May 1999.

121. *Ibid.*

122. On 15 February 2000, the CIA released a study that reported a sharp increase in Colombian cocaine production. The CIA said cocaine production reached 520 tons in 1999, up from 435 tons in 1998, and 230 in 1995.

CHAPTER TEN

The Peacemaker

A political victory ... the return of your absent friend ... and you think good days are preparing for you. Do not believe it. Nothing can bring you peace but yourself. Nothing can bring you peace but the triumph of principles. —Ralph Waldo Emerson, *Self-Reliance,* 1841.

No one in Colombia had ever seen a protest like it before. On Sunday, October 24, 1999, the same day the government officially opened peace talks in Uribe, millions of Colombians took to the streets and waved white flags of all sizes with the words "No Más" (No More). The protesters wore white tee shirts with green ribbons and peacefully demanded an end to the most brutal violence in the hemisphere. They passionately wanted an end to the conflict, an end to the kidnappings, and an end to the massacres. The marches were big news and were broadcast live on Colombian television stations. Foreign correspondents compared the marches to the early days of the 1960s antiwar movement in the United States. All in all, it was the largest peace protest in the history of the nation. Approximately six million Colombians in 17 cities across the country participated in the nonviolent demonstration.

Thousands also participated abroad; Colombian exiles held simultaneous peace rallies in cities throughout the world, including New York, Houston, Los Angeles,

Miami, Washington, Paris, London, Madrid, Caracas, Venezuela and Lima, Peru. Organizers in Colombia claimed inspiration from nonviolent leaders Mohandas Gandhi and Martin Luther King, Jr., and said they hoped they would establish a trend in Colombia to end the violence that bred indifference and apathy among the masses. Organizers also said that the nation was sick and tired of the bloodshed and wanted to bring an end to the long period of violence in Colombia by increasing pressure on the government and the belligerents.

The main targets of the peace march were the guerrillas, paramilitary death squads and drug traffickers who inflicted the violence on the innocent citizens of the nation. However, many marchers urged the government to produce more visible advances in the peace negotiations. Others voiced regret with the slow pace of negotiations. Overall, President Pastrana's peace process had stumbled since the government agreed to withdraw government troops and create a demilitarized zone for the FARC guerrillas in November of 1998.

After the missed opportunity in January 1999, when Sureshot failed to show up at the peace table in San Vicente del Caguán, Pastrana settled on a sweeping negotiating agenda in May. But the talks deadlocked when the President demanded that an international verification committee be allowed to enter the zone to monitor rebel activity. Faced with determined FARC opposition to the idea, Pastrana dropped the demand and proceeded with the talks.

Overall, the peace process was an exasperating experience for the President. He gave Sureshot every opportunity to wage peace, but Pastrana had absolutely nothing to show for his efforts. It seemed every time he made a concession to the FARC they asked for more, without offering anything in exchange. The one-sided negotiations damaged the credibility of the talks. The major stumbling block in his discussions with the FARC was the paramilitary death squads. The FARC wanted Pastrana to stop the death squads from conducting massacres. The President responded that he was doing everything in his power and had already fired two generals for tolerating paramilitary actions. The FARC wanted him to do more and cringed when the President routinely denied the that armed forces had any active role in the death squads. Despite the lack of progress, Pastrana maintained his optimism. After 14 months in office, the President continued to argue that a peace accord was not an impossible dream. Admirably, his enthusiasm for peace never wavered. To all, it appeared that Andrés Pastrana was as dedicated to his role of "Peacemaker" in October of 1999 as he had been when he first assumed office in August 1998.

Meanwhile, the government and the FARC attempted to jump-start the peace process with face-to-face negotiations. "Either we will destroy ourselves, or we will rebuild ourselves," peace commissioner Víctor Ricardo said in Uribe, a small ranching town in the southern demilitarized zone 125 miles from Bogotá. Unfortunately, Ricardo's outstanding reputation for fairness was under attack. The Harvard-educated political scientist, who had wandered through mountains and jungles in search of peace, was now the antagonist of the extreme right in Colombia. Hardcore Conservatives made it well known that they thought Ricardo was entirely too sympathetic to the cause of the guerrillas. As a result, rumors swirled around Bogotá that the President's commissioner was the top target of death squads that were enemies of the peace process. Consequently, friends cautioned Ricardo to tone down the rhetoric calling for strong social reforms or risk suffering with the same fate as the beloved comic Garzón. To his credit, Ricardo ignored the warnings and showed his fearlessness in his opening remarks at the peace talks.

"Whoever thinks that the mass marches of today and tomorrow are exclusively against the guerrillas is wrong," Ricardo declared. "No, ladies and gentlemen. What those multitudes want, what they ask for, what they will have is social, political and economic justice that creates conditions for peace…. Today, millions of Colombians are demanding that we begin negotiations, and now we are…. Our historic responsibility is to stay at the negotiating table until we have a peace treaty." Ricardo also shed light on the guidelines for the talks. "There are only three subjects that are not in discussion. Respect for private property, democracy as a system of government, and recognition of national boundaries."

Raúl Reyes, the FARC spokesman and key negotiator, opened his remarks by saying, "We ratify our desire for peace with social justice … this will put to test the government's will to permit structural transformations." Camouflage-clad FARC soldiers carrying AK-47, American AR-15 and Dragunov sniper rifles put their own spin on the "No More" messages. On dusty streets controlled by the FARC, guerrilla soldiers displayed banners that demanded: "No More Unemployment," "No More Massacres," and "No More Torture." Townspeople in Uribe wore shirts with the message "No More Gringo Military," a reference to the stepped-up U.S. military aid being used by the government to fight guerrilla units that protect the illegal drug trade. Reyes even went as far as to issue a warning to Washington, "No more meddling of the North American state in the internal affairs of Colombia."

After the opening remarks, 13 government representatives and ten FARC delegates began reviewing a 12-point negotiating program while seated under a canopy in Uribe's elementary school. The agenda envisioned the eventual disarmament of the guerrillas in return for sweeping reforms to ease poverty, redistribute land to peasants and combat political corruption. Reyes reiterated that the FARC was ready to set up a pilot program to persuade peasant farmers to switch from drug crops to legal produce in the municipality of Cartagena del Chairá. The proposed site of the crop experiment was adjacent to the demilitarized zone but not included in it. If government security forces withdrew from there as well, it would leave the FARC with a self-ruling enclave stretching from almost the southern border with Ecuador to within a few hours of Bogotá. In rejecting the FARC's earlier crop substitution plan, the Pastrana government said it was unprepared to pull security forces out of an area even broader than the existing demilitarized zone.

Pastrana and Sureshot did not attend the talks in Uribe. Their presence would only be required during the final stages of the negotiations. In reality, few Colombians expected a quick solution at the peace table. Political analysts predicted a final peace deal could take years, perhaps even a decade. As such, most Colombians expected a continuation of the warfare. A Gallup poll published in *Cambio* magazine the morning of the marches indicated that 80 percent of Colombians disapproved of the way the Pastrana government was handling the peace negotiations, and only 16 percent of the individuals polled believed the FARC leaders would negotiate in good faith.[1] A separate poll in *El Tiempo* reported the chilling news that two-thirds of Colombia's top business leaders favored calling in foreign troops to crush the guerrillas.[2]

The day of the marches, Antonio Navarro Wolff, the former M-19 guerrilla turned congressman, looked at the big picture when he warned that the war in Colombia had turned into a stalemate, and a military victory was impossible. "The two sides must realize that the war is unwinnable," he told Bogotá's *Caracol* television. "If either side thinks they can win the war, there will be no peace treaty." For the most part, the news in Colombia was thoroughly negative.

"The image of the peace process now has turned bleak and languid," wrote former Foreign Minister Rodrigo Pardo in *El Espectador* the morning after the marches. "But the government and the guerrillas must be moved by so many feet marching at the same time." At the conclusion of the brief Uribe peace talks both parties agreed to reconvene on November 2, in nearby San Vicente del Caguán, to continue the dialogue that they hoped would produce a lasting peace treaty.

Ricardo refused to divulge his "private strategy" for peace but did say that he wanted to "create spaces of confidence" and that the government needed to enact multimillion-dollar development programs to counter years of state neglect in war-torn regions. The strongest admission the President's peace commissioner volunteered in regard to the government's official position was, "We have said peace has a price but we are not prepared to make peace at any price."

Washington's fears that the corruption-ridden Colombian military was losing the war against the "Unholy Alliance" of FARC guerrillas and drug traffickers was pushing the United States to step up its involvement with the Colombian armed forces, despite their long history of human rights abuses.[3] The $289 million aid package in 1999 included the partial funding for the 950-man army special counternarcotics battalion, a CIA-sponsored intelligence center and listening post deep in Colombia's Amazon jungle[4] and substantial support for General Serrano's National Police forces. The decision to "cautiously reengage" the Colombian military was a dramatic shift from previous policy, but now that the FARC was financing its war efforts with revenue from drug traffickers, Washington considered the guerrillas "fair game." U.S. officials said they had little choice in the decision, given the FARC's growing involvement in drug trafficking.[5]

Secretary of State Madeleine Albright examined the complexities of the Colombian situation in a thoughtful op-ed piece in the *New York Times*.[6] Albright explained how both the guerrillas and paramilitaries used the drug trade to finance their operations. She also wrote, "Colombia's problems extend beyond its borders and have implications for regional security and stability. To turn the tide, President Pastrana must wage a comprehensive effort. And he needs … and deserves … international support that focuses on more than drug interdiction and eradication." The Secretary of State concluded her foreign policy essay by stating "Colombia's people are engaged in a vital test of democracy, a test they must pass for themselves. But they should know that we understand the many dimensions and long-term nature of the problems they

face, and that we will do all we can to help them."

Despite the strong show of support by Albright, the plan to help Colombia was generating strong reservations among some within the administration who feared the United States was being drawn more deeply into a convoluted civil conflict.[7] "It is going to be a very dangerous mess," said a senior official who had worked on Colombia. "And we are going to be in the middle of that mess."[8] Not since the Central American civil wars of the 1980s had the United States attempted to come to the aid of a Latin American ally threatened by an insurgency.

Officials still remembered the brutal 1980 paramilitary murder of El Salvador's most respected Roman Catholic Church leader, Archbishop Oscar Arnulfo Romero, as he celebrated Mass in San Salvador. Romero's murder and other horrors in Central America weighed heavily on the minds of many officials in the White House and increased the discomfort with the growing role in Colombia. Without a doubt, though, the clear winner in the administration's debate was Andrés Pastrana, whose biggest achievement as President in his first year in office was making sure Colombia would not walk the plank into the unknown alone.

In October 1999, the United States Congress was studying a new aid package that would greatly expand American involvement in Colombia. One of Colombia's strongest congressional allies was Speaker of the House Dennis Hastert, Republican of Illinois. In September, President Pastrana was in Washington seeking billions in economic and military assistance to rally a reeling Colombia. Hastert was in a key position to dictate the legislation and Colombia had good reason to expect that its request would be favorably heard. However, there was disagreement among American lawmakers over what the

Congressman Dennis Hastert in Colombia examines a National Police commando figure offered by General Rosso José Serrano. *Courtesy of Gil Macklin*

money should buy. About 60 Democrats demanded in a June letter that Colombia improve its human rights record before it received more U.S. aid. The Democrats were determined that Congress did not "tip-toe" around the human rights problem in Colombia.

Pastrana was seeking $3.5 billion in U.S. assistance over the next three years for "peace, prosperity and strengthening the state." He also was quietly pleading with American lawmakers "to look the other way" and not let the human rights issue derail the aid package. The Clinton administration made no formal commitment to Pastrana, but was thinking along the lines of $1.5 billion spread over three years. Although the White House did not speak

in absolute terms, one thing was certain, senior officials did not want to be outflanked by Republicans Gilman and Burton as they were with the 1999 aid package.

On Capitol Hill, lawmakers were quoting a figure of nearly $1 billion per year flowing from drug traffickers to rebel forces. "This is our war as much as Colombia's war," said Indiana Representative Dan Burton.[9] "The billions we're talking about for dealing with the drug problem down there is not enough."

From the opposite end of the political spectrum, Senator Christopher Dodd, Democrat of Connecticut, a Latin American specialist on the Senate Foreign Relations Committee, said he was concerned about excessive U.S. involvement in the rebel war. But he said the problem the guerrillas posed to the Colombian government could not be exaggerated. "Colombia is a country that is on the brink of losing its sovereignty," Dodd said.[10]

During his trip to Washington in September Pastrana explained he wanted U.S. military equipment, technical support, training and intelligence as his government assembled a special battalion of 950 members dedicated to helping police fight narcotraffickers. The force could grow to 4,000 within three years, he said. In an example of how the force might work, Pastrana described a scenario in which police using helicopters to spray defoliants on coca crops came under fire from rebels on the ground—a common occurrence in Colombia. The proposed counternarcotics battalion could be used to suppress the hostile fire, serving both a counterinsurgency and counternarcotics role. Pastrana also met with James Wolfensohn, President of the World Bank, and Enrique Iglesias, head of the Inter-American Development Bank, to discuss dealing with the social impact of the war on drugs.

The gray area between the war on drugs and the war against the guerrillas protecting the Colombian drug trade had many American lawmakers worried. Language approved by the House Armed Services Committee and accompanying the House-passed defense authorization bill for the year 2000 said the committee supported the war on drugs but "remains concerned about the prospect of U.S. military personnel being drawn into Colombia's war." In August 1999, Army Secretary Louis Caldera told an interviewer, "It is hard to separate the missions, because a lot of the insurgents are involved in drug trafficking. It they are involved in drug trafficking, then we have to go after them, regardless of whether the line gets blurred or not."

State Department spokesman James Rubin said that the Pentagon was required to plan for various military contingencies, including possible use of force in Colombia, but that did not mean such an option was actively being considered by the administration. He said the guerrilla situation and the drug problem were linked, but the priority for the U.S. policy was narcotrafficking. "We do not intend to provide counterinsurgency aid to the government of Colombia," Rubin said.

A major problem for Colombia was President Pastrana's creation of the demilitarized zone. It enraged Republicans on Capitol Hill. "Support for increased military aid to Colombia should be dependent on the restoration of government access to the narco-guerrillas' 16,000 square-mile zone of impunity," Representative Benjamin Gilman said after a meeting with Pastrana in September.[11] Gilman was one of the most respected Americans in Colombia and was someone who could lecture Pastrana. Democrats also strongly urged Pastrana to be more aggressive in meeting the combined guerrilla and drug trafficking challenge.

Representative Dan Burton was also ticked off at Pastrana. Burton, who along with Gilman had the strongest record of helping Colombia on Capitol Hill, said Pastrana lost credibility during his September trip to Washington by not bringing along General Rosso José Serrano, "the most effective drug fighter" in the world. "President Pastrana knows how much influence General Serrano carries with the Congress," Burton said, adding that it would be difficult to support aid unless the bulk of it went to the police. Stung by the criticism, President Pastrana told a reporter, "The President of Colombia is President Pastrana, not General Serrano."[12]

Luis Alberto Moreno, Colombia's Ambassador to Washington, was counting on House Speaker Hastert. "He is the one

Left to right: CIA Director John Deutch, FBI Director Louis Freeh, and Congressman Ben Gilman discus the war on drugs in Washington, D.C. *Courtesy of Gil Macklin*

most committed member at the leadership level of your Congress who understands what needs to be done and is willing to do it," he said. "Every time you talk to him, he is very focused on it."[13] Before he was speaker, Hastert went to Colombia four times, helicoptering to remote police bases in the rain forest, and visiting wounded members of the National Police in hospitals. Now that he had risen from relative obscurity to his present position amid the turmoil of impeachment and a sex scandal in the Republican leadership, Hastert was bringing to his office forceful opinions on Colombia just as U.S. policy towards Bogotá was reaching a critical juncture. "I think the oldest democracy in the South-ern Hemisphere is in great jeopardy," declared Hastert. "I'm concerned about Colombia because of the implications it has for our kids ... the heroin and cocaine that comes into our country."[14]

The internal debate in the White House reflected major concerns that the U.S. could be drawn more deeply into a longstanding civil conflict. The one point of agreement among senior officials was that something had to be done. However, the political and financial constraints of the federal budget were starting to emerge as a problem for Colombia. Neither the White House nor Republican lawmakers wanted to be the first to break the balanced budget limits by embracing an expensive foreign aid program. Another major problem for Colombia was continued allegations by major human rights organizations that members of the army acted "hand in glove" with paramilitary groups and cooperated in civilian killings and even massacres.

In November 1997, Democratic Senator Patrick Leahy of Vermont authored Section 570 of the Foreign Operations Appropriations Act. The new law prohibited distribution of U.S. aid to military units whose members were found to have committed gross violations of human rights. The so-called "Leahy Amendment" would guarantee that the human rights viewpoint would be included in the Colombian aid package. This was particularly important since Pastrana's architect of the $3.5 billion request, Minister Jaime Ruíz, openly admitted that "a bit more than half" of the money Colombia requested was earmarked for strengthening and restructuring the army.[15] Ruíz made it clear that Colombia was hedging. "A country cannot bet everything on a peace process," he said.[16] Therefore, Democrats in Congress armed with the Leahy Amendment were prepared to make sure that human rights organizations would have their say before funds would start pouring into the coffers of the Colombian armed forces.

Republicans initiated the important legislation providing aid for Colombia. Republican Senators Paul Coverdell of Georgia and Mike DeWine of Ohio drafted a massive military aid package for Colombia in the fall of 1999. The $1.5 billion three-year proposal (2000–2002 fiscal years) provided for $540 million for helicopters and other equipment to attack new coca and opium poppy crops in southern Colombia; $405 million for air interdiction and enhanced law enforcement programs; $365 million to enhance regional drug interdiction; $120 million to develop alternative opportunities to growing drug crops

in Colombia, Bolivia and Peru; and $70 million to bolster democracy and human rights in Colombia. Powerful political actors lined up to support the legislation.

President Pastrana praised the Republican plan, calling it "a good starting point." General Charles Wilhelm, the chief of American military forces in Latin America, stressed the importance of the aid package "For negotiations [peace] to succeed. I'm convinced that the government must strengthen its negotiating position, and I believe that increased leverage at the negotiating table can only be gained on Colombia's battlefields."[17]

Senate Foreign Relations Committee Chairman Jesse Helms said, "Without U.S. help, Colombia could lose this war ... or seek to appease the narco guerrillas."[18] The Republican Senator from North Carolina supported the military package. "We must bolster Colombia's security forces ... beginning with its counter-narcotics battalions ... to fight the well-armed narco terrorists."[19]

"This crisis is not overstated," Coverdell said. "The situation in Colombia is indeed dismal and is reaching emergency proportions. I firmly believe U.S. assistance is needed, and needed now, to address the situation."

Undersecretary of State Thomas R. Pickering, who was coordinating the administration's policy toward Colombia, told the Senate Foreign Relations Committee in October that aid was essential because "Colombia's national sovereignty was increasingly threatened by well-armed and ruthless guerrillas, paramilitaries and narco trafficking interests, which are inextricably linked."[20] Additionally, Colombian and U.S. officials cited consistent intelligence reports that the FARC was buying shoulder-launched surface-to-air missiles and that the use of such missiles would "change the threat envelope considerably."[21] The shoulder-launched surface-to-air missiles were capable of striking the new sophisticated S-70 Black Hawk and 18 UH-1N "Superhuey" helicopters, according to intelligence officials.

Despite the powerful alignment of White House and Republican supporters and the overwhelming agreement in Washington that Colombia was in desperate need of help, the aid package stalled. The defeat took place in early November when the Coverdell-DeWine Colombian legislation fell victim to budget bickering and White House fear of overloading its foreign aid request.[22] In the final hours, the Administration decided it could go only so far in arguing for increases in foreign aid against Republican charges it was tapping into Americans' retirement funds.[23] "The budget negotiations just got too complicated," said a senior administration official. "The trade-offs were pernicious ... we need a package that doesn't come at the expense of the Middle East, debt relief and Kosovo."[24]

The real problem for Colombia was that lawmakers were worried about the American elections in the year 2000. Democrats and Republicans had resorted to using the budget battle to grapple for political advantage in the upcoming struggle for control of Congress and the White House. As such, neither party wanted to be guilty of dipping into Social Security funds or raising taxes in any form whatsoever. On another front, presidential scholars focused on the end of Clinton's reign. "The eighth year is not a productive time," said George C. Edwards, Director of the Center for Presidential Studies at Texas A&M University.[25] "Everybody does not put politics aside and come together for the common good in the eighth year. Believing in that is like believing in the tooth fairy."

"The only winners here are the narcos and the guerrillas," said Ambassador Luis Alberto Moreno in response to the defeat of the Coverdell–DeWine aid package.

However, other officials in Washington and Bogotá could not hide their disappointment that President Clinton dropped the ball on Colombia. A fuming *Semana* magazine registered Colombia's deep sense of rejection and reported that Washington's handling of the aid package was a slap in the face to the nation.[26] The press in Bogotá immediately began to question Pastrana's failure to deliver on what was widely touted in Colombia as a done deal and openly suggested that the President's heralded friendship with Bill Clinton had proved of little value.

Troubled by the negative reaction in Bogotá, Secretary of State Albright called President Pastrana on Monday, November 8, to reassure him that despite the lack of action in Congress, the U.S. had not turned its back on him. Two days later, the White House released a statement by the President reaffirming his support for Colombia.[27] The press release said President Clinton would ask Congress early the next year to boost economic and antinarcotics aid to Colombia. "More funding is needed if we are to gain the upper hand in the fight against drugs and help Colombia on the path to stable democracy," the statement read. Finally, behind the scenes, Sandy Berger, the President's influential National Security Advisor, was working the corridors of power to make sure that everyone knew that Clinton was "emphatic" that White House officials work hand in hand with Congress to secure a new aid package for Colombia in early 2000.

The day after the White House release of the President's statement, Amnesty International reported that it would oppose the renewal of U.S. military aid to Colombia.[28] The organization said that its research showed that human rights violations were on the rise and that right-wing paramilitaries in Colombia had grown over the last five years, despite U.S. support for the government. "We are opposing the

U.S. renewal of aid to the army until there are clear guarantees that it won't be used for human rights violations," Susan Lee, Amnesty's researcher on Colombia, told a news conference. During a recent three-week research visit to Colombia, Lee reported that Amnesty compiled shocking reports of the terror tactics used by the paramilitaries in complicity with the army.[29]

"Killings have been conducted with chain saws, victims have been dismembered alive.... There are reports of the paramilitaries playing football with victims' heads," Lee said. Moreover, Amnesty International reported that communities would greet the arrival of the army with relief, only to see soldiers don the armbands of the paramilitaries. "The complicity is that blatant," she stated.[30] Lee also said that people were no longer reporting human rights violations because they feared reprisals. "The statistics are a gross underestimate, but there have been 198 massacres (incidents involving at least five victims) in the country so far this year according to the national ombudsman's office," Lee said. "The guerrilla uprising in Colombia and the government's attempts to stamp it out have also led to 1.5 million people being internally displaced. That number is growing." Lee believes the government's programs were designed to disguise the problem of internal refugees. "There are 300,000 this year compared with 200,000 last year," she said.[31]

Two days later, on November 13, the U.S. announced it would begin training two new Colombian army antidrug battalions in the spring of 2000. Political analysts said the move would give Washington a more direct role in the war against drugs and guerrillas. General Keith Huber, operations director of the U.S. Army's Miami-based Southern Command, said that each of the elite units would comprise some 950 men — similar to the Colombian

army's first antidrug battalion — that the units were awaiting funding. Huber, who served as a Special Forces adviser during the civil war in El Salvador in the 1980s, briefed reporters on the sidelines of a two-day conference about Colombia at the U.S. Army War College in Carlisle, Pennsylvania.[32]

"This is a war, a conflict that we must win collectively. Drugs are a chemical and a weapon of mass destruction that kill our children one at a time," Huber said. "The enemy in Colombia is a business enterprise and if you want to look at how to defeat that you must look at how they grow [the drugs], process it and transport it." Given a worse case scenario, Huber admitted that the guerrillas could take power "if we lose the confidence of the majority."

Although congressional funding was not yet authorized to pay for the new units, Pentagon sources said if necessary, funding could be drawn from the Department of Defense budget with little or no accountability to Congress. Political analysts warned that under the pretext of fighting drugs Washington could be sucked into the quagmire of Colombia's jungle guerrilla war. "Some people are making the same mistakes they made with Vietnam in 1963," said Cynthia Watson, associate dean of the National War College in Washington, D.C. "Colombia is not the first place where the potential for mission creep is great."[33]

The operation to cripple the drug traffickers in Colombia was a daunting challenge. A new generation of drug traffickers, light-years ahead of the traditional Medellín and Cali cartels, were using the internet and other modern technology, which sharply increased cocaine and heroin production and smuggling.[34] "It is a whole new generation of traffickers who have carefully studied and learned from the mistakes of the groups that went before them," said General Serrano.[35] "They maintain an extremely low profile, they mix their licit and illicit businesses, they don't carry out terrorist acts and they operate in small, autonomous cells. They are much harder to fight than previous groups because they are much harder to find."

Unlike the previous organizations, the new Colombian traffickers contracted out most of their work to specialists, who worked on a job-by-job basis rather than as part of an integrated structure that would be easier to detect, according to law enforcement officials. Most Colombian cocaine was sold in bulk to Mexican drug trafficking organizations, which also underwent major changes in the last several years, and the Mexican traffickers assumed the risk of transporting and distributing the drugs in the United States, they said. "When you take out the leadership of an organization now, you find that underneath there is really not an integrated structure," one U.S. official said.[36] Furthermore, unlike the previous waves of Colombian drug traffickers, who were allied mostly with far-right paramilitary death squads, the current leadership was prospering by dealing with all sides in the Colombian conflict, particularly the FARC. "We estimate there are several hundred small cartels now operating in an atomized fashion…. They are smarter, less visible and cause us all kinds of trouble," the official explained.[37]

General Fernando Tapias was saber-rattling. The general was not happy with the peace process and wanted everybody to know it. Tapias was breaking ranks with the President and offering a hawkish solution to Colombia's peace process. It was a calculated move designed to gain him a greater role in the decision making and diminish the President's control of Colombia's destiny. "If the United States wanted to stop drug trafficking in Colombia it could do it in two or three years," he said.[38] "What we're asking for is the help to end

it … what is needed is a different recipe." General Tapias was clearly inching closer to the camp of hard-core Colombian Conservatives who no longer had faith in the peace process.

"The fundamental thing we have to tell them [the U.S.] is that they have the technology, and we're putting up the dead and wounded. So let's get together and start moving forward," Tapias explained.[39] "The Colombian peace process is never going to work as long as we have armed groups that are rolling in money and that can buy anything they want on the black market for arms. They could [not] care five cents about it [peace] because they have access to everything."[40]

His remarks were made as the government was preparing to reopen peace talks with the FARC in October 1999. Tapias was a proud military leader and regularly defended his troops against charges of human rights violations. To Tapias, international human rights organizations that reported paramilitary abuses in the countryside were Communists and were secretly working with the guerrillas to destroy constitutional democracy in Colombia. Moderates in the Colombian military command warned Tapias that his warmonger rhetoric and tainted characterization of human rights organizations would make passage of U.S. aid in Washington more difficult. However, he ignored the advice, verbally elbowed Pastrana, and basically told the nation what they needed was a warrior, not a peacemaker.

The President denied a fallout with Tapias. Nonetheless, in December 1999 *El Espectador* reported its second major scoop of the year (the first was the January disclosure that the U.S. had met with the FARC in Costa Rica). The paper told a spellbound nation that Colombia's two top generals, Fernando Tapias and Jorge Mora, resigned in November to protest the handling of the peace process but President

Pastrana refused to accept their resignations, narrowly averting the second crisis in the military high command in 1999.[41] Generals Tapias and Mora were widely credited with reversing the tide of the battle with the FARC and reportedly challenged President Pastrana's powers vested in Peace Commissioner Víctor Ricardo. The two generals had forced the FARC to abandon its tactic of large-unit assaults and return to small-scale hit-and-run guerrilla warfare.

Tapias and Mora were confident after a series of American-aided battlefront victories against the FARC, and they had seen enough of the peace talks. Consequently, they wanted Pastrana to put an end to the demilitarized zone. The Generals accused the FARC of launching offensives from the safe haven and wanted Pastrana to give the military the opportunity to wipe out the guerrilla base camps in the demilitarized zone. Part of the secret terms that established the safe haven allowed the government to enter the demilitarized zone with only 48 hours' notice. However, some Colombians feared that a military invasion of the zone would cause FARC to use surface-to-air missiles to destroy American Black Hawk and Huey helicopters.

It was the greatest challenge of the Peacemaker's presidency. In essence, the senior generals wanted Pastrana to oust Ricardo and seek a military solution to the civil conflict. *El Espectador* cited unnamed sources within the presidential palace that said President Pastrana considered firing Ricardo.[42] Pastrana and Ricardo were the two most powerful doves in the nation, and if Ricardo was axed, it was certain to be interpreted as a sure sign that the Peacemaker was terminating the peace process.

"The president succeeded in heading off the crisis and persuaded the generals to remain in their posts," *El Espectador* said. "But the episode, which has been kept quiet, implied a high political cost for the government and has put peace commissioner Víctor Ricardo's post at risk."[43] Ricardo was the architect of the historic meeting between Sureshot and Pastrana before the President took office in August 1998. The generals wanted to map out a new strategy for peace without Ricardo and were willing to submit their resignations to convince the President that they would not take no for an answer. Overall, the military was deeply distrustful of Ricardo over his adoption of a conciliatory tone with the FARC and wanted him out of the picture.

Ultimately, the President convinced the generals to stay onboard. Journalists speculated that a "deal" was struck but the government denied it. One indication of a possible deal was Pastrana's fresh verbal attacks on the FARC. Calling the guerrillas "cowardly and arrogant," Pastrana abandoned the language of a peacemaker and adopted a more bellicose tone that the press speculated was designed to please Generals Tapias and Mora and the score of other senior military commanders behind the scenes who supported them.

On December 30, 1999, Colombian citizens knew something was amiss when President Pastrana made the uncharacteristic move of vetoing a critical human rights bill that was praised by the United Nation's High Commissioner for Human Rights.[44] The vetoed legislation, called the "Genocide Bill," would have set mandatory jail terms for heinous crimes in Colombia. Pastrana defended his veto by saying it could lead to the prosecution of soldiers fighting the country's civil war. Congress approved the legislation, which was drafted for the sole purpose of cleaning up Colombia's dismal human rights record, on November 30, 1999, and expected the President to endorse it. The groundbreaking section of the vetoed legislation said that civilian courts rather than military courts would be permitted to try soldiers accused of human rights violations. Pastrana attempted to justify his decision by arguing that the new bill was unacceptable because it could "impede fulfillment of the constitutional and legal functions of the public [security] forces." Human rights officials dismissed his explanations, though, and said that the President had failed to implement one of the most important judicial reforms in the history of Colombia. Military courts in Colombia rarely held anyone accountable for massacres and had a miserable history of incompetence and corruption, the human rights officials in Bogotá said.

Pastrana specifically objected to the first article of the bill, which called for a maximum 60-year jail term for anyone involved in killings aimed at the partial or total destruction of a political group.[45] The President explained that it would be unconstitutional to subject security force members to possible "genocide charges" for fighting the guerrilla army. The vetoed legislation would have meant that a 45- to 60-year prison term was the maximum penalty for genocide, as Colombia did not have a death penalty. In vetoing the legislation, President Pastrana eliminated prison terms of up to 40 years for anyone convicted of "forced disappearance," a legal term for abduction with probable intent to kill, and up to 15 years in jail for torture.[46] "This really disqualifies the government when it comes to its commitment in terms of human rights," said Vivian Morales, an independent lawmaker who was a leading proponent of the legislation. "They don't want to commit themselves to clear ground rules."[47]

Meanwhile the violence in Colombia reached new heights. There was a total of 1,863 Colombians massacred in 1999, an average of five a day and an increase of 40 percent over the 1,336 victims in 1998, according to the official statistics from the Colombian Federal Human Rights Ombudsman.[48] Government human rights officials identified a massacre as any killing involving three or more fatalities and said there were 402 such cases in 1999, a 74 percent increase over 1998.[49] The government report blamed ultrarightist paramilitary groups, who targeted leftists and suspected rebel sympathizers, for 37.8 percent of the mass killings (International Human Rights organizations attributed 70 percent of the massacres in Colombia to death squads). Guerrillas were deemed responsible for about 17 percent of the massacres, and Colombia's security forces were blamed for 2 percent, according to the report. Responsibility for the remainder of the killings cited in the report was placed on unidentified "armed gunmen."

Year-end statistics were piling up. That same week, the Colombian National Police reported preliminary figures indicating that 23,172 Colombians were murdered in 1999, three every hour, compared to 23,096 in 1998.[50] (By comparison, in 1998, the United States, with a population of about 270 million, had 16,914 murders.) The National Police also said that they carried out fewer drug hauls, seizing about 30 tons of pure cocaine and semirefined cocaine base in 1999, compared to a record 54.5 tons in 1998, a 45 percent decline. From the private sector, a watchdog group said Colombia set a world record in abductions. A total of 2,945 kidnappings took place in Colombia, compared with 2,216 in 1998, the independent group reported.[51]

On January 2, 2000, the Colombian Army released official 1999 battlefield casualties.[52] At least 419 FARC and 267 ELN guerrillas were killed in combat, according to the army. The Colombian armed forces reportedly suffered 263 casualties during the year and the paramilitary death squads who were responsible for the most massacres in Colombia were practically unscathed with the loss of only 26 members

Colombian National Police blow craters to destroy a narcoguerrilla airstrip in eastern Colombia. *Courtesy of Gil Macklin*

in 1999, according to official statistics released by the army. Another grim statistic of Colombia's war zone was that the 480-mile pipeline connecting the Caño Limón oil field with the Caribbean port of Coveñas was attacked a record 79 times in 1999, according to a spokesman for the state-owned oil company Ecopetrol.

Internationally, the French media watchdog group Reporters Without Borders reported that Colombia had dropped to second deadliest place in the world for journalists in 1999 with six journalists killed; Sierra Leone was the deadliest with ten journalists killed. Finally, the DEA reported that Colombia was expected to produce 330 to 440 tons of pure cocaine in the year 2000, compared to 220 tons in 1999.

It also reported that Colombian coca fields covered approximately 220,000 acres of land at the end of 1999 compared with only 81,000 acres in 1992.

At the end of 1999 Colombia was a nation in serious need of good news. Collectively, the 40 million citizens of the country were living in one of the most violent societies on the face of the earth. Outside of the President and Víctor Ricardo there were few well-known optimists in Bogotá and the only two clear-cut heroes in the country were General Rosso José Serrano and the dashing Colombian auto-racing star Juan Pablo Montoya. Tragically, government human rights officials continued to report that approximately 90 percent of all crimes committed in Colombia went unpunished. Officials attributed the rampant violence in Colombia to a weak, intimidated and notoriously ineffective judicial system. The same officials also voiced tremendous concern for the future. As bad as things were in Colombia, they feared it would get worse.

As people throughout the world celebrated the approach of the new millennium, many human rights activists in Colombia were disheartened. They worried about a possible shift in the balance of power at the highest levels of government, and they cited President Pastrana's veto of the Genocide bill as proof of the new order. To them, the veto by the President was the first signal that his administration was caving in to military pressure. They wondered aloud how the President could side with heavily armed soldiers in the military and leave innocent unarmed victims of violence, especially the poor and helpless women and children in the countryside, without viable legal protection. Looking to the future, they feared that the President was going to abandon the careful practice of conflict resolution and turn the war over to the armed forces so they could attempt to seek a military solution.

By and large, the President's performance in office made him highly unpopular and *El Espectador* let everyone in Bogotá know it with a harsh headline that read "Pastrana Fails."[53] The paper based its headline on the results of a national poll that indicated that most Colombians disapproved of the President's leadership because of the protracted war and the fact that he presided over the country's worst recession in 100 years. A total of 68 percent Colombians had an unfavorable image of the President, according to the poll in *El Espectador*. Moreover, 85 percent of those surveyed said he failed to take adequate measures to reduce Colombia's 18.1 percent unemployment rate, which was the highest in the hemisphere.[54] The poll also

showed that 78 percent of Colombians disapproved of Pastrana's anticrime efforts and 79 percent believed he had done too little to fight kidnapping. The survey of 1,504 adults was conducted by the highly regarded National Consultancy Centre on January 3–4 and had a margin of error of 2.5 percent.

El Tiempo reported the results of another national survey on December 30, 1999.[55] The survey indicated that 41 percent of Colombians believed peace "may never be made" with the FARC, and that 25 percent of those surveyed said it could take up to ten years or more to reach a negotiated settlement of the war. Only 18 percent of respondents said peace was possible within the next five years, while 16 percent said they did not know how long it would take or declined to answer the question. The respected Napoleón Franco polling firm conducted the survey in Colombia's five leading cities from December 18–20. It was based on interviews with 410 adults from across the social spectrum and had a margin of error of 4.8 percent.

A disturbing mark of the national gloom, and the creeping influence of the guerrillas, was unveiled in the *El Tiempo* survey. When the adults in the survey were asked what group or individual did the most to help Colombia progress as a nation in 1999, 28 percent of the respondents answered "No One." That was the single most popular response. The runner-up on a list that included President Pastrana and the armed forces among others, was "Guerrillas," who actually were endorsed by 12 percent of those polled.[56] Remarkably the guerrillas outdistanced the President of the Republic the armed forces, among others, as doing the most to help the nation progress, according to the survey in the most powerful and respected newspaper in Colombia.

On Sunday evening, January 9, 2000, paramilitary death squad boss Carlos

Castaño admitted for the first time before a national television audience that his organization financed their operations by taxing the drug trade.[57] "The self-defense forces are where they are because there is money. The war has become economic," said Castaño, dressed in green fatigues. "Why don't we be frank and tell the world what's really going on in Colombia?"[58] Castaño was interviewed by the Caracol television network in Catatumbo, a violent, coca-growing region in northeast Colombia near the border with Venezuela. The security-conscious Castaño, who was surrounded by armed guards with his back to the camera, said "If we come in and retake an area we have to earn income from where it exists," Castaño said. "Here [coca] is the economy, and that's how I finance myself."

The confession by the death squad chief confirmed what Colombian and U.S. law enforcement officials had reported for years. Up until the national broadcast by Caracol the death squads had vehemently denied any link to the drug trade and claimed that their organization was a self-defense group that protected lawful Colombians from guerrilla violence. The decision to publicly admit involvement in the drug trade opened the possibility that the armed forces would have no choice but to pursue them. However, with a paramilitary army of approximately 5,000 soldiers and after suffering a minuscule 26 combat casualties in 1999 compared with much higher ratios for the guerrillas, one Colombian political analyst dismissed the thought. Paramilitary death squads hunted guerrillas; as a result the Colombian armed forces were reluctant to eliminate anyone fighting the same enemy, the analyst explained. Castaño said that his organization charged a 40 percent tax on peasants who produce coca, the raw material for cocaine.

"Paramilitaries forced me off my plot of land and I had to come to the city with my husband and five children to beg and live in poverty," said peasant protester Josefina Jaimes after she joined a group of refugees that smashed their way into the Bogotá headquarters of the International Red Cross and took 37 officials hostage.[59] The mob of some 100 displaced peasants, that included women and children, had been living in makeshift plastic tents outside the Red Cross headquarters and were protesting the rancid conditions in the bulging shantytowns in and around Bogotá.

The International Red Cross played a crucial role in Colombia. Red Cross representatives visited hostages and oversaw their release when invited to do so. Moreover, officials regularly provided Colombian families with information and training in due process and the international laws of war between states established in Hague Regulations of 1899 and 1907 and the Geneva Conventions of 1949. Unfortunately, Protocols I and II, 1977 additions to the Geneva Conventions, were the only provisions that directly applied to internal (as opposed to international) armed conflicts. President Samper and Interior Minister Serpa officially adopted the 1977 Geneva Convention provisions in Colombia. (Protocol I came into effect in March 1994 and Protocol II followed in February 1996.) Protocols I and II offered precise and detailed standards for the protection of civilians and combatants rendered "hors de combat" by their capture or wounding. The Red Cross also assisted wounded civilian victims and when appropriate, officials presented the government with cases of alleged human rights abuses by armed actors.

The evening of the attack, Tuesday, January 4, 2000, the protestors released 33 Red Cross officials but continued to hold four hostages, including the head of the mission in Colombia, Rolin Wavre. The International Committee of the Red Cross responded to the takeover of its facility by suspending all operations in Colombia. It was an unusual move. The Red Cross operated in the world's most dangerous war zones and rarely shut down operations in a nation. The recent exceptions were in the breakaway republics of Chechnya and East Timor, but those situations involved the complete breakdown of law and order.

Colombia was not at that point. However, the hopelessness among the poor and the repeated broken promises of the government to address the problem of poverty were creating a dangerous undercurrent of unrest among the nearly four million impoverished Colombians in Bogotá. The attack on the most important humanitarian organization in the world was a sure sign that things in Colombia were spinning out of control. The Pastrana government was well aware if it did not improve the grim standard of living of the poor in the five major cities of Bogotá, Medellín, Cali, Barranquilla and Bucaramanga, the FARC would breed at a perilous rate.

The Red Cross considered the Colombian refugee problem the biggest in the world outside Africa and wanted a peaceful end to the "violent occupation" of its headquarters. As a result, Bogotá police chief General Argemiro Serna did not order security forces to physically oust the protesters. Many of the protestors had been forced out of their homes at gunpoint and were now demanding that the government provide housing, health care and education for their children. "We're not going to leave here until our demands have been met," said protester Gustavo Cepeda, from northern Guajira province.

"We deplore this violent occupation of our delegation and also the fact that our delegates are being held forcibly in our offices," said Corinne Adam, spokeswoman for the Swiss-based humanitarian agency in Geneva.[60] The Red Cross had no active role in trying to negotiate an end to the dispute. "We are neither mediators nor neutral intermediaries, we just accompanied the parties in the discussions," the spokeswoman said. The Red Cross, which had 60 foreign delegates and 220 Colombian staff in Colombia, was headed by Jakob Kellenberger in Geneva.

Sixteen days later, the Red Cross partly resumed its activities in Colombia. "While this unacceptable situation continues, the delegates have provisionally reorganized themselves in order to resume the Red Cross humanitarian engagement," said an official. The protestors had released the hostages but still occupied the Red Cross building. "We are responding to the call of the victims of the conflict ... and for that reason we have decided to partially resume operations," released hostage Rolin Wavre told a news conference.[61]

President Clinton kept his word. At a White House briefing on Tuesday, January 11, 2000, Secretary of State Albright and drug czar Barry McCaffrey announced a massive infusion of aid to Colombia. The package totaled $1.6 billion over a two-year period. If approved by Congress, at least 80 percent of the aid would be used to finance an intense air and ground war against the FARC in southern Colombia with an additional 30 Black Hawk and 33 Huey helicopters. The package also included funds for a new sophisticated RG-8A reconnaissance plane along with air base and radar enhancements and further upgrades to add night-vision systems to aging Colombian planes. The night-vision upgrades were a sure sign the Colombian government was considering high-tech raids on drug sites under the cover of darkness. "This is not a counter insurgency program," Albright said. "This is a counter narcotics program."[62]

The Secretary of State's statement was based on the administration's strong conviction that the guerrilla "unholy alliance" with drug traffickers made them "fair game" for attack. "This will not just benefit the people of Colombia, but American children," McCaffrey said. "We are experiencing an explosion of cocaine and heroin from Colombia flowing to the 4.1 million Americans addicted to drugs."[63]

Not everyone was impressed with the speed with which the White House came to the rescue of Colombia. Congressmen Dan Burton, Benjamin Gilman and John Mica were of the conviction that the Clinton administration was responsible for the deteriorating situation in Colombia. "Someone should be held accountable for this disaster at our doorstep," Mica said. The trio of House Republicans had held countless hearings and sponsored intense congressional efforts to warn the White House that Colombia was a democracy at risk. They were extremely frustrated that resources already approved by Congress had failed to be provided to the government of Colombia in a timely fashion.

Other Republicans were more cordial about the White House proposal. "I finally welcome the White House plan to provide timely and needed assistance," said Senator Coverdell. "There is simply too much at stake not to take action." The basic framework of how the Administration's package would be distributed was the responsibility of the Office of Management and Budget, the State Department, the Pentagon, and the Office of National Drug Policy Control. Moreover, the White House planed to brief congressional leaders on the specific spending allocations before the package was officially made public. The aid package was of such great significance that the White House also planned to assemble a permanent secretariat to manage the aid process.

Bipartisan cooperation for the White House proposal was expected although some Republicans and Democrats reportedly had competing views on how the U.S.

aid would be spent, according to congressional staffers. Republicans were keen on maintaining strong support for General Serrano's National Police and were suspicious of the "dubious" human rights record of the Colombian armed forces. Democratic Senators Leahy of Vermont and Edward Kennedy of Massachusetts were expected to sharply question past failures and potential pitfalls of U.S. policy in Colombia and were known to want more cash directed at social reforms and diplomatic peace efforts.

A senior State Department official stressed the aid package was not set in stone and the administration was willing to listen to critics and incorporate their suggestions. Charles Gillespie, a former ambassador to Colombia now at the Forum for International Policy, said there had never been a better ... and more crucial ... time to act in Colombia. "Can you control how deeply and widely you go in? If the U.S. can't do that, then we are in terrible shape," he said.[64]

That weekend Madeleine Albright flew to Colombia to discuss the two-year $1.6 billion aid package with President Pastrana. The Secretary of State landed in the peaceful sun-soaked seaside resort of Cartegena for a private dinner with Pastrana and Nobel laureate Gabriel García Márquez on January 14. On the eve of her arrival, Raúl Reyes, the FARC's chief peace negotiator, announced from San Vicente del Caguán that the White House funding was the first step toward a U.S. invasion of Colombia.[65]

"I vow on behalf of President Clinton and in very close partnership with President Pastrana to seek 100 years of peace and democracy ... for both our nations," Albright announced at a news conference in Cartagena. "We are sharing a very important moment ... and are fully in harmony on high priority objectives." The Secretary of State was the highest U.S.

official to visit Colombian since President George Bush paid a visit to Cartagena more than a decade earlier.

Prior to leaving for a scheduled visit to Panama, the Secretary of State warned Colombia that U.S. support depended on Bogotá taking "appropriate action against human rights [abuses]."[66] Albright praised the progress Colombia had already made on human rights issues but said that the $1.6 billion aid package depended on President Pastrana making more gains. "Our support for Plan Colombia ... rests on the assumption that you will continue to take appropriate action against human rights violators ... whether those violators are military, paramilitary, guerrilla or just plain criminals," she said.

One U.S. official traveling with Albright could not hide the contempt building inside the White House and used stronger language. "Colombia should attack the right-wing paramilitary groups if Pastrana's plan is to work ... it is absolutely clear that if the government of Colombia wants to wage a vigorous law-and-order program, it has to go out and attack the paramilitaries," the official told foreign correspondents.[67]

A week later the U.S. lectured the Colombian military high command on the importance of building a strong tradition of guaranteeing human rights. "Government forces will strengthen the hand of Marxist rebels and terrorists if they fail to stamp out human rights abuses in their ranks," U.S. Army Secretary Louis Caldera told Colombian armed forces leaders at Bogotá's Army War College.[68] "Even the most well-intentioned government will be rejected by citizens whose trust has been eroded by the behavior of the government's security forces," Caldera said.

The U.S. Army Secretary did not refer to paramilitaries, but warned that in a conflict like Colombia's, abuses by the security forces could lead disaffected civilians to provide "weapons, supplies, intelligence, and even manpower to the insurgents, who were free to roam undetected within the civilian population, free to attack at will.[69] That these local civilians may have been coerced through intimidation to assist the enemy in the past is no reason to further push them into his arms through atrocities that undercut the moral superiority of the government's forces over terrorists," said Caldera.[70] "Real headway is possible if every single soldier, down to the lowest-ranking private, appreciates that due process and respect for human rights are fundamental to the military's larger mission, and understands that any violations will have severe legal and professional repercussions."

Days prior to the Army Secretary's speech, innocent civilians were being killed at an unprecedented rate across the country. It started on January 16 when about 2,000 Colombian troops, backed by helicopter gun ships, attacked a FARC column of 100 guerrillas approximately 40 miles east of Bogotá.

"We're going after these bandits," said General Mora.[71] Shortly afterwards, General Tapias announced the army had killed 44 FARC guerrillas but he was only able to produce 12 rebel corpses to reporters at the Apiay military base.[72] *El Espectador* said independent confirmation of the rebel casualties was not possible but reported that at least nine civilians were killed in the combat along with at least five soldiers and one policeman. Military sources hailed the battle as the first victory for the army's Rapid Deployment Force, the new elite unit with U.S. Black Hawk helicopters equipped with "mini guns" capable of firing 2,000 rounds a minute. The Rapid Deployment Force entered the battle accompanied by the army's 13 Brigade. "This is an elite force that is made up of some of the army's best men equipped with some of the most modern methods of electronic warfare," said an army spokesman in Bogotá.

However, local Colombian television camera teams at the scene of the battle reported a different dimension of the outcome. Television cameras captured images of Black Hawk helicopters blasting off hundreds of rounds of tracer bullets and pounding the mountain region with rockets before dawn. At daybreak the television camera crews entered the battle zone and showed the bodies of several dead civilians. They also filmed frightened local villagers shouting out of shattered windows for help from passing Red Cross teams.[73]

Civilian casualties continued on January 18, when paramilitary death squads executed 26 unarmed peasants in two raids in the northern region of the nation. In the village of La Loma, in Antioquía province, some 50 heavily armed paramilitary gunmen in combat fatigues dragged 19 unarmed peasants from their homes, bound their hands behind their backs and shot them in front of other villagers, according to local government official Eliécer Agudelo.[74] In a separate attack, seven peasants were executed by paramilitary death squads in Estados Unidos, a hamlet in northern Cesar province, according to local police.[75]

The death squads struck again the next day, killing 16 unarmed peasants. Some villagers were killed simply for being friendly to guerrillas who passed through dressed as civilians, a local official said. "Here a peasant sells a soft drink or bread to someone, without asking who they are," said Jorge Eliécer Agudelo, town manager in Yarumal, near where the killings took place. "That's their only sin."[76] Paramilitaries killed a total of nine men in hamlets outside Yarumal and murdered another seven peasants in a village outside Becerril, a rural town in northern Cesar State, according to National Police operations director General Alfonso Arellano. In Becer-

ril, paramilitaries called out the seven victims' names from lists, dragged them from their homes and riddled them with bullets in the village's main plaza, police said.[77]

The rampage continued on January 20, when death squads conducted execution-style murders of ten men in a rural corner of Antioquía province. All of the paramilitary killings reportedly were in retaliation for ELN guerrilla bombings of rural power facilities.[78] The ELN bombings were to protest the sale of state owned power generator ISAGEN, power grid group ISA, and the coal mining agency Carbocol. The sales were cornerstones of a privatization program mandated by the International Monetary Fund (IMF) and expected to bring some $2 billion into state coffers in 2000 to ease the government's public spending deficit.

"For each electrical facility that is attacked, we will execute 10 rural guerrillas," a paramilitary statement read.[79] Despite statements to the contrary, Pastrana and the Colombian armed forces were unable to stop the murder of civilians. Moreover, the death squads were able to administer their own brand of Colombian paramilitary justice with no apparent fear of interference from government security forces. Tragically, local newspapers reported that most of the civilian victims were mistaken for guerrillas.

The ELN lost patience with Pastrana's management of the nation's assets and wanted to gain his attention with a series of explosions meant to cripple sections of the nation's energy apparatus. "The ruling class listens only to the voice of dynamite and rifles," Nicolás "Gabino" Rodríquez, the head of the National Liberation Army, said in a radio interview.[80] Rodríquez and his 5,000 ELN guerrillas had decided to start blowing up electricity producing sites to prevent the state sale of energy assets. The rebel attacks on energy structures forced school closings, shut businesses and

Illicit coca fields photographed from a Black Hawk helicopter. *Courtesy of Gil Macklin*

prompted utilities to announce energy rate increases. Hundreds of rural towns as well as the nation's second-largest city, Medellín, weathered severe energy rationing when the explosives planted by the ELN damaged or toppled 22 electrical facilities across the mountainous region of central Colombia.

"The popular revolution has the responsibility of protesting how the government is managing policy-making in the country. We'll keep on dynamiting as much as we can," said Gabino.[81] "The discussion of the sale of assets in the energy industry is deficient. It's stupid to give all our assets to foreign companies just to cover up for corruption and bad management. The poor will always be the most affected by any measure or attack. But we simply want to delay any sale unless it is fully discussed, to flesh out its implica-

tions for the nation's coffers and draw attention to state officials responsible for corruption within the mining and energy industries.

"The Pastrana clan has always benefited with privatizations and all those processes, as well as Colombia's oligarchy. We want that to stop," the ELN chief told the Caracol Radio station.[82] Left unsaid by Gabino was that President Pastrana continued to anger the ELN by refusing to duplicate the demilitarized FARC safe haven and vacate government troops from a vast ELN northern Colombian stronghold. The explosions were creating havoc. In Medellín, a city of over 2.5 million, many restaurants and offices were operating by candlelight after dark. City schools were closed indefinitely, forcing more than 650,000 students to stay home. In the neighboring province of Chocó, the ELN explosions caused 14 towns to lose power altogether.

The multiple killing spree continued on January 28 when gunmen clad in army combat fatigues dragged 11 victims from their homes, killing them execution style.[83] The death squad reportedly checked to make sure the names of the victims were included on a list of suspected leftists or rebel sympathizers before killing them, police spokesmen said. The spokesmen added that the head of a local police civilian review board was among the 11 men and women killed and that the gunmen carried off at least two villagers in the predawn raid.

The behavior of the paramilitary death squads was raising the level of debate in Washington. American officials were angered that the death squads acted as if they would never be brought to justice. The paramilitary units didn't fear local media reports of the massacres, and they were not concerned that their actions would prompt surviving peasants to rush into the arms of the guerrillas to seek revenge. The arrogance prompted officials in Washington to think the death squads were mistaking the drug war for the Cold War. Moreover, death squad actions suggested they did not believe the Cold War was over, and they were expecting to receive military and political support as long as they were anti–Communist, the officials said.

If so they were making an enormous mistake, according to State Department officials. During the Cold War, U.S. aided anti–Communist groups targeted Jacobo Arbenz's Guatemala and Salvador Allende's Chile. However, the code of conduct in the drug war was quite different than that of the Cold War. In the drug war, President Clinton was concerned about supporting people involved in human rights violations and stressed the greater good of fighting drugs.

The impunity the paramilitary death squads enjoyed in Colombia was starting to make senior officials in the Clinton administration very uncomfortable. What President Pastrana's military high command needed was a clear determination to radically challenge its "sclerotic" internal ethos. Some former White House officials nervous that death squad activities could torpedo U.S. aid hoped Pastrana would duplicate what Bill Clinton did at the CIA. Unknown to many Americans, the CIA underwent the "Scrub" in 1995 when Director John Deutch ordered a far-reaching review of all assets. Deutch followed the outline of a blueprint authored by the previous Director, James Woolsey, and introduced an analytical valuation of CIA assets to determine the justification for a wide range of operations.

Shortly after the highly unpopular Scrub was concluded, the CIA dropped approximately 1,000 agents because of poor information or insufficient value.[84] Moreover, the results of the comprehensive Scrub prompted Deutch to fire the former chief of the CIA Latin American division.[85] President Clinton chose George J. Tenet, the former Special Assistant to the President and Senior Director for Intelligence Programs at the National Security Council, to assist in the CIA transformation in July 1995. Tenet, a former New Yorker, was sworn in as Director two years later to manage the approximately $29 billion spent each year by the intelligence organization. (The exact amount of CIA spending is classified, although $29 billion is generally accepted at the 1999 figure.) To his credit, Tenet dramatically raised the diversity of talent in the CIA. He was also responsible for nurturing increased CIA cooperation with the DEA on counternarcotics and with the FBI on terrorists.

What Pastrana needed was someone in the military to sanitize the Colombian armed forces the way Woolsey, Deutch and Tenet changed the ethos of the CIA. Former intelligence professionals in Washington said until the senior military command in Bogotá implemented a widely respected system that fostered a tradition of transparency and completely eliminated the suppression of wrongdoing, the armed forces would continue to be associated with paramilitary death squad impunity in Colombia. They also said high-quality "actionable" intelligence would be required to help President Pastrana make sure that the constitution and not military chieftains guided the ship of state in Colombia.

"What we have here is hunger, misery and exploitation and that's not going to end with rifles, machine guns or bombs," said Sureshot when asked to comment on the $1.6 billion emergency assistance President Clinton wanted to give Colombia.[86] "I think the ones who came up with this [aid] agreement have committed a grave error. The problems here are of a social order, it's not a problem of weaponry," Sureshot said in a live broadcast over national radio. The public comment by the Comandante of the FARC army took place in a small village outside of San Vicente where government representatives and the guerrilla negotiating team met in late January 2000 to inaugurate a new initiative called the "minimum agenda for halting the war." Sureshot was now speaking to the press on a regular basis from the safety of the demilitarized zone.

Pablo Beltrán, a veteran leader of the ELN confident that President Pastrana would soon create a safe haven for his 5,000 guerrilla fighters in the northeastern province of Bolívar, said the White House aid "is supposedly for the fight against drug trafficking, but it is really for the armed forces." Speaking to reporters during "the São Paolo Forum," an annual gathering of Latin American left wing organizations in Nicaragua, Beltrán asked, "How can they expect us to disarm when

they're reinforcing the army? Our fight will have to grow, and we will not disarm."

"The FARC disagrees with this aid from the United States because assistance should be for social spending and peace, not for increasing the conflict with the blessing of the few who directly benefit from the war," said Sureshot. "We can be attacked by the security forces when the President considers it convenient, since we are an organization that has taken up arms against the state. But it's wrong that they should do this with the participation of the United States, under the slanderous pretext that we have links to the drug trade." The FARC was angry that President Clinton defended the aid package because of "the intersection of narco-traffickers and political rebels" in Colombia.[87] Sureshot called Clinton's defense of the aid an "invention" of the press and a crude pretext to deepen American involvement in Colombia.[88]

The FARC was in denial regarding its accountability in the production of drugs in Colombia. Its leaders naively continued to defend their role in the drug trade as free of criminal behavior. They protested allegations that they were international drug traffickers, which technically was correct. The FARC was not actively involved in the transportation network that moved drugs from the interior of the country to destinations outside the borders of Colombia. However, there was no way the FARC could deny links to the drug trade; nor could they reasonably refute President Clinton's "intersection" charge.

The FARC guarded illegal crops, provided security for labs and established military perimeters around jungle airstrips so guerrillas could unload incoming weapons and supplies, and drug traffickers could load outgoing cocaine and heroin. Moreover, the FARC generated a steady cash flow by taxing farmers that grew illicit crops. In some cases poor cash starved farmers were forced to pay FARC tax collectors in coca leaves. In other instances the FARC forced farmers to pay taxes by processing poppy latex into a vastly more valuable morphine base, which was convertible to heroin at a 1:1 weight ratio. The FARC would then inventory the illegal commodities and convert the tax receipts to cash or supplies on scheduled dates with large drug traffickers.

In reality, the FARC maintained a massive financial alliance with the drug trade that generated about $2 million a day, according to former DEA officials. At best, one could objectively call the FARC a highly organized and disciplined military organization. By definition they were revolutionaries because they took up arms against the state, but the FARC also had many sinister facades. The guerrillas were common criminals because they earned millions of dollars kidnapping innocent Colombians. They were human rights violators for recruiting children and training them to be guerrilla warriors. They were cold-blooded murderers for the senseless execution of Americans Terence Freitas, Ingrid Washinawatok and Lahe'ena'e Gay. And without a doubt they were narcobandits because they generated a fortune enabling traffickers to successfully grow, process and transport drugs in areas they controlled.

However, the FARC downplayed its income-generating criminal activities and wanted to promote its role in Colombia as the noble army of the poor. Its members hoped the world would see them as a group of modern day Robin Hoods who stole from the rich and gave to the poor. Sureshot preached that the FARC was the army of the common people and that their sole purpose was to correct the injustices of poverty inside the Republic of Colombia. The FARC published manifestos, declarations, documents, programs, platforms and agreements outlining the need for social reforms and greater political inclusion. To a great

extent President Pastrana, Peace Commissioner Víctor Ricardo and educated Colombians agreed that poverty was the root of the nation's problems and that the government needed to dramatically improve its social programs for the lower classes.

All the propaganda aside, Sureshot and his army of FARC guerrillas wanted power. Their objective was control of Colombia. The peril to Bogotá and Washington was that the FARC was gaining wider acceptance in Colombia because of the government's long history of failure with social reforms. The danger to Pastrana and Clinton was that the poor had lost faith in the politicians in Bogotá and had more confidence in the FARC's ability to bring about sweeping changes in the economy. To the poor, Sureshot was a credible political voice for huge social spending. Moreover, the relentless persecution of innocent Colombians by the death squads and the government's unwillingness to go after the paramilitaries enabled Sureshot to fill his ranks with large numbers of dedicated peasants waiting to take up arms to make Colombia a socialist state.

In many ways Sureshot was a political genius. He had a marvelous ability to persuade. Each day millions of poor and hungry Colombians passively hoped the FARC could improve the miserable standard of living in the country. Moreover, by anointing the FARC the protector of the lower classes, and by reminding the poor of the government's brutal violence in the 1950s, of the elite rule of the National Front in the 1960s, of the corruption of the 1970 presidential elections and the betrayal of the Patriotic Union political party (UP) in the late 1980s and early 1990s, Sureshot managed to downplay the FARC's criminal activities and highlight its role as the nation's political and social savior.

The key to Sureshot's revolutionary rhetoric was that the ruling class could not be trusted. He portrayed the poverty in

Colombia as a form of enforced state repression. In that regard, the government was its own worst enemy. Large landowners and ruling class elites always defeated significant land and social reforms. The prudent management of the economy, the virtues of uninhibited trade, open markets and privatizations were the first concerns of the ruling class that controlled the political and economic process in Colombia.

The FARC leadership understood this and the critical propaganda value of attacking the ruling class. By condemning rich urban dwellers for living in "towers filled with dollars," Sureshot was able to raise enormous support with the poor in the large cities of Colombia, and it was the poor in the large cities of Colombia that presented the greatest threat to the stability of the Pastrana government. Although Colombian military intelligence downplayed the danger to Bogotá from urban guerrillas, stating that there were fewer than 500 armed FARC soldiers in the city, simple logic argued otherwise.

In early 2000 Bogotá was bulging with more than eight million Colombians. Over half of them were poor and well over 60 percent of the very poor were unemployed. Sadly, many of the poor who were working were making less than $26 a month. The lack of adequate government services for the poor played into the hands of the FARC. Moreover, many of the poor flocking to the big cities were displaced countryside peasants who traditionally had much more faith in the integrity of the guerrillas than the government's armed forces.

The FARC was mobilizing the poor in Bogotá aggressively. One small example of peasant-FARC cooperation in Bogotá was the intelligence networks in poor neighborhoods. The FARC established foolproof systems of "spreading the word" to mark the presence of a single stranger in many poor barrios of the capital. The FARC also

acquired the capability to assemble hundreds of poor men, women and children in a matter of minutes with the "spreading the word" system, to crowd a neighborhood and circumvent a surprise visit by police or the army.

The FARC was also getting outside help. Former Nicaraguan Sandinista guerrilla leaders instructed the FARC on the importance of using leftist business connections to infiltrate the nation's commerce. Colombian military intelligence publicly denied that the FARC had successfully completed an infiltration of Bogotá's commercial centers. However, it was common knowledge that the FARC had successfully penetrated every major city in Colombia with dozens of wide ranging business enterprises.

In Bogotá, for example, the FARC owned over 300 restaurants, of all scales from the poor neighborhood bodega, to middle-class business cafeterias to upscale expensive eateries in the Zona Rosa. The FARC also owned one of the largest messenger services in Bogotá. Although Sureshot was not able to duplicate the success of the ELN, squeezing millions of dollars out of oil and gas companies by threatening production and exploration disruptions, he was starting to generate considerable income by using his urban guerrillas to "shake down" many legitimate businesses in the big cities with the threat of harm or kidnapping.

The end result of the FARC's activities in Bogotá and other major cities was that they provided fresh recruits, additional income to finance the war, and aided the guerrilla intelligence apparatus. The FARC realized they could not match the real time intelligence the Colombian armed forces received from the United States, but their sophisticated system of wiretaps and coded communication network did manage to successfully coordinate information and supplies. In essence, the FARC was slowly establishing a strong organizational ability to operate in the population centers of Colombia. It was premature to assume that they could conduct an effective war against the Colombian armed forces in the major commercial areas of the country in 2000, but within a few years it would be within their grasp.

Under close inspection, there was no doubt that the FARC was making long-term plans to take control of power. Sureshot made it known he would not let the U.S. real-time intelligence and American-made Black Hawk and Huey helicopters defeat his army. In an attempt to offset the air superiority, the FARC was in the process of integrating their savannah, jungle and mountain base camps with civilian human shields to prevent heavy aerial strafing and bombing. However, given the Colombian armed forces dubious human rights history the FARC realized that they ran the risk of suffering heavy casualties.

However, they were prepared to use the government's brutality to their advantage. The FARC planned to use the killing of innocent women and children as the propaganda catalyst to move the civil war for control of Colombia out of the rural arena and into the large urban commercial centers of the country. If fighting in the open countryside was no longer militarily possible the FARC was prepared to change the code of combat. If needed, it was ready to speed up plans and initiate a bloody "eye-for-an-eye" campaign of urban terrorism to take the struggle against the state to the doorsteps of the rich in the big cities.

If open urban warfare started, the struggle for the control of Colombia would begin in earnest. It was critical that the government acted with extreme caution, because if the armed forces and murderous paramilitary death squads conducted widespread random attacks on innocent civilians in response to the FARC's terrorism,

duplicating the savage army and police violence of more than a half-century earlier, the defenseless poor Colombians bearing the brunt of the brutality would more than likely flock to the guerrillas for protection and tip the scales of power in favor of Sureshot and his FARC revolutionary warriors. Moreover, the White House would be in the uncomfortable position of having a partnership with an abusive and ineffective military that undermined democracy.

In April 1948, when the legendary Colombian populist Jorge Eliécer Gaitán was mysteriously assassinated, there was no army of the common people for the poor *campesinos* of the *pueblo* to turn to. At the dawn of the new millennium that was no longer the case. In the year 2000, Sureshot, the lone guerrilla veteran of *La Violencia,* through a combination of shrewd military acumen and manipulative criminal activities, had positioned his veteran army of guerrillas for the possible control of Colombia. The FARC was no longer a bunch of peasants with pitchforks; Sureshot had thousands of left-wing workers and university students waiting for the right moment to join his revolutionary army of guerrilla fighters. The only thing the FARC lacked in order for the revolution to be successful was the Colombian masses.

Therefore, if Sureshot and the senior leadership of the FARC convinced the millions of destitute Colombians throughout the nation to angrily reject the government and take up arms with their guerrilla army, the Colombian government would fall within days. With the widespread support of the poor, Sureshot would duplicate the revolutions of the Sandinista army in Nicaragua and of Fidel Castro in Cuba. If the poor in the countryside united with the poor in the big cities, Sureshot would undoubtedly topple the government and establish a socialist state in Colombia.

In recent years, U.S. troops entered

Grenada in 1983, Panama in 1989, and Haiti in 1994 to combat small conventional opposition forces. A U.S. military intervention in Colombia would dwarf each of those campaigns. Moreover, combat in Colombia would include jungle and possibly urban warfare. Therefore, if U.S. troops entered Colombia they would face two veteran guerrilla armies (the FARC and ELN) that had combined strength of well over 25,000 fighters and occupied regions that included populations that were extremely sympathetic to the revolutionaries. The U.S. would also have to face the possibility that other smaller guerrilla groups in neighboring countries would join the struggle and the conflict could conceivably spill over and impact brittle governments in the region such as those of Venezuela, Panama and Ecuador.

American leaders would be wise to consider how much trouble 250,000 Russian soldiers and airmen using high-tech military equipment had subduing 5,000 guerrilla fighters in Chechnya. Certainly the White House would be negligent if it wasn't mindful of what the head of the FBI said about the Colombian insurgents in Congressional hearings. "These narco-guerrillas are the best funded, best trained, best equipped and certainly the most well rewarded in the history of guerrilla warfare," Louis Freeh said.

In the words of Peter Romero, Acting Assistant Secretary of State for Western Hemisphere affairs, "The region's outstanding record of democratization since the apex of military rule some 20 years ago cannot be taken for granted." Latin America's population "has the most unequal distribution of income in the world," with the top 10 percent receiving 40 percent of total income while the bottom 30 percent gets 7.5 percent, Romero pointed out.

Certainly, if Colombia's civil war exploded into the heart of Colombia's high-population centers, a rescue plan would

seriously challenge Washington's commitment to stay out of the fight in Colombia. At the very least, a war for the survival of democracy in Colombia would require the presence of an international peacekeeping force. However, given the hemisphere's reluctance to get involved in Colombia, the United States would probably be the only nation Bogotá could count on for crucial support.

The American military experts in the U.S. Defense Department willing to speak to the press about Colombia feared being drawn more deeply into Bogotá's growing civil war. "I am personally concerned," one senior military official said.[89] "Here's the dilemma: do you just let them [Colombia] go down the tubes? It is far preferable for us to try to train them and equip them than it is for American troops to ultimately have to be there."[90]

In Congress, the depth of the U.S. military commitment to Colombia also raised the important question about the length of American aid to Bogotá beyond the expiration of the White House package in 2001. "This aid is a down payment on a multiyear strategy requiring hundreds of millions of dollars a year," said Democrat Senator Patrick Leahy.[91] "Yet the administration has not explained in any detail what its goals are … at what cost, or what the risks are."[92]

Regrettably, a scenario that includes the possible downfall of the Colombian government will place the President of the United States at the brink of a military intervention strongly reminiscent of John F. Kennedy's "domino theory" deployment of American soldiers in Vietnam. However, given the fact that the Cold War no longer dominates American foreign policy, and given the lessons learned in Vietnam, events in Bogotá clearly indicate that the drug-contaminated civil war cannot be resolved with a military solution. To that end, the United States cannot afford to march another generation of young Americans off to war and then inform them decades afterwards it was a big mistake.

In this light, President Pastrana's peace process is a historic opportunity for Colombia to rid itself of its dysfunctional system of elite rule. They cannot afford to fail. Colombia desperately needs an earnest mechanism for the practice of conflict resolution, and Pastrana and his Peace Commissioner are doomed to failure if they do not eliminate the horrid dirty war of paramilitary death squad massacres. The honest solution to the conflict in Colombia is the implementation of significant social reforms and the introduction of greater political inclusion.

However, in order for Colombia to find peace on earth and end its long history of violence its leaders must summon the courage to vigorously exterminate the criminal elements of its armed forces. The worst human rights disaster in the hemisphere can only be resolved when the Colombian government nurtures the triumph of democratic principles and abandons its institutional culture of denial. Otherwise, the doomsday guerrilla thesis of a prolonged battle in the rural areas and then an escalated door-to-door fight to the finish in the big cities of Colombia remains a stark reality.

Notes

1. Karl Penhaul, Reuters, "Colombia Peace Talks Restart Amid Massive Marches," Bogotá, 24 October 1999.

2. *Ibid.*

3. Douglas Farah, *Washington Post*, "U.S. to Aid Colombian Military," Washington, 27 December 1998.

4. *Ibid.*

5. *Ibid.*

6. Madeleine K. Albright, *New York Times*, "Colombia's Struggles, and How We Can Help," Washington, 10 August 1999.

7. Tim Golden and Steven Lee Myers, *New York Times*, "U.S. Plans Big Aid Package to Rally a Reeling Colombia," New York, 15 September 1999.

8. *Ibid.*

9. John Diamond, *Chicago Tribune*, "Capitol Hill Divided Over Colombian Aid Appeal," Washington, 23 September 1999.

10. *Ibid.*

11. *Ibid.*

12. David Briscoe, Associated Press, "Plan Would Boost Aid to Colombia," Washington, 23 September 1999.

13. Mike Dorning, *Chicago Tribune*, "In Drug War, Hastert in Colombia's Corner," Washington, 15 October 1999.

14. *Ibid.*

15. Larry Rohter, *New York Times*, "Plan to Strengthen Colombia Nudges U.S. for $3.5 Billion," Bogotá, 18 September 1999.

16. *Ibid.*

17. Larry Rohter, *New York Times*, "Like Carrot, Stick Fails with Rebels in Colombia," Bogotá, 27 September 1999.

18. Anthony Boadle, Reuters, "U.S. Closer to Boosting Military Aid to Colombia," Washington, 6 October 1999.

19. *Ibid.*

20. Douglas Farah, *Washington Post*, "Pact Near on Aid to Colombia," Washington, 9 October 1999.

21. Douglas Farah, *Washington Post*, "Colombian Rebels Tap E. Europe for Arms," Washington, 4 November 1999

22. Karen DeYoung, *Washington Post*, "Drug Aid for Colombia Is Stalled," Washington, 10 November 1999.

23. *Ibid.*

24. *Ibid.*

25. David M. Shribman, *Boston Globe*, "The Presidency, Bill Clinton's Long Goodbye," Washington, 14 November 1999.

26. *Semana*, "Estados Unidos, El tío conejo. A pesar de que es muy probable que el paquete de ayuda para el país sea aprobado a comienzos de 2000 la forma en que Washington manejó el tema fue una bofetada para Colombia," Bogotá, 15 Noviembre de 1999.

27. Office of the Press Secretary, The White House, "Statement by the President," 10 November 1999.

28. Reuters, "Amnesty Opposes U.S. Aid to Colombia," London, 11 November 1999.

29. *Ibid.*

30. *Ibid.*

31. *Ibid.*

32. Karl Penhaul, Reuters, "U.S. Steps Up Drug War in Colombia," Carlisle, Pennsylvania, 13 November 1999.

33. *Ibid.*

34. Douglas Farah, *Washington Post,* "New Colombian Drug Smugglers Hold Tech Advantage," Bogotá, 15 November 1999.

35. *Ibid.*

36. *Ibid.*

37. *Ibid.*

38. Tom Brown, Reuters, "Colombia Military Chief Urges Broader U.S. Commitment," Bogotá, 2 October 1999.

39. *Ibid.*

40. *Ibid.*

41. Reuters, "Colombian Leader Heads Off Military Crisis—Report," Bogotá, 11 December 1999.

42. *Ibid.*

43. *Ibid.*

44. Vivian Sequera, Associated Press, "Genocide Law Setback in Colombia," Bogotá, 30 December 1999.

45. Reuters, "Colombia's Pastrana Vetoes Heinous Crimes Act," Bogotá, 30 December 1999.

46. *Ibid.*

47. *Ibid.*

48. Reuters, "Surge in Mass Killings in Colombia in '99," Bogotá, 29 December 1999.

49. *Ibid.*

50. *Ibid.*

51. Associated Press, "Colombia Breaks Kidnap World Record," Bogotá, 28 January 2000.

52. Reuters, "975 Fighters Die in Colombia in 1999," Bogotá, 2 January 2000.

53. Reuters, "Colombia's Pastrana Highly Unpopular, Poll Says," Bogotá, 7 January 1999.

54. *Ibid.*

55. Reuters, "Colombians See More War in New Millennium," Bogotá, 30 December 1999.

56. *Ibid.*

57. Vivian Sequera, Associated Press, "Colombia Militias Tax Drug Trade," Bogotá, 10 January 2000.

58. *Ibid.*

59. Karl Penhaul, Reuters, "Colombia Peasant Refugees Storm ICRC HQ," Bogotá, 4 January 2000.

60. Reuters, "ICRC Deplores Occupation of Bogotá office," Geneva, 6 January 2000.

61. Associated Press, "Red Cross Resumes Colombia Work," Geneva, 20 January 2000.

62. Frank Davies, *San Jose Mercury News,* "U.S. Readies Huge Aid Package for Colombia," Washington, 12 January 2000.

63. *Ibid.*

64. Elaine Monaghan, Reuters, "Analysis—U.S. Plans in Colombia Stir Fears of War," Washington, 14 January 2000.

65. Steve Dudley, *Washington Post,* "Albright Discusses Anti-Drug Aid in Colombia," Cartagena, 15 January 2000.

66. Agence France-Presse, "US Aid Depends on Colombia's Approach to Human Rights; Albright," Cartagena, 15 January 2000.

67. *Ibid.*

68. Reuters, "U.S. Tells Colombia Army to Halt Rights Abuses," Bogotá, 21 January 2000.

69. *Ibid.*

70. *Ibid.*

71. Karl Penhaul, Reuters, "Colombian Army Claims 44 Dead Rebels, Hunts Others," Bogotá, 16 January 2000.

72. *Ibid.*

73. *Ibid.*

74. Reuters, "Colombia Death Squads Kill 26 Peasants," Bogotá, 18 January 2000.

75. *Ibid.*

76. Jared Kotler, Associated Press, "Suspected Rightist Militias Kill 16," Bogotá, 19 January 2000.

77. *Ibid.*

78. Reuters, "Suspected Colombia Death Squad Kills 10," Bogotá, 21 January 2000.

79. *Ibid.*

80. Jared Kotler, Associated Press, "Colombian Rebels Vow More Sabotage," Bogotá, 20 January 2000.

81. *Bloomberg News,* "Colombia Rebel Leader Rodriguez on Power Pylon Attacks: Comment," Bogotá, 20 January 2000.

82. *Ibid.*

83. Reuters, "Paramilitary Gang Kills at Least 11 Colombians," Bogotá, 28 January 2000.

84. Nurith C. Aizenman, *New Republic,* "Can George Tenet Save the CIA," 22 March 1999.

85. *Ibid.*

86. Tom Brown, Reuters, "Rebel Chieftain Slams U.S. Aid to Colombia," Bogotá, 29 January 2000.

87. *Ibid.*

88. *Ibid.*

89. Tim Golden, *New York Times,* "U.S. Antidrug Plan to Aid Colombia Is Facing Hurdles," Washington, 6 February 2000.

90. *Ibid.*

91. John Donnelly, *Boston Globe,* "Details of $1.3 Billion in Antidrug Aid to Colombia Prompt Questions," Washington, 10 February 2000.

92. *Ibid.*

Afterword

In August of 2000, the most popular public figure in Colombia resigned from civil service because he was "tired of seeing his officers die." General Rosso José Serrano decided to step down after nearly 2,000 Colombian police died in the line of duty since he took over as National Police Chief in 1994. "I've been to so many police officers' funerals I can't bear another," he said. The 40-year police veteran, whose reputation for valor and honesty made him Colombia's most revered public official, was arguably the most highly regarded international law enforcement official in the world, according to the new DEA Administrator Donnie R. Marshall. The charismatic Serrano was a fierce fighter of corruption, firing or forcing into retirement over 8,000 officers during his tenure. As a result, many dedicated middle and lower class Colombians were carefully working behind the scenes to convince Serrano to run as a "populist" candidate for Chief of State in the 2002 presidential elections.

On August 22, 2000, President Clinton signed a waiver authorizing distribution of a much needed $1.3 billion U.S. aid package called "Plan Colombia" to help the government in Bogotá fight drug traffickers, even though the Bogotá administration had not met all the human rights conditions set by Congress. The waiver touched off a storm of protest. Senator Paul D. Wellstone (D-Minn.) declared, "after an honest and objective assessment of the human rights situation in Colombia, it should be clear to all that certifying Colombia today is impossible: The military maintains links to the paramilitaries; the government of Colombia has not vigorously pursued members of paramilitaries; and many members of the armed forces who are credibly accused of human rights violations have not been suspended." The Clinton waiver also drew complaints from Senator Patrick J. Leahy (D-Vt.) who said, "We need to see a consistent good-faith effort to curb human rights abuses [from Colombia], and we don't even see that."

Nevertheless, President Clinton made a one-day visit to the Caribbean town of Cartagena on August 30, 2000, and promoted the merits of "Plan Colombia" by telling the world it was propeace and that Colombia was "in the fight of their lives." The White House successfully defended the President, saying that the aid package would strengthen Pastrana's democratic government and give it leverage to force the FARC guerrillas to finally negotiate in good faith. Moreover, they added that as bad as the situation in Colombia was, without the immediate aid the violence and instability would worsen if the drug traffickers and guerrillas increased their power base. The White House added that the U.S. could not lead the hemisphere without joining its neighbors in facing its challenges. The U.S. felt it must assist states in combating drug trafficking because it was the insatiable appetite for drugs in the U.S. that was the major cause of the problem. Consequently, it was clear that although lawlessness in Colombia was a major concern to many Americans, the sophisticated military might of the FARC which now included the ability to "lock on" to flights with hostile missile radar weapons was a far greater priority to President Clinton.

To that end, the Clinton administration was sensitive to international criticism. Remarks from Venezuelan President Hugo Chavez regarding "Plan Colombia" irked the White House. U.S. Conservatives were already openly alarmed for some time of a possible Havana-Caracas-Bogotá axis. These fears were fueled by repeated pleas for Latin American unity by President Chavez, which offered increased closeness of ties between Venezuela and Cuba as an example to the rest of the region. Moreover, Chavez regularly annoyed American conservatives by condemning the "cursed individualism" of unrestrained capitalism and for his nation's key role in supporting higher oil prices with OPEC production controls. However, the White House had been very patient with Chavez and was disappointed when the Venezuelan President warned that Colombia's U.S.-backed efforts to combat drug traffickers and guerrillas could engulf much of South America in a Vietnam-like war. "It would be very dangerous if the operation leads to a military escalation of the conflict," Chavez said. "It could lead us to a Vietnamization of the whole Amazon region."

Chavez's criticism was the first time that a South American leader had cautioned that "Plan Colombia" could degenerate into guerrilla warfare of continental dimensions. Weeks earlier, Brazil's Foreign Minister Luiz Felipe Lampreia stressed the "autonomy" of Latin America's largest country, and told Secretary of State Madeleine Albright it would not participate in the major Washington campaign to help battle Colombian drug traffickers. Brazil, which shared a long Amazon jungle border with Colombia, feared that a huge military assault would drag it into Colombia's savage civil war or send droves of refugees into Brazil. Brazil was also fearful that, if provoked, drug traffickers would exploit the vastness of its frontier territory to seek out new markets within its border.

All in all, the White House was feeling isolated. Even Britain urged Colombia to improve its human rights record before it was willing to finance an international plan to stamp out drug production. Complicating matters further, British Cabinet Minister Mo Mowlam, one of the architects of the Northern Ireland peace accords, took a swipe at a major component of U.S. policy when she voiced strong opposition to the widespread use of herbicides on drug crops. The British were concerned that large-scale crop spraying intended to eradicate illegal coca plantations would poison people living nearby. Mowlam made her remarks during a trip to Bogotá on September 14, 2000. She also said Britain and most of Europe were withholding large amounts of aid in the antidrug war unless Colombian security forces underwent further reforms. President Pastrana had hoped to convince European allies to contribute billions of dollars in antidrug aid. However, only two European countries — Spain and Norway — pledged a total of $120 million by mid–September of 2000.

Adding to the White House woes, the Colombian Armed Forces lost a major American ally in November 2000. Representative Benjamin A. Gilman, the departing Chairman of the House International

Relations Committee, abruptly withdrew his support from the decision to funnel $1.3 billion in mostly military aid to Colombia, arguing that the United States was on the brink of a "major mistake." Gilman sent a letter to White House drug czar Barry McCaffrey, saying that the American plan to increase the role of the Colombian military in the drug fight would end disastrously because the history of corruption and human rights abuses by the military had undermined its political support in Colombia. Gilman called on the Clinton administration to redirect its assistance, including at least 40 Black Hawk helicopters, from the military to the National Police in Colombia. "If we fail early on with Plan Colombia, as I fear, we could lose the support of the American people." "If we lose public support, we will regret we did not make the mid-course corrections for Colombia," concluded Gilman.

A month later, in December of 2000, the United Nation's top human rights official accused the Colombian government of doing little to stop killings by right-wing paramilitary groups. "The government, despite a commitment voiced to me very strongly, has not in practice tackled adequately the violence by paramilitary groups," said U.N. human rights official Mary Robinson. "I'm aware of certain commitments made but I'm looking at the practical implementation and I would have to say I have grave concerns about the process of tackling this problem in an effective way," she said. Robinson, who served as Ireland's President from 1990 to 1997, also had harsh words for the FARC, which she accused of violating international humanitarian law with the "deplorable" national campaign of kidnappings.

At the end of the year the final report card for 2000 was in. The statistics were staggering. The Colombian National Police reported that 25,660 people met violent deaths in 2000, a 5 percent increase

from the 1999 total of 24,358. An average of 71 violent deaths a day took place in war-ravaged Colombia, according to the report. The National Police also reported that Colombia still had the dubious honor of being the kidnapping capital of the world, beating its own record in 2000 when the total rose 7 percent to register 3,162 victims. There was a total of 2,959 kidnappings reported in 1999, the report said. The statistics confirmed what most Colombians already knew: The situation in Colombia was out of control and Pastrana was incapable of doing something about the "scorched earth" mentality of the death squads or the guerilla intentions to grab "power" by force. A Gallup survey published by *Cambio* magazine on January 7, 2001, showed that Colombians were losing faith in President Pastrana. The gloomy poll found that 73 percent of respondents believed the peace process was going badly and just 19 percent saw progress. "What is certain is that on this second anniversary, the peace process is lacking oxygen," the country's most respected daily, *El Tiempo*, said in an editorial, urging international mediation to help Colombia emerge from "this black night."

President Pastrana made his first trip to Washington to meet privately with President George W. Bush for 45 minutes on February 27, 2001. During the White House meeting President Bush reportedly made a strong point of instructing Pastrana to improve the dismal human rights situation in Colombia but said he would continue with President Clinton's "Plan Colombia" initiative but with "better management." Behind the scenes, Republican insiders were saying President Bush considered Colombia the biggest threat to regional stability and was rethinking policy because it lacked international support. The insiders said President Bush was keenly aware that on February 1, 2001, the European parliament adopted a resolution on "Plan

Colombia," with an almost unanimous vote: 474 in favor, only 1 against. It was the strongest statement thus far, stressing that Europe was keeping clear distance from the U.S. military approach towards Colombia. The parliament advocated a European developmental carrot in Colombia rather than the U.S. military stick.

While Pastrana was in Washington, the State Department released a report slamming Colombia's human rights record. "In global terms, I think it is a fair report of the realities we are living in Colombia," said President Pastrana after meeting with Henry Hyde (R-Ill.), the new Chairman of the House International Relations Committee. Those realities included soldiers and police committing murders, security forces working with right-wing paramilitary death squads and high-ranking officials rarely being held accountable for crimes the State Department said in its annual report examining human rights worldwide. "Members of the security forces collaborated with paramilitary groups that committed abuses, in some instances allowing such groups to pass through roadblocks, sharing information or providing them with supplies or ammunition," the report stated.

Perhaps the most shocking statistic of the Colombian reality was that 56.3 percent of Colombia — 21.6 million citizens — suffered from extreme poverty, making less than $55 a month, according to the Colombian Departamenta Nacional de Planeación (DNP). Moreover, in early 2001, Bogotá was inundated with displaced *campesinos* attempting to escape the war in the countryside, raising the population of residents in the capital to over 8 million Colombians. Those human rights activists who had not fled Colombia in terror from right-wing death squads estimated the FARC guerrilla organization now had hundreds of thousands of urban sympathizers in the major cities of Colombia — some

with suitcases filled with weapons ready to be used for a revolution. Additionally, veteran Bogotá social workers now feared that the FARC could muster a clandestine urban militia of over 10,000 well-armed revolutionaries and bandits from the worker unions, universities and from the ranks of the 4 million poor Colombians crowded into the downtrodden barrios of Bolivar, Kennedy and Soacha. Included in the estimate were small units of dangerously mobile urban youth gangs that were prepared to use dirt motorbikes to strike designated targets and escape within seconds.

The key to the success of the FARC and ELN guerrillas in Colombia was the massacres of the paramilitary death squads. It was also obvious that as long as the Colombian high military command continued its slaughterhouse activities with the death squads and as long as the privileged Colombian oligarchy exempted all high school and college graduates from duty in the war zone, more and more poor would reject the legitimacy of the government. Moreover, President Pastrana was fond of saying that Colombia was united and that 95 percent of its citizens believed in democracy and the rule of law. However, the true reality of Colombia was that millions of poor *campesinos* were hungry and had lost faith in a government that could not protect them or provide for them. Also security forces blatantly conducted illegal actions that were not consistent with the leadership of the nation.

In the spring of 2001, the citizens of Colombia were well aware that the government was not capable of attaining a military victory against the FARC and ELN guerrillas. As a result some of the brightest minds in the nation reasoned that there were truly only two possibilities for peace in Colombia. One was that President George W. Bush, Secretary of State Colin Powell, Vice President Dick Cheney, Secretary of Defense Donald Rumsfeld and National

Security Adviser Condoleezza Rice, hand in hand with Congress, "rebuild" Colombia in partnership with the guerrillas. The other possibility was that the Colombian "pueblo" finally break the grip of the powerful ruling elite and elect an incorruptible populist President of impeccable character who was willing to implement significant social, judicial, and land reforms to cleanse the nation of its dishonest culture of denial, and unite the wholesome people of Colombia under one flag.

Bibliography

Abel, Christopher. *Política, Iglesia y Partidos en Colombia*. Bogotá: Universidad Nacional de Colombia, 1987.

Agee, Philip. *Inside the Company: CIA Diary*. Middlesex: Penguin, 1975.

Anderson, Jon L. *Che Guevara: A Revolutionary Life*. New York: Grove Press, 1997.

Anderson, Paul. *Janet Reno, Doing the Right Thing*. New York: John Wiley & Sons, 1994.

Art, Robert J. *Robert Jervis: International Politics*. 4th ed. New York: HarperCollins, 1996.

Auerbach, Jerold S. *Unequal Justice: Lawyers and Social Change in Modern America*. London: Oxford University Press, 1976.

Baily, Thomas A. *A Diplomatic History of the American People*. 8th ed. New York: Appleton-Century-Crofts, 1969.

Bareño, Leonel Pérez. *Multinacionales, Estado y Petróleo: El Contrato de Asociación en Colombia*. Bogotá: Corpes Orinoquia, 1998.

Bell-Villada, Gene H. *García Márquez: The Man and His Works*. Chapel Hill: University of North Carolina Press, 1990.

Bergquist, Charles W. *Coffee and Conflict in Colombia 1886–1910*. Durham: Duke University Press, 1978.

Berry, Albert R., Ronald G. Hellman and Mauricio Solaun, editors. *Politics of Compromise: Coalition Government in Colombia*. New Haven: Yale University Press, 1971.

Berry, Albert R., and Miguel Urrutia. *Income Distribution in Colombia*. New Haven: Yale University Press, 1976.

Blair, John M. *The Control of Oil*. New York: Pantheon Books, 1976.

Braun, Herbert. *Our Guerrillas, Our Sidewalks*. Niwot: University Press of Colorado, 1994.

_____. *The Assassination of Gaitán: Public Life and Urban Violence in Colombia*. Madison: University of Wisconsin Press, 1985.

Broderick, Walter J. *Camilo Torres: A Biography of the Priest-Guerrillero*. New York: Doubleday, 1975.

Bushnell, David. *The Making of Modern Colombia: A Nation in Spite of Itself*. Berkeley: University of California Press, 1993.

Cañón, Luis M. *La Crisis: Cuatro Años a Bordo del Gobierno de Samper*. Bogotá: Planeta, 1998.

Carrigan, Ana. *The Palace of Justice, A Colombian Tragedy*. New York: Four Walls Eight Windows, 1993.

Chalarca, Jose. *El Café en la Vida de Colombia*. Bogotá: Carvajal S.A., 1987.

Chepesiuk, Ron. *Hard Target: The United States War Against International Drug Trafficking, 1982–1997*. Jefferson, N.C.: McFarland, 1999.

Clawson, Patrick L., and Rensselaer W. Lee III. *The Andean Cocaine Industry*. New York: St. Martin's Press, 1998.

Coatsworth, John H., and Alan M. Taylor, editors. *Latin America and the World Economy Since 1800*. Cambridge: Harvard University Press, 1998.

Corporacíon Observatorio Para La Paz. *Las Verdaderas Intenciones de las FARC*. Bogotá: Intermedio Editores, 1999.

Country Review Colombia 1998/1999. Commercial Data International.

Dix, Robert H. *The Politics of Colombia.* New York: Praeger, 1987.

Dominguez, Jorge I., and Abraham F. Lowenthal. *Constructing Democratic Governance, Latin America and the Caribbean in the 1990's, Themes and Issues.* Baltimore: Johns Hopkins University Press, 1996.

Donadío, Alberto. *Yo, El Fiscal.* Bogotá: Circulo de Lectores, 1996.

Drexler, Robert W. *Colombia and the United States: Narcotics Traffic and a Failed Foreign Policy.* Jefferson, N.C.: McFarland, 1997.

Duzan, Maria Jimena. *Death Beat; A Colombian Journalist's Life Inside the Cocaine Wars.* New York: HarperCollins, 1994.

Enrique, Jorge. *Robledo Castillo, El Café en Colombia: Un Análisis Independiente.* Bogotá: El Ancora Editores, 1998.

Escobar, Arturo. *Encountering Development, The Making and Unmaking of the Third World.* Princeton: Princeton University Press, 1995.

Frechette, Barbara. *El poder compartido.* Bogotá: Norma, 1999.

Galán, Luis Carlos. *Ni Un Paso Atras, Siempre Adelante!* Bogotá: Fundacion Luis Carlos Galán, 1991.

Giraldo, Javier S.J. *Colombia: The Genocidal Democracy.* Monroe: Common Courage Press, 1996.

Graebner, Norman A. *An Uncertain Tradition: American Secretaries of State in the Twentieth Century.* New York: McGraw-Hill, 1961.

Hanratty, Dennis M., and Sandra W. Meditz. *Colombia: A Country Study.* Washington, D.C.: Government Printing Office, 1990.

Hargrove, Thomas R. *Long March to Freedom.* New York: Ballantine Books, 1995.

Harrison, Lawrence E. *The Pan-American Dream.* Boulder: Westview Press, 1997.

Holt, Pat M. *Secret Intelligence and Public Policy: A Dilemma of Democracy.* Washington, D.C.: Congressional Quarterly, 1995.

Human Rights Watch. *Political Murder and Reform in Colombia: The Violence Continues.* New York: Americas Watch, 1992.

_____. *State of War: Political Violence and Counterinsurgency in Colombia.* New York: Americas Watch, 1993.

_____. *Generation Under Fire: Children and Violence in Colombia.* New York: Americas Watch, 1994.

_____. *Colombia's Killer Networks: The Military-Paramilitary Partnership and the United States.* New York: Americas Watch, 1996.

_____. *War Without Quarter: Colombia and International Humanitarian Law.* New York: Americas Watch, 1998.

_____. *The Ties That Bind: Colombia and Military-Paramilitary Links.* New York: Americas Watch, 2000.

Junguito, Roberto, and Diego Pizano. *El Comercio Exterior y la Politica Internacional del Café.* Bogotá: Fedesarrollo, 1993.

_____. *Producción de Café en Colombia.* Bogotá: Fedesarrollo, 1991.

Kleiman, Mark A.R. *Against Excess: Drug Policy for Results.* New York: Basic Books, 1992.

Kline, Harvey F. *Colombia: Democracy Under Assault.* 2d ed. Boulder: Westview Press, 1990.

Levine, Daniel H. *Popular Voices in Latin America Catholicism.* Princeton: Princeton University Press, 1992.

Mackenzie, Angus. *Secrets: The CIA's War at Home.* Berkeley: University of California Press, 1997.

Márquez, Julio Ortiz. *El Hombre Que Fue un Pueblo: Jorge Eliécer Gaitán.* Bogotá: Página Maestra, 1998.

Martz, John D. *The Politics of Clientelism: Democracy and the State of Colombia.* New Brunswick: Transaction Publishers, 1997.

_____. *United States Policy in Latin America.* Lincoln: University of Nebraska Press, 1995.

Maullin, Richard L. *The Fall of Dumar Aljure, A Colombian Guerrilla and Bandit.* Santa Monica: Rand, 1968.

McCullough, David. *The Path Between the Seas: The Creation of the Panama Canal 1870–1914.* New York: Simon & Schuster 1977.

Medina, Serna. *Santiago: La Verdad Sobre las Mentiras.* 2d ed. Bogotá: Planeta, 1997.

The National Catholic Almanac. Paterson: St. Anthony's Guild, 1952.

Osterling, Jorge P. *Democracy in Colombia.* New Brunswick: Transaction Publishers, 1989.

Pearce, Jenny. *Colombia: Inside the Labyrinth.* London: Latin American Bureau, 1990.

Pilger, John. *Hidden Agendas.* New York: The New Press, 1998.

Riley, Kevin Jack. *Snow Job? The War Against International Cocaine Trafficking.* New Brunswick: Transaction Publications, 1996.

Samper, Ernesto. *Colombia Sale Adelante!* Bogotá: E.C.M., 1989.

Sharpless, Richard E.. *Gaitán of Colombia: A Political Biography.* Pittsburgh: University of Pittsburgh Press, 1978.

Stassen, Glen. *Just Peacemaking, Ten Practices for Abolishing War.* Cleveland: Pilgrim Press, 1998.

Strong, Simon. *Whitewash: Pablo Escobar.* London: Macmillan Publishers, 1995.

Vargas, Mauricio. *Tiro Directo.* Bogotá: Planeta, 1998.

Vargas, Mauricio, and Jorge Lesmes. *Edgar Tellez, el Presidente que se iba a caer.* Bogotá: Planeta, 1996.

Westerfield, H. Bradford. "Inside CIA's Private World: Declassified Articles from the Agency's Internal Journal 1955–1992." New Haven: Yale University Press, 1995.

White, John Kenneth. *Still Seeing Red: How the Cold War Shapes the New American Politics.* Boulder: Westview Press, 1998.

Woolner, Ann. *Washed in Gold: The Story of the Biggest Money Laundering Investigation in United States History.* New York: Simon & Schuster, 1994.

Zinn, Howard. *The Politics of History.* 2nd ed. Chicago: University of Illinois Press, 1990.

_____. *The Twentieth Century: A People's History.* (Revised & Updated Edition.) New York: Harper Perennial, 1998.

_____. *You Can't Be Neutral on a Moving Train: A Personal History of Our Times.* Boston: Beacon Press, 1994.

Official Documents

American Embassy, Colombia. Country Commercial Guide Fiscal Year 1999. Bogotá, 1998.

Bureau of Democracy, Human Rights, and Labor, U.S. Department of State. 1999 Country Reports on Human Rights Practices: Colombia. Washington: Government Printing Office, 2000.

Bureau of Inter-American Affairs, U.S. Department of State. Background Notes. Colombia. Washington: Government Printing Office, 1998.

Central Intelligence Agency. Factbook on Intelligence: The Intelligence Community. Washington: CIA Publications, 1998.

Central Intelligence Agency. The World Factbook: Colombia. Washington: CIA Publications, 1999.

Central Intelligence Agency Secret Report. Cuban Subversive Activities in Latin America: 1959–1968, 16 February 1968.

Hearing Before the Committee on International Relations House of Representatives, One Hundred Fifth Congress, Second Session. U.S. Counter-Narcotics Policy Toward Colombia. Washington: Government Printing Office, 26 February 1998.

Hearing Before the Committee on International Relations House of Representatives, One Hundred Fifth Congress, Second Session. U.S. Counter-Narcotics Policy Toward Colombia. Washington: Government Printing Office, 31 March 1998.

Hearing Before the Committee on International Relations House of Representatives, One Hundred Fifth Congress, Second Session. Colombian Heroin Crisis. Washington: Government Printing Office, 24 June 1998.

U.S. Department of State Special Memorandum to White House for Mr. Henry A. Kissinger. Colombia to Hold Presidential and Congressional Elections, Sunday, April 19. Washington, 17 April 1970.

U.S. Embassy Confidential Report, Department of State. Alfonso Lopez Michelsen: The Man, His Enemies and His Political Views. Bogotá, 26 March 1973.

U.S. Embassy Confidential Report, Department of State. Army Kills Ciro Trujillo Castaño. Bogotá, 7 October 1968.

U.S. Embassy Confidential Report, Department of State. Belisario Betancur Talks About Changes in Society and His Political Ambitions. Bogotá, 9 December 1971.

U.S. Embassy Confidential Report, Department of State. Church Finds Some Sour Apples Among the First Fruits of Reform. Bogotá, 12 May 1969.

U.S. Embassy Confidential Report, Department

of State. Communist Comment on Counterinsurgency in Colombia. Bogotá, 19 June 1967.

U.S. Embassy Confidential Report, Department of State. Communist Party Publicly Attacks Castro-Oriented, Pro-Guerrilla Warfare Thesis of Central Committee Member. Bogotá, 19 December 1967.

U.S. Embassy Confidential Report, Department of State. Extremists and the University Reform Issue. Bogotá, 19 November 1968.

U.S. Embassy Confidential Report, Department of State. Half-Year of Guerrilla Activity. Bogotá, 3 January 1968.

U.S. Embassy Confidential Report, Department of State. Increasing Guerrilla Action. Bogotá, 31 December 1969.

U.S. Embassy Confidential Report, Department of State. Initial Visit of Dr. Pastrana as Official Candidate to Medellín, Marinilla and the Hinterland: Assessment of the Visit. Bogotá, 16 December 1969.

U.S. Embassy Confidential Report, Department of State. Jump in Kidnappings. Bogotá, 31 October 1969.

U.S. Embassy Confidential Report, Department of State. Political Biweekly. Bogotá, 13 March 1970.

U.S. Embassy Confidential Report, Department of State. Political Panorama: Magic Names. Bogotá, 2 July 1970.

U.S. Embassy Confidential Report, Department of State. Political Roundup, Events Following the general elections in Colombia April 19. Bogotá, 8 May 1970.

U.S. Embassy Confidential Report, Department of State. Political Situation: Final Vote Count and Claim of Vote Irregularities. Bogotá, 19 June 1970.

U.S. Embassy Confidential Report, Department of State. Pre-Election Report. Bogotá, 12 April 1970.

U.S. Embassy Confidential Report, Department of State. Situation of the Colombian Traditional Parties. Bogotá, 15 May 1970.

U.S. Embassy Confidential Report, Department of State. Some Observations on Democracy, the Political Environment and Local Government in Colombia. Bogotá, 18 July 1967.

U.S. Embassy Confidential Report, Department of State. The Internal Security Situation: Identification of the Threat. Bogotá, 21 November 1967.

U.S. Embassy Official Report, Department of State. Analysis of Election Statistics. Bogotá, 4 December 1969.

U.S. Embassy Official Report, Department of State. Campesino Is Awakening but Does Not Signify Impending Revolution. Bogotá, 8 September 1971.

U.S. Embassy Official Report, Department of State. Government Reaction to Wave of Violence. Bogotá, 31 January 1973.

U.S. Embassy Official Report, Department of State. Peasant "Invasions" in Valle. Bogotá, 19 November 1971.

U.S. Embassy Official Report, Department of State. Visit to Department of Huila. Bogotá, 20 March 1970.

U.S. Embassy Official Report, Department of State. Voter Abstention in Colombia. Bogotá, 3 May 1968.

U.S. Embassy Secret Report, Department of State. Colombian Military Security Capability Analysis: The Army Cannot Eliminate Present Ground Threat. Bogotá, 15 December 1967.

U.S. Embassy Secret Report, Department of State. Colombian Security Agency Disrupts Colombian Communist Party Subversive Efforts and Implicates USSR. Bogotá, 24 May 1968.

U.S. Embassy Secret Report, Department of State. David Rockefeller Visit and Comments on President Lleras. Bogotá, 1 February 1968.

U.S. Embassy Secret Report, Department of State. FY 1973–75 Country Analysis and Strategy Paper (CASP) for Colombia. Bogotá, 29 January 1971.

U.S. Embassy Secret Report, Department of State. FY 1974–75 Country Analysis and Strategy Paper (CASP) for Colombia. Bogotá, 13 March 1973.

U.S. Embassy Secret Report, Department of State. Host Country Resources and Effort — Military, National Police, DAS. Bogotá, 1 August 1970.

U.S. Embassy Secret Report, Department of State. Internal Security: Alertness to Potential Insurgency. Bogotá, 18 August 1967.

U.S. Embassy Secret Report, Department of State. No Agreement to Extend the National Front. Bogotá, 30 October 1972.

U.S. Embassy Secret Report, Department of State. We Expect State of Siege to Be in Force Indefinitely. Bogotá, 22 April 1970.

Index

267